Canadian Immigration Made Easy

Canadian Immigration Made Easy

How to Immigrate into Canada (All Classes) with Employment Search Strategies for Skilled Workers

With Do-It-Yourself And Step-By-Step Settlement And Job Search Guide

A 4 –in-1 Publication

by

Tariq Nadeem

ISBN: 0-9780460-4-8 (Paperback)
ISBN: 0-9780460-5-6 (e-book)

Library and Archives Canada Cataloguing in Publication

Nadeem, Tariq, 1966-
Canadian immigration made easy : how to immigrate into Canada (all classes) with employment search strategies for skill workers : with do-it-yourself and step-by-step settlement and job search guide : a 4 in 1 publication / by Tariq Nadeem. -- 2nd ed.

Includes bibliographical references.
ISBN-13: 978-0-9780460-4-0
ISBN-10: 0-9780460-4-8

1. Emigration and immigration law--Canada. 2. Immigrants--Employment--Canada. 3. Job hunting--Canada. I. Title.

KE4454 N23 2007 342.7108'2 C2006-905876-8
KF4483.I5N23 2007

This book is printed on acid free paper.

This publication is designed to provide accurate and authoritative information that is up-to-date and current at the time of this publication. It is sold with the understanding that the publisher is not engaged in rendering any professional services.

Self-Help Publishers does not endorse any product or service in this publication. Any service or services provider listed in this publication assume full liability for their products and services and any claims direct or indirect arising from them.

Send your wholesale inquiries in U.S.A to Ingram Book Group, Baker & Taylor, and Nacscorp.
In United Kingdom and Europe send your wholesale inquiries to Bertram and Blackwell's.

For retail purchase visit your local Amazon and Barns and Nobles online bookstores or checkout with your local bookstore.

For reprint/co-publishing rights contact Self-Help Publishers at 3-445 Pioneer Dr. Kitchener ,ON, N2P 1L8 Canada or visit www.selfhelppublishers.com

Manufactured in United States of America and United Kingdom simultaneously by arrangements with Self-Help publishers.

Cover design and layout by Lisa Walter – Publishing date: January 01, 2007

ACKNOWLEDGEMENT & CREDITS

© Her Majesty the Queen in Right of Canada, represented by the Minister of Public works and Government Services, 2007.

Statistics Canada information is used with the permission of Minister of Industry, as Minister responsible for Statistics Canada. Information on the availability of the wide range of data from Statistics Canada can be obtained from Statistics Canada's Regional Offices, its World Wide Web site at http://www.statcan.ca and its toll-free access number 1-800-263-1136

Introduction to Canada, facts and figures – CIA -The world factbook
Manage your impression – Put Your Best Foot Forward.

World-wide quality of living survey
http://www.mercerhr.co.uk/pressrelease/details.jhtml?idContent=1173105

Canadian Economy in Brief
http://www.fin.gc.ca/ECONBR/ecbr06-03e.html

Budget in Brief
http://www.fin.gc.ca/budget06/brief/briefe.htm

Where Does Your Tax Dollar Go
http://www.fin.gc.ca/taxdollar/text/html/pamphlet_e.html

Top Ten Ways to Get Canadian Experience - Do You Have International Experience By Shawn Mintz of A.C.C.E.S www.accestrain.com.

"Strategizing for Employment in the Canadian Workplace" Ms. Irena Valenta

I also thank Mrs. Ambreen Tariq for her assistance and help in dealing with technicalities of this publication.

DISCLAIMER

Federal government of Canada and Provincial governments of Canada and their ministers, employees, agents , directors, author, editor shall not be liable for any losses, claims, demands, injuries, causes of action, actions, damages suffered by the user or users of this publication.

Portions of this book have been provided courtesy of Citizenship and Immigration Canada. The Government of Canada does not endorse or support any annotations or commentary included in this publication. These are the sole responsibility and choice of the author.

DEDICATION

This book is dedicated to all those peace lovers who believe in democratic values with its true implementation and practice. And to all those who believe in human and animal rights. To those who wishes to make Canada their homeland.

To those who encourage people to focus on productive outcomes that advance and unite civilization. To those with peaceful imagination that seek to minimize alienation and celebrate interdependence rather than self sufficiency, inclusion rather then exclusion, openness, opportunity and hope rather than limits, suspicion and grievance. To all those who act to keep this planet in one piece.

If there is to be peace in the world,
There must be peace in the nations.

If there is to be peace in the nations,
There must be peace in the cities.

If there is to be peace in the cities,
There must be peace between neighbors.

If there is to be peace between neighbors,
There must be peace in the home.

If there is to be peace in the home,
There must be peace in the heart.

Lao Tzu (570-490 B.C.)

PREFACE

Migrating from one country and culture to another is a giant and bold step in anyone's life. This publication is my humble effort to save the newcomer's hard earned money and time. I also wish to provide the prospective immigrants from around the world the necessary information and tools in advance to plan their new life well before arriving to Canada. Further, I am trying my best to well equip these perspective immigrants to meet the new challenges with courage, and to face the unexpected. in a professional manner.

Many new immigrants also come with horror stories. An example of those cited by our former Federal Minister of Citizenship and Immigration Canada, Honorable Mr. Denis Coderre who also was very well informed about all the complaints filed by prospective and new immigrants, especially about those unscrupulous immigration consultants who also undermined the reputation of honest and legitimate immigration consultants, lawyers and advisors. Immigration Canada has thousands of complaints about these consultants. I would like to refer to a news article in the daily "Toronto Star" dated Sept.7, 2002. According to the newspaper, Mr. Coderre used a stopover in Hong Kong and cited horror stories of such consultants who urged their clients to lie on their applications, or who falsely claimed that extortionate fees often in excess of $ 10,000 – would guarantee a visa which has never been the case.

Our current Federal Minister of Citizenship and Immigration Honorable Mr. Monte Solberg and his staff is actively addressing the old and current issues to refine and harmonize the Canadian immigration policy to meet the challenges of 21st century .

I must thank and appreciate the cooperation of Ms. Nicole Hudon and Ms. Christine Way of Crown Copyright and Licensing who have guided me to obtain the necessary copyright clearance.

I am sure, you would like what you have in your hands. ***Thanks for checking it out!***

INTRODUCTION

This book features all classes of Canadian immigration under the new Immigration and Refugee Protection Act (IRPA), which was put into effect on June 28, 2002. In previous edition a brief introduction has been given about every class. But this 2nd edition is the most comprehensive edition of this publication in which application guides for all classes have been integrated with latest and up-to-date changes that lead to Canadian immigration with respect to eligibility requirements and how to prepare your application, fill-up the forms and submit to your local Canadian High commission office..

The immigration polices and rules are reviewed from time to time by Citizenship and Immigration Canada (CIC) based on results and objectives. Therefore, CIC constantly updates its website, *www.cic.gc.ca,* to incorporate new changes to deliver up-to-date information to their clients.

In view of the above, web links have been provided for most of the information in this book, hence, encouraging readers to extract or verify particular information by visiting the CIC website before taking any action towards filing their application.

Hopefully this approach will provide the latest and up-to-date information to meet your needs when it comes to Canadian Immigration.

The employment search and settlement part of this book will provide almost every bit of information, which is necessary for new immigrants to successfully settle within any geographical region of their choice in Canada.

An industry veteran, Ms. Irena Valenta, has designed a strategy for employment search in a Canadian workplace to help foreign trained skilled workers to find employment in their field in a professional and efficient manner.

I believe this book will prove to be an asset for every reader who wishes to start a new life in Canada.

CONTENTS

PART ONE

PART TWO

HOW TO IMMIGRATE TO CANADA

Business Immigrant Program

FEDERAL SKILLED WORKER CLASS

PROVINCIAL NOMINEES

FAMILY CLASS

The Economy in Brief

PART THREE

WELCOME TO CANADA
YOUR GUIDE TO START A NEW LIFE WITH SUCCESS

PART FOUR

WORKING IN CANADA
YOUR GUIDE TO CANADIAN LIVING

CANADA

The Land of Peace Lovers and Intelligent Communities

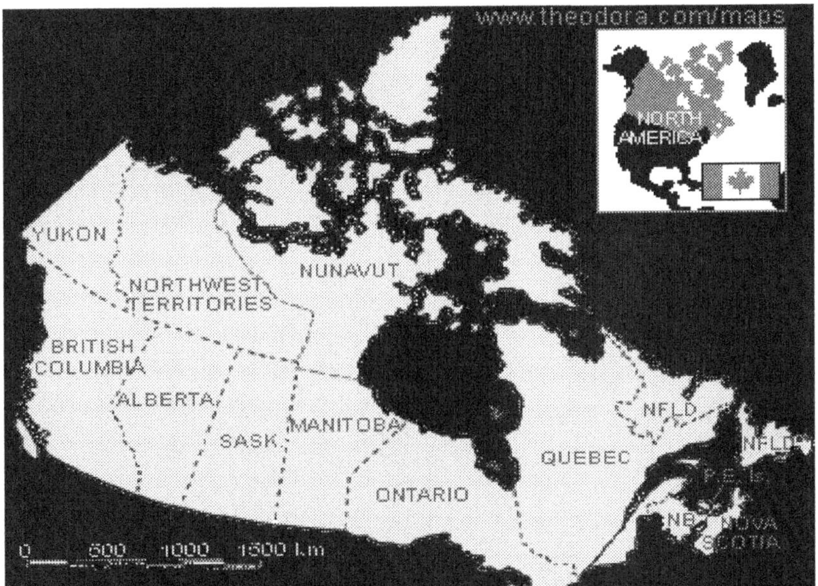

PART ONE

LETS LEARN ABOUT CANADA

CANADA

Introduction

Background:

A land of vast distances and rich natural resources, Canada became a self-governing dominion in 1867 while retaining ties to the British crown. Economically and technologically the nation has developed in parallel with the US, its neighbor to the south across an unfortified border. Canada's paramount political problem is meeting public demands for quality improvements in health care and education services after a decade of budget cuts. Canada also faces questions about integrity in government following revelations regarding a corruption scandal in the federal government that has helped revive the fortunes of separatists in predominantly francophone Quebec.

Geography

Location:

Northern North America, bordering the North Atlantic Ocean on the east, North Pacific Ocean on the west, and the Arctic Ocean on the north, north of the conterminous US

Geographic coordinates:

60 00 N, 95 00 W

Map references:

North America

Area:
total: 9,984,670 sq km
land: 9,093,507 sq km
water: 891,163 sq km

Area - comparative:
somewhat larger than the US

Land boundaries:
total: 8,893 km
border countries: US 8,893 km (includes 2,477 km with Alaska)

Coastline:
202,080 km

Maritime claims:
territorial sea: 12 nm
contiguous zone: 24 nm
exclusive economic zone: 200 nm
continental shelf: 200 nm or to the edge of the continental margin

Climate:
varies from temperate in south to subarctic and arctic in north

Terrain:
mostly plains with mountains in west and lowlands in southeast

Elevation extremes:
lowest point: Atlantic Ocean 0 m
highest point: Mount Logan 5,959 m

Natural resources:
iron ore, nickel, zinc, copper, gold, lead, molybdenum, potash, diamonds, silver, fish, timber, wildlife, coal, petroleum, natural gas, hydropower

Land use:
arable land: 4.57%
permanent crops: 0.65%
other: 94.78% (2005)

Irrigated land:
7,850 sq km (2003)

Natural hazards:
continuous permafrost in north is a serious obstacle to development; cyclonic storms form east of the Rocky Mountains, a result of the mixing of air masses from the Arctic, Pacific, and North American interior, and produce most of the country's rain and snow east of the mountains

Environment current issues:
air pollution and resulting acid rain severely affecting lakes and damaging forests; metal smelting, coal-burning utilities, and vehicle emissions impacting on agricultural and forest productivity; ocean waters becoming contaminated due to agricultural, industrial, mining, and forestry activities

Environment international agreements:

party to: Air Pollution, Air Pollution-Nitrogen Oxides, Air Pollution-Persistent Organic Pollutants, Air Pollution-Sulfur 85, Air Pollution-Sulfur 94, Antarctic-Environmental Protocol, Antarctic-Marine Living Resources, Antarctic Seals, Antarctic Treaty, Biodiversity, Climate Change, Climate Change-Kyoto Protocol, Desertification, Endangered Species, Environmental Modification, Hazardous Wastes, Law of the Sea, Marine Dumping, Ozone Layer Protection, Ship Pollution, Tropical Timber 83, Tropical Timber 94, Wetlands
signed, but not ratified: Air Pollution-Volatile Organic Compounds, Marine Life Conservation

Geography - note:

second-largest country in world (after Russia); strategic location between Russia and US via north polar route; approximately 90% of the population is concentrated within 160 km of the US border

People

Population:
33,098,932 (July 2006 est.)

Age structure:
0-14 years: 17.6% (male 2,992,811/female 2,848,388)
15-64 years: 69% (male 11,482,452/female 11,368,286)
65 years and over: 13.3% (male 1,883,008/female 2,523,987) (2006 est.)

Median age:
total: 38.9 years
male: 37.8 years
female: 39.9 years (2006 est.)

Population growth rate:
0.88% (2006 est.)

Birth rate:
10.78 births/1,000 population (2006 est.)

Death rate:
7.8 deaths/1,000 population (2006 est.)

Net migration rate:
5.85 migrant(s)/1,000 population (2006 est.)

Sex ratio:
at birth: 1.05 male(s)/female
under 15 years: 1.05 male(s)/female
15-64 years: 1.01 male(s)/female
65 years and over: 0.75 male(s)/female
total population: 0.98 male(s)/female (2006 est.)

Infant mortality rate:
total: 4.69 deaths/1,000 live births
male: 5.15 deaths/1,000 live births
female: 4.22 deaths/1,000 live births (2006 est.)

Life expectancy at birth:
total population: 80.22 years
male: 76.86 years
female: 83.74 years (2006 est.)

Total fertility rate:
1.61 children born/woman (2006 est.)

HIV/AIDS - adult prevalence rate:
0.3% (2003 est.)

HIV/AIDS - people living with HIV/AIDS:
56,000 (2003 est.)

HIV/AIDS - deaths:
1,500 (2003 est.)

Nationality:
noun: Canadian(s)
adjective: Canadian

Ethnic groups:
British Isles origin 28%, French origin 23%, other European 15%, Amerindian 2%, other, mostly Asian, African, Arab 6%, mixed background 26%

Religions:
Roman Catholic 42.6%, Protestant 23.3% (including United Church 9.5%, Anglican 6.8%, Baptist 2.4%, Lutheran 2%), other Christian 4.4%, Muslim 1.9%, other and unspecified 11.8%, none 16% (2001 census)

Languages:
English (official) 59.3%, French (official) 23.2%, other 17.5%

Literacy:
definition: age 15 and over can read and write
total population: 99%
male: 99%
female: 99% (2003 est.)

Government

Country name:

conventional long form: none
conventional short form: Canada

Government type:

constitutional monarchy that is also a parliamentary democracy and a federation

Capital:

name: Ottawa
geographic coordinates: 45 25 N, 75 40 W
time difference: UTC-5 (same time as Washington, DC during Standard Time)
daylight saving time: +1hr, begins second Sunday in March; ends first Sunday in November
note: Canada is divided into six time zones

Administrative divisions:

10 provinces and 3 territories*; Alberta, British Columbia, Manitoba, New Brunswick, Newfoundland and Labrador, Northwest Territories*, Nova Scotia, Nunavut*, Ontario, Prince Edward Island, Quebec, Saskatchewan, Yukon Territory*

Independence:

1 July 1867 (union of British North American colonies); 11 December 1931 (independence recognized)

National holiday:

Canada Day, 1 July (1867)

Constitution:
made up of unwritten and written acts, customs, judicial decisions, and traditions; the written part of the constitution consists of the Constitution Act of 29 March 1867, which created a federation of four provinces, and the Constitution Act of 17 April 1982, which transferred formal control over the constitution from Britain to Canada, and added a Canadian Charter of Rights and Freedoms as well as procedures for constitutional amendments

Legal system:
based on English common law, except in Quebec, where civil law system based on French law prevails; accepts compulsory ICJ jurisdiction, with reservations

Suffrage:
18 years of age; universal

Executive branch:
chief of state: Queen ELIZABETH II (since 6 February 1952), represented by Governor General Michaelle JEAN (since 27 September 2005)
head of government: Prime Minister Stephen HARPER (since 6 February 2006)

cabinet: Federal Ministry chosen by the prime minister usually from among the members of his own party sitting in Parliament

elections: none; the monarchy is hereditary; governor general appointed by the monarch on the advice of the prime minister for a five-year term; following legislative elections, the leader of the majority party or the leader of the majority coalition in the House of Commons is automatically designated prime minister by the governor general

Legislative branch:

bicameral Parliament or Parlement consists of the Senate or Senat (members appointed by the governor general with the advice of the prime minister and serve until reaching 75 years of age; its normal limit is 105 senators) and the House of Commons or Chambre des Communes (308 seats; members elected by direct, popular vote to serve for up to five-year terms)

elections: House of Commons - last held 23 January 2006 (next to be held in 2011)
election results: House of Commons - percent of vote by party - Conservative Party 36.3%, Liberal Party 30.2%, New Democratic Party 17.5%, Bloc Quebecois 10.5%, Greens 4.5%, other 1%; seats by party - Conservative Party 124, Liberal Party 103, New Democratic Party 29, Bloc Quebecois 51, other 1

Judicial branch:

Supreme Court of Canada (judges are appointed by the prime minister through the governor general); Federal Court of Canada; Federal Court of Appeal; Provincial Courts (these are named variously Court of Appeal, Court of Queens Bench, Superior Court, Supreme Court, and Court of Justice)

Political parties and leaders:
Bloc Quebecois [Gilles DUCEPPE]; Conservative Party of Canada (a merger of the Canadian Alliance and the Progressive Conservative Party) [Stephen HARPER]; Green Party [Elizabeth MAY]; Liberal Party [Bill GRAHAM]; New Democratic Party [Jack LAYTON]

Political pressure groups and leaders:
NA

International organization participation:
ACCT, AfDB, APEC, Arctic Council, ARF, AsDB, ASEAN (dialogue partner), Australia Group, BIS, C, CDB, CE (observer), EAPC, EBRD, ESA (cooperating state), FAO, G-7, G-8, G-10, IADB, IAEA, IBRD, ICAO, ICC, ICCt, ICFTU, ICRM, IDA, IEA, IFAD, IFC, IFRCS, IHO, ILO, IMF, IMO, Interpol, IOC, IOM, IPU, ISO, ITU, MIGA, MINUSTAH, MONUC, NAFTA, NAM (guest), NATO, NEA, NSG, OAS, OECD, OIF, OPCW, OSCE, Paris Club, PCA, PIF (partner), SECI (observer), UN, UNAMSIL, UNCTAD, UNDOF, UNESCO, UNHCR, UNMOVIC, UNRWA, UNTSO, UPU, WCL, WCO, WFTU, WHO, WIPO, WMO, WToO, WTO, ZC

Diplomatic representation in the US:

chief of mission: Ambassador Michael WILSON
chancery: 501 Pennsylvania Avenue NW, Washington, DC 20001
telephone: [1] (202) 682-1740
FAX: [1] (202) 682-7726
consulate(s) general: Atlanta, Boston, Buffalo, Chicago, Dallas, Denver, Detroit, Los Angeles, Miami, Minneapolis, New York, San Francisco, Seattle
consulate(s): Anchorage, Houston, Philadelphia, Phoenix, Raleigh, San Diego

Diplomatic representation from the US:

chief of mission: Ambassador David H. WILKINS
embassy: 490 Sussex Drive, Ottawa, Ontario K1N 1G8
mailing address: P. O. Box 5000, Ogdensburgh, NY 13669-0430
telephone: [1] (613) 238-5335, 4470
FAX: [1] (613) 688-3082
consulate(s) general: Calgary, Halifax, Montreal, Quebec, Toronto, Vancouver, Winnipeg

Flag description:

two vertical bands of red (hoist and fly side, half width), with white square between them; an 11-pointed red maple leaf is centered in the white square; the official colors of Canada are red and white

Economy

Economy - overview:

As an affluent, high-tech industrial society in the trillion dollar class, Canada resembles the US in its market-oriented economic system, pattern of production, and affluent living standards. Since World War II, the impressive growth of the manufacturing, mining, and service sectors has transformed the nation from a largely rural economy into one primarily industrial and urban. The 1989 US-Canada Free Trade Agreement (FTA) and the 1994 North American Free Trade Agreement (NAFTA) (which includes Mexico) touched off a dramatic increase in trade and economic integration with the US. Given its great natural resources, skilled labor force, and modern capital plant, Canada enjoys solid economic prospects. Top-notch fiscal management has produced consecutive balanced budgets since 1997, although public debate continues over how to manage the rising cost of the publicly funded healthcare system. Exports account for roughly a third of GDP. Canada enjoys a substantial trade surplus with its principal trading partner, the US, which absorbs more than 85% of Canadian exports. Canada is the US' largest foreign supplier of energy, including oil, gas, uranium, and electric power.

GDP (purchasing power parity):

$1.111 trillion (2005 est.)

GDP (official exchange rate):

$1.035 trillion (2005 est.)

GDP - real growth rate: 2.9% (2005 est.)

GDP - per capita (PPP): $33,900 (2005 est.)

GDP - composition by sector:
agriculture: 2.2%
industry: 29.4%
services: 68.4% (2005 est.)

Labor force: 16.3 million (December 2005)

Labor force - by occupation: agriculture 2%, manufacturing 14%, construction 5%, services 75%, other 3% (2004)

Unemployment rate: 6.8% (2005 est.)

Population below poverty line: 15.9%; note - this figure is the Low Income Cut-Off (LICO), a calculation that results in higher figures than found in many comparable economies; Canada does not have an official poverty line (2003)

Household income or consumption by percentage share:
lowest 10%: 2.8%
highest 10%: 23.8% (1994)

Distribution of family income - Gini index: 33.1 (1998)

Inflation rate (consumer prices): 2.2% (2005 est.)

Investment (gross fixed):	20.5% of GDP (2005 est.)
Budget:	*revenues:* $159.6 billion *expenditures:* $152.6 billion; including capital expenditures of $NA (2004)
Public debt:	69.6% of GDP (2005 est.)
Agriculture - products:	wheat, barley, oilseed, tobacco, fruits, vegetables; dairy products; forest products; fish
Industries:	transportation equipment, chemicals, processed and unprocessed minerals, food products, wood and paper products, fish products, petroleum and natural gas
Industrial production growth rate:	2.6% (2005 est.)
Electricity - production:	566.3 billion kWh (2003)
Electricity - consumption:	520.9 billion kWh (2003)
Electricity - exports:	22 billion kWh (2004)
Electricity - imports:	33 billion kWh (2004)
Oil - production:	2.4 million bbl/day (2004)

Oil - consumption: 2.3 million bbl/day (2004)

Oil - exports: 1.6 million bbl/day (2004)

Oil - imports: 963,000 bbl/day (2004)

Oil - proved reserves: 178.9 billion bbl
note: includes oil sands (2004 est.)

Natural gas - production: 165.8 billion cu m (2003 est.)

Natural gas - consumption: 90.95 billion cu m (2003 est.)

Natural gas - exports: 91.52 billion cu m (2003 est.)

Natural gas - imports: 8.73 billion cu m (2003 est.)

Natural gas - proved reserves: 1.673 trillion cu m (2004)

Current account balance: $24.96 billion (2005 est.)

Exports: $364.8 billion f.o.b. (2005 est.)

Exports - commodities: motor vehicles and parts, industrial machinery, aircraft, telecommunications equipment; chemicals, plastics, fertilizers; wood pulp, timber, crude petroleum, natural gas, electricity, aluminum

Exports - partners:	US 84.2%, Japan 2.1%, UK 1.8% (2005)
Imports:	$317.7 billion f.o.b. (2005 est.)
Imports - commodities:	machinery and equipment, motor vehicles and parts, crude oil, chemicals, electricity, durable consumer goods
Imports - partners:	US 56.7%, China 7.8%, Mexico 3.8% (2005)
Reserves of foreign exchange and gold:	$33.02 billion (2005 est.)
Debt - external:	$439.8 billion (30 November 2005)
Economic aid - donor:	ODA, $2.6 billion (2004)
Currency (code):	Canadian dollar (CAD)
Exchange rates:	Canadian dollars per US dollar - 1.2118 (2005), 1.301 (2004), 1.4011 (2003), 1.5693 (2002), 1.5488 (2001)
Fiscal year:	1 April - 31 March

Communications

Telephones - main lines in use: 18.276 million (2005)

Telephones - mobile cellular: 16.6 million (2005)

Telephone system: *general assessment:* excellent service provided by modern technology
domestic: domestic satellite system with about 300 earth stations
international: country code - 1-xxx; 5 coaxial submarine cables; satellite earth stations - 5 Intelsat (4 Atlantic Ocean and 1 Pacific Ocean) and 2 Intersputnik (Atlantic Ocean region)

Radio broadcast stations: AM 245, FM 582, shortwave 6 (2004)

Television broadcast stations: 80 (plus many repeaters) (1997)

Internet country code: .ca

Internet hosts: 3,934,223 (2006)

Internet users: 21.9 million (2005)

Transportation

Airports:
1,337 (2006)

Airports - with paved runways:
total: 509
over 3,047 m: 18
2,438 to 3,047 m: 15
1,524 to 2,437 m: 151
914 to 1,523 m: 248
under 914 m: 77 (2006)

Airports - with unpaved runways:
total: 828
1,524 to 2,437 m: 66
914 to 1,523 m: 355
under 914 m: 407 (2006)

Heliports:
319 (2006)

Pipelines:
crude and reined oil 23,564 km; liquid petroleum gas 74,980 km (2005)

Railways:
total: 48,467 km
standard gauge: 48,467 km 1.435-m gauge (2005)

Roadways:
total: 1,042,300 km
paved: 415,600 km (including 17,000 km of expressways)
unpaved: 626,700 km (2005)

Waterways:
631 km
note: Saint Lawrence Seaway of 3,769 km, including the Saint Lawrence River of 3,058 km, shared with United States (2003)

Merchant marine:
total: 173 ships (1000 GRT or over) 2,129,243 GRT/2,716,340 DWT
by type: bulk carrier 62, cargo 10, chemical tanker 9, container 2, passenger 6, passenger/cargo 63, petroleum tanker 13, roll on/roll off 8
foreign-owned: 7 (Germany 3, Netherlands 1, Norway 1, US 2)
registered in other countries: 111 (Australia 1, Bahamas 18, Barbados 8, Cambodia 6, Cyprus 2, Denmark 1, Honduras 1, Hong Kong 28, Liberia 2, Malta 18, Marshall Islands 6, Panama 4, Russia 1, Saint Vincent and the Grenadines 6, US 4, Vanuatu 5) (2006)

Ports and terminals:
Fraser River Port, Halifax, Montreal, Port Cartier, Quebec, Saint John's (Newfoundland), Sept Isles, Vancouver

Military

Military branches:	Canadian Forces: Land Forces Command, Maritime Command, Air Command, Canada Command (homeland security) (2006)
Military service age and obligation:	16 years of age for voluntary military service; women comprise approximately 11% of Canada's armed forces (2001)
Manpower available for military service:	*males age 16-49:* 8,216,510 *females age 16-49:* 8,034,939 (2005 est.)
Manpower fit for military service:	*males age 16-49:* 6,740,490 *females age 16-49:* 6,580,868 (2005 est.)
Manpower reaching military service age annually:	*males age 18-49:* 223,821 *females age 16-49:* 212,900 (2005 est.)
Military expenditures - percent of GDP:	1.1% (2003)

Transnational Issues

Disputes - international: managed maritime boundary disputes with the US at Dixon Entrance, Beaufort Sea, Strait of Juan de Fuca, and around the disputed Machias Seal Island and North Rock; working toward greater cooperation with US in monitoring people and commodities crossing the border; uncontested sovereignty dispute with Denmark over Hans Island in the Kennedy Channel between Ellesmere Island and Greenland

Illicit drugs: illicit producer of cannabis for the domestic drug market and export to US; use of hydroponics technology permits growers to plant large quantities of high-quality marijuana indoors; transit point for ecstasy entering the US market; vulnerable to narcotics money laundering because of its mature financial services sector

This page was last updated on 14 November, 2006

World-Wide Quality of Living Survey

- Zurich scores highest for quality of living, Baghdad ranks lowest
- Cities in Canada, Europe and Australia dominate the top of the rankings
- Honolulu is the highest ranking city in the US; Houston is the lowest
- London remains at position 39; Birmingham and Glasgow both climb one place to joint 55th position

Zurich ranks as the world's top city for quality of living, according to a survey by Mercer Human Resource Consulting. The city scores 108.2 and is only marginally ahead of Geneva, which scores 108.1, while Vancouver follows in third place with a score of 107.7. In contrast, Baghdad is the lowest ranking city in the survey, scoring just 14.5.

The analysis is part of an annual World-wide Quality of Living Survey, covering more than 350 cities, to help governments and multinational companies place employees on international assignments. Each city is based on an evaluation of 39 criteria, including political, social, economic and environmental factors, personal safety and health, education, transport, and other public services. Cities are ranked against New York as the base city, which has an index score of 100.

"When multinational companies set up expatriate assignments they have to provide attractive reward packages to compensate employees for any negative changes to their quality of living," Yvonne Sonsino, Principal at Mercer, commented. "Moving abroad can be a big upheaval for expatriates and their families, so international assignments tend to carry large price tags, particularly if they are in cities with low living standards facing political unrest or terrorist threats." She added: "Many companies use benchmark data to help them structure pay deals at the right level."

Europe and the Middle East

Almost half the top 30 scoring cities are in Western Europe. In this region, Vienna follows Zurich and Geneva in 4th position with a score of 107.5. Other highly-rated cities include Düsseldorf (107.2), Frankfurt (107.0) and Munich (106.8) in positions 6, 7 and 8 respectively. Athens remains the lowest scoring city in Western Europe, scoring 86.8 at position 79.

London is the UK's highest ranking city and is stable at position 39 (score 101.2). The two other UK cities covered in the survey are Birmingham and Glasgow, which both score 98.3 and climb one place to joint 55th position. Dublin has dropped two places to 24th position, scoring 103.8, mainly due to increased traffic congestion.

As predicted, cities in Eastern Europe such as Budapest, Ljubljana, Prague, Vilnius, Tallinn and Warsaw continue to benefit from incremental score increases and are gradually climbing the rankings.

"The standard of living in many Eastern European cities is gradually improving, as the countries that most recently joined the EU attract greater investment," commented Slagin Parakatil, Senior Researcher at Mercer. "Yet cities such as Dubai may still offer a wider variety of facilities demanded by expatriates – for example, well-connected international airports and better opportunities for recreation and leisure activities – compared to many Eastern European cities."

Positions for most cities in Europe and the Middle East are generally unchanged, with the exception of Cairo which has tumbled nine places to position 131 and scores 71.2 due to the political turmoil and terrorist attacks in the city and surrounding area.

Baghdad ranks as the least attractive city for expatriates for a third consecutive year, with a score of 14.5.

Americas

Honolulu, the highest ranking city in the U.S., drops two positions to 27th with a score of 103.3. San Francisco remains at 28th position and scores 103.2. Boston, Washington, Chicago and Portland follow in positions 36, 41, 41 and 43 respectively (scores 101.9, 100.4, 100.4 and 100.3) while Houston remains the lowest ranking city in the U.S. at position 68 (score 95.4). Overall, U.S. cities continue to slip slightly or remain stable in the rankings, except Chicago which has moved up 11 places due to decreased crime rates.

"Economies in the developed world tend to be relatively stable overall. Fluctuations in the quality of living in these regions are usually driven by factors such as increased air pollution, crime rates and traffic congestion, or external events like terrorism, disease outbreaks or natural disasters," said Mr. Parakatil.

In South America, scores vary considerably due to differences in economic and political stability. "Argentina's steady economic recovery is likely to push its cities up in the rankings in the next few years," commented Mr. Parakatil.

Asia-Pacific

Auckland and Wellington have both moved up the rankings from 8th to 5th and 14th to 12th places respectively, mainly due to strong internal stability relative to other cities, while Sydney remains at position 9 with a score of 106.5.

In Asia, Singapore ranks 34th (score 102.5) followed by Tokyo, Japan's highest scoring city, at position 35 (score 102.3). Hong Kong's modern and efficient infrastructure, including its airport (which is considered one of best in the world), has pushed it up from 70th to 68th position with a score of 95.4.

The top-ranking city in China is Shanghai in 103rd place (score 80.1). "Beijing and Shanghai are on the rise and should experience rapid improvements in quality of living in the coming years. This is mainly due to greater international investment driven by the availability and lower cost of labour and manufacturing expertise," explained Mr. Parakatil.

Though cities in India generally rank lower than their Chinese counterparts, they are also showing signs of development in the region.

"The quality of living in Indian cites such as Mumbai and Bangalore is increasing slowly but steadily, primarily due to India's improved political relationships with other countries," said Mr. Parakatil. "Investment from multinationals setting up operations in India may prompt further improvements, boost economic growth and contribute to economic stability. In turn, this will encourage the local authorities to focus on improving quality of living standards."

Other low-ranking cities for overall quality of living include Congo in Brazzaville (score 30.3) and Bangui in the Central African Republic and Khartoum in Sudan (30.6 and 31.7).

The overall quality of living ranking is based on an evaluation of 39 criteria. New York has been used as the base score for quality of living, which has a total index equal to 100.

Mercer's study is based on detailed assessments and evaluations of 39 key quality of living determinants, grouped in the following categories:

- ***Political and social environment*** (political stability, crime, law enforcement, etc.)

- ***Economic environment*** (currency exchange regulations, banking services, etc.)
- ***Socio-cultural environment*** (censorship, limitations on personal freedom, etc.)
- ***Medical and health considerations*** (medical supplies and services, infectious diseases, sewage, waste disposal, air pollution, etc.)
- ***Schools and education*** (standard and availability of schools, etc.)
- ***Public services and transportation*** (electricity, water, public transport, traffic congestion, etc.)
- ***Recreation*** (restaurants, theatres, cinemas, sports and leisure, etc.)
- ***Consumer goods*** (availability of food/daily consumption items, cars, etc.)
- ***Housing*** (housing, household appliances, furniture, maintenance services, etc.)
- ***Natural environment*** (climate, record of natural disasters)

***Notes**: Data was collected largely between September and November 2005 and is updated regularly to take account of changing circumstances. In particular, the assessments will be revised in the case of any new developments. Only 215 cities have been considered in the Quality of Living 2006 rankings.*

Canada - The World's Best Country to Live in

Vancouver is Third in World in Annual Quality of Life Survey

Vancouver ranked third overall in the 2005 annual "Quality of Life Survey", published by Mercer Human Resource Consulting. This year's score matches Vancouver's previous score in the 2004 Quality of Life survey.

Geneva and Zurich, Switzerland were tied for first place with scores of 106.5. **Vancouver's** score was 106, which tied it with Vienna, Austria. Other Canadian cities, Toronto, Ottawa, Montreal , and Calgary took 14th, 20th, 22nd and 25th place, respectively.

All five Canadian cities in the survey were praised for their relatively high levels of "personal safety and security" and for being in a politically stable country, according to a report from CBC News (see below).

- **Vancouver 3rd in world in quality of life survey**
- *CBC News, March 14, 2005*
- **World-wide quality of life survey**
- *Mercer Human Resource Consulting, March 14, 2005*

For almost a decade (up to the year 2001), Canada was ranked ***number one*** among 175 countries in the United Nation's Quality of Life survey.

Canada still manages to maintain a relatively high standard today. According to the 2004 UN Human Development Index, Canada was ranked fourth overall.

What is the United Nations Human Development Index?

The United Nations Human Development Index **(HDI)** examines the health, education and wealth of each nation's citizens by measuring:

- life expectancy
- educational achievement -- adult literacy plus combined primary,
- secondary and tertiary enrolment; and standard of living -- real GDP per capita based on PPP exchange rates.

The UN also computes a Gender-Related Development Index that extends the HDI to take into account gender differences in the ranking criteria. Canada ranks well in this category: 2nd in 2002, 1st in 1997, and 2nd in 1996.

Canada has the best educated people and the highest literacy rate in the world. Canadians live longer than anyone on the planet, except people in Japan and Iceland.

Vancouver, the best city in the Americas

In a similar vein, the Geneva-based Corporate Resources Group compares more that one hundred major international cities in their annual 'quality of life' survey. Rankings are compiled by using 42 factors covering political and economic stability, crime, pollution, health, environment, education, infrastructure and leisure facilities.

In 2004, Condé Nast Traveler magazine voted Vancouver the "Best City in the Americas" at its annual Readers' Choice Awards ceremony held in New York. Vancouver won the top spot over Victoria and Quebec City.

Canada's Financial Performance in an International Context

Introduction

This annex reviews Canada's financial position on a comparable basis with those of the other Group of Seven (G7) countries (United States, United Kingdom, France, Germany, Japan and Italy). For Canada, the relevant measure is the total government financial position, which consists of the federal, provincial-territorial and local government sectors, as well as the Canada Pension Plan and the Quebec Pension Plan.

On a total government, National Accounts basis:

- Canada was the only G7 country to record a surplus in 2003, 2004 and 2005.
- The Organisation for Economic Co-operation and Development (OECD) projects that Canada will be the only G7 country to record a surplus in both 2006 and 2007.
- Canada's total government sector net debt burden declined to an estimated 26.4 per cent of gross domestic product (GDP) in 2005, and has been the lowest in the G7 since 2004.

Looking at the fiscal positions of the federal governments in Canada and the United States:

- In 2004–05 the Canadian federal government posted a surplus of C$1.5 billion or 0.1 per cent of GDP, while the U.S. federal government incurred an "on-budget" deficit of US$494 billion or 4.0 per cent of GDP.

- For 2005–06, the federal government in Canada is forecasting a surplus of C$8 billion or 0.6 per cent of GDP, while the U.S. Administration is projecting an on-budget deficit of US$602 billion or 4.6 per cent of GDP.

- As a result of continued surpluses in Canada and the deterioration in U.S. federal finances, the federal market debt-to-GDP ratio in Canada fell below the U.S. figure in 2003–04 for the first time since 1977–78, with the gap expected to widen in 2005–06.

Comparing Fiscal Results Across Countries

- Two important factors need to be taken into account in making international comparisons: differences in accounting practices among countries, and differences in financial responsibilities among levels of government within countries.

- For these reasons, international comparisons rely on the standardized System of National Accounts estimates for the total government sector (i.e. the combined national and subnational levels). The OECD produces a complete series of estimates based on this system. Unless otherwise indicated, the data presented in this annex are based on the December *2005 OECD Economic Outlook*.

Comparing Fiscal Results Between the Canadian and the U.S. Federal Governments

- It is important to note that there are certain fundamental differences in the accounting practices and expenditure responsibilities of the Canadian and U.S. federal governments. The U.S. federal budgetary balance includes the substantial surpluses in the Social Security system, whereas surpluses in the Canada Pension Plan are not included in the Canadian federal figures. For this reason, the Canadian federal balance is more comparable with the "on-budget" balance in the U.S. (excluding Social Security), while U.S. government debt is more comparable with federal market debt in Canada.

Canada is Expected To Be The Only G7 Country To Record A Surplus In 2006 And 2007

Chart A1.1
Total Government Financial Balances
(National Accounts Basis)

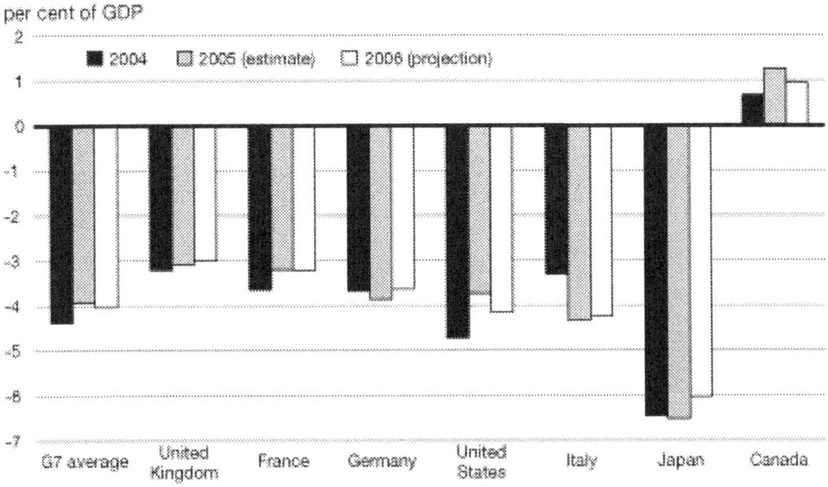

Source: *OECD Economic Outlook*, No. 78 (December 2005).

- Canada was the only G7 country to record a surplus in 2005, according to OECD estimates of the total government sector financial position. This was the third consecutive year in which Canada was the only G7 country in surplus. Canada's surplus for 2005 was estimated at 1.3 per cent of GDP, compared to an average deficit of 3.9 per cent in the G7 countries.

- The OECD expects that Canada will continue to be the only G7 country to post a total government surplus again in 2006 and in 2007.

Canada Has The Lowest Net Debt Burden In The G7

Chart A1.2

Total Government Net Financial Liabilities

(National Accounts Basis)

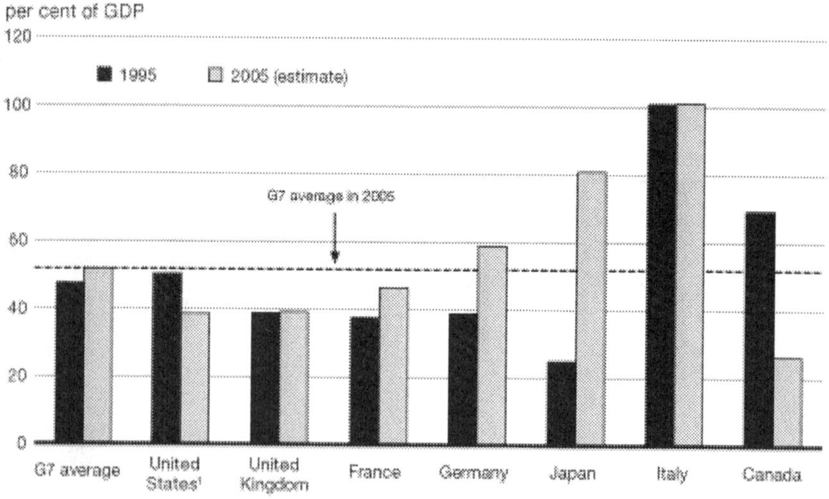

[1]Adjusted to exclude certain government employee pension liabilities to enhance comparability with other countries' debt measures.

Sources: *OECD Economic Outlook*, No. 78 (December 2005); Federal Reserve, *Flow of Funds Accounts of the United States* (December 2005); Department of Finance Canada calculations.

- Canada currently has the lowest ratio of total government net financial liabilities[1] to GDP among G7 countries. Canada's ratio was estimated at 26.4 per cent of GDP in 2005, a significant decline from the peak in 1995. The OECD estimates that Canada will continue to have the lowest net debt burden in both 2006 and 2007. In contrast, the debt burdens of all other G7 countries are projected to continue to increase.

The Federal Government in Canada Has Maintained A Budgetary Surplus Since 1997–98, Unlike The U.S.

Chart A1.3
Federal Budgetary Balances
(Public Accounts Basis)

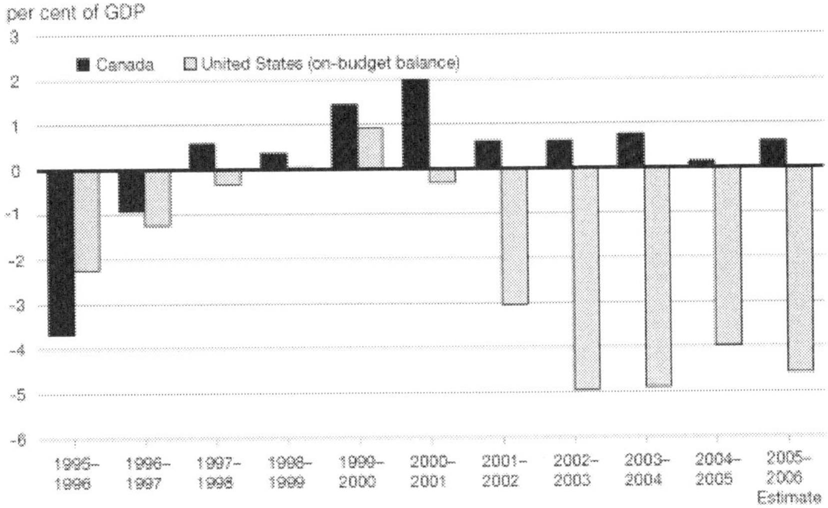

Note: This chart shows the budgetary balance for Canada and the on-budget balance for the U.S. for fiscal years ending March 31 and September 30 respectively.

Sources: Canada—Department of Finance Canada. U.S.—Budget of the United States Government, fiscal year 2007.

- Like the Canadian federal government, the U.S. federal government moved from large deficits to surpluses in the latter half of the 1990s. However, since 2000–01 the U.S. has returned to deficits whereas Canada has recorded successive surpluses.

- The Canadian federal government posted a surplus of C$1.5 billion or 0.1 per cent of GDP in 2004–05, while the U.S. federal government incurred an "on-budget" deficit of US$494 billion or 4.0 per cent of GDP. Even when Social Security surpluses are included, the U.S. "unified budget" deficit was US$318 billion or 2.6 per cent of GDP in 2004–05.

- While the Canadian federal government is expecting a surplus of C$8 billion in 2005–06, the U.S. on-budget deficit is expected to increase to US$602 billion or 4.6 per cent of GDP (with a unified budget deficit of US$423 billion). The U.S. Administration does not project a return to balanced budgets for at least the next five years.

The Federal Market Debt-To-GDP Ratio In Canada Fell

Chart A1.4
Federal Market Debt
(Public Accounts Basis)

per cent of GDP

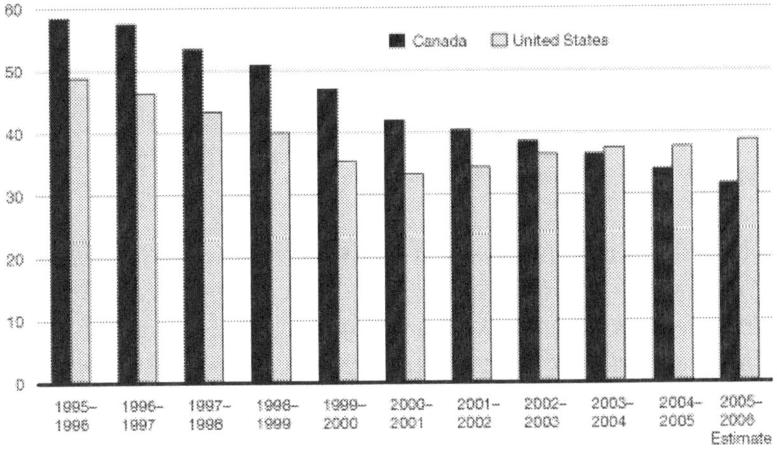

Note: This chart shows market debt for Canada and debt held by the public for the U.S. for fiscal years ending March 31 and September 30 respectively. These two measures are the most comparable measures of the federal debt burden of the two countries.

Sources: Canada—Department of Finance Canada. U.S.—Budget of the United States Government, fiscal year 2007.

- As a result of continued surpluses at the federal level in Canada and the deterioration in U.S. federal finances, the federal market debt-to-GDP ratio in Canada fell below the U.S. figure in 2003–04 for the first time since 1977–78.
- The Canadian federal market debt-to-GDP ratio fell to 33.8 per cent in 2004–05 while the U.S. figure rose for the fourth consecutive year to 37.4 per cent. This gap is expected to widen in 2005–06 as the Canadian ratio is expected to fall to 31.5 per cent while the U.S. ratio is expected to rise to 38.5 per cent.

[1] *The OECD uses the term "net financial liabilities" to mean "net debt" of the total government sector.*

Where Canadians Tax Dollar Goes

In the fiscal year ended March 31, 2005, Canada's federal government collected $198.4 billion in taxes and other revenues. That represents a bit over 15 per cent of our country's $1.3-trillion economy. This fanfold provides a quick overview of where that money went—and how it was raised.

About These Numbers

The federal government calculates its finances over a 12-month "fiscal year" that ends every March 31. This presentation is based on the *Annual Financial Report of the Government of Canada* for the most recent completed fiscal year, 2004–05. *Where Your Tax Dollar Goes* is updated annually, after the Government's final financial results become available. Please note that numbers may not total 100 per cent due to rounding.

1. Interest Payments

The largest single federal spending item in 2004–05 was interest payments on Canada's public debt (that is, money borrowed by the central government over the years, which has not yet been repaid to the lenders). These payments—to institutions and people who hold federal bonds, treasury bills and other forms of the debt—cost $34.1 billion. That's just over 17 cents of every tax dollar

2. Transfer Payments

Cash payments that go directly to individuals, to provincial and territorial governments, and to other organizations are called "transfers." There are three major categories of transfers. Combined, they made up more than half of all federal spending—just over 55 cents of each tax dollar ($109.6 billion).

Transfers to Persons

The biggest transfer category was Major Transfers to Persons. These direct payments to people cost about 21 1⁄2 cents of every tax dollar ($42.6 billion).

- This included payments to eligible elderly Canadians through Old Age Security payments, the Guaranteed Income Supplement and the Allowance for spouses. After interest on the federal debt, this support for seniors was the second largest spending item in the federal budget—14 cents of your tax dollar ($27.9 billion).

- The other major transfer to people was employment insurance (EI) benefits to eligible unemployed workers (including for periods of unemployment due to sickness, pregnancy, parental leave and caring for gravely ill or dying family members). And funding also went to programs that assist people to prepare for, find and maintain jobs. Altogether, EI payments cost about 7 1⁄2 cents of every tax dollar ($14.7 billion).

Support for Families and Children

In 2004–05, the federal government also provided nearly $12 billion in direct cash payments to help low- and modest-income families—especially those with children—through the Canada Child Tax Benefit ($8.7 billion) and the goods and services tax (GST) credit ($3 billion). Since these payments are subtracted from ("netted against") personal income tax and GST revenues, they are not included in the spending calculations presented to Parliament in each year's federal budget.

Funding for Provinces

The federal government also funds several Major Transfers to Other Levels of Government. These payments—totalling almost $42 billion in 2004–05—help provinces and territories pay for health care, post-secondary education and other social services.

Since 1996, much of this support came through a single program, the Canada Health and Social Transfer. However, to improve transparency and accountability, the federal, provincial and territorial First Ministers agreed to divide this funding into two separate programs starting in 2004.

- The Canada Health Transfer in 2004–05 provided provinces and territories with cash support for health programs equal to more than 71⁄2 cents of each tax dollar ($15.2 billion).

- The Canada Social Transfer—to support post-secondary education, social assistance and other social programs—gave provinces and territories cash funding representing 4 cents of each federal tax dollar ($7.9 billion).

Further major transfers included the equalization and Territorial Formula Financing programs, which together equal more than 61⁄2 cents of every tax dollar ($13.3 billion). These are payments from Ottawa to less-affluent provinces, and to the three territories, to help them provide public services reasonably comparable to those that wealthier provinces can deliver.

There were also a variety of other federal transfers, such as funding to reduce medical wait times, for early learning and child care, and under an agreement with Newfoundland and Labrador and Nova Scotia about offshore resource revenues. Together, these helped boost transfer funding by almost 3 cents of each tax dollar ($5.5 billion).

Support for Health Care

Federal support for health care goes beyond cash payments under the Canada Health Transfer, the equalization program, and initiatives such as the $4.2-billion Wait Times Reduction Fund.

For example, in 1977 the federal government agreed to let the provinces take over a share of its taxes to supplement direct cash transfers. In 2004–05, these "tax points" added some $16 billion to provincial finances for programs such as health care.

There is also direct health-related spending by the federal government itself, which contributed some $6 billion last year. This included funding for First Nations health services; health care for veterans; and programs for health protection, disease prevention, health information and health-related research.

For more information, consult *Total Federal Support for Health, Post-Secondary Education, and Social Assistance and Social Services (2004–05)* on the Department of Finance Canada website at www.fin.gc.ca.

Other Grants and Contributions

Other transfer programs by various federal departments provide funds to individuals, governments and other organizations and groups for specific public policy purposes.

In 2004–05, spending on these federal grants, contributions and subsidies added up to $25 billion, or just over 121⁄2 cents of each tax dollar. This included:

- Over $6 billion in transfers for First Nations and Aboriginal peoples (bringing total federal spending in this area to some $9 billion).

- Some $2.8 billion in assistance to farmers and other food producers.
- About $3.6 billion in foreign aid and other international assistance.
- Over $3.6 billion in support for research and development, infrastructure, regional development and assistance to businesses.

Further funding went to student assistance programs, health research and promotion, the arts, amateur sports, and multiculturalism and bilingualism.

Other Program Expenses

After transfers, the bulk of federal tax dollars went to cover the operating costs of government itself: the more than 130 departments, agencies, Crown corporations and other federal bodies that provide programs and services for Canadians.

In 2004–05, these operating costs (such as salaries and benefits, facilities and equipment, and supplies and travel) made up a bit under 27 cents of each tax dollar ($53.1 billion).

But a large share of this spending—close to 11 1⁄2 cents of each tax dollar—went to just three organizations.

Federal Government's Budgetary Expenditures

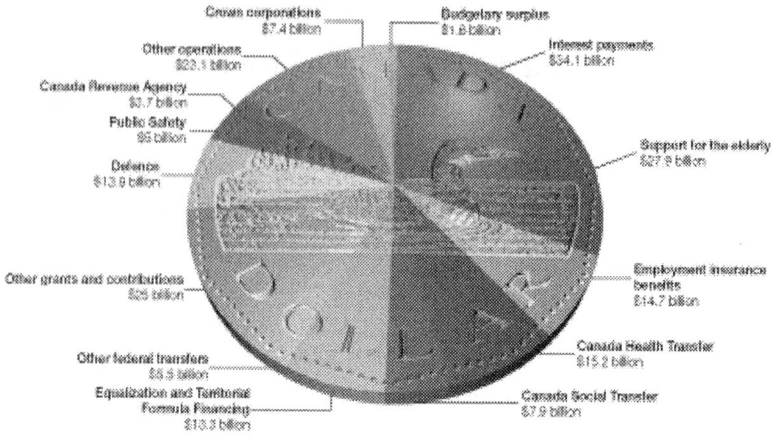

Defence

First, spending by the Department of National Defence on Canada's military forces last year made up 7 cents of each taxpayer dollar ($13.9 billion).

Public Safety

Next, operating costs of the Department of Public Safety and Emergency Preparedness were just over 21⁄2 cents of your tax dollar ($5 billion). This includes funding for the Royal Canadian Mounted Police, the federal prison system, and border traffic and security operations.

Canada Revenue Agency

And third, there was funding for the Canada Revenue Agency, which administers the federal tax system (and also collects personal income taxes for all provinces except Quebec). Its operations cost about 2 cents of each tax dollar ($3.7 billion).

Other Operations

A further $23.1 billion—just over 11 1/2 cents of each tax dollar—was spent on the operations of the other federal departments and agencies.

These included major departments such as: Environment; Fisheries and Oceans; Health; Human Resources Development; Industry; Justice; Natural Resources; Public Works; Transport; and Veterans Affairs.

As well, funding went to federal agencies such as the Canadian Food Inspection Agency, Parks Canada and the Canadian International Development Agency.

Paying for Parliament

One of the smallest slices of federal operating spending goes to Parliament itself—the House of Commons, the Senate and the Library of Parliament.

In 2004–05, the combination of salaries and benefits for Members of Parliament, Senators and parliamentary staff, and spending on facilities and services, totalled about $468 million. That's about one-quarter of a cent of every tax dollar.

Crown Corporations

The last portion of Other Program Expenses in 2004–05 went to Crown corporations (organizations owned directly or indirectly by the Government). This cost $7.4 billion, or a bit over 3.7 cents of your tax dollar. But the bulk of this funding went to just three organizations:

- The Canada Mortgage and Housing Corporation, which helps support home ownership and affordable housing, received $2.1 billion.

- The Canadian Broadcasting Corporation—our national television and radio networks—received $1 billion.

- Atomic Energy of Canada Limited recorded a $2.3-billion expense last year for environmental liabilities.

Funding was also provided to cultural organizations (including the National Gallery of Canada, the Canadian Museum of Civilization and the Canada Council for the Arts), to enterprises like VIA Rail, and to the Canadian Tourism Commission.

4. Budgetary Surplus
(Debt Reduction)

The remaining 0.8 cents of the 2004–05 tax dollar was the budgetary surplus—how much money was left after paying for all federal programs, operations and interest on the debt ($1.6 billion).

This surplus was not money available for future spending. Government accounting principles mean that any surplus at year-end automatically goes to help reduce the federal debt.

Together with other surpluses recorded in recent years, this has helped cut the federal debt by $63 billion. And lower debt means the Government and taxpayers are saving $3 billion a year in interest costs.

Where the Money Comes From

The federal government's budgetary revenues came from a variety of taxes and other sources.

- Personal income tax is the biggest revenue source. In 2004–05, it provided $89.8 billion in federal funding. That's more than 45 per cent of all federal revenues.

- Revenues from the goods and services tax provided $29.8 billion, or 15 per cent of total federal funds.

- Corporate income tax raised about $30 billion, just over 15 per cent of federal finances.

- A number of other taxes—such as non-resident taxes, customs import duties, energy taxes and excise taxes on alcohol and tobacco—made up $16.7 billion, or nearly 8½ per cent of revenues.

- As well, employment insurance premiums, which are treated as part of general revenues, contributed $17.3 billion to federal finances, or 8.7 per cent of the total.

- And other revenues—such as earnings by Crown corporations and the sale of goods and services—provided the remaining $14.9 billion, or 7½ per cent of total revenues. This included a one-time $2.6-billion net gain from the sale of the federal government's remaining shares in Petro-Canada.

Federal Government's Budgetary Revenues

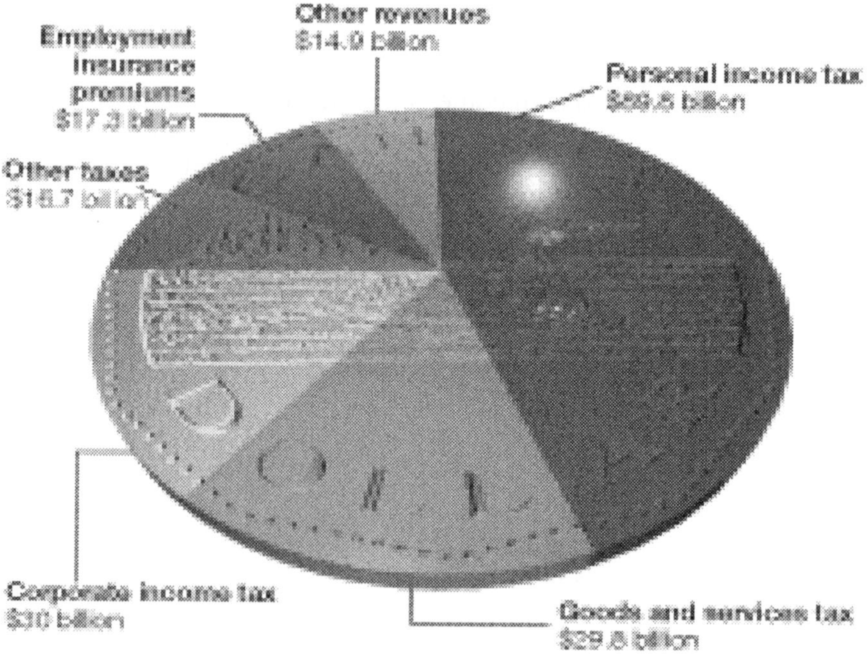

How Can I Get More Information?

A multimedia version of this document—which also includes direct links to other online material on federal finances—is available on the Internet at www.fin.gc.ca.

General information on the Government of Canada and its operations is available by phoning:

1 800 O-Canada (1 800 622-6232)
1 800 926-9105
(TTY for the speech and hearing impaired)

You can also obtain copies of this fanfold and other documents prepared by the Department of Finance Canada from the:

Distribution Centre
Department of Finance Canada
Room P-135, West Tower
300 Laurier Avenue West
Ottawa, Ontario K1A 0G5
Phone (613) 995-2855
Fax: (613) 996-0518
E-mail: services-distribution@fin.gc.ca

Population of Census Metropolitan Areas, (2001 Census Boundaries)

	2000	2001	2002	2003	2004
	persons (thousands)				
Total census metropolitan areas	**19,332.2**	**19,959.7**	**20,285.3**	**20,526.2**	**20,754.8**
Toronto (Ont.)	4,747.2	4,883.8	5,020.4	5,114.5	5,203.6
Montréal (Que.)	3,471.3	3,507.4	3,547.1	3,577.4	3,607.2
Vancouver (B.C.)	2,040.3	2,076.1	2,111.3	2,140.6	2,160.0
Ottawa-Gatineau (Ont.-Que.)	1,078.5	1,102.9	1,118.8	1,131.6	1,142.7
Calgary (Alta.)	952.5	976.8	1,002.0	1,018.9	1,037.1
Edmonton (Alta.)	946.9	961.5	979.9	990.8	1,001.6
Quebec (Que.)	692.6	696.4	701.6	705.5	710.8
Hamilton (Ont.)	678.8	689.2	697.9	704.8	710.3
Winnipeg (Man.)	686.4	690.1	693.7	697.1	702.4
London (Ont.)	445.0	449.6	454.5	457.6	459.7
Kitchener (Ont.)	423.4	431.3	438.7	444.7	450.1
St. Catharines-Niagara (Ont.)	390.3	391.7	393.2	394.4	394.9
Halifax (N.S.)	366.3	369.1	373.8	376.9	379.8
Windsor (Ont.)	313.7	320.8	325.9	328.6	330.9
Victoria (B.C.)	321.8	325.4	326.8	328.2	330.2
Oshawa (Ont.)	301.8	308.5	315.8	324.0	332.0
Saskatoon (Sask.)	230.3	230.8	231.8	232.6	234.0
Regina (Sask.)	198.0	196.8	196.5	197.3	198.6
St. John's (N.L.)	175.9	176.2	177.5	178.7	179.9
Sherbrooke (Que.)	155.6	157.0	158.7	160.4	162.3
Greater Sudbury (Ont.)	162.2	161.5	161.0	161.1	161.1
Abbotsford (B.C.)[1]	`	SDR1DE	155.2	156.3	160.1
Kingston (Ont.)[1]	..	152.7	154.4	155.7	156.5
Saguenay (Que.)	159.4	157.8	156.2	155.0	154.2
Trois-Rivières (Que.)	140.6	140.1	140.0	140.4	141.2
Saint John (N.B.)	126.6	126.0	126.1	126.3	126.5
Thunder Bay (Ont.)	126.8	126.6	126.2	126.8	127.1

Note: Population as of July 1.

1. Abbostford and Kingston became census metropolitan areas in 2001.

Source: Statistics Canada, CANSIM, table 051-0034 and Catalogue nos. 91-213-XIB and 91-213-XPB.

Last modified: 2005-03-23.

Population By Mother Tongue, By Provinces And Territories (2001 Census)

	Canada	Newfoundland and Labrador	Prince Edward Island	Nova Scotia	New Brunswick
	number				
Total Population	**29,639,035**	**508,080**	**133,385**	**897,570**	**719,710**
Single responses[1]	29,257,885	507,425	132,855	893,195	713,770
English	17,352,315	499,750	125,125	832,660	465,170
French	6,703,325	2,110	5,665	34,025	236,665
Non-official languages	5,202,245	5,495	2,065	26,510	11,935
Chinese	853,745	520	130	2,125	1,215
Cantonese	322,315	50	0	425	190
Mandarin	101,790	25	20	115	105
Hakka	4,565	0	0	15	10
Chinese, n.o.s.	425,085	445	115	1,505	915
Italian	469,485	115	60	865	510
German	438,080	340	190	3,015	1,420
Polish	208,375	75	65	960	220
Spanish	245,495	55	55	700	510
Portuguese	213,815	105	15	355	150
Punjabi	271,220	90	0	275	80
Ukrainian	148,085	20	20	320	105
Arabic	199,940	215	145	4,035	535
Dutch	128,670	90	480	1,980	855
Tagalog (Pilipino)	174,060	130	20	335	150
Greek	120,360	35	0	1,110	165
Vietnamese	122,055	60	10	480	110
Cree	72,885	0	0	30	10
Inuktitut (Eskimo)	29,010	550	10	10	15
Other non-official languages	1,506,965	3,090	860	9,930	5,815
Multiple responses[2]	381,145	650	530	4,375	5,940
English and French	112,575	330	440	2,555	5,255
English and non-official language	219,860	310	85	1,660	550
French and non-official language	38,630	0	0	125	105
English, French and non-official language	10,085	10	0	35	35

Source: Statistics Canada, Census of population.

Last modified: 2005-01-27.

Population by mother tongue, by census metropolitan areas (2001 Census)

	Toronto	Hamilton	St. Catharines–Niagara	Kitchener	London
	number				
Total Population	**4,647,955**	**655,055**	**371,400**	**409,765**	**427,215**
Single responses[1]	4,556,475	647,370	367,255	405,390	423,345
English	2,684,195	503,045	300,035	316,175	350,030
French	57,485	9,840	13,915	5,710	5,465
Non-official languages	1,814,795	134,485	53,295	83,515	67,850
Chinese	348,010	7,310	1,830	4,715	3,425
Cantonese	145,490	1,765	235	1,000	670
Mandarin	35,315	745	160	645	325
Hakka	2,085	0	15	20	0
Chinese, n.o.s.	165,120	4,795	1,420	3,055	2,420
Italian	195,960	22,680	13,760	2,165	4,075
German	43,665	7,720	7,550	15,090	4,835
Polish	79,875	11,565	4,485	5,525	7,015
Spanish	83,245	5,470	1,885	4,660	4,745
Portuguese	108,935	8,805	385	10,915	6,645
Punjabi	95,950	3,990	185	2,515	635
Ukrainian	26,675	3,680	2,335	765	1,375
Arabic	46,575	5,660	1,290	1,685	5,800
Dutch	13,565	5,895	4,490	2,090	5,300
Tagalog (Pilipino)	77,220	2,630	740	435	770
Greek	50,165	2,410	660	1,585	2,060
Vietnamese	36,555	2,810	500	2,935	1,720
Cree	110	20	10	10	0
Inuktitut (Eskimo)	10	0	0	0	0
Other non-official languages	608,280	43,840	13,200	28,415	19,435
Multiple responses[2]	91,480	7,685	4,150	4,375	3,865
English and French	7,810	1,265	1,315	600	795
English and non-official language	77,430	5,935	2,540	3,625	2,730
French and non-official language	4,585	370	210	95	225
English, French and non-official language	1,655	110	85	55	120

Source: Statistics Canada, Census of population.

Last modified: 2005-01-27.

Frequency of language of work in Toronto, by areas (2001 Census)

Toronto	Total - Frequency of language of work	Only	Mostly	Equally	Regularly
	Number				
English	**2,692,890**	2,413,945	197,010	42,695	39,240
French	**70,150**	2,655	5,765	9,710	52,020
Chinese, not otherwise specified	**42,565**	12,940	7,735	4,110	17,780
Cantonese	**33,375**	10,495	6,770	2,770	13,340
Punjabi	**15,230**	2,325	1,485	2,615	8,805
German	**4,075**	110	220	580	3,165
Mandarin	**8,015**	2,090	1,420	655	3,850
Portuguese	**23,560**	4,335	3,590	2,880	12,755
Spanish	**18,780**	1,420	1,535	2,675	13,150
Vietnamese	**5,275**	910	570	575	3,220
Korean	**6,820**	1,265	1,470	675	3,410
Italian	**32,285**	1,890	2,030	4,630	23,735
Other languages	**79,975**	7,310	7,850	11,905	52,910

Source: Statistics Canada, Census of Population. Last modified: 2005-01-27

Frequency of language of work in Montreal, by census metropolitan areas (2001 Census)

Montréal	Total - Frequency of language of work	Only	Mostly	Equally	Regularly
	Number				
English	**1,068,440**	145,165	223,810	156,590	542,875
French	**1,729,840**	806,620	547,715	156,970	218,535
Chinese, not otherwise specified	**7,275**	2,885	1,150	1,095	2,145
Cantonese	**1,020**	395	175	50	400
Punjabi	**1,140**	200	95	285	560
German	**1,615**	45	160	240	1,170
Mandarin	**470**	125	175	30	140
Portuguese	**3,365**	240	395	635	2,095
Spanish	**16,860**	720	1,145	3,270	11,725
Vietnamese	**2,195**	555	300	325	1,015
Korean	**290**	65	45	15	165
Italian	**18,165**	885	1,485	4,535	11,260
Other languages	**31,470**	3,450	3,205	7,120	17,695

Source: Statistics Canada, Census of Population. Last modified: 2005-01-27

Frequency of language of work in Vancouver, by census metropolitan areas (2001 Census)

Vancouver	Total - Frequency of language of work	Only	Mostly	Equally	Regularly
	Number				
English	**1,112,005**	991,620	77,330	17,500	25,555
French	**17,470**	825	1,795	1,730	13,120
Chinese, not otherwise specified	**38,215**	11,110	7,515	4,050	15,540
Cantonese	**31,475**	9,930	6,130	2,560	12,855
Punjabi	**18,920**	4,970	2,055	3,040	8,855
German	**2,575**	135	240	355	1,845
Mandarin	**14,400**	3,705	2,900	1,400	6,395
Portuguese	**610**	95	75	50	390
Spanish	**5,390**	440	515	610	3,825
Vietnamese	**3,360**	900	465	480	1,515
Korean	**5,230**	1,325	1,155	490	2,260
Italian	**1,580**	15	120	195	1,250
Other languages	**23,410**	2,250	3,090	2,955	15,115
Source: Statistics Canada, Census of Population.					
Last modified: 2005-01-27.					

Definitions

Language of work: Refers to the language used most often at work by the individual at the time of the census. Other languages used at work on a regular basis are also collected.

Frequency of language of work: Indicates that a language is spoken at work by the respondent either most often or on a regular basis.

Only: Indicates that this is the only language spoken at work by the respondent.

Mostly: Indicates that this is the only language spoken most often at work while at least one other language is spoken on a regular basis by the respondent.

Equally: Indicates that this language has been reported with another language as the one spoken most often at work by the respondent.

Regularly: Indicates a language that was reported as being used on a regular basis at work. (A respondent must report a language spoken most often at work in order to have a language spoken regularly at work.)

Census metropolitan areas: Area consisting of one or more adjacent municipalities situated around a major urban core. To form a census metropolitan area, the urban core must have a population of at least 100,000.

Population projections for 2011 and 2016, at July 1

	2011			2016		
	Both sexes	Male	Female	Both sexes	Male	Female
	thousands			thousands		
All ages[1]	**33,361.7**	**16,511.6**	**16,850.2**	**34,419.8**	**17,044.8**	**17,375.0**
0-4	**1,666.4**	855.1	811.3	**1,708.7**	877.0	831.7
5-9	**1,715.8**	880.0	835.9	**1,741.8**	893.6	848.2
10-14	**1,863.6**	957.7	905.9	**1,790.1**	919.8	870.3
15-19	**2,175.0**	1,117.7	1,057.2	**1,945.5**	1,001.3	944.2
20-24	**2,241.4**	1,143.6	1,097.8	**2,261.2**	1,154.1	1,107.1
25-29	**2,263.5**	1,148.5	1,115.0	**2,336.4**	1,185.9	1,150.5
30-34	**2,293.0**	1,163.2	1,129.8	**2,360.0**	1,197.4	1,162.6
35-39	**2,278.1**	1,150.7	1,127.4	**2,367.1**	1,197.7	1,169.4
40-44	**2,370.3**	1,192.6	1,177.8	**2,324.0**	1,171.9	1,152.1
45-49	**2,681.7**	1,350.4	1,331.3	**2,385.2**	1,201.3	1,183.8
50-54	**2,637.4**	1,317.5	1,319.9	**2,657.5**	1,335.4	1,322.1
55-59	**2,318.3**	1,145.2	1,173.2	**2,588.5**	1,285.6	1,302.9
60-64	**2,011.3**	984.1	1,027.2	**2,251.4**	1,102.5	1,149.0
65-69	**1,495.8**	719.7	776.1	**1,907.4**	920.2	987.2
70-74	**1,112.7**	519.9	592.8	**1,365.7**	641.3	724.4
75-79	**879.7**	392.6	487.2	**957.2**	429.4	527.8
80-84	**666.2**	269.5	396.7	**688.1**	286.7	401.4
85-89	**422.5**	141.1	281.4	**452.9**	162.7	290.1
90 and over	**269.0**	62.6	206.4	**331.0**	80.7	250.2

Note: Figures represent the medium-growth projection and are based on 2000 population estimates.

1. Due to rounding, the totals may not always add up to the sum of the figures.

Source: Statistics Canada, CANSIM, table 052-0001.

Last Modified: 2005-02-01.

Population by religion, by provinces and territories (2001 Census)

	Canada	Quebec	Ontario	Manitoba	Saskatchewan
	number				
Total population	**29,639,035**	**7,125,580**	**11,285,550**	**1,103,700**	**963,150**
Catholic	12,936,905	5,939,715	3,911,760	323,690	305,390
Protestant	8,654,850	335,590	3,935,745	475,185	449,195
Christian Orthodox	479,620	100,375	264,055	15,645	14,280
Christian not included elsewhere	780,450	56,750	301,935	44,535	27,070
Muslim	579,640	108,620	352,530	5,095	2,230
Jewish	329,995	89,915	190,795	13,040	865
Buddhist	300,345	41,380	128,320	5,745	3,050
Hindu	297,200	24,525	217,555	3,835	1,585
Sikh	278,410	8,225	104,785	5,485	500
Eastern religions	37,550	3,425	17,780	795	780
Other religions	63,975	3,870	18,985	4,780	6,750
No religious affiliation	4,900,090	413,190	1,841,290	205,865	151,455

Source: Statistics Canada, Census of Population.

Last modified: 2005-01-25.

Population by religion, by provinces and territories (2001 Census)

	Canada	Alberta	British Columbia	Yukon
	number			
Total population	**29,639,035**	**2,941,150**	**3,868,875**	**28,520**
Catholic	12,936,905	786,360	675,320	6,015
Protestant	8,654,850	1,145,460	1,213,295	9,485
Christian Orthodox	479,620	44,475	35,655	150
Christian not included elsewhere	780,450	123,140	200,345	1,010
Muslim	579,640	49,040	56,220	60
Jewish	329,995	11,085	21,230	35
Buddhist	300,345	33,410	85,540	130
Hindu	297,200	15,965	31,500	10
Sikh	278,410	23,470	135,310	100
Eastern religions	37,550	3,335	9,970	190
Other religions	63,975	10,560	16,205	330
No religious affiliation	4,900,090	694,840	1,388,300	11,015

Source: Statistics Canada, Census of Population.

Last modified: 2005-01-25.

Consumer Price Index (monthly)

	February 2004	January 2005	February 2005	January 2005 to February 2005	February 2004 to February 2005
	1992 = 100			%	
Canada					
All items	**123.2**	**125.3**	**125.8**	**0.4**	**2.1**
Food	123.4	126.8	**126.6**	-0.2	2.6
Shelter	119.0	122.4	**122.6**	0.2	3.0
Household operations and furnishings	115.2	115.3	**115.5**	0.2	0.3
Clothing and footwear	104.0	100.0	**103.0**	3.0	-1.0
Transportation	141.9	146.3	**147.0**	0.5	3.6
Health and personal care	117.7	119.0	**119.7**	0.6	1.7
Recreation, education and reading	126.6	125.5	**126.3**	0.6	-0.2
Alcoholic beverages and tobacco products	141.1	145.1	**145.2**	0.1	2.9
Special aggregates					
All items excluding food	123.2	125.1	**125.7**	0.5	2.0
All items excluding energy	121.7	123.4	**123.7**	0.2	1.6
Energy	141.9	149.1	**152.3**	2.1	7.3

Sources: Statistics Canada, CANSIM, table 326-0001 and Catalogue nos. 62-001-XPB and 62-010-XIB.

Last Modified: 2005-03-22.

Construction price indexes, by selected metropolitan areas, New housing price indexes (monthly)

	January 2004	December 2004	January 2005	December 2004 to January 2005	January 2004 to January 2005
	1997 = 100			% change	
Canada	**119.9**	**125.8**	**126.1**	**0.2**	**5.2**
House only	127.1	134.1	**134.5**	0.3	5.8
Land only	106.0	110.0	**110.2**	0.2	4.0
Metropolitan areas (house and land)					
St. John's (N.L.)	114.5	122.3	**123.2**	0.7	7.6
Charlottetown (P.E.I.)	107.5	111.0	**111.0**	0.0	3.3
Halifax (N.S.)	121.1	121.8	**121.8**	0.0	0.6
Saint John, Fredericton and Moncton (N.B.)	103.6	107.2	**107.8**	0.6	4.1
Québec (Que.)	126.9	131.3	**131.8**	0.4	3.9
Montréal (Que.)	130.8	138.7	**139.4**	0.5	6.6
Ottawa-Gatineau (Ont.-Que.)[1]	141.7	151.0	**151.8**	0.5	7.1
Toronto and Oshawa (Ont.)	122.8	129.1	**129.2**	0.1	5.2
Hamilton (Ont.)	123.3	131.3	**131.6**	0.2	6.7
St. Catharines-Niagara (Ont.)	124.4	135.2	**136.0**	0.6	9.3
Kitchener (Ont.)[2]	122.4	129.3	**129.2**	-0.1	5.6
London (Ont.)	117.5	122.5	**123.3**	0.7	4.9
Windsor (Ont.)	102.1	103.0	**104.5**	1.5	2.4
Greater Sudbury and Thunder Bay (Ont.)[3]	96.7	99.0	**99.0**	0.0	2.4
Winnipeg (Man.)	116.4	125.6	**127.5**	1.5	9.5
Regina (Sask.)	128.5	136.9	**136.9**	0.0	6.5
Saskatoon (Sask.)	115.9	123.9	**123.9**	0.0	6.9
Edmonton (Alta.)	127.0	132.4	**132.6**	0.2	4.4
Calgary (Alta.)	135.3	140.2	**140.5**	0.2	3.8
Vancouver (B.C.)	99.0	102.7	**102.7**	0.0	3.7
Victoria (B.C.)	101.4	107.8	**108.4**	0.6	6.9

1. Formerly Ottawa-Hull.

2. Formerly Kitchener-Waterloo.

3. Formerly Sudbury-Thunder Bay.

Sources: Statistics Canada, CANSIM, table 327-0005 and Catalogue no. 62-007-XPB.

Last modified: 2005-03-09.

Employment by major industry groups, seasonally adjusted, by provinces (monthly)

	February 2004	January 2005	February 2005	January 2005 to February 2005	February 2004 to February 2005
	employment (thousands)			% change	
Canada - All industries	**15,844.4**	**16,057.4**	**16,084.0**	**0.2**	**1.5**
Goods-producing sector	3,943.5	4,037.0	4,006.7	-0.8	1.6
Agriculture	328.3	317.1	324.8	2.4	-1.1
Forestry, fishing, mining, oil and gas	281.6	297.2	300.6	1.1	6.7
Utilities	128.5	122.1	119.7	-2.0	-6.8
Construction	913.3	1,005.3	994.3	-1.1	8.9
Manufacturing	2,291.7	2,295.4	2,267.3	-1.2	-1.1
Services-producing sector	11,900.9	12,020.4	12,077.2	0.5	1.5
Trade	2,494.6	2,542.5	2,548.5	0.2	2.2
Transportation and warehousing	815.9	792.9	798.0	0.6	-2.2
Finance, insurance, real estate and leasing	923.0	985.1	989.2	0.4	7.2
Professional, scientific and technical services	1,002.5	1,030.1	1,032.9	0.3	3.0
Business, building and other support services[1]	627.4	622.4	635.8	2.2	1.3
Educational services	1,049.1	1,047.8	1,068.3	2.0	1.8
Health care and social assistance	1,724.1	1,722.1	1,732.0	0.6	0.5
Information, culture and recreation	735.2	721.0	736.0	2.1	0.1
Accommodation and food services	1,003.6	1,026.0	1,005.8	-2.0	0.2
Other services	702.1	708.5	707.6	-0.1	0.8
Public administration	823.3	821.9	823.2	0.2	0.0

1. Formerly Management of companies, administrative and other support services.

Source: Statistics Canada, CANSIM table 282-0088.

Last modified: 2005-03-11.

Average hourly wages of employees by selected characteristics and profession, unadjusted data, by provinces (monthly)

	February 2004		February 2005		February 2004 to February 2005
Canada	number of employees[1] (thousands)	average hourly wage ($)	number of employees[1] (thousands)	average hourly wage ($)	% change in hourly wage
15 years and over	**13,146.4**	**18.53**	**13,320.0**	**18.98**	**2.4**
15 to 24 years	2,157.9	10.56	2,210.6	10.79	2.2
25 to 54 years	9,550.1	20.08	9,569.9	20.57	2.4
55 years and over	1,438.3	20.18	1,539.5	20.85	3.3
Men	6,610.3	20.22	6,705.9	20.77	2.7
Women	6,536.1	16.82	6,614.1	17.17	2.1
Full-time	10,593.2	19.85	10,746.7	20.35	2.5
Part-time	2,553.2	13.05	2,573.3	13.28	1.8
Union coverage[2]	4,267.5	21.40	4,305.8	21.88	2.2
No union coverage[3]	8,878.9	17.15	9,014.2	17.60	2.6
Permanent job[4]	11,695.4	18.99	11,810.1	19.47	2.5
Temporary job[5]	1,451.0	14.84	1,509.9	15.13	2.0
Management occupations	947.5	29.12	912.3	30.14	3.5
Business, finance and administrative occupations	2,619.3	17.70	2,650.8	18.00	1.7
Natural and applied sciences and related occupations	860.7	26.28	927.7	26.79	1.9
Health occupations	796.8	21.98	823.6	22.05	0.3
Occupations in social science, education, government service and religion	1,133.7	24.41	1,169.7	24.37	-0.2
Occupations in art, culture, recreation and sport	291.3	18.58	309.7	19.85	6.8
Sales and service occupations	3,391.8	12.33	3,432.4	12.72	3.2
Trades, transport and equipment operators and related occupations	1,837.7	18.36	1,848.1	19.10	4.0
Occupations unique to primary industry	190.9	16.60	216.2	16.79	1.1
Occupations unique to processing, manufacturing and utilities	1,076.7	16.45	1,029.4	16.84	2.4

1. Those who work as employees of a private firm or business or the public sector.
2. Employees who are members of a union and employees who are not union members but who are covered by a collective agreement or a union contract.
3. Employees who are not members of a union or not covered by a collective agreement or a union contract.
4. A permanent job is one that is expected to last as long as the employee wants it, given that business conditions permit. That is, there is no pre-determined termination date.
5. A temporary job has a predetermined end date, or will end as soon as a specified project is completed. Includes seasonal jobs; temporary, term or contract jobs including work done through a temporary help agency; casual jobs; and other temporary work.

Sources: Statistics Canada, CANSIM tables 282-0069 and 282-0073.

Last modified: 2005-03-11.

Selected economic indicators, Canada and United States (monthly and quarterly)				
	Latest period		Change from previous period	Annual change
Canada - Labour market [1,2]				
		thousands	%	
Labour force(SA)	February 2005	17,293	0.2	1.2
Employment (SA)	February 2005	16,084	0.2	1.5
		%		
Unemployment rate (SA)	February 2005	7.0	0.0	-4.1
		$millions	%	
Gross Domestic Product at market prices (SAAR)[3] (Chained 1997 dollars)	4th quarter 2004	1,059,417	0.6	3.1
		index	%	
Consumer Price index (1992=100)	February 2005	125.8	0.4	2.1
			%	
Stock market (closing quotations at month end)[4] (1975=1000)	February 2005	9,668.3	5.0	10.0

SA - seasonally adjusted

SAAR - seasonally adjusted at annual rates

1. Labour Force Survey for Canada, Payroll Survey for the United States.
2. Canadian estimates are drawn from a household survey while American estimates use a business survey and provide somewhat different coverage and definitions.
3. In Canadian dollars.
4. S&P/TSX Composite Index for Canada, and Dow Jones Composite Index for United States.

Sources: Statistics Canada, CANSIM, tables 176-0046, 282-0087, 326-0001, 379-0018, 451-0006, 451-0009 and 451-0010.

Last modified: 2005-03-22.

	Latest period		Change from previous period	Annual change
United States – Labour market [1,2]				
		thousands	%	
Labour force(SA)	February 2005	148,132	0.1	1.1
Employment (SA)	February 2005	140,144	-0.1	1.3
		%		
Unemployment rate (SA)	February 2005	5.4	3.8	-3.6
		$billion	%	
Gross Domestic Product at market prices (SAAR)[3] (Chained 2000 dollars)	3rd quarter 2004	10,891	1.0	4.0
		index	%	
Consumer Price index (1982-84=100)	February 2005	191.8	0.6	3.0
			%	
Stock market (closing quotations at quarter end)[3,4]	February 2005	10,766.2	2.6	1.7
SA - seasonally adjusted				
SAAR - seasonally adjusted at annual rates				
1. Labour Force Survey for Canada, Payroll Survey for the United States.				
2. Canadian estimates are drawn from a household survey while American estimates use a business survey and provide somewhat different coverage and definitions.				
3. In U.S. dollars.				
4. S&P/TSX Composite Index for Canada, and Dow Jones Composite Index for United States.				
Sources: Statistics Canada, CANSIM, tables 176-0046, 282-0087, 326-0001, 379-0018, 451-0006, 451-0009 and 451-0010.				
Last modified: 2005-03-24.				

Imports, exports and trade balance of goods on a balance-of-payments basis, by country or country grouping

	1999	2000	2001	2002	2003	2004
	$ millions					
Exports	**369,034.9**	**429,372.2**	**420,657.1**	**413,795.3**	**400,010.0**	**430,357.6**
United States[1]	309,116.8	359,021.2	352,083.1	347,068.9	330,375.3	351,936.8
Japan	10,125.9	11,297.4	10,124.8	10,152.5	9,785.7	9,955.4
United Kingdom	6,002.9	7,273.3	6,912.9	6,184.8	7,697.8	9,447.1
Other European Economic Community countries	14,383.8	16,846.3	16,712.0	16,372.0	16,420.5	17,655.6
Other OECD[2]	9,947.2	12,059.0	12,129.2	12,174.1	12,668.6	14,211.6
Other countries[3]	19,458.4	22,875.1	22,695.0	21,843.0	23,062.1	27,151.0
Imports	**327,026.0**	**362,336.7**	**350,682.5**	**356,580.9**	**341,832.7**	**363,123.4**
United States[1]	249,485.3	266,511.1	254,949.4	255,093.2	239,870.7	249,981.3
Japan	10,592.2	11,729.8	10,572.0	11,732.9	10,644.9	10,029.4
United Kingdom	7,685.4	12,289.3	11,952.9	10,178.8	8,826.8	9,205.9
Other European Economic Community countries	20,765.8	21,136.5	23,197.0	25,860.8	25,982.7	27,052.5
Other OECD[2]	13,257.2	19,067.6	18,645.5	19,680.7	19,676.5	22,362.4
Other countries[3]	25,240.1	31,602.5	31,365.6	34,034.5	36,831.1	44,491.8
Balance	**42,008.9**	**67,035.5**	**69,974.6**	**57,214.4**	**58,177.3**	**67,234.2**
United States[1]	59,631.5	92,510.1	97,133.7	91,975.7	90,504.6	101,955.5
Japan	-466.3	-432.4	-447.2	-1,580.4	-859.2	-74.0
United Kingdom	-1,682.5	-5,016.0	-5,040.0	-3,994.0	-1,129.0	241.2
Other European Economic Community countries	-6,382.0	-4,290.2	-6,485.0	-9,488.8	-9,562.2	-9,396.9
Other OECD[2]	-3,310.0	-7,008.6	-6,516.3	-7,506.6	-7,007.9	-8,150.8
Other countries[3]	-5,781.7	-8,727.4	-8,670.6	-12,191.5	-13,769.0	-17,340.8

1. Includes also Puerto Rico and Virgin Islands.

2. Organisation for Economic Co-operation and Development excluding the United States, Japan, United Kingdom and the other European Economic Community.

3. Countries not included in the European Economic Community or the OECD.

Source: Statistics Canada, CANSIM, table 228-0003.

Last modified: 2005-02-10.

Life expectancy at birth, by provinces

	Males	Females
	years	
Canada		
1920-22	59	61
1930-32	60	62
1940-42	63	66
1950-52	66	71
1960-62	68	74
1970-72	69	76
1980-82	72	79
1990-92	75	81
1990-92		
Newfoundland and Labrador	74	80
Prince Edward Island	73	81
Nova Scotia	74	80
New Brunswick	74	81
Quebec	74	81
Ontario	75	81
Manitoba	75	81
Saskatchewan	75	82
Alberta	75	81
British Columbia	75	81
Source: Statistics Canada.		
Last modified: 2005-02-17.		

Average weekly earnings, health care and social assistance, provinces and territories

	1999	2000	2001	2002	2003
	$[1]				
Canada	**544.79**	**562.39**	**581.34**	**605.12**	**612.92**
Newfoundland and Labrador	572.79	617.40	630.23	646.71	619.48
Prince Edward Island	521.90	542.49	569.18	599.49	602.10
Nova Scotia	508.16	525.72	555.00	581.66	599.76
New Brunswick	499.90	516.99	536.38	564.91	586.68
Quebec	529.55	543.53	562.77	587.15	591.40
Ontario	568.12	585.69	601.94	624.90	634.47
Manitoba	443.22	450.06	469.32	497.54	506.61
Saskatchewan	494.48	506.36	527.61	547.62	571.94
Alberta	543.64	565.06	590.89	615.84	617.75
British Columbia	574.97	595.07	612.49	634.62	642.55
Yukon	642.47	668.75	686.91	717.30	733.12
Northwest Territories including Nunavut	784.48	848.60	..	..	..
Northwest Territories	..	..	856.72	864.82	974.92
Nunavut	..	..	713.83	775.81	829.83

1. Unadjusted for seasonal variation.

Source: Statistics Canada, CANSIM, table 281-0027 and Catalogue no. 72-002-XIB.

Last Modified: 2005-02-18.

Household size, by provinces and territories (2001 Census)

	2001				
	Canada	Quebec	Ontario	Manitoba	Saskatchewan
	number				
Total households[1]	**11,562,975**	**2,978,115**	**4,219,410**	**432,550**	**379,680**
1-person households	2,976,875	880,765	990,160	121,760	105,150
2-person households	3,772,430	981,660	1,327,325	139,535	127,270
3-person households	1,875,215	486,465	697,860	63,395	53,200
4-person households	1,843,800	427,695	737,405	64,185	54,430
5-person households	741,525	147,665	309,795	28,495	26,160
6-person or more households	353,135	53,860	156,870	15,185	13,470
Total persons in households	**29,522,300**	**7,097,850**	**11,254,730**	**1,090,625**	**956,630**
Average number of persons in household	**2.6**	**2.4**	**2.7**	**2.5**	**2.5**

Source: Statistics Canada, Census of Population.

Last modified : 2005-01-04.

Average weekly earnings (including overtime), educational and related services, by provinces and territories

	2000	2001	2002	2003
	$			
Canada	**673.88**	**694.30**	**725.27**	**747.88**
Newfoundland and Labrador	714.37	716.98	734.16	766.84
Prince Edward Island	705.42	699.68	709.18	708.35
Nova Scotia	606.49	653.34	697.12	693.92
New Brunswick	659.52	661.21	662.74	674.40
Quebec	663.50	708.53	745.02	780.89
Ontario	689.31	699.65	735.34	748.12
Manitoba	643.42	655.98	644.68	691.86
Saskatchewan	657.07	664.16	705.66	738.55
Alberta	620.22	638.99	679.87	713.51
British Columbia	712.46	729.71	740.92	759.71
Yukon	899.54	928.44	962.30	830.61

Note: Excludes owners or partners of unincorporated businesses and professional practices, the self-employed, unpaid family workers, persons working outside Canada, military personnel, and casual workers for whom a T4 is not required.

Source: Statistics Canada, CANSIM, table 281-0027 and Catalogue no. 72-002-XIB.

Last modified: 2005-02-18.

Average time spent on household activities, by sex

	1998		
	Total population[1]	Participants[2]	Participation rate[3]
	Both Sexes		
	hours per day		%
Activity group, total	**24.0**	**24.0**	**100**
Total work	**7.8**	**8.0**	**98**
Paid work and education	4.2	8.3	51
Paid work and related activites	3.6	8.3	44
Paid work	3.3	7.7	43
Activities related to paid work	0.0	0.6	8
Commuting	0.3	0.8	38
Education and related activities	**0.6**	**6.2**	**9**
Unpaid work	**3.6**	**3.9**	**91**
Household work and related activities	3.2	3.6	90
Cooking and washing up	0.8	1.0	74
Housekeeping	0.7	1.7	41
Maintenance and repair	0.2	2.5	6
Other household work	0.4	1.3	30
Shopping for goods and services	0.8	1.9	43
Child care	0.4	2.2	20
Civic and voluntary work	0.3	1.9	18
Personal care	10.4	10.4	100
Night sleep	8.1	8.1	100
Meals (excluding restaurant meals)	1.1	1.2	92
Other personal activities	1.3	1.3	95
Free time	**5.8**	**5.9**	**97**
Socializing including restaurant meals	1.9	2.9	66
Restaurant meals	0.3	1.6	19
Socializing in homes	1.3	2.4	55
Other socializing	0.3	2.6	12
Television, reading and other passive leisure	2.7	3.2	85
Watching television	2.2	2.8	77
Reading books, magazines, newspapers	0.4	1.3	32
Other passive leisure	0.1	1.1	9
Sports, movies and other entertainment events	0.2	2.7	6
Active leisure	1.0	2.4	40
Active sports	0.5	2.0	24
Other active leisure	0.5	2.3	22

Note: Averaged over a seven-day week.

1. The average number of hours per day spent on the activity for the entire population aged 15 years and over (whether or not the person reported the activity).

2. The average number of hours per day spent on the activity for the population that reported the activity.

3. The proportion of the population that reported spending some time on the activity.

Source: Statistics Canada, CANSIM, table 113-0001 . Last modified: 2004-09-02.

Average income after tax by economic family types

	1998	1999	2000	2001	2002
	$ constant 2002				
Economic families[1], two people or more	**54,600**	**55,800**	**57,600**	**60,300**	**60,500**
Elderly families[2]	40,000	41,600	41,200	42,700	43,400
Married couples only	38,700	40,500	39,900	41,500	42,000
All other elderly families	44,700	45,200	45,700	47,300	48,400
Non-elderly families[3]	56,900	58,100	60,200	63,100	63,200
Married couples only	54,500	53,900	54,800	59,300	59,000
No earner	26,600	27,100	27,300	30,900	28,800
One earner	43,600	44,500	43,700	48,100	45,800
Two earners	61,800	60,800	61,400	65,500	65,700
Two parent families with children[4]	60,500	62,100	64,300	67,100	67,700
No earner	21,700	21,400	20,900	23,500	24,200
One earner	45,800	46,000	45,900	48,200	49,900
Two earners	61,600	62,500	64,900	67,000	67,200
Three or more earners	75,000	78,400	81,600	84,500	83,800
Married couples with other relatives	75,400	78,600	82,200	83,700	82,700
Lone-parent families[4]	29,500	29,900	32,600	34,100	33,000
Male lone-parent families	40,600	39,100	42,200	41,200	42,100
Female lone-parent families	27,500	28,200	30,600	32,500	30,800
No earner	15,500	16,100	15,600	16,600	15,800
One earner	28,400	28,900	30,400	31,600	30,400
Two or more earners	43,900	43,400	48,000	49,600	44,400
All other non-elderly families	51,300	52,400	53,700	56,400	58,000
Unattached individuals	**22,800**	**23,600**	**24,100**	**25,300**	**25,900**
Elderly male	24,300	23,900	23,200	25,200	24,600
Non-earner	21,800	22,300	21,400	23,000	22,500
Earner	38,700	33,200	31,500	35,200	32,400
Elderly female	19,800	19,900	20,300	21,400	21,900
Non-earner	19,200	19,400	19,600	20,500	21,500
Earner	27,400	26,900	28,600	31,700	26,800
Non-elderly male	25,200	25,700	27,300	28,200	28,400
Non-earner	9,600	9,300	9,200	10,800	10,100
Earner	28,200	28,700	30,000	30,800	31,300
Non-elderly female	21,200	23,000	22,600	23,900	25,200
Non-earner	9,900	9,600	9,500	11,000	11,300
Earner	24,700	27,000	26,200	27,200	28,300

Note: Average income after tax is total income, which includes government transfers, less income tax.

1. An economic family is a group of individuals sharing a common dwelling unit who are related by blood, marriage (including common-law relationships) or adoption.
2. Families in which the major income earner is 65 years of age and over.
3. Families in which the major income earner is less than 65 years of age.
4. With children less than 18 years of age.

Source: Statistics Canada, CANSIM, table 202-0603 and Catalogue no. 75-202-XIE. , Last modified: 2005-01-21.

Average household expenditures, by provinces and territories

	2003			
	Canada		Newfoundland and Labrador	
Household Characteristics				
Estimated number of households	11,803,420		193,690	
	Average expenditure per household	**Households reporting expenditures**	**Average expenditure per household**	**Households reporting expenditures**
	$	%	$	%
Total expenditures	**61,152**	**100.0**	**48,919**	**100.0**
Total current consumption	43,755	100.0	36,196	100.0
Food	6,791	100.0	6,147	100.0
Shelter	11,584	99.9	7,593	99.7
Household operation	2,870	100.0	2,564	100.0
Household furnishings and equipment	1,751	94.0	1,605	95.2
Clothing	2,436	99.1	2,442	98.5
Transportation	8,353	98.1	7,140	94.8
Health care	1,588	97.2	1,344	97.0
Personal care	834	99.4	722	99.9
Recreation	3,591	98.0	3,266	97.3
Reading materials and other printed matter	283	84.1	201	80.2
Education	1,007	44.5	790	43.5
Tobacco products and alcoholic beverages	1,489	84.7	1,470	85.8
Games of chance (net amount)	272	73.9	281	75.5
Miscellaneous	904	90.2	631	79.8
Personal income taxes	12,370	91.9	8,723	79.2
Personal insurance payments and pension contributions	3,505	81.2	2,986	73.9
Gifts of money and contributions	1,522	73.1	1,015	86.5
Source: Statistics Canada, CANSIM, table 203-0001.				
Last modified: 2005-01-24.				

Experienced labour force 15 years and over by industry, by census metropolitan areas (2001 Census)

	2001				
	Toronto	Hamilton	St. Catharines–Niagara	Kitchener	
	number				
Total labour force	**2,564,585**	**345,505**	**191,930**	**232,860**	**231,080**
All industries		340,295	189,285	229,885	
Agriculture, forestry, fishing and hunting	9,425	4,320	5,435	2,160	4,200
Mining and oil and gas extraction	2,660	475	460	195	230
Utilities	15,765	1,825	1,435	860	1,000
Construction	124,395	19,565	10,575	12,970	11,970
Manufacturing	395,970	64,775	32,845	59,810	36,500
Wholesale trade	151,870	17,385	6,950	10,980	9,825
Retail trade	272,680	39,940	23,530	24,895	26,575
Transportation and warehousing	123,135	15,090	8,630	9,400	10,045
Information and cultural industries	100,760	8,005	2,940	4,650	5,010
Finance and insurance	177,210	15,500	5,875	12,365	12,075
Real estate and rental and leasing	56,890	6,125	2,445	3,190	4,045
Professional, scientific and technical services	246,655	17,990	7,150	12,570	11,435
Management of companies and enterprises	4,840	340	165	1,045	140
Administrative and support, waste management and remediation services	121,490	14,070	8,150	8,030	10,880
Educational services	143,985	23,710	11,695	16,200	17,145
Health care and social assistance	189,450	35,735	16,810	17,110	28,130
Arts, entertainment and recreation	47,870	5,990	7,960	3,400	3,900
Accommodation and food services	141,560	20,550	19,250	12,895	15,190
Other services (except public administration)	110,745	16,255	9,295	10,280	11,290
Public administration	84,655	12,645	7,695	6,880	7,425
Source: Statistics Canada, Census of Population.					
Last modified: 2005-02-17.					

Employed labour force by place of work, by provinces and territories (2001 Censuses)

	2001				
	Place of work status				
	Total	Worked at home	Worked outside Canada	No fixed workplace address	Usual place of work
	number				
Canada	**14,695,130**	**1,175,760**	**68,520**	**1,273,450**	**12,177,410**
Newfoundland and Labrador	188,815	11,570	590	15,865	160,790
Prince Edward Island	63,935	5,690	185	6,100	51,965
Nova Scotia	402,295	26,990	2,260	40,765	332,280
New Brunswick	325,335	20,215	1,520	30,050	273,545
Quebec	3,434,265	224,685	9,245	225,685	2,974,650
Ontario	5,713,900	406,230	33,930	466,945	4,806,790
Manitoba	549,990	54,310	1,605	43,335	450,730
Saskatchewan	479,735	86,500	870	40,370	352,000
Alberta	1,608,840	165,865	6,020	189,920	1,247,035
British Columbia	1,883,975	171,390	12,235	210,510	1,489,835
Yukon	15,860	1,065	35	1,605	13,155
Northwest Territories	18,810	795	15	1,435	16,565
Nunavut	9,380	455	10	855	8,065
Source: Statistics Canada, Census of Population.					
Last modified: 2004-09-01.					

Employed labour force by place of work, by census metropolitan areas (1996 and 2001 Censuses)

	2001				
	Place of work status				
	Total	Worked at home	Worked outside Canada	No fixed workplace address	Usual place of work
	number				
St. John's	80,090	4,015	335	5,695	70,040
Halifax	182,480	10,755	1,510	15,765	154,450
Saint John	55,865	2,645	170	4,930	48,120
Saguenay	65,520	2,685	65	3,915	58,850
Québec	343,745	17,895	840	22,130	302,875
Sherbrooke	74,960	4,430	165	4,675	65,685
Trois-Rivières	60,950	3,205	140	3,765	53,845
Montréal	1,678,715	93,120	5,325	107,745	1,472,530
Ottawa-Gatineau	561,870	34,435	2,365	35,275	489,795
Oshawa	150,690	7,860	400	11,770	130,660
Toronto	2,413,100	152,285	12,755	201,450	2,046,610
Hamilton	325,795	19,580	1,310	26,505	278,400
St. Catharines-Niagara	180,470	10,735	1,755	12,955	155,030
Kitchener	220,080	12,450	825	15,895	190,905
London	215,690	14,600	970	18,420	181,710
Windsor	149,810	5,245	6,975	7,645	129,950
Greater Sudbury	70,530	3,035	115	5,730	61,645
Thunder Bay	57,065	2,570	165	4,545	49,775
Winnipeg	345,730	17,035	955	25,655	302,085
Regina	100,465	5,945	235	7,515	86,780
Saskatoon	114,615	8,260	335	10,075	95,950
Calgary	540,370	38,600	2,725	61,085	437,965
Edmonton	503,355	32,325	1,810	54,130	415,090
Vancouver	995,320	80,285	9,040	102,590	803,400
Victoria	155,730	14,390	820	15,705	124,810
Source: Statistics Canada, Census of Population.					
Last modified: 2004-09-01.					

Exchange rates, interest rates, money supply and stock prices

	2000	2001	2002	2003	2004
	US$ per $ Canadian				
Exchange rate	**0.6732**	**0.6456**	**0.6368**	**0.7138**	**0.7685**
	%				
Selected interest rates					
Bank rate (last Wednesday of the month)	5.77	4.31	2.71	3.19	2.50
Prime business loan rate	7.27	5.81	4.21	4.69	4.00
Chartered bank typical mortgage rate					
1 year	7.85	6.14	5.17	4.84	4.59
3 years	8.17	6.88	6.28	5.82	5.65
5 years	8.35	7.40	7.02	6.39	6.23
Consumer loan rate	11.71	10.06	9.36	9.51	9.24
90 day prime corporate paper rate	5.71	3.87	2.66	2.94	2.31
	$ millions				
Money supply					
Gross M1	106,155	119,001	132,968	143,632	161,404
M2	491,645	517,448	550,030	581,721	617,337
M3	666,880	702,436	744,492	788,196	859,559
	1975 = 1000				
Toronto Stock Exchange 300 index	**9,607.74**	**7,731.72**	**7,036.18**	**7,161.60**	**8,646.14**
Sources: Statistics Canada, CANSIM, tables 176-0036, 176-0043, 176-0047 and 176-0064; Bank of Canada, *Bank of Canada Review*, Ottawa.					
Last modified: 2005-03-18.					

TD Canada Trust Exchange Rate as of **Fri Dec 15 18:05:03 EDT 2006**

	Client Buys (Pays Canadian)	**Client Sells (Receives Canadian)**
US Dollar	1.176	1.133
Sterling Pound	2.299	2.221
Euro	1.554	1.476

Employment by industry

	2000	2001	2002	2003	2004
	thousands				
All industries	**14,758.6**	**14,946.7**	**15,307.9**	**15,665.1**	**15,949.7**
Goods-producing sector	3,826.0	3,779.4	3,881.4	3,930.6	3,992.7
Agriculture	373.7	322.7	324.2	328.3	324.1
Forestry, fishing, mining, oil and gas	276.0	279.6	271.0	281.1	285.7
Utilities	113.7	122.3	131.0	130.4	133.0
Construction	808.7	825.4	864.3	907.4	952.8
Manufacturing	2,253.9	2,229.5	2,291.0	2,283.4	2,297.0
Services-producing sector	10,932.6	11,167.3	11,426.5	11,734.4	11,957.0
Trade	2,303.3	2,363.9	2,401.6	2,457.6	2,503.6
Transportation and warehousing	773.8	779.3	760.3	789.3	809.3
Finance, insurance, real estate and leasing	861.2	878.2	891.1	912.2	955.0
Professional, scientific and technical services	937.4	985.5	985.5	1,000.7	1,010.1
Business, building and other support services[1]	533.0	535.7	579.6	607.9	630.1
Educational services	973.5	981.3	1,008.5	1,029.3	1,038.4
Health care and social assistance	1,499.6	1,543.1	1,622.2	1,683.2	1,736.7
Information, culture and recreation	664.9	711.6	714.2	714.2	732.7
Accommodation and food services	935.4	944.3	984.9	1,006.8	1,006.8
Other services	685.6	665.1	685.5	713.0	705.1
Public administration	765.0	779.2	793.0	820.3	829.2

1. Formerly Management of companies, administrative and other support services.

Source: Statistics Canada, CANSIM, table 282-0008 and Catalogue no. 71F0004XCB.

Last modified: 2005-02-17.

Crimes by type of offence

	1999	2000	2001	2002	2003
	rate per 100,000 population				
All incidents	**8,530.4**	**8,432.6**	**8,453.7**	**8,507.0**	**8,884.8**
Criminal Code offences (excluding traffic offences)	7,751.7	7,666.5	7,655.4	7,708.3	8,132.4
Crimes of violence	958.2	984.4	983.8	969.2	962.8
Homicide	1.8	1.8	1.8	1.9	1.7
Attempted murder	2.3	2.5	2.3	2.2	2.2
Assaults (level 1 to 3)[1]	728.0	761.6	763.9	751.6	746.5
Sexual assault	78.5	78.2	77.5	78.1	74.1
Other sexual offences	10.9	10.2	8.7	8.8	8.0
Robbery	94.5	88.1	88.0	85.0	89.6
Other crimes of violence[2]	41.3	41.3	41.1	40.8	40.7
Property crimes	4,275.7	4,080.9	4,003.5	3,974.5	4,121.4
Breaking and entering	1,046.1	955.9	900.9	878.7	899.5
Motor vehicle theft	530.8	522.4	543.5	516.3	540.7
Theft over $5,000	74.0	69.6	67.2	63.2	63.6
Theft $5,000 and under	2,231.2	2,160.5	2,126.3	2,127.8	2,220.4
Possession of stolen goods	96.4	93.0	86.9	95.8	103.6
Frauds	297.2	279.6	278.8	292.8	293.5
Other *Criminal Code* offences	2,517.9	2,601.2	2,668.1	2,764.6	3,048.3
Criminal Code offences (traffic offences)	387.0	366.4	387.6	374.9	
Impaired driving	282.9	258.2	266.7	255.2	243.6
Other traffic offences[3]	125.4	124.9	123.0	122.9	122.7
Federal statutes	391.7	399.8	410.7	423.8	386.2
Drugs	263.6	287.0	288.2	295.8	271.8
Other federal statutes	128.1	112.7	122.5	127.9	114.4

1. "Assault level 1" is the first level of assault. It constitutes the intentional application of force without consent, attempt or threat to apply force to another person, and openly wearing a weapon (or an imitation) and accosting or impeding another person. "Assault with weapon or causing bodily harm" is the second level of assault. It constitutes assault with a weapon, threats to use a weapon (or an imitation), or assault causing bodily harm. "Aggravated assault level 3" is the third level of assault. It applies to anyone who wounds, maims, disfigures or endangers the life of complainant.
2. Includes unlawfully causing bodily harm, discharging firearms with intent, abductions, assaults against police officers, assaults against other peace or public officers and other assaults.
3. Includes dangerous operation of motor vehicle, boat, vessel or aircraft, dangerous operation of motor vehicle, boat, vessel or aircraft causing bodily harm or death, driving motor vehicle while prohibited and failure to stop or remain.

Source: Statistics Canada, CANSIM, table 252-0013.

Last Modified: 2004-11-18.

Weather conditions in capital and major cities

Definitions and notes	Annual Average		
	Snowfall	Total precipitation	Wet days
	cm	mm	number
St. John's	322.1	1,482	217
Charlottetown	338.7	1,201	177
Halifax	261.4	1,474	170
Fredericton	294.5	1,131	156
Québec	337.0	1,208	178
Montréal	214.2	940	162
Ottawa	221.5	911	159
Toronto	135.0	819	139
Winnipeg	114.8	504	119
Regina	107.4	364	109
Edmonton	129.6	461	123
Calgary	135.4	399	111
Vancouver	54.9	1,167	164
Victoria	46.9	858	153
Whitehorse	145.2	269	122
Yellowknife	143.9	267	118
International comparisons			
Beijing, China	30	623	66
Cairo, Egypt	...	22	5
Capetown, South Africa	...	652	95
London, England	...	594	107
Los Angeles, U.S.A.	...	373	39
Mexico City, Mexico	...	726	133
Moscow, Russia	161	575	181
New Delhi, India	...	715	47
Paris, France	...	585	164
Rio de Janeiro, Brazil	...	1,093	131
Rome, Italy	...	749	76
Sydney, Australia	...	1,205	152
Tokyo, Japan	20	1,563	104
Washington, D.C.	42	991	112

Sources: For Canada, *Climate Normals 1961–1990*, Climate Information Branch, Canadian Meteorological Centre, Environment Canada; for International data, *Climate Normals 1951–1980*.

Last modified: 2005-02-16.

Top 15 countries of origin for overnight visitors to Canada			
	2003		
	Overnight trips		
Country of origin	Trips	Nights spent	Spending in Canada
	thousands		C$ millions
U.S.A.	14,232	56,723	7,288
United Kingdom	691	8,961	945
France	275	4,180	365
Germany	253	3,942	345
Japan	250	2,994	348
Australia	136	1,765	206
South Korea	133	3,341	222
Mexico	132	2,101	206
Netherlands	104	1,499	124
Hong Kong	87	1,623	106
Switzerland	83	1,605	150
Mainland China	77	2,329	143
Taiwan	68	1,079	78
India	67	1,297	57
Italy	57	727	68
Source: Statistics Canada, Culture, Tourism and the Centre for Education Statistics.			

Top 15 countries visited by Canadians			
	2003		
	Overnight visits		
Country visited	Visits	Nights spent	Spending in country
	thousands		C$ millions
U.S.A.	12,666	97,333	8,075
Mexico	716	7,375	790
United Kingdom	684	8,624	821
France	509	6,468	671
Cuba	495	4,408	451
Dominican Republic	415	3,983	403
Germany	331	3,297	278
Italy	248	3,279	384
Netherlands	165	1,401	110
Spain	154	2,017	199
Switzerland	125	911	98
Japan	122	1,643	193
Mainland China	115	2,245	197
Austria	109	586	77
Australia	99	2,685	195
Source: Statistics Canada, Culture, Tourism and the Centre for Education Statistics.			
Last modified: 2004-10-15.			

Household Internet use at home by Internet activity

	1999	2000	2001	2002	2003
	% of all households				
E-mail	26.3	37.4	46.1	48.9	52.1
Electronic banking	8.0	14.7	21.6	26.2	30.8
Purchasing goods and services	5.5	9.6	12.7	15.7	18.6
Medical or health information	15.6	22.9	30.1	32.8	35.6
Formal education/training	9.2	19.0	22.9	24.3	24.9
Government information	12.7	18.9	25.6	29.2	32.2
General browsing	24.3	36.2	44.3	46.1	48.5
Playing games	12.3	18.2	24.4	25.7	27.9
Chat groups	7.5	11.0	13.7	14.0	14.4
Other Internet services	10.0	17.7	21.1	24.8	23.5
Obtain and save music	7.8	17.8	23.3	24.3	20.6
Listen to the radio	5.0	9.3	12.3	12.3	13.1
Find sports related information	..	17.3	22.1	23.8	24.6
Financial information	..	18.5	22.8	23.5	25.0
View the news	..	20.4	26.2	27.2	30.2
Travel information/arrangements	..	21.9	27.4	30.4	33.6
Search for a job	..	12.2	16.2	18.0	19.6
Source: Statistics Canada, CANSIM, table 358-0006 and Catalogue no. 56F0003X (free).					
Last modified: 2005-03-18.					

Home Ownership Rate by Ethno-Racial Group in the City of Toronto, 1996

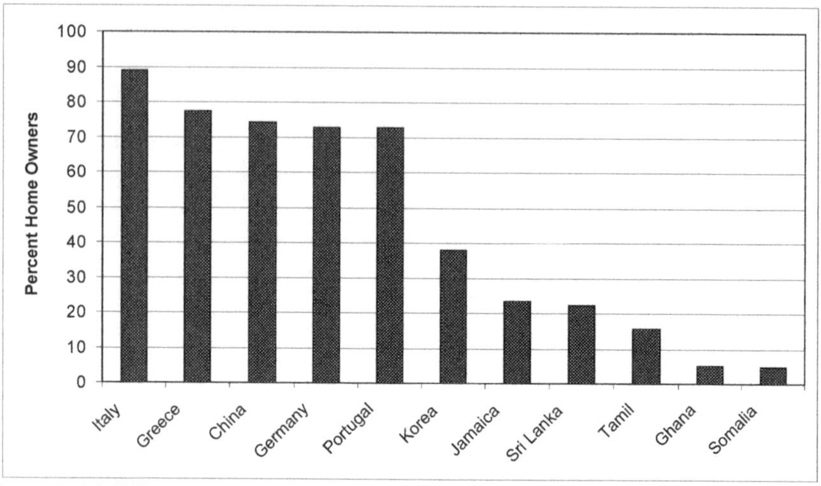

Source: Ornstein 2000

Home Ownership Rate of Immigrants Living in the Toronto CMA in 1996 by Period of Immigration

Source: Murdie and Teixeira, 2001 (Original Data - Statistics Canada, Census of Canada, 1996, Public Use Micro data – Individual File).

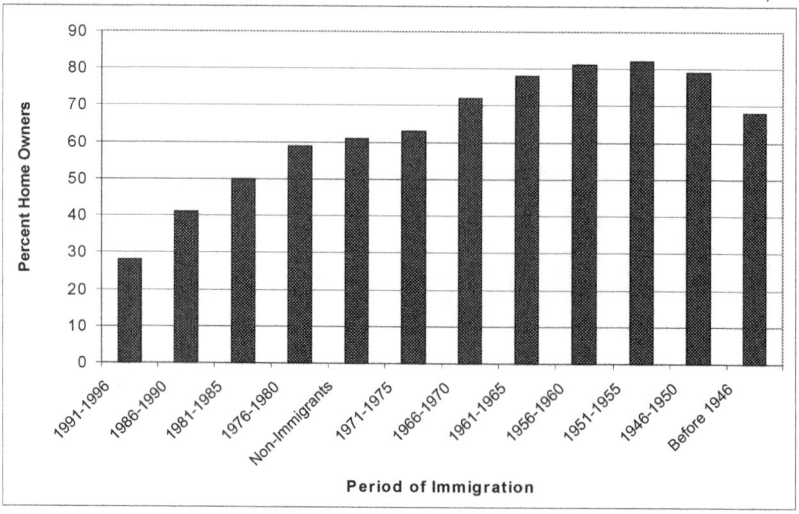

Backgrounder
Citizenship Fast Facts

History

- The year 2006 marks the 59th anniversary of Canadian citizenship.
- In 1947, Canada became the first Commonwealth country to gain its own citizenship act.
- Before that, Canadians were considered British subjects living in Canada, not Canadian citizens.
- The prime minister at the time, William Lyon Mackenzie King, became the first Canadian citizen.

Citizenship

- Since the first citizenship act was enacted, almost 5.7 million people have been granted Canadian citizenship.
- In 2005, citizenship grants were up by 2% from 2004: 196,068 individuals took the oath of citizenship in 2005, compared to 193,025 in the previous year.
- According to the 2001 census, about 84% of eligible immigrants are Canadian citizens.
- In 2005, 2,575 citizenship ceremonies were held across Canada.

See the table below for the number of people who took the oath of citizenship in 2005, 2004 and 2003.

Province	2005	2004	2003
Alberta	12,217	12,743	10,353
British Columbia	33,782	32,059	29,365
Manitoba	2,315	3,244	2,505
New Brunswick	634	361	374
Newfoundland and Labrador	269	278	175
Nova Scotia	1,696	1,043	910
Northwest Territories	58	59	35
Nunavut	1	16	8
Ontario	115,605	122,668	87,611
Prince Edward Island	100	79	138
Quebec	28,119	18,698	19,189
Saskatchewan	612	1,249	1,286
Yukon	67	20	75
Outside Canada / Unspecified	593	508	3,093
Total	**196,068**	**193,025**	**155,117**

Top 10 countries of birth for new Canadians in 2005

Country		**Total**	**%**
1.	China	25,480	12.99
2.	India	21,720	11.07
3.	Pakistan	12,229	6.23
4.	Philippines	10,835	5.52
5.	South Korea	5,381	2.74
6.	England	5,017	2.55
7.	United States	5,009	2.55
8.	Iran	4,947	2.52
9.	Sri Lanka	4,446	2.26
10.	Romania	4,432	2.26
	Other	**96,572**	49.25
	Top 10 countries	**99,496**	50.74
	Total Canada	**196,068**	**100.0**

Immigration

- 262,236 immigrants came to Canada in 2005.
- In 2005, the top five provinces of destination were Ontario (140,533), British Columbia (44,767), Quebec (43,308), Alberta (19,399), Manitoba (8,097).

According to the 2001 census, almost one out of every five Canadian residents (18.4%) was born outside the country.

PART TWO

HOW TO IMMIGRATE TO CANADA

Immigrating to Canada

Every year, Canada welcomes thousands of new residents. Coming to Canada as an immigrant is an exciting opportunity, but also a great challenge.

If you are interested in immigrating to Canada, you have a number of options when applying for permanent residence status. Read about these programs and decide which class suits you and your family best.

- **Skilled Worker Class Immigration:**
  Canada values the skills and experiences that foreign professionals and workers bring with them. Check to see if your skills and experience qualify you to come to Canada as a skilled worker.

- **Business Class Immigration:**
  Canada has a strong economic culture. If you have experience running or investing in businesses, you may qualify to come to Canada as a business immigrant.

- **Provincial Nomination:**
  Most Canadian provinces have programs that encourage immigrants to settle in those provinces and benefit their economies. Learn about settling in one of Canada's provinces as a provincial nominee.

- **Family Class Immigration:**
  Family class immigration reunites families in Canadian homes. Learn how to sponsor your family member or come to Canada as a member of the family class.

- **International Adoption:**
  Adopting children from abroad can be a long process. This is to protect children's rights. Learn about what you need to do to bring an adoptive child to Canada.

- **Quebec-Selected Immigration:**
  Quebec is responsible for selecting immigrants who wish to settle in Quebec. Find out how to apply to be selected to settle in Quebec.

Business Class Applicants

"Investors"

Investor – Regulatory Requirements

"investor" means a foreign national who

a. has business experience;
b. has a legally obtained net worth of at least $800,000; and
c. indicates in writing to an officer that they intend to make or have made an investment.

"business experience" in respect of

a. an investor, other than an investor selected by a province, means a minimum of two years of experience consisting of
   i. two one-year periods of experience in the management of a qualifying business and the control of a percentage of equity of the qualifying business during the period beginning five years before the date of application for a permanent resident visa and ending on the day a determination is made in respect of the application;
   ii. two one-year periods of experience in the management of at least five full-time job equivalents per year in a business during the period beginning five years before the date of application for a permanent resident visa and ending on the day a determination is made in respect of the application, or
   iii. a combination of a one-year period of experience described in subparagraph (i) and a one-year period of experience described in subparagraph (ii);

"full-time job equivalent" means 1,950 hours of paid employment.

"minimum net worth" means

a. in respect of an entrepreneur, other than an entrepreneur selected by a province, $300,000; and
b. in respect of an entrepreneur selected by a province, the minimum net worth required by the laws of the province.

"net assets", in respect of a qualifying business or a qualifying Canadian business, means the assets of the business, minus the liabilities of the business, plus shareholder loans made to the business by the foreign national who is making or has made an application for a permanent resident visa and their spouse or common-law partner.

"net income", in respect of a qualifying business or a qualifying Canadian business, means the after tax profit or loss of the business plus remuneration by the business to the foreign national who is making or has made an application for a permanent resident visa and their spouse or common-law partner.

"net worth", in respect of an investor, other than an investor selected by a province, means the fair market value of all of the assets of the investor and their spouse or common-law partner minus the fair market value of all of their liabilities;

"percentage of equity" means

a. in respect of a sole proprietorship, 100 per cent of the equity of the sole proprietorship controlled by a foreign national or their spouse or common-law partner;
b. in respect of a corporation, the percentage of the issued and outstanding voting shares of the capital stock of the corporation controlled by a foreign national or their spouse or common-law partner; and
c. in respect of a partnership or joint venture, the percentage of the profit or loss of the partnership or joint venture to which a foreign national or their spouse or common-law partner is entitled.

"qualifying business" means a business — other than a business operated primarily for the purpose of deriving investment income such as interest, dividends or capital gains — for which, during the year under consideration, there is documentary evidence of any two of the following:

a. the percentage of equity multiplied by the number of full-time job equivalents is equal to or greater than two full-time job equivalents per year;
b. the percentage of equity multiplied by the total annual sales is equal to or greater than $500,000;
c. the percentage of equity multiplied by the net income in the year is equal to or greater than $50,000; and
d. the percentage of equity multiplied by the net assets at the end of the year is equal to or greater than $125,000.

What is a Canadian Business ?

Canadian Business

Only some businesses qualify as **Canadian businesses** for the purpose of satisfying your residency obligations. To qualify as a Canadian business, the business must meet **one** of these three definitions:

1. The business is incorporated under Canadian or provincial laws and has an ongoing operation in Canada.
2. The business is an enterprise, other than a corporation described above, that has an ongoing operation in Canada **and** satisfies the following conditions:
    - It is capable of generating revenue and is carried on in anticipation of profit; **and**
    - Canadian citizens, permanent residents or Canadian businesses as defined above hold a majority of voting or ownership interests.
3. The business is an organization or enterprise created by the laws of Canada or by the laws of a province of Canada.

Excluded businesses

An enterprise, corporation or organization is **not** a Canadian business if it exists primarily to allow permanent residents to comply with their residency obligations during a stay outside Canada.

Qualifying Employment outside Canada

The phrase "employed on a full-time basis by a Canadian business or in the public service of Canada" means:

- you are an employee of, or under contract to provide services to, either a Canadian business, the public service of Canada or the public service of a Canadian province; and
- you are assigned as a term of your employment or contract on a full-time basis to either:
    1. a position outside Canada;
    2. an affiliated enterprise outside Canada; or
    3. a client of the Canadian business or the public service outside Canada.

Immigrant Investors: Application Process

The following is an outline of the process that must be followed when applying to immigrate to Canada as an immigrant investor.

What you need to know

- Follow the steps below to apply as an immigrant investor for permanent residence status in Canada. You may wish to print this page for future reference.
-

  until a determination is made on your application.
- Download applications from this Web site or visit a Canadian embassy, high commission or consulate near you for print copies.

  Please consult the CIC fee schedule for more information.

Steps in the Immigrant Investor Application Process

You may wish to review the following steps in the immigrant investor application process before proceeding.

1. **Complete an application form**
   The application consists of the following components. All components must be completed. If you cannot download or print the forms from this Web site, you may obtain copies from the Canadian embassy, high commission or consulate nearest you.
   - General information for all applicants
     - Guide for Business Applications
       [IMM 4000] available in PDF format
       (The guide is also available in HTML format)
   - Forms to be completed
     - Application for permanent residence
       [IMM 0008 GENERIC]
     - Schedule 1 Background/Declaration
       [IMM 0008 SCHEDULE 1]
     - Schedule 6 Economic Classes — Business Immigrants
       [IMM 0008 SCHEDULE 6]
     - Additional Family Information
       [IMM 5406]
     - Use of a Representative
       [IMM 5476]

2. **Submit your application for processing**
   Submit your completed application, supporting documents and fees to the visa office where you must apply. The visa

office staff will advise you if they need any further documentation.

3. **You may be contacted for an interview**
Once your application has been examined, you may be required to attend an interview to substantiate the information in your application or provide additional supporting information.
4. **CIC will accept or reject your application**
A letter will be sent to you indicating your acceptance or rejection.
5. **Make your investment**
You will make your $400,000 investment only if you are accepted and all immigration matters have been addressed in the visa office in which you applied.

When and How to Make an Investment

WHEN

You must make the $400,000 investment within the time frame given to you in the letter from the visa office processing your application for permanent residence (generally **within 30 days**). You will be instructed to make the investment by the visa office near the end of the application process. Your permanent resident visa will not be issued until your investment is made.

HOW

Facilitators
Although it is not a requirement, we recommend that you use the services of one of the approved facilitators listed on our Web site. These facilitators are financial institutions, approved by CIC, that are members of the Canada Deposit Insurance Corporation.

CIC pays a commission to facilitators to market the IIP and to assist you with the administrative requirements of making and ultimately redeeming your $400,000 investment. Each facilitator has all the necessary forms required in order to make your investment.

CIC has set up administrative processes to support the pledging of your investment as security for a loan. Your facilitator will have a variety of financing options available in the event that you wish to finance your investment.

Making the Investment without a Facilitator

The investment of CAN $400,000 can only be made by an electronic funds transfer [Acrobat PDF, 73 k], also known as a "wire transfer." The electronic funds transfer must include the following information:

- Your surname and first names;
- Your address;
- Your immigration file number (B number); and
- The location of the visa office processing your application.

Required Documentation

You must also sign and submit two original copies of the Subscription Agreement [Acrobat PDF, 53 k]. Please note that if you are unable to print the Subscription Agreement, you can request one from any visa office. Please ensure that:

- Your name and immigration file number (B number) appear on page 1; and
- Your signature and the date the agreement was signed appear on page 5.

With your Subscription Agreement, please submit a cover letter with the same information that must be included with your electronic funds transfer. Send the completed Subscription Agreement with cover letter to:

Business Immigration
Citizenship and Immigration Canada
Jean Edmonds Tower North
300 Slater Street, 7th Floor
Ottawa, ON
K1A 1L1
Canada

When received, Business Immigration will execute the Subscription Agreement and return one copy to you at the address provided. The promissory note will also be sent to you, so be sure to keep us informed of any address changes that might occur from the time of investment until the maturity date of the promissory note. We can be reached by fax at (613) 941-9014.

Return of Subscription Agreement and Promissory Note

Once both the Subscription Agreement and investment are received, Business Immigration will send a notification to the visa office processing your application indicating that the investment portion of your immigration requirements has been met. The visa office will then contact you with further instructions.

Withdrawal of Application in Investor Category

If you decide that you do not want to pursue your application in the investor category, but have already made the investment, immediately contact both Business Immigration and the visa office processing your application to begin the refund process. The investment cannot be refunded if you have been issued a permanent resident visa.

Refusal of Application in Investor Category

We do not recommend payment until your application has been approved. If you have paid and your application is not approved, you can request a refund of your investment. CIC will refund your investment within 90 days of receipt of a signed request for refund.

Seeking Help in the Application Process

While use of an immigration consultant is not necessary, you may choose to have someone represent you in your application process. A representative is someone who has your permission to conduct business on your behalf with Citizenship and Immigration Canada (CIC) and the Canada Border Services Agency (CBSA).

You may have **one** representative only. Your representative may be a family member, a member of a non-governmental or religious organization, a member of the Canadian Society of Immigration Consultants, a member of a Canadian provincial or territorial law society, or a member of the Chambre des notaires du Québec.

What Happens Next?

After you are approved, you should make sure that you understand your obligations and that you take all the necessary steps to protect your permanent resident status.

Immigrant Investor Program: Facilitators

Although it is not a requirement, we recommend that you use the services of one of the approved facilitators listed on our Web site. These facilitators are financial institutions, approved by CIC, that are members of the Canada Deposit Insurance Corporation (CDIC).

Through CIC, participating provinces pay a commission to facilitators to market the Immigrant Investor Program (IIP) and to assist you with the administrative requirements of making and ultimately redeeming your $400,000 investment. Each facilitator has all the necessary forms in order to make your investment.

CIC has set up administrative processes to support the pledging of your investment as security for a loan. Your facilitator will have a variety of financing options available in the event that you wish to finance your investment.

To contact one of the banks or other financial institutions that have been chosen by CIC to help immigrant investors, please see the list of approved financial institutions below.

Immigrant Investor Facilitators

The following is the list of the CDIC members participating in the IIP. Contact the program official at the bank or credit union you wish to use for your financing.

CIBC
Ms. Teresa Tazumi
Director, Asian Banking
199 Bay Street
Commerce Court West, 7th Floor
Toronto, Ontario
M5L 1A2
Tel.: (416) 980-8452
Fax: (416) 980-4378
E-mail: TeresaM.Tazumi@cibc.com
Internet Site: www.cibc.com or www.cibcasianbanking.com

Computershare Trust Company of Canada
Mrs. Sophie Brault
Corporate Trust Officer
1500 University Street, 7th Floor
Montréal, Quebec
H3A 3S8
Tel.: (514) 982-7888, x7455
Fax: (514) 982-7677
E-mail: Sophie.Brault@computershare.com
Internet Site: www.computershare.com

Desjardins Trust Inc.
Mr. Marc Audet
Vice-President
East Tower, 27th Floor
2 Complexe Desjardins
P.O. Box 992, Station Desjardins
Montréal, Quebec
H5B 1C1
Tel.: (514) 499-8440
Fax: (514) 982-9579
E-mail: cic_inquiry@immigrantinvestor.com
Internet Site: www.immigrantinvestor.com

Habib Canadian Bank
Mr. Muslim Hassan
Chief Operating Officer
918 Dundas Street East, Suite 1B
Mississauga, Ontario
L4Y 4H9
Tel.: (905) 276-5300
Fax: (905) 276-5400
E-mail: muslim@habibcanadian.com
Internet Site: www.habibcanadian.com

HSBC Bank Canada
Mr. Eric G. Major
Managing Director
Global Immigrant Investor Programs
Suite 1100
885 West Georgia Street
Vancouver, British Columbia
V6C 3E8
Tel.: (604) 631-8086
Fax: (604) 631-8073
E-mail: Eric_Major@hsbc.ca
Internet Site: www.hsbc.ca/iip

Industrial Alliance Trust Inc.
Mr. Alain Nadon
Program Director
Immigrant Investor Program
2200 McGill College, Suite 320
Montréal, Quebec
H3A 3P8
Tel.: (514) 499-1170
Fax: (514) 499-1063
E-mail: alain.nadon@iatrust.ca
Internet Site: www.inalco.com

Korea Exchange Bank of Canada
Mr. See Mok Kim
Vice-President
Business Operations Department
Madison Centre, Suite 1101
4950 Yonge Street
Toronto, Ontario
M2N 6K1
Tel.: (416) 222-5200, ext. 251
Fax: (416) 222-8180
E-mail: kimseee@keb.co.kr
Internet site: www.kebcanada.com

Laurentian Bank of Canada
Ms. Johanne Sheehy
Private Banking
1981 McGill College Avenue
Mezzanine Level
Montréal, Quebec
H3A 3K3
Tel.: (514) 284-4000
Fax: (514) 284-4009
Internet Site: www.laurentianbank.com/en/02_consumers/
08_gestion_privee/04_Immigrant/_fr.htm

MCAP Inc.
Mr. Glenn Doré
President
New Canadian Plan
1 Westmount Square, Suite 1250
Montréal, Quebec
H3Z 2P9
Tel.: (514) 989-1909 ext. 22
Fax: (514) 989-1088
E-mail:canada@newcanadianplan.com
Internet Site: www.newcanadianplan.com

National Bank of Canada
Mr. Fouad Boustani
Senior Manager
Immigrant Investor Program and
Electronic Banking Services Retail
500 Place d'Armes, 5th Floor
Montréal, Quebec
H2Y 2W3
Tel.: (514) 394-6490
Fax: (514) 394-6915
E-mail: iip.canada@nbc.ca
Internet Site: www.nbc.ca/immigrantinvestor

Royal Bank of Canada
Ms. Ritu Narayan
Program Manager
Global Private Banking
Royal Bank Plaza, South Tower
200 Bay Street, Suite 600, P.O Box 88
Toronto, Ontario
M5J 2J5
Tel.: (416) 974-0250
Fax: (416) 974-6102
E-mail: gpbimmigrantinvestor@rbc.com
Internet Site: www.rbc.com/canada/
cad_immigrant_investor_prog.html

Scotiabank
Mr. Guy Pilote
Associate Director
ScotiaMcLeod
Scotia Tower
1002 Sherbrooke Street West, Suite 2140
Montréal, Quebec
H3A 3L6
Tel.: (514) 350-7764
Fax: (514) 350-7794
E-mail: guy_pilote@scotiamcleod.com
Internet Site: www.scotiabank.com/immigrantinvestor

Toronto-Dominion Bank
Mr. Ramon Yu
Managing Director
Two Pacific Place
88 Queensway, Suite 3415
Hong Kong
Tel.: (852) 2846-4160
Fax: (852) 2845-9191
E-mail: Ramon.Yu@td.com
Internet Site: www.td.com

Immigrant Investors: Know the Rules

Permanent resident status gives you the right to live in Canada. The following provides additional information on obligations relevant to investor immigrants and all permanent residents of Canada.

What happens after you are approved

After you have become a permanent resident to Canada:

- Meet your obligations as a permanent resident
- Enjoy the benefits of living in Canada

Repayment of Your Investment

If you made your investment directly, contact Business Immigration for instructions on how to proceed with the redemption of your CAN $400,000 promissory note approximately two to three months before the end of the five-year allocation period. If you used the services of a facilitator when you made your investment, please contact the facilitator.

Please note that CIC has 30 days from the maturity date of your promissory note to repay your investment. Before redemption can occur, the original promissory note must be returned to CIC along with your contact information and signature for verification purposes. Please inform Business Immigration or your facilitator of any changes in your contact information during your five-year holding period.

Residency Requirements

As a permanent resident, you enjoy all the benefits of living in Canada. However, as a permanent resident, you must comply with a residency obligation during every five-year period. An examiner will meet with you to determine if the residency conditions have been met.

Please refer to the *After you arrive...* section of our Web site offering information and advice on programs for newcomers, finding help in your community, residency obligations for permanent residents, and other useful resources.

More Information

Additional information pertaining to the Immigrant Investor Program is available in the application guide and through supporting links and resources. Potential applicants may also wish to review information about Canadian immigration regulatory requirements before proceeding with their applications. Additional support is also available through Canadian embassies and consulates, immigration lawyers, and Canadian commercial banks.

Applying for Permanent Residence
Business Class Applicants

Investors
Entrepreneurs
Self-employed Persons

Overview

Canada welcomes successful business people who are seeking new opportunities and challenges. The Business Immigration Program is designed to encourage and facilitate the admission of these individuals. Both the federal and provincial/territorial governments welcome business immigrants and offer services to help immigrants start a business and settle in Canada.

This **application kit** provides information on how to qualify as a business immigrant and how to apply for permanent residence in Canada. It states the requirements and features of the three business immigrant classes: investors, entrepreneurs and self-employed persons. The **application kit** also contains instructions on how to complete the five **application forms**: *Application for Permanent Residence in Canada* (IMM 0008, Generic), *Background/Declaration* (IMM 0008, Schedule 1), *Economic Classes - Business Immigrants* (IMM 0008, Schedule 6), *Additional Family Information* (IMM 5406) and *Use of a representative* (IMM 5476).

While the information in this application pertains to immigration to any place in Canada, the province of Quebec, under the *Canada-Quebec Accord*, operates its own business immigration program. Quebec's rules may differ from those in this application kit. Immigrants in the Quebec program must intend to live in Quebec and must be selected by Quebec. If you want to settle in Quebec, contact the responsible Quebec Immigration Office (see Appendix E) or request this information from one of our visa offices. The responsible Quebec Immigration office will send you an application, which includes a *Demande de Certificat de sélection* form, to be completed and returned to the appropriate address. If your application is approved, you will be issued a *Certificat de sélection du Québec* (CSQ) (see Definitions). You must then complete our forms and send them along with the original of the CSQ to one of our visa offices.

Separate application kits are also available for skilled worker and family class immigrants. A skilled worker immigrant is someone with specific experience and occupational skills that are readily transferable to the Canadian labour market. Family class immigrants are sponsored to come to Canada by a relative such as a parent, spouse or common-law partner. If you think you may qualify in one of these categories, you can find the appropriate application at www.cic.gc.ca or at any of our visa offices.

It is an offence under the *Immigration and Refugee Protection Act* to knowingly make a false or misleading statement in support of an application for permanent residence in Canada.

Definitions

Read the following carefully:

Accompanying family member: A spouse, common-law partner or dependent child of the principal applicant who intends to obtain permanent resident status in Canada. Accompanying family members can travel separately from the principal applicant but must not arrive in Canada before the principal applicant.

Business experience:

- In respect of an **investor,** means:
    - The management of a **qualifying business** and the control of a **percentage of equity** of a qualifying business for at least two years in the period beginning five years before the date of application; or
    - The management of at least five **full-time job equivalents** per year in a business for at least two

years in the period beginning five years before the date of application.

- In respect of an **entrepreneur**, means:
  - The management of a **qualifying business** and the control of a **percentage of equity** of a qualifying business for at least two years in the period beginning five years before the date of application.

Certificat de sélection du Québec **(CSQ):** A document issued by the Ministère des Relations avec les citoyens et de l'Immigration (MRCI), indicating that an immigration candidate has been accepted to live in the province of Quebec upon arrival in Canada.

Common-law partner: A person who is living in a conjugal relationship with another person, either of the same or opposite sex, who has done so for a period of at least one year.

Dependent children: Daughters and sons, including children adopted before the age of 18, who:

- are under the age of 22 and do not have a spouse or common-law partner; or
- have been continuously enrolled and in attendance as full-time students in an educational institution and financially supported by their parents since turning 22 (or since marrying or entering into a common-law relationship if this happened before the age of 22); or
- depend substantially on the financial support of their parents since turning 22 and are unable to support themselves due to a medical condition.

Educational credential: Any diploma, degree, trade or apprenticeship credential issued for the completion of a program of study or training at a recognized educational or training institution.

Family member: A spouse, common-law partner, dependent child, or dependent child of a dependent child of the principal applicant.

The spouse or common-law partner of the principal applicant's dependent child is also considered a family member.

Full-time equivalent studies: With respect to part-time or accelerated studies, the period that would have been required to complete those studies on a full-time basis.

Full-time job equivalent: Defined as 1,950 hours of paid employment.

Net assets: Assets minus liabilities plus shareholder loans from the applicant and their spouse or common-law partner.

Net income: After tax profit or loss plus remuneration to the applicant and their spouse or common-law partner.

Net worth: The fair market value of the assets of the applicant and their spouse or common-law partner minus the fair market value of all their liabilities.

Percentage of equity:

- In respect of a sole proprietorship, 100% of the equity of a sole proprietorship.
- In respect of a corporation, the percentage of the issued and outstanding voting shares of the capital stock of the corporation controlled by the applicant or their spouse or common-law partner.
- In respect of a partnership or joint venture, the percentage of the profit or loss of a partnership or joint venture to which the applicant or their spouse or common-law partner is entitled.

Post-secondary credential: Any diploma, certificate, or other credential other than a university credential issued for the completion of a program of study or training at a recognized educational or training institution.

Qualifying business: A business—other than a business operated primarily for the purpose of deriving investment income such as interest, dividends or capital gains—for which, in each of any two years in the period beginning five years before the date of application and ending on the date of the interview decision, there is proof of any two of the following:

1. That the percentage of equity multiplied by the number of full-time job equivalents is equal to or greater than two full-time job equivalents per year;
2. That the percentage of equity multiplied by the total annual sales is equal to or greater than $500,000;
3. That the percentage of equity multiplied by the net income in the year is equal to or greater than $50,000; and
4. That the percentage of equity multiplied by the net assets at the end of the year is equal to or greater than $125,000.

Qualifying Canadian business: A business operated in Canada by an entrepreneur—other than a business operated primarily for the purpose of deriving investment income, such as interest, dividends or capital gains—for which there is, in any year within the period of three years after the day the entrepreneur becomes a permanent resident, proof of any two of the following:

1. That the percentage of equity multiplied by the number of full-time job equivalents is equal to or greater than two full-time job equivalents per year;
2. That the percentage of equity multiplied by the total annual sales is equal to or greater than $250,000;
3. That the percentage of equity multiplied by the net income in the year is equal to or greater than $25,000; and
4. That the percentage of equity multiplied by the net assets at the end of the year is equal to or greater than $125,000.

Relevant experience: In respect of a **self-employed person**, means

- For at least two years in the period beginning five years before the date of application:

- Self-employment in cultural activities or athletics; or
- Participation, at the world-class level, in cultural activities or athletics; or
- Farm management experience.

Spouse: A person of the opposite sex who is 16 years of age or older and to whom the applicant is legally married.

Visa office: A Canadian immigration office outside Canada, located at a Canadian Embassy, High Commission or Consulate.

All monetary amounts mentioned throughout this application are in Canadian dollars.

Types of Business Applicants

Canada has three classes of business immigrants: **investors, entrepreneurs** and **self-employed persons**. You must choose to apply under only **one** of these classes, even if you meet the requirements for more than one class. Features of each type are listed below to help you make that decision. Note that you cannot change the class you are applying under once you have submitted your application.

Investors

Investors must have business experience. They must have **either:**

a. managed a qualifying business and controlled a percentage of equity of a qualifying business for at least two years in the period beginning five years before the date of application, or
b. they must have managed at least five full-time job equivalents per year in a business for at least two years in the period beginning five years before the date of application.

The investor class applicant must have a net worth of at least $800,000. They are required to make an investment of $400,000, paid to the Receiver General of Canada. The investment is subsequently allocated to participating provinces and territories in Canada. These governments use the funds for job creation and economic development. The full amount of the investment (without interest) is repaid to the investor after five years. The exact date of repayment depends on when the $400,000 is received by Citizenship and Immigration Canada. At the latest, the amount would be returned five years and 3 months after the date of payment. The return of the investment is fully guaranteed by participating provinces and territories.

Features of the Investor Program

- Investors are not required to start a business in Canada;
- Investments are fully guaranteed by provinces and territories that participate in the program;
- The provinces and territories control the investment during the five year lock-in period; and
- No immigration conditions are imposed upon admission to Canada.

Under the *Canada-Quebec Accord*, the province of Quebec operates its own immigrant investor program. All investors in the Quebec program must intend to live in Quebec and must be selected by Quebec. In common with the federal program, investors in the Quebec program must invest $400,000 and have a net worth of $800,000.

Entrepreneurs

Entrepreneurs must have business experience. They must have managed a qualifying business and controlled a percentage of equity of a qualifying business for **at least two years** in the period beginning five years before the date of application.

The entrepreneur class applicant must have a net worth of at least $300,000. Additionally, they must have the intention and the ability to:

1. Control a percentage of equity of a qualifying Canadian business equal to or greater than 33 1/3 %;
2. Provide active and ongoing management of the qualifying Canadian business; and
3. Create at least one incremental full-time job equivalent for one or more Canadian citizens or permanent residents other than the entrepreneur applicant and their family members.

Entrepreneurs are required to sign a declaration stating they intend and will be able to meet the conditions of permanent residence.

Features of the Entrepreneur Program

- A minimum net worth requirement of $300,000;
- A requirement that within three years of becoming a permanent resident, the entrepreneur must have controlled and have actively managed a qualifying Canadian business for a period of at least one year, and that the business must have created employment opportunities for others; and
- All family members are admitted under the same conditions as the principal applicant; the conditions are removed once the entrepreneur satisfies the conditions.

Under the *Canada-Quebec Accord*, the province of Quebec operates its own immigrant entrepreneur program. All entrepreneurs in the Quebec program must intend to live in Quebec and must be selected by Quebec. In common with the federal programs, entrepreneurs in the Quebec program must have a net worth of $300,000.

Self-employed persons

Self-employed immigrants must have **relevant experience (see** Definitions**)**. Points are awarded for relevant experience within the five-year period immediately preceding the date of application.

Features of the Self-employed persons program

- No immigration conditions are imposed on this class.
- Self-employed immigrants must have the experience, intention and ability to:
    - establish a business that will, at a minimum, create an employment opportunity for themselves and that will make a significant contribution to cultural activities or athletics in Canada; or
    - purchase and manage a farm in Canada.

Selection Criteria

You must first meet the definition of the one class you are applying under (investor, entrepreneur or self-employed person) to be eligible for selection. If you successfully meet the definition, you are then assessed against five selection factors: age, education, official languages, experience and adaptability. For each selection factor, a specific number of selection points are allotted. The following tables will help you estimate how many points you would earn for each factor. It is important that you make a careful assessment before you apply because you must pay certain fees, one of which is non-refundable (the processing fee) even if your application is refused. If you have a score lower than a total of 35 points, your application may be refused. The pass mark for all three classes of business immigrants is 35.

Investors and Entrepreneurs

Factor 1: Business experience (maximum 35 points)

Business experience must have been obtained within the period beginning five years before the date of application.

Two years business experience	20
Three years business experience	25
Four years business experience	30
Five years business experience	35

Factor 2: Age (maximum 10 points)

Points are given for your age at the time your application is received

Age	Total Points
16 or under	0
17	2
18	4
19	6
20	8
21-49	10
50	8
51	6
52	4
53	2
54 and over	0

Factor 3: Education (maximum 25 points)

You have not completed secondary school (also called high school)	0
You have obtained a secondary school credential	5
You have obtained a one-year post-secondary educational credential and completed at least 12 years of full-time of full-time equivalent studies.	12
You have obtained a one-year post-secondary educational credential and completed at least 13 years of full-time or full-time equivalent studies	15
You have obtained a one-year university credential at the bachelor's level and completed at least 13 years of full-time or full-time equivalent studies.	15
You have obtained a two-year post-secondary educational credential and completed at least 14 years of full-time or full-time equivalent studies.	20
You have obtained a two-year educational credential at the bachelor's level and completed at least 14 years of full-time or full-time equivalent studies.	20
You have obtained a three-year post-secondary educational credential and completed at least 15 years of full-time or full-time equivalent studies.	22
You have obtained two or more university educational credentials at the bachelor's level and completed at least 15 years of full-time or full-time equivalent studies.	22
You have obtained a Master's or PhD and completed at least 17 years of full-time or full-time equivalent studies.	25

Factor 4: English and French language ability (maximum 24 points)

To assess your English and French language ability, first decide which language you are most comfortable with. This language is your **first official language.** The language you feel less comfortable communicating with is your **second official language.** Next, award points according to your ability to read, write, listen to and speak English and French. The following two tables define the levels of language proficiency and how points are allotted for each level:

Skill Level	**Criteria**
High proficiency	You can communicate effectively in most community and workplace situations. You speak, listen to, read and write the language very well.
Moderate proficiency	You can make yourself understood and you understand what others are saying in most workplace and community situations. You speak, listen to, read and write the language well.
Basic proficiency	You do not meet the above criteria for moderate proficiency but still have some ability to speak, listen to, read or write the language.
No proficiency	You have no ability whatsoever in speaking, listening to, reading or writing the language.

Calculating your language points

First official language	**Read**	**Write**	**Listen**	**Speak**	**Maximum score per category**
High proficiency	4	4	4	4	16
Moderate proficiency	2	2	2	2	8
Basic proficiency	1	1	1	1	2
No proficiency	0	0	0	0	0
Maximum possible score for all four abilities in first official language =					**16**
Second official language	**Read**	**Write**	**Listen**	**Speak**	**Maximum score per category**
High proficiency	2	2	2	2	8
Moderate proficiency	2	2	2	2	8
Basic proficiency	1	1	1	1	2
No proficiency	0	0	0	0	0
Maximum possible score for all four abilities in second official language =					**8**
Maximum possible score total for both official languages =					**24**

Factor 5: Adaptability (maximum 6 points)

A maximum of 6 points for adaptability can be earned by any combination of the following elements:

You have made a business exploration trip to Canada in the period beginning five years before the date of your application.	6
You have participated in joint federal-provincial business immigration initiatives.	6

If you wish to be assessed for adaptability points, it is necessary that your province of destination provide you with documentation indicating that it is satisfied that you have met one or both of the above elements.

For the purpose of awarding points:

a. a trip to Canada becomes a business exploration trip to Canada only when a province has deemed it to be so; and
b. each province establishes individually, what constitutes participation in a joint federal-provincial business immigration initiative.

If you wish to earn points for adaptability, you should first contact the provincial or territorial government contact for the province/territory to which you are destined. Consult the list in Appendix F Provincial and Territorial Government Contacts. The province can then provide you with appropriate documentation indicating that, in their view, you have met the regulatory requirements. You must submit this documentation to the visa office

Self-employed Persons

Factor 1: Business experience (maximum 35 points)

Business experience must have been obtained within the period beginning five years before the date of application.

Two years business experience	20
Three years business experience	25
Four years business experience	30
Five years business experience	35

Factor 2: Age (maximum 10 points)

Points are given for your age at the time your application is received.

Age	Total Points
16 or under	0
17	2
18	4
19	6
20	8
21-49	10
50	8
51	6
52	4
53	2
54 and over	0

Factor 3: Education (maximum 25 points)

You have not completed secondary school (also called high school)	0
You have obtained a secondary school credential	5
You have obtained a one-year post-secondary educational credential and completed at least 12 years of full-time of full-time equivalent studies.	12
You have obtained a one-year post-secondary educational credential and completed at least 13 years of full-time or full-time equivalent studies	15
You have obtained a one-year university credential at the bachelor's level and completed at least 13 years of full-time or full-time equivalent studies.	15
You have obtained a two-year post-secondary educational credential and completed at least 14 years of full-time or full-time equivalent studies.	20
You have obtained a two-year educational credential at the bachelor's level and completed at least 14 years of full-time or full-time equivalent studies.	20
You have obtained a three-year post-secondary educational credential and completed at least 15 years of full-time or full-time equivalent studies.	22
You have obtained two or more university educational credentials at the bachelor's level and completed at least 15 years of full-time or full-time equivalent studies.	22
You have obtained a Master's or PhD and completed at least 17 years of full-time or full-time equivalent studies.	25

Factor 4: English and French language ability (maximum 24 points)

To assess your English and French language ability, first decide which language you are most comfortable with. This language is your **first official language.** The language you feel less comfortable communicating with is your **second official language.** Next, award points according to your ability to read, write, listen to and speak English and French. The following two tables define the levels of language proficiency and how points are allotted for each level:

Skill Level	**Criteria**
High proficiency	You can communicate effectively in most community and workplace situations. You speak, listen, read and write the language very well.
Moderate proficiency	You can make yourself understood and you understand what others are saying in most workplace and community situations. You speak, listen, read and write the language well.
Basic proficiency	You do not meet the above criteria for moderate proficiency but still have some ability to speak, listen to, read or write the language.
No proficiency	You have no ability whatsoever in speaking, listening to, reading or writing the language.

Calculating your language points

First official language	**Read**	**Write**	**Listen**	**Speak**	**Maximum score per category**
High proficiency	4	4	4	4	16
Moderate proficiency	2	2	2	2	8
Basic proficiency	1	1	1	1	2
No proficiency	0	0	0	0	0
Maximum possible score for all four abilities in first official language =					**16**
Second official language	**Read**	**Write**	**Listen**	**Speak**	**Maximum score per category**
High proficiency	2	2	2	2	8
Moderate proficiency	2	2	2	2	8
Basic proficiency	1	1	1	1	2
No proficiency	0	0	0	0	0
Maximum possible score for all four abilities in second official language =					**8**
Maximum possible score total for both official languages =					**24**

Factor 5: Adaptability (maximum 6 points)

A maximum of 6 points for adaptability can be earned by any combination of the following elements:

1. Your accompanying spouse or common-law partner's level of education	
Secondary school (high school) diploma or less	0
A one or two-year post-secondary educational credential **and** at least 13 years of education	3
A three-year post secondary educational credential **and** at least 15 years of education	4
A three-year university credential **and** at least 15 years of education	4
A Master's or PhD **and** at least 17 years of education	5
2. You or your accompanying spouse or common-law partner has studied in Canada	
Not at all, or anything less than two years post-secondary education in Canada	0
Obtained a Canadian post-secondary educational credential of at least two years since the age of 18	5
3. You or your accompanying spouse or common-law partner has worked in Canada	
Not at all, or less than one year full-time work in Canada	0
Worked full-time in Canada for at least one year	5
4. You or your accompanying spouse or common-law partner has family in Canada	
No	0
Have a parent, grandparent, aunt, uncle, sister, brother, nephew, niece, child or grandchild who is a Canadian citizen or permanent resident living in Canada	5

Your Score

For all three business classes, use the table below to calculate your total score. The pass mark is 35. The maximum possible score for each class is 100. The pass mark is variable and is determined, on an ongoing basis, by the Minister of Citizenship and Immigration Canada.

The officer reviewing your application will first determine whether or not you meet the definition of the class you are applying under (investor, entrepreneur or self-employed person). If you meet the definition, the officer will then assess your score against the selection criteria. If there is a difference between the points you give yourself and the points the officer awards you, the officer's assessment will prevail.

FACTOR		**Maximum Points**	**Your Score**
1	Business experience / Relevant experience	**35**	
2	Age	**10**	
3	Education	**25**	
4	Language proficiency	**24**	
5	Adaptability	**6**	
Total		**100**	

Funds Required to Settle in Canada

The Government of Canada provides no financial support to business immigrants. All business applicants must establish that they have enough money to support themselves and their family members for at least one year after they arrive in Canada. This is normally satisfied by the net worth requirement. Nonetheless, you should research the cost of living in the region of Canada where you intend to live and have access to enough capital for your initial establishment.

You should be aware that Canadian legislation requires persons entering Canada to declare cash funds of $10,000 CDN or more. You will have to disclose these funds to a Canadian official upon arrival. Cash funds means money (coins or bank notes), securities in bearer form (stocks, bonds, debentures, treasury bills, etc.) and negotiable instruments in bearer form (bank drafts, travellers' cheques, money orders, etc.).

Fees

The processing fee:

- **is non**-refundable whether your application is approved or not;
- must be paid when you send your application to the visa office;
- must be paid by the principal applicant and each accompanying family member.

Use the table below to calculate the amount required in **Canadian dollars (CDN$)**.

Important:

For information on how to pay your fees, such as the acceptable payment method, consult the Web site of the visa office to which you will be applying (follow the links in www.cic.gc.ca). Your processing fee payment must accompany your completed application. If it does not, your application will be returned to you.

Processing Fee	**Number of People**	**Amount per Person**	**Amount Due**
Principal applicant	1	$1050	$1050
Spouse or common-law partner		x $550	
Each dependent child who is 22 years of age or older or who is married or in a common-law relationship, regardless of age		x $550	
Each dependent child under 22 years of age and not married or in a common-law relationship		x $150	
Total			**$**

Right of Permanent Residence Fee

- **$490 per person** for you (the principal applicant) and your spouse or common-law partner (if applicable). Dependent children are exempt.
- You will need to pay this fee before your application for permanent residence can be finalized. **We will send you a request to pay this fee** when we are ready to issue the permanent resident visa.

How to Apply to Immigrate to Canada

STEP 1. Collect the documents you need to support your application. These are listed in the Appendix A Checklist. The Checklist will tell you how many copies of the application form the visa office needs. It will also tell you which documents must be originals and which should be photocopies, and whether a certified translation in English or French is required.

STEP 2. Photocopy the forms. Page two of the *Application for Permanent Residence in Canada* (IMM 0008, Generic) form asks for details of family members. There is space for three family members on the form. If you have more than three family members, photocopy this page before you start to fill it in so you have enough space for everyone.

You, the principal applicant, must complete *Schedule 6: Economic Classes - Business Immigrants.* You, your spouse or common-law partner and each dependent child aged 18 or over (whether accompanying you or not) must each complete *Schedule 1: Background/Declaration.* This application kit provides only one copy of each form. Before you start to fill them in, be sure to make enough photocopies for your needs.

STEP 3. Complete the *Additional Family Information* form (IMM 5406). You, your spouse or common-law partner and each dependent child aged 18 or over (whether accompanying you or not) must each complete this form. It is very important that you also list on this form any other children you may have (even if they are already citizens or permanent residents of Canada). This includes adopted children, step-children, married children and any of your children who have been adopted by others or are in the custody of an ex-spouse or common-law partner. Where custody arrangements have been made, you must provide copies of the custody documents.

STEP 4. Complete the *Use of a Representative* form (IMM 5476) if you paid someone to help you complete your application or if you want us to discuss your application with someone other than yourself.

STEP 5. Obtain a police certificate/clearance from every country in which you or your family members aged 18 years or over have lived for six months or longer since reaching the age of 18 (see Appendix B).

STEP 6. Use the instructions in the Fees section to calculate the fees you must send with your application. Pay the fees according to instructions on the Web site of the visa office to which you will be applying. Do not mail cash.

STEP 7. Use the Checklist to verify that you have all of the required documents. It is important to note that the visa office may request additional information at any time during the application process.

STEP 8. Submit your completed application to the Canadian visa office responsible for:

- the country in which you are residing, provided you have been lawfully admitted to that country for at least one year; or
- your country of nationality.

To find out which visa office will serve you, consult our Web site at www.cic.gc.ca/english/offices/apply-where.html or contact a Canadian embassy, consulate or high commission.

Print your name and address on the top left-hand side of the envelope. If mailing, make sure that your envelope has sufficient postage. The post office will return your application to you if it does not have enough postage.

If you do not fully complete and sign the forms, your application will be returned to you unprocessed.

Completing the Forms

The following pages do not contain instructions for all the boxes on the forms. Most questions are clear; instructions are provided only when necessary. Attach a separate sheet of paper if you need more space and indicate the number of the question you are answering.

You must answer all questions. If you leave any sections blank, your application will be returned to you and processing will be delayed. If any sections do not apply to you, answer "N/A" ("Not applicable"). Print clearly with a black pen or use a typewriter. Be sure to make enough photocopies before you start.

If your application is accepted and information you provide on the forms changes before you arrive in Canada, you must inform, in writing, the visa office to which you applied. You must do this even if your visa has already been issued.

WARNING! It is a serious offence to give false or misleading information on this form. We may check to verify your responses.

Application for Permanent Residence in Canada (IMM 0008, Generic)

This form must be completed by the principal applicant. Page two of the form asks for details of dependent family members. There is space for three family members on the form. If you have more than three family members, photocopy this page before you start to fill it in so you have enough space for everyone.

At the top of the form, there are three boxes:

Category under which you are applying

Check the "Economic Class" box.

Number of family members

Write the total number of people included in your application, including yourself and any family members, whether they are accompanying you to Canada or not.

Preferred Language

Correspondence: Decide which of English or French you are more comfortable reading and writing, and check the appropriate box.

Interview: You may be selected for an interview. Interviews can be conducted in English or French. You may also be interviewed in another language of your choice; however, you will be responsible for the cost of hiring an interpreter.

Instructions on how to fill out the rest of the form are listed below.

1. Print your full **family name** (surname) as it appears on your passport or on the official documents that you will use to obtain your passport. Print all of your **given names** (first, second or more) as they appear on your passport or official documents. Do not use initials.

5. If you are a citizen of more than one country, give details on a separate page.

10. This section requires you to give details of your past marriages or common-law relationships (see Definitions). If you have never had a spouse or common-law partner other than your current one, check the "No" box and proceed to Question 11. If you have, check the "Yes" box and provide the details requested. If you have had more than two previous spouses or common-law partners, give details on a separate page.

12. Check the box that best describes the highest level of education you have completed. If you have not completed secondary school, check the "No secondary" box.

    Secondary education: the level of schooling after elementary and before college, university, or other formal training. Also called high school.

    Trade/Apprenticeship: completed training in an occupation, such as carpentry or auto mechanics.

    Non-university certificate/diploma: training in a profession that requires formal education but not at the university level (for example, dental technician or engineering technician).

Bachelor's degree: An academic degree awarded by a college or university to those who complete the undergraduate curriculum; also called a baccalaureate. Examples include a Bachelor of Arts (BA), Bachelor of Science (BSc) or Bachelor of Education (BEd).

Master's degree: An academic degree awarded by the graduate school of a college or university. You must have completed a Bachelor's degree before a Master's degree can be earned.

PhD: the highest university degree, usually based on at least three years graduate study and a dissertation. Normally, you must have completed a Master's degree before a PhD can be earned.

14. This is the address we will use to mail correspondence regarding your application. Print your address in English and, if applicable, also in your own native script.

19. Cards issued by a foreign national, provincial, municipal or other government, as well as cards issued by a recognized international agency such as the Red Cross, can be used to identify yourself. If you have such a card, print the number in the space provided. Photocopy both sides of the card and attach the photocopy to your application. If you do not have an identity card, print "N/A".

Details of family members

Given name(s)

Print all of your family members's **given names** (first, second or more) as they appear on his or her passport or official documents. Do not use initials.

Country of citizenship

If your family member is a citizen of more than one country, give details on a separate page.

Relationship to you

Indicate whether the family member is your spouse, common-law partner, daughter or son.

Will accompany you to Canada

Tell us if your family member will come to Canada with you. He or she must immigrate before the visa expires, but may arrive in Canada after you.

Education

Indicate the level of education your family member has successfully completed. Use the categories listed in Question 11.

Photos

Ask a photographer to provide you with a set of photos of yourself and each of your family members included in your application, whether they will be accompanying you or not. Consult the Web site of the visa office to which you are applying for the number of photos you need (follow the links from www.cic.gc.ca).

Photos must comply with specifications given at Appendix C, Photo Specifications. Make sure you give a copy of these specifications to the photographer.

- **On the back of one photo (and only one) in each set**, write the name and date of birth of the person appearing in the photo as well as the date the photo was taken.
- Enclose each set of photos in separate envelopes. Write the family member's name, date of birth and relationship to you on the corresponding envelope and close the envelope with a paper clip.
- Photos must not be stapled, scratched, bent or bear any ink marks.
- Note that the visa office may also require additional photos at a later date.

Background / Declaration
(IMM 0008, Schedule 1)

1. Write all of your given names. Do not use initials.

6. Indicate your current status in the country where you now live (for example, citizen, permanent resident, visitor, refugee, no legal status, etc.).

10. Provide details of all post-secondary education. Begin with the most recent program completed.

11. You must account for every month since your 18th birthday. Under "Activity", print your occupation or job title if you were working. If you were not working, enter what you were doing (for example, unemployed, studying, travelling, etc.). Attach another sheet if necessary.

15. Give a complete address including the street, town or city, province or region, and country. If there was no street or street number, explain exactly the location of the house or building.

Declaration

Read the statements carefully. Sign and date in the boxes provided. By signing, you certify that you fully understand the questions asked, and that the information you have provided is complete, truthful, and correct. If you do not sign, the application will be returned to you.

Economic Classes - Business Immigrants (IMM 0008, Schedule 6)

All questions on this form must be completed by the principal applicant.

1. Choose the one class you are applying under. Refer to section Types of Business Applicants for information on the different classes.

4. To assess your English and French language ability, refer to the tables in section Selection Criteria.

6. If yes, give details such as the dates of your trip, which cities you were in and what businesses or organizations you visited.

7. If yes, give details such as the name of the initiative, the federal departments and provincial governments involved and the dates of your participation.

8. You must complete all sections of this question (A to E) for every business in which you had ownership. Photocopy page two and complete a separate copy for every business.

13. The last option box under relationship, "spouse or common-law partner," applies only to the principal applicant.

15. **B and G: Real Property** includes any property of significant value, such as real estate, boats, aircraft and high-value automobiles.

    J:Total Funds refers to the amount of available and transferable money you have available for settlement in Canada (indicate amount in Canadian dollars).

16. **Complete this section if you are applying in the Entrepreneur Class.** If you do not check "Yes" your application will be returned to you.

Additional Family Information (IMM 5406)

Before you begin writing on this form, make enough photocopies for yourself and for each person who must complete it. You, your spouse or common-law partner and each dependent child aged 18 or over (whether accompanying you or not) must complete this question. All sections must be answered. If any sections do not apply, answer “NOT APPLICABLE” or “N/A”.

It is very important that you list on this form any other children (even if they are already permanent residents of Canada or Canadian citizens) that you, your spouse or common-law partner or your dependent children might have who are not included in your *Application for Permanent Residence in Canada* (IMM 0008, Generic). This includes married children and any of your children who have been adopted by others, or are in the custody of an ex-spouse or common-law partner.

Use of a Representative (IMM 5476)

Complete this form if you are appointing a representative.

If you have dependent children aged 18 years or older, they are required to complete their own copy of this form if a representative is also conducting business on their behalf.

A **representative** is someone who has your permission to conduct business on your behalf with Citizenship and Immigration Canada. When you appoint a representative, you also authorize CIC to share information from your case file with this person.

You are not obliged to hire a representative. We treat everyone equally, whether they use the services of a representative or not. If you choose to hire a representative, your application will not be given special attention nor can you expect faster processing or a more favourable outcome.

The representative you appoint is authorized to represent you only on matters related to the application you submit with this form. You can appoint only **one** representative for each application you submit.

There are two types of representatives:

Unpaid representatives

- friends and family members who do not charge a fee for their advice and services
- organizations that do not charge a fee for providing immigration advice or assistance (such as a non-governmental or religious organization)
- consultants, lawyers and Québec notaries who do not, and will not, charge a fee to represent you

Paid representatives

If you want us to conduct business with a representative who is, or will be charging a fee to represent you, he or she must be authorized. Authorized representatives are:

- immigration consultants who are members in good standing of the Canadian Society of Immigration Consultants (CSIC)
- lawyers who are members in good standing of a Canadian provincial or territorial law society and students-at-law under their supervision
- notaries who are members in good standing of the *Chambre des notaires du Québec* and students-at-law under their supervision

If you appoint a paid representative who is not a member of one of these designated bodies, your application will be returned. For more information on using a representative, visit our Web site.

Section B.

5. Your representative's full name

If your representative is a member of CSIC, a law society or the *Chambre des notaires du Québec*, print his or her name as it appears on the organization's membership list.

8. Your representative's declaration

Your representative must sign to accept responsibility for conducting business on your behalf.

Section D.

10. Your declaration

By signing, you authorize us to complete your request for yourself and your dependent children under 18 years of age. If your spouse or common-law partner is included in this request, he or she must sign in the box provided.

Release of information to other individuals

To authorize CIC to release information from your case file to someone other than a representative, you will need to complete form *Authority to Release Personal Information to a Designated Individual* (IMM 5475) which is available on our Web site and from Canadian embassies, high commissions and consulates abroad.

The person you designate will be able to obtain information on your case file, such as the status of your application. However, he or she will **not** be able to conduct business on your behalf with CIC.

You must notify us if your representative's contact information changes or if you cancel the appointment of a representative.

What Happens Next?

Checking your application status

You can find out the current status of your application by logging on to e-Client Application Status. You may also phone our Call Centre.

If you do not want your information available on-line, you can remove on-line information by logging on to e-Client Application Status. You may also call our Call Centre and ask an agent to do this for you.

Current processing times are updated weekly.

The decision on your application

An officer will decide if an interview is necessary. If so, you will be informed of the time and place. Your spouse or common-law partner and dependent children aged 18 or over may also be asked to come to the interview. The officer may ask about your job, experience, education, reasons for migrating, plans and preparations. The officer may also ask about your family, health, financial situation, or past difficulties with the law. There may also be questions to determine your ability to settle successfully in Canada.

If your application is successful, the Canadian visa office will ask you to submit your passports. You and your family members must have valid passports in order to receive your visas. Diplomatic, official or similar passports cannot be used to immigrate to Canada. You must have ordinary (non-official) passports when you arrive. The validity of your visas cannot exceed the validity of your passports. The Canadian visa office may request that your passports be renewed prior to submission.

For how long is my permanent resident visa valid?

The validity date is based on the earlier of:

- your passport validity dates or your family members' passport validity dates; or
- the medical validity dates. Medical examination results are valid for 12 months after the initial medical examination.

If you do not use your visa within its validity, you must re-apply for immigration to Canada. Permanent resident visas cannot be extended once issued.

Employment and settlement services

Settlement services vary between regions and provinces. You can learn about them from:

- Citizenship and Immigration Canada at: www.cic.gc.ca/english/newcomer;
- Human Resources and Social Development: www.hrsdc.gc.ca; and,
- from some provincial governments or provincial organizations.

Arriving in Canada

When you arrive, you must present your *Confirmation of Permanent Residence* to a Canadian customs or immigration officer at your first port of entry. The officer will check your *Confirmation of Permanent Residence* and passport and ask you questions similar to those on the *Application for Permanent Residence in Canada* (IMM 0008, Generic) to verify that you are of good character and in good health. You may also be required to show proof of your funds.

The permanent resident card

You will be issued a permanent resident card as part of the arrival process. Cards will be mailed to your home address soon after you become a permanent resident. For information on the permanent resident card, visit our Web site.

Permanent resident status

Some conditions apply:

- You will remain a permanent resident until you become a Canadian citizen, however, you must spend at least two years of each five year period in Canada
- You may leave and re-enter Canada as often as you wish
- If you spend more than two years of a five-year period outside Canada, you may lose your permanent resident status (certain conditions apply)

Rights

As permanent residents, you and your family will have the right to:

- Live, study and work in Canada for as long as you remain permanent residents.
- Access most social benefits accorded to Canadian citizens (see "Limitations" below)
- Apply for Canadian citizenship and a Canadian passport (once you have been a legal resident of Canada for three of the previous four years)

Limitations

There are a few limitations on permanent residents:

- You cannot vote in certain elections.
- You may be ineligible for certain jobs requiring high-level security clearances
- If you or any of your family members commit a serious crime, you or your family members risk being deported from Canada

Obligations

As permanent residents, you will also have the same legal obligations as Canadians, such as paying taxes and respecting all federal, provincial and municipal laws.

Appendix A
Checklist

This document is available in PDF format only. The checklist is one of the forms you will need to mail with your application. Make sure you print this document and attach it when completed to your application

Mailing Your Application

Submit your completed application to the Canadian visa office responsible for:

- the country in which you are residing, provided you have been lawfully admitted to that country for at least one year; or
- your country of nationality.

To find out which visa office will serve you, consult our Web site at www.cic.gc.ca/english/offices/apply-where.html or contact a Canadian embassy, consulate or high commission.

Appendix B
Obtaining Police Certificates and Clearances

Security Requirements

You and your family members (spouse/common-law partner and dependent children) must not be any risk to Canada. You and all your family members aged 18 and over who are not Canadian citizens or permanent residents must undergo background checks. This also applies to your family members who do not intend to join you in Canada.

For each country in which you or your family members have lived for more than six months during the past 10 years, you must provide a police certificate, clearance or record of no information. If you or your family members were under 18 years of age when you lived in one of those countries, you do not need to provide a police certificate for that country. It is your responsibility to contact the police or relevant authorities.

We will also do our own background checks to determine if you have any arrests or criminal convictions, or if you are a security risk to Canada.

How to apply for police certificates

For the following countries, police certificates should not be obtained before applying for immigration. You may receive special instructions at a later date about police certificates for these countries.

Afghanistan	Honduras	Thailand
Costa Rica	Hong Kong	Ukraine
Fiji	Poland	United Kingdom
French Polynesia	Singapore	Venezuela

If you have lived in one of the countries listed below, you will need additional forms before applying for immigration. If you do not have the forms, contact the visa office for more information.

Argentina	South Korea	
Russia	Sri Lanka	

Criminality

Generally, persons with a criminal conviction are not admitted into Canada. However, if a prescribed period has passed after they have completed their sentence or committed an offence and during which they were not convicted of a subsequent offence, they may be deemed to have been rehabilitated. If they are not deemed to have been rehabilitated, they may, under special circumstances, be eligible to apply for rehabilitation.

Offences outside Canada

If you were convicted of or committed a criminal offence **outside** Canada, you may be deemed to have been rehabilitated if 10 years have passed since you have completed the sentence imposed upon you or since you have committed the offence, if the offence is one that would, in Canada, be an indictable offence punishable by a maximum term of imprisonment of less than 10 years. If the offence is one that would, in Canada, be prosecuted summarily and if you were convicted of two or more such offences, that period is five years after the sentence imposed was served or to be served.

Offences in Canada

If you have a criminal conviction **in** Canada, you must seek a pardon from the National Parole Board of Canada before you apply for immigration to Canada. For further information, contact:

Clemency and Pardons Division
National Parole Board
410 Laurier Avenue West
Ottawa ON K1A 0R1
Telephone: 1-800-874-2652 (Callers in Canada and the United States only)
Facsimile: 1-613-941-4981
Web site: www.npb-cnlc.gc.ca (the guide which includes application forms can be downloaded from the Web site)

If you have had two or more summary convictions in Canada, you may be deemed rehabilitated and no longer inadmissible if

- five years have passed since the sentence imposed was served or to be served,
- you have had no subsequent convictions and
- you have not been refused a pardon.

See the table below for a summary of the types of offences and length of rehabilitation periods.

If you or any of your family members have committed a criminal offence, you must provide, in addition to any police certificates or clearances, a full description of the circumstances surrounding the offence and the court record. This information will be reviewed by the visa office and you will receive further instructions.

We will also do our own background checks in all countries in which you and your family members have lived. These checks will determine if you have any arrests or criminal convictions, or if you are a security risk to Canada.

The following table gives a summary of the type of offences and length of rehabilitation periods.

Conviction or offence	**Rehabilitation period**	
	When deemed rehabilitated[1]	When eligible to apply for rehabilitation
Conviction of an offence outside Canada that, if committed in Canada, would be an indictable offence punishable by a maximum term of imprisonment of less than ten years	At least ten years after completion of the sentence imposed	Five years after completion of the sentence imposed
Commission of an offence outside Canada that, if committed in Canada, would be an indictable offence punishable by a maximum term of imprisonment of less than ten years	At least ten years after commission of the offence	Five years after commission of the offence

Conviction or offence	**Rehabilitation period**	
	When deemed rehabilitated[1]	When eligible to apply for rehabilitation
Conviction or commission of an offence outside Canada, that, if committed in Canada, would be punishable by a maximum term of imprisonment of ten years or more	Not applicable	Five years from completion of the sentence or commission of the offence
Conviction for two or more offences outside Canada that, if committed in Canada, would constitute summary conviction offences	At least five years after the sentences imposed were served or to be served	Not applicable
Conviction for two or more summary conviction offences in Canada	At least five years after the sentences imposed were served or to be served	Must apply for a pardon
Conviction for two or more indictable offences in Canada	Not applicable	Must apply for a pardon

[1]The person must not have committed or been convicted of any other indictable offence.

Appendix C
Photo Specifications

Notes to the applicant

TAKE THIS WITH YOU TO THE PHOTOGRAPHER

- Immigration photographs are **not** the same as passport photographs.
- Make sure that you provide the correct number of photographs specified on the Web site of the visa office to which you apply.

Notes to the photographer

The photographs must:

- show a full front view of the person's head and shoulders showing full face centred in the middle of the photograph;
- have a **plain white background**;
- be identical (black and white or colour) produced from the same untouched negative, or exposed simultaneously by a split-image or multi-lens camera;

The photographs must:

- measure between 25 mm and 35 mm (1" and 1 3/8") from chin to crown
- have a 35 mm x 45 mm (1 3/8" x 1 3/4") finished size

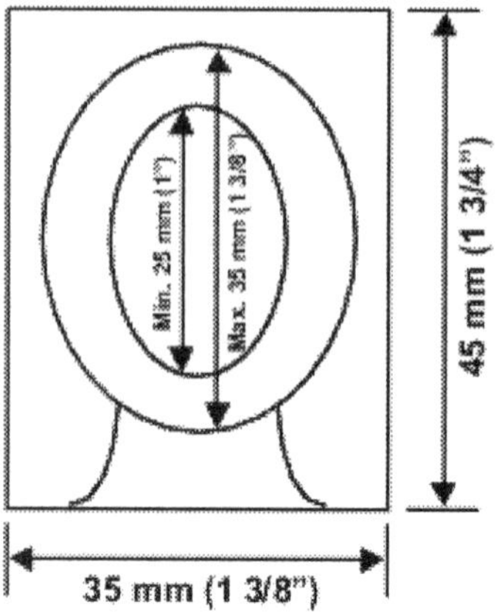

Appendix D
Medical Examinations

Medical requirements

You and your family members, whether accompanying you or not, must undergo and pass a medical examination in order to come to Canada. To pass the medical examination you or your family members must not have a condition that is a danger to public health or safety or would cause excessive demand on health or social services in Canada.

Medical instructions will normally be sent to you after you submit your application to the visa office. The medical examination is valid for 12 months from the date of the first medical examination. If your visa is not processed in this time, you must undergo another complete medical examination.

Your own doctor cannot do the medical examination. You must see a physician on Canada's list of Designated Medical Practitioners

(DMPs). Note that the physician is only responsible for conducting a medical examination; he or she cannot give you any advice on the immigration process.

Excessive demand

"Excessive demand" refers to the burden placed on Canada's health or social services due to ongoing hospitalization or medical, social or institutional care for physical or mental illnesses, or special education or training. Individuals may be denied admittance to Canada due to the high costs of their care. The factors considered during the medical assessment include whether or not hospitalization or medical, social or institutional care are required and whether potential employability or productivity could be affected.

Will I receive a copy of the medical report?

All medical reports and x-rays for the medical examination become the property of the Canadian Immigration Medical Authorities and cannot be returned to you. The physician will not tell you the results of the medical; however, he or she will let you know if you have a health problem. The officer and not the physician makes the final decision on whether a medical examination has been passed for immigration purposes. The visa office will inform you in writing if there is a problem with your medical examination.

My children are studying abroad and cannot return home for their immigration medical examination. What should I do?

Whenever possible, the same physician should perform the medical examination for all family members. If this is not possible, advise the visa office that your family members are unable to present themselves and the visa office will arrange to have their medical examinations done by a physician in their area. The visa office will send you a copy of the *Medical Report: Section A, Client Identification & Summary* (IMM 1017), along with the address of the physician closest to your family members. The visa office will fill in your family members' dates of birth, eye colour and other necessary data and attach their photographs to the forms.

The Visa Office & Number section of this form (IMM 1017) must have the name of the visa office where your application is being processed. The physician doing the medical examination of your family members must also forward their complete medical reports to the same Canadian medical office that received your report. Your family members' medical examination reports will be matched with your file, as the Medical Report form will carry your file number.

Appendix E
Quebec Immigration Offices

You may also visit the Internet site of the *Ministère des Relations avec les citoyens et de l'Immigration* of the province of Québec at: www.immq.gouv.qc.ca/anglais.

Immigration Offices **Address and Telephone**	**Countries Served**
Brussels Service d'immigration du Québec Délégation générale du Québec 46, avenue des Arts, 7e étage 1000 Bruxelles BELGIQUE Phone: (32.2) 512.0036 Fax: (32.2) 514.2641	Belgium
Buenos Aires Service d'immigration du Québec Edificio Laminar Plaza Ing. Butty 240, piso 3 C1001 AFB Buenos Aires ARGENTINA Phone: 54-11- 4343-2033 Fax: 54-11-4343-2122	Argentina, Paraguay, Uruguay
Damascus Service d'immigration du Québec a/s Ambassade du Canada Autostrade Mezzeh, C.P. 3394 Damas SYRIE Phone: (963.11) 611.6851 or 611.6692 Fax: (963.11) 613.1600	Afghanistan, Azerbaijan, Bahrain, Bhutan, Cyprus, Egypt, India, Iran, Iraq, Jordan, Kuwait, Lebanon, Maldives, Nepal, Oman, Pakistan, Qatar, Saudi Arabia, Sri Lanka, Sudan, Syria, Turkey, United Arab Emirates, Yemen
Hong Kong Service d'immigration du Québec a/s Consulat général du Canada Exchange Square Tower 1, 13th floor 8, Connaught Place HONG KONG Phone: (852) 2810.7183 Fax: (852) 2845.3889	Australia, Bangladesh, Brunei, Burma (Myanmar), Cambodia, China, Fiji, French Polynesia, Hong Kong, Indonesia, Japan, Korea, Laos, Macao, Malaysia, Micronesia, New Caledonia, New Guinea, New Zealand, Papua, Philippines, Singapore, Taiwan, Thailand, Vietnam

Mexico Service d'immigration du Québec Délégation du Québec Avenida Taine 411 Colonia Bosques de Chapultepec 11580 Mexico, D.F. MEXIQUE Phone: (52.555) 250.8208 Fax: (52.555) 250.8332	Antigua, Barbados, Belize, Bolivia, Brazil, Chile, Colombia, Costa Rica, Cuba, Dominica, El Salvador, Ecuador, Falkland Islands, French Guiana, Grenada, Guatemala, Guyana, Haiti, Honduras, Jamaica, Mexico, Netherlands, Antilles, (and Antilles not mentioned elsewhere), Nicaragua, Panama, Peru, Puerto Rico, St. Lucia, St. Vincent, Surinam, Trinidad and Tobago, Venezuela
Montréal Unité de traitement des DPI - Africa (except Egypt and Sudan) 276, St-Jacques 4e étage Montréal (Québec) H2Y 1N3 CANADA Fax: (514) 873-9265	Azores, Algeria, Angola, Benin, Botswana, Burkina Faso, Burundi, Cameroon, Canaries, Cape Verde islands, Central African Republic, Chad, Comoros, Congo, Djibouti, Guinea Equatorial, Ethiopia, Gabon, Gambia, Ghana, Guinea-Bissau, Guinea, Ivory Coast, Kenya, Lesotho, Liberia, Libya, Madagascar, Malawi, Mali, Malta, Marocco, Mauritania, Mozambique,Namibia, Niger, Nigeria, Principe, Ruanda, Sao Tome, Senegal, Seychelles, Sierra Leone, Somalia, South Africa, St. Helena,Swaziland, Tanzania, Togo, Tunisia, Uganda, Western Sahara, Zaire, Zambia, Zimbabwe
New York Service d'immigration du Québec Délégation générale du Québec One Rockefeller Plaza 26th Floor New York, NY 10020 U.S.A. Phone: (212) 843.0960 Fax: (212) 376.8984	United States, Bermuda, St. Pierre and Miquelon
Paris Service d'immigration du Québec Délégation générale du Québec 87-89, rue La Boétie 75008 Paris FRANCE Phone: in France: (01) 53.93.45.45 outside of France	Andorra, Denmark, Estonia, Finland, France, Gibraltar, Great Britain, Greece, Greenland, Guadeloupe, Iceland, Ireland, Israel, Italy, Reunion, Latvia, Liechtenstein, Lithuania, Luxembourg, Madeira, Martinique, Mauritius, Monaco, Norway, Netherlands, Portugal, San Marino, Spain, Sweden, Switzerland, Vatican City

(33.1) 53.93.45.45 Fax: in France (01) 53.93.45.40 outside of France (33.1) 53.93.45.40	
Vienna Service d'immigration du Québec a/s Ambassade du Canada Laurenzerberg 2 Bürocenter Stiege 2, 2.OG A-1010 Vienne AUTRICHE Phone: (43.1) 53138.3005 Fax: (43.1) 53138.3443	Albania, Armenia, Austria, Belarus, Bosnia-Herzegovina, Bulgaria, Croatia, Czech Republic, Georgia, Germany, Hungary, Kazakhstan, Kirghizistan, Moldavia, Mongolia, Ouzbekistan, Poland, Romania, Russia, Slovakia, Slovenia, Tajikistan, Turkmenistan, Ukraine, Yugoslavia

Appendix F
Provincial and Territorial Government Contacts

Business Immigrant Program:
Provincial and Territorial Partners

Provincial Information

Many provinces and territories provide valuable information and services to assist business immigrants in setting up and successfully operating businesses in Canada. You may wish to visit the provincial or territorial Web sites for more information. These Web sites also have information about the geographic, economic and social aspects of the provinces or territories.

Some provinces also have business immigration programs as part of the Provincial Nominee Program.

Alberta
Economic Immigration Program http://www.alberta-canada.com/investLocate/economicImmigrationProgram.cfm 4th Floor, Commerce Place 10155 – 102 Street Edmonton, Alberta T5J 4L6 Tel.: (780) 427-6375 Fax: (780) 427-6560

British Columbia

Business Immigration

http://www.businessimmigration.gov.bc.ca

Suite 730, World Trade Centre
999 Canada Place
Vancouver, British Columbia
V6C 3E1
Tel.: (604) 775-2227
Fax: (604) 660-4092
E-mail: bus.imm@gov.bc.ca

Manitoba

Business Immigration

http://www.gov.mb.ca/labour/immigrate/immigration/3_2.html

9th Floor, 213 Notre-Dame Avenue
Winnipeg, Manitoba
R3B 1N3
Tel.: 1-800-665-8332
Fax: (Canada 001) 204-948-2256
E-mail: immigratemanitoba@gov.mb.ca

New Brunswick

Immigrating to New Brunswick

http://www.gnb.ca/immigration/english/
immigrating/immigrate_NB.asp

Investment and Immigration
Department of Business New Brunswick
P.O. Box 6000
Fredericton, New Brunswick
E3B 5H1
Tel.: 1 506 453-3981
Fax: 1 506 444-4277
E-mail: immigration@gnb.ca

Newfoundland and Labrador
Department of Innovation, Trade and Rural Development http://www.intrd.gov.nl.ca/intrd Department of Innovation, Trade and Rural Development P.O. Box 8700, Confederation Building St. John's, Newfoundland and Labrador A1B 4J6 Tel.: (709) 729-7000 Fax: (709) 729-0654 E-mail: ITRDinfo@gov.nl.ca
Nova Scotia
Business and Immigration http://www.novascotiaimmigration.com/default.asp?mn=1.4&id=190&pagesize=1&sfield=MenuId&search=4 Office of Immigration P.O. Box 1535 1741 Brunswick Street, Suite 110A Halifax, Nova Scotia B3J 2Y3 Tel.: (902) 424-5230 Fax: (902) 424-7936 E-mail: immigration@gov.ns.ca
Northwest Territories
Government of the Northwest Territories http://www.gov.nt.ca P.O. Box 1320 Yellowknife, Northwest Territories X1A 2L9

Nunavut Territory
Government of Nunavut http://www.gov.nu.ca/Nunavut Economic Development and Innovation Division Department of Economic Development and Transportation Government of Nunavut P.O. Box 612 Pangnirtung, Nunavut X0A 0R0 Fax: (867) 473-2663
Ontario
Immigration and Settlement http://www.gov.on.ca/citizenship/english/ citdiv/immigrat/index.html 6th floor, 400 University Avenue Toronto, Ontario M7A 2R9 Tel.: 1-800-267-7329 E-mail: immigration@gov.on.ca
Prince Edward Island
Business Immigration http://www.gov.pe.ca/immigration/index.php3 P.O. Box 2000 Charlottetown, Prince Edward Island C1A 7N8 Tel.: (902) 368-4000 E-mail: Island@gov.pe.ca

Quebec

Business Immigrants to Quebec follow the rules set out in the Canada-Quebec Accord on Immigration.

- General information on immigrating to Quebec
- Business immigration to Quebec

Saskatchewan

Government of Saskatchewan

http://www.gov.sk.ca

Immigration
2nd Floor, 1919 Saskatchewan Drive
Regina, Saskatchewan
S4P 3V7
Tel.: 1-866-727-5427
E-mail: http://www.gov.sk.ca/contact-webmaster/webmaster.cgi

Yukon Territory

Yukon Government

http://www.gov.yk.ca/index.html

Box 2703
Whitehorse, Yukon
Y1A 2C6

Business Immigrant Links: FAQs

The following page provides answers to commonly asked questions about immigrating to Canada as a Business Immigrant.

Business Immigrant Program

Why does Canada have a Business Immigration Program?

The three business classes seek to attract experienced business people to Canada to support the development of a strong and prosperous Canadian economy.

Business immigrants are expected to own and manage businesses in Canada, or in the case of the investor program, pay CAN$400,000 for future investment by the provinces and territories to support their economies and create jobs.

What do business immigrants bring to Canada?

The business programs allow experienced business people to immigrate to Canada and apply their capital, entrepreneurial skills and knowledge of markets and technology within the Canadian economy.

What are the principal differences between investors, entrepreneurs and self-employed persons?

Investors must make a CAN$400,000 investment but are not subject to monitoring or other regulatory requirements once they arrive in Canada.

Entrepreneurs come to Canada subject to the monitored, regulatory condition that they invest and participate in the management of a business of a given size in Canada that creates at least one additional job for someone other than their immediate family.

Self-employed persons are selected based on their intention and ability to create a job for themselves in cultural or athletic activities or to purchase and manage a farm in Canada, but are not subject to monitoring or other regulatory requirements once they arrive in Canada.

What will I have to do to satisfy CIC that my net worth has been legally obtained?

You will have to satisfy the visa officer that no portion of your net worth was obtained as a result of criminal activity. You should be able to explain material disparities between your net income over the years and your present net worth, and to comply with reasonable requests for documents to back up both your income sources and the components of your net worth.

What type of documents will I be required to submit in support of my application?

In addition to the usual documents in support of any application for immigration to Canada, you will be required to provide documents supporting your past business experience, such as the following:

- financial statements;
- corporate and personal income tax returns;
- tax assessments;
- bank statements;
- business licences;
- minute books;
- letters of reference; and
- promotional material.

Where can I get application forms?

Application forms for investors, entrepreneurs and self-employed persons are available on our site. If you cannot download or print the forms from this site, you may obtain copies from the visa office near you.

Where do I apply?

You must apply in your country of residence, your country of nationality or the country where you have been legally admitted for at least one year.

How long will it take for my application to be processed?

The length of time it takes to process your application is different in each visa office. For estimated times, please visit the Application Process Times section of this site.

Where can I find information about starting up a business in Canada?

Our Business Immigration Links page provides several sites where you may obtain more information about starting a business in Canada.

Immigrant Investor FAQ's

What are the requirements for qualifying as an investor?

To meet the definition, you must have at least two years of business experience, and demonstrate legally obtained net worth of at least CAN$800,000. You must then obtain a minimum of 35 points in a selection grid designed to determine whether you will be able to become economically established in Canada.

Before a visa is issued, you must make an investment of CAN$400,000 to CIC.

What is the procedure for becoming an investor?

You must apply for immigration to Canada, satisfy a visa officer that you meet the definition of an investor, be awarded at least 35 assessment points and pass the medical and admissibility checks.

You will then be directed, in writing, to make a CAN$400,000 investment to Citizenship and Immigration Canada, after which a visa may be issued to you.

What are the business experience requirements?

You can meet the business experience requirements if you have owned a percentage of a business of a specified size for a minimum of two full years, or if you have managed a minimum of five full-time job equivalents in a business of any size for a minimum of two full years, or a combination of one-year periods in either.

Does the business experience have to be recent?

You can go back as far as five years before the date of your application (and up until a determination is made on your application by a visa officer).

What is meant by "business"?

A business is a commercial enterprise carried on for the purpose of profit. This does not exclude businesses that are not currently generating profits or professional practices, but it does exclude governmental organizations, not-for-profit organizations, and others.

Who is responsible for the investment operations of the program?

CIC administers the cash management aspects of the program by acting as agent for the participating provinces. Each investor must make their CAN$400,000 investment with CIC. Their investment will be returned by CIC after approximately five years and two months.

What documents do I receive after I pay my investment?

You will receive a Zero Interest Promissory Note that is not transferable (you may not sell it), but that may be pledged as collateral for a loan. At the maturity date, you will return the promissory note to CIC for repayment of your $400,000 investment.

Why do you recommend that I make my investment through a CIC-approved facilitator?

CIC has set up administrative procedures with a number of facilitators to assist in the payment and redemption of your $400,000 investment. These services are available to you at no cost (CIC pays their fees). Additionally, facilitators offer a variety of financing options in the event you should want to finance the payment of your investment or to pledge your promissory note as collateral for a loan in the future.

How big is the Immigrant Investor Program?

Including the Quebec program, over $3 billion has been raised since the inception of the Immigrant Investor Program in 1986.

In 2004, the Quebec and federal programs raised $272,000,000 and $718,800,000 respectively from 2,477 principal applicants and their families.

Where do most immigrant investors come from?

Investors come from all over the world. Currently, the majority of investors are from China, Taiwan, Korea and Hong Kong, but there are also substantial numbers of investors applying from the Middle East and elsewhere.

In 2002, the selection criteria for business immigrants were modified in the *Immigration and Refugee Protection Regulations.* Why?

While the Immigrant Investor Program was substantially altered on April 1,1999, with respect to the administration of the CAN$400,000 investment, the rules governing the selection attributes of the investor, entrepreneur and self-employed programs had remained largely unchanged since their inception.

The Auditor General of Canada, noting that the business definitions were vague and therefore difficult to apply, suggested that the selection criteria be amended to make them clearer to both economic immigrants and the program administrators, and to make it easier to achieve the Program's objectives.

What changed for investors?

- An objective standard for business experience was established.
- The net worth requirement of CAN$800,000 remained unchanged; however, the requirement that the net worth be created by the investor's own activities was removed and replaced by a requirement that the net worth be legally obtained.
- Spousal assets are now included when assessing net worth (Quebec calculates its own net worth in accordance with its own laws).
- The selection grid was altered to provide the flexibility to adjust the weight of the various criteria.

However, the most significant change in the investor and entrepreneur programs was the introduction of more objective measures for business experience. It is generally agreed that business experience is the best predictor of future business success. The definition of business experience has been modified to ensure that only experienced businesspeople can qualify for the business programs.

Entrepreneur Immigrant

What are the requirements for qualifying as an entrepreneur?

To meet the definition, you must have at least two years of business experience and demonstrate a legally obtained net worth of at least CAN$300,000. You must then obtain a minimum of 35 points in a selection grid designed to determine whether you will be able to become economically established in Canada.

You will be required to indicate in writing that you have the intention and ability to meet given business conditions in Canada. After taking up permanent residence in Canada, you will have three years to meet these conditions.

What is the procedure to become an entrepreneur?

You must apply for immigration to Canada, satisfy a visa officer that you meet the definition of an entrepreneur, be awarded at least 35 assessment points and pass the medical and admissibility checks.

You will also be subject to conditions after you take up permanent residence in Canada.

What are the business experience requirements?

You can meet the business experience requirements if you have owned a percentage of a business of a specified size for a minimum of two full years.

Does the business experience have to be recent?

You can go back as far as five years before the date of your application (and up until a decision is made on your application by a visa officer).

What is meant by "business"?

A business is a commercial enterprise carried on for the purpose of profit. This does not exclude businesses that are not currently generating profits or professional practices, but it does exclude governmental organizations, not-for-profit organizations, and others.

What will I have to do to satisfy CIC that my net worth has been legally obtained?

You will have to satisfy the visa officer that no portion of your net worth was obtained as a result of criminal activity. You should be able to explain material differences between your net income over the years and your present net worth, and to comply with reasonable requests for documents to back up both your income sources and the components of your net worth.

Who do I contact to see about meeting my business conditions in Canada?

You will be given a pamphlet with instructions and contact information for the CIC offices in your province of destination. You will be expected to make contact with the appropriate CIC office within six months of landing to report your address and telephone number and to provide evidence of your efforts to meet your conditions after 18 months.

How big is the Entrepreneur Program?

Over the past five years, approximately 1,000 entrepreneurs (principal applicants) a year have landed in Canada.

Where do most entrepreneurs come from?

Entrepreneurs come from all over the world. Currently, the majority of entrepreneurs are from China, Taiwan, Korea and Hong Kong, but there are also large numbers of them applying from the Middle East and elsewhere.

In 202, the selection criteria for business immigrants were modified in the Immigration and Refugee Protection Regulations. Why?

The Auditor General of Canada, noting that the business definitions were vague and therefore difficult to apply, suggested that the selection criteria be amended to make them clearer to both economic immigrants and the program administrators, and to make it easier to achieve the Program's objectives.

What changed for entrepreneurs?

- An objective standard for business experience was established.
- The minimum net worth requirement of CAN$300,000 was introduced.
- The selection grid was revised to provide the flexibility to adjust the weight of the various criteria.
- Objective, transparent conditions were introduced, and an additional year was granted for their completion.

Self-Employed Immigrant

What are the requirements for qualifying as a Self-employed Person?

To meet the definition, you must demonstrate that you have at least two years of relevant experience, you have the intention and the ability to be self-employed in Canada, and you have the intention and the ability to make a significant contribution to specified economic activities in Canada.

You must then obtain a minimum of 35 points in a selection grid designed to determine whether you will be able to become economically established in Canada.

What is the procedure for becoming a self-employed person?

You must apply for immigration to Canada, satisfy a visa officer that you meet the definition of a self-employed person, be awarded at least 35 assessment points and pass the medical and admissibility checks.

What constitutes relevant experience?

Relevant experience is limited to:

1. self-employment in cultural activities or athletics;
2. participation at a world-class level in cultural activities or athletics; or
3. farm management experience.

Does the relevant experience have to be recent?

You can go back as far as five years before the date of your application (and up until a decision is made on your application by a visa officer).

What is meant by "cultural activities"?

We refer here to occupations generally considered to be part of Canada's artistic and cultural diversity. Examples include, but are not limited to, authors and writers, creative and performing artists, musicians, painters, sculptors and other visual artists, technical support and occupations in motion pictures, creative designers, craftspeople, etc. More examples may be found on the National Occupational Classification Web site.

What are specified economic activities?

You must have the intention and ability to be self-employed in Canada in cultural or athletic activities, or to purchase and manage a farm.

What is meant by a "significant contribution"?

There is no formal definition of what constitutes a "significant contribution." The intention of the requirement is to give visa officers the ability to use their judgment and allow them to recognize that a contribution to athletics or the arts, even at less than a national standard, may still be of significant benefit at the local level.

For example, a music teacher with reasonable qualifications will be in a better position to make a significant contribution if destined to a small town rather than a big city.

Please note that you must have contributed to economic activities "in Canada." While this does not preclude activities outside of Canada, there must exist a significant contribution in Canada for Canada.

Are there any reporting requirements once I am landed in Canada?

No. Unlike the entrepreneur program, there are no conditions to be met after taking up permanent residence in Canada.

Are there any net worth requirements?

Unlike the investor and entrepreneur programs, there are no regulated minimum net worth requirements. However, you will have to satisfy a visa officer that you have sufficient capital to settle yourself and your family in Canada and to finance the specified economic activities that your selection was based on.

How big is the Self-Employed Persons Program?

Over the past five years, approximately 600 self-employed persons (principal applicants) a year have landed in Canada.

Is there information available on how to set up my business once I am in Canada?

Many provinces provide valuable information and services to assist business immigrants in setting up and successfully operating businesses in Canada. You may wish to visit the following site for more information: http://www.cic.gc.ca/english/business/bi-provinces.html.

For more information, you may write to us at the following e-mail address: Nat-Business-Immigration@cic.gc.ca

Statistical Information: Applications Processed at Canadian Visa Offices

Business Class – Federal
April 2005 to March 2006

Citizenship and Immigration Canada staff work at locations around the world. Officers in Canadian embassies, high commissions and consulates process applications abroad for permanent residence for people wishing to immigrate to Canada.

The tables below show the number of months that were required to approve or refuse applications at visa offices around the world.

The length of time it takes to finalize applications may be different at different visa offices.

Past processing times may not indicate the length of time it will take to finalize applications in the future.

Read more information about submitting applications from outside of Canada.

> Citizenship and Immigration Canada has made a commitment to finalize 1,000 federal investor cases in 2006. These cases will be processed in the order in which they have been received at visa offices around the world. Applications submitted before July 2004 will be assessed in 2006. Applications received from July 2004 on will not likely be finalized before 2007.

Months Required to Finalize Applications [see note]

ALL REGIONS				
	30% of cases finalized in: (months)	**50% of cases finalized in: (months)**	**70% of cases finalized in: (months)**	**80% of cases finalized in: (months)**
Processing Times at Visa Offices in All Regions	33	44	53	60
AFRICA AND THE MIDDLE EAST				
	30% of cases finalized in: (months)	**50% of cases finalized in: (months)**	**70% of cases finalized in: (months)**	**80% of cases finalized in: (months)**
Processing Times at Visa Offices in Africa and the Middle East	56	67	73	76

Processing Times at Individual Visa Offices in Africa and the Middle East	**30% of cases finalized in: (months)**	**50% of cases finalized in: (months)**	**70% of cases finalized in: (months)**	**80% of cases finalized in: (months)**
Abidjan	-	-	-	-
Accra	-	-	-	-
Cairo	-	-	-	-
Damascus	60	68	73	77
Nairobi	-	-	-	-
Pretoria	-	-	-	-
Rabat	-	-	-	-
Tel Aviv	20	27	32	35

ASIA AND PACIFIC				
	30% of cases finalized in: (months)	**50% of cases finalized in: (months)**	**70% of cases finalized in: (months)**	**80% of cases finalized in: (months)**
Processing Times at Visa Offices in Asia and Pacific	28	46	56	62
Processing Times at Individual Visa Offices in Asia and Pacific	**30% of cases finalized in: (months)**	**50% of cases finalized in: (months)**	**70% of cases finalized in: (months)**	**80% of cases finalized in: (months)**
Beijing	48	53	57	59
Colombo	-	-	-	-
Hong Kong	26	60	65	68
Islamabad	31	39	47	52
Kuala Lumpur	8	12	20	23
Manila	7	12	14	16
New Delhi	-	-	-	-
Seoul	25	32	48	51
Singapore	43	46	49	51
Sydney	-	-	-	-
Taipei	21	23	26	28

EUROPE				
	30% of cases finalized in: (months)	**50% of cases finalized in: (months)**	**70% of cases finalized in: (months)**	**80% of cases finalized in: (months)**
Processing Times at Visa Offices in Europe	38	49	54	59
Processing Times at Individual Visa Offices in Europe	**30% of cases finalized in: (months)**	**50% of cases finalized in: (months)**	**70% of cases finalized in: (months)**	**80% of cases finalized in: (months)**
Ankara	-	-	-	-
Berlin	9	10	14	35
Bucharest	-	-	-	-
Kyiv	-	-	-	-
London	42	50	57	61
Moscow	50	53	55	57
Paris	48	50	52	53
Rome	29	35	56	68
Vienna	5	7	14	19
Warsaw	-	-	-	-

THE AMERICAS				
	30% of cases finalized in: (months)	**finalized in: (months)**	**70% of cases finalized in: (months)**	**80% of cases finalized in: (months)**
Processing Times at Visa Offices in the Americas	34	39	44	47

Processing Times at Individual Visa Offices in the Americas	**30% of cases finalized in: (months)**	**50% of cases finalized in: (months)**	**70% of cases finalized in: (months)**	**80% of cases finalized in: (months)**
Bogota	-	-	-	-
Buenos Aires	-	-	-	-
Buffalo	35	39	44	47
Caracas	-	-	-	-
Guatemala City	-	-	-	-
Havana	-	-	-	-
Kingston	-	-	-	-
Lima	-	-	-	-
Mexico City	9	11	14	15
Port-au-Prince	-	-	-	-
Port of Spain	19	24	27	28
Santiago	-	-	-	-
Sao Paulo	-	-	-	-

* Processing times are presented only where an office has finalized 10 or more cases in the category in the above-mentioned 12-month time period.

* Processing time may change time to time.

Applying for Permanent Residence

Federal Skilled Worker Class

Who Are Skilled Workers

Skilled workers are people whose education and work experience will help them find work and make a home for themselves as permanent residents in Canada. Applying to come to Canada as a Skilled Worker is not difficult. You will find all the information and forms you need to make your application here. **http://www.cic.gc.ca/english/applications/index.html.**

Refer to www.cic.gc.ca often. The rules for applying as a Skilled Worker can change. Before you apply, make sure your application follows the current rules. After you apply, check back for information about the steps to follow. You can also check the status of your application while it is in process through this website. **http://www.cic.gc.ca/english/e-services/index.html**

Will You Qualify As a Skilled Worker?

Skilled workers are people who may become permanent residents because they are able to become economically established in Canada.

To be accepted as a Skilled Worker, applicants must:

- meet the minimum work experience requirements;
- prove that they have the funds required for settlement; and
- earn enough points in the six selection factors to meet the pass mark.

The following categories will help you determine if you can apply as Skilled Worker. You can assess your chances of being accepted. Consult each of the following areas for the current regulations regarding:

Minimum Work Experience Requirements

Skilled workers are people who may become permanent residents because they have the ability to become economically established in Canada.

You must meet the following minimum work experience requirements to allow you to apply as a skilled worker:

- You must have at least one year of full-time work experience. You must have been paid for this work.
- Your work experience must be in the category of **Skill Type 0**, or **Skill Level A or B** on the Canadian National Occupational Classification (NOC). (See below for instructions.)
- You must have had this experience within the last 10 years.

What are Skill Types

Skill Type 0 : These are the management occupations. All kinds of managers in their field of expertise fall under type 0.

Skill Level A: These are the occupations that required **university degree** at the bachelor's or master's or doctorate level for example Engineers, Physicians, Lawyers, Teachers.

Skill Level B: These are the occupations that requires college education or apprenticeship training for example 2 or 3 years diploma in the field of engineering / information technology or management sciences. Their designations may vary as Associate Engineer, Technologist and Technicians

- To know more about **Skill Type 0** or **Skill Level A or B,** visit this link **http://cnp2001noc.worklogic.com/e/matrix.pdf**

National Occupation Classification (NOC)

The NOC is a classification system for jobs in the Canadian economy. It describes duties, skills, talents and work settings for occupations.

National Occupation Classification List

The following occupations are listed in Skill Type 0, Skill Level A or B of the National Occupation Classification List.

Code	A
0632	Accommodation Service Managers
5135	Actors and Comedians
1221	Administrative Officers
0114	Administrative Services Managers (other)
0312	Administrators - Post-Secondary Education and Vocational
2146	Aerospace Engineers
2222	Agricultural and Fish Products Inspectors
8252	Agricultural and Related Service Contractors and Managers
2123	Agricultural Representatives, Consultants and Specialists
2271	Air Pilots, Flight Engineers and Flying Instructors
2272	Air Traffic Control and Related Occupations
2244	Aircraft Instrument, Electrical and Avionics Mechanics, Technicians and Inspectors
7315	Aircraft Mechanics and Aircraft Inspectors
3234	Ambulance Attendants and Other Paramedical Occupations

5231	Announcers and Other Broadcasters
8257	Aquaculture Operators and Managers
2151	Architects
2251	Architectural Technologists and Technicians
0212	Architecture and Science Managers
5113	Archivists
5244	Artisans and Craftpersons
1235	Assessors, Valuators and Appraisers
5251	Athletes
5225	Audio and Video Recording Technicians
3141	Audiologists and Speech-Language Pathologists
5121	Authors and Writers
7321	Automotive Service Technicians, Truck Mechanics and Mechanical Repairers
Code	**B**
6252	Bakers
0122	Banking, Credit and Other Investment Managers
2221	Biological Technologists and Technicians
2121	Biologists and Related Scientists
7266	Blacksmiths and Die Setters
7262	Boilermakers
1231	Bookkeepers
7281	Bricklayers
5224	Broadcast Technicians
4163	Business Development Officers and Marketing Researchers and Consultants

0123	Business Services Managers (other)
6251	Butchers and Meat Cutters - Retail and Wholesale
Code	**C**
7272	Cabinetmakers
7247	Cable Television Service and Maintenance Technicians
3217	Cardiology Technologists
7271	Carpenters
9231	Central Control and Process Operators, Mineral and Metal Processing
6241	Chefs
2134	Chemical Engineers
2211	Chemical Technologists and Technicians
2112	Chemists
3122	Chiropractors
2231	Civil Engineering Technologists and Technicians
2131	Civil Engineers
6215	Cleaning Supervisors
5252	Coaches
4131	College and Other Vocational Instructors
7382	Commercial Divers
0643	Commissioned Officers, Armed Forces
0641	Commissioned Police Officers
4212	Community and Social Service Workers
0213	Computer and Information Systems Managers

2281	Computer and Network Operators and Web Technicians
2147	Computer Engineers (Except Software Engineers)
2174	Computer Programmers and Interactive Media Developers
7282	Concrete Finishers
5132	Conductors, Composers and Arrangers
1226	Conference and Event Planners
2224	Conservation and Fishery Officers
5112	Conservators and Curators
2234	Construction Estimators
2264	Construction Inspectors
0711	Construction Managers
7311	Construction Millwrights and Industrial Mechanics (Except Textile)
7215	Contractors and Supervisors, Carpentry Trades
7212	Contractors and Supervisors, Electrical Trades and Telecommunications
7217	Contractors and Supervisors, Heavy Construction Equipment Crews
7216	Contractors and Supervisors, Mechanic Trades
7214	Contractors and Supervisors, Metal Forming, Shaping and Erecting Trades
7219	Contractors and Supervisors, Other Construction Trades, Installers, Repairers
7213	Contractors and Supervisors, Pipefitting Trades
6242	Cooks
1227	Court Officers and Justices of the Peace
1244	Court Recorders and Medical Transcriptionists
7371	Crane Operators
1236	Customs, Ship and Other Brokers

Code	D
5134	Dancers
2172	Database Analysts and Data Administrators
2273	Deck Officers, Water Transport
3222	Dental Hygienists and Dental Therapists
3223	Dental Technologists, Technicians and Laboratory
3113	Dentists
3221	Denturists
3132	Dietitians and Nutritionists
2253	Drafting Technologists and Technicians
7372	Drillers and Blasters D Surface Mining, Quarrying and Construction
6214	Dry Cleaning and Laundry Supervisors
Code	**E**
4214	Early Childhood Educators and Assistants
4162	Economists and Economic Policy Researchers and Analysts
5122	Editors
4166	Education Policy Researchers, Consultants and Program Officers
4143	Educational Counsellors
7332	Electric Appliance Servicers and Repairers
2241	Electrical and Electronics Engineering Technologists and Technicians
2133	Electrical and Electronics Engineers
7333	Electrical Mechanics
7244	Electrical Power Line and Cable Workers
7241	Electricians (Except Industrial and Power System)

3218	Electroencephalographic and Other Diagnostic Technologists, n.e.c.
2242	Electronic Service Technicians (Household and Business
7318	Elevator Constructors and Mechanics
4213	Employment Counsellors
2274	Engineer Officers, Water Transport
2262	Engineering Inspectors and Regulatory Officers
0211	Engineering Managers
1222	Executive Assistants
6213	Executive Housekeepers
Code	**F**
0721	Facility Operation and Maintenance Managers
4153	Family, Marriage and Other Related Counsellors
8253	Farm Supervisors and Specialized Livestock Workers
8251	Farmers and Farm Managers
5222	Film and Video Camera Operators
1112	Financial and Investment Analysts
1111	Financial Auditors and Accountants
0111	Financial Managers
1114	Financial Officers (other)
0642	Fire Chiefs and Senior Firefighting Officers
6262	Firefighters
8261	Fishing Masters and Officers
8262	Fishing Vessel Skippers and Fishermen/women
7295	Floor Covering Installers

6212	Food Service Supervisors
2122	Forestry Professionals
2223	Forestry Technologists and Technicians
6272	Funeral Directors and Embalmers
Code	**G**
7253	Gas Fitters
2212	Geological and Mineral Technologists and Technicians
2144	Geological Engineers
2113	Geologists, Geochemists and Geophysicists
7292	Glaziers
0412	Government Managers - Economic Analysis, Policy Development
0413	Government Managers - Education Policy Development and Program Administration
0411	Government Managers - Health and Social Policy Development and Program Administration
6234	Grain Elevator Operators
5223	Graphic Arts Technicians
5241	Graphic Designers and Illustrators
Code	
6271	Hairstylists and Barbers
3151	Head Nurses and Supervisors
3123	Health Diagnosing and Treating (Other Professional Occupations)
4165	Health Policy Researchers, Consultants and Program Officers
7312	Heavy-Duty Equipment Mechanics
0112	Human Resources Managers

Code	I
1228	Immigration, Employment Insurance and Revenue Officers
2141	Industrial and Manufacturing Engineers
2252	Industrial Designers
7242	Industrial Electricians
2233	Industrial Engineering and Manufacturing Technologists and Technicians
2243	Industrial Instrument Technicians and Mechanics
2171	Information Systems Analysts and Consultants
2263	Inspectors in Public and Environmental Health and Occupational Health and Safety
4216	Instructors (other)
4215	Instructors and Teachers of Persons with Disabilities
7293	Insulators
1233	Insurance Adjusters and Claims Examiners
6231	Insurance Agents and Brokers
1234	Insurance Underwriters
0121	Insurance, Real Estate and Financial Brokerage Managers
5242	Interior Designers
7264	Ironworkers

Code	J
7344	Jewellers, Watch Repairers and Related Occupations
5123	Journalists
4111	Judges
1227	Justices of the Peace
Code	**L**
2254	Land Survey Technologists and Technicians
2154	Land Surveyors
2225	Landscape and Horticultural Technicians and Specialists
2152	Landscape Architects
8255	Landscaping and Grounds Maintenance Contractors and Managers
4112	Lawyers and Quebec Notaries
1242	Legal Secretaries
0011	Legislators
5111	Librarians
5211	Library and Archive Technicians and Assistants
0511	Library, Archive, Museum and Art Gallery Managers
3233	Licensed Practical Nurses
1232	Loan Officers
8241	Logging Machinery Operators

Code	M
7316	Machine Fitters
7231	Machinists and Machining and Tooling Inspectors
0512	Managers - Publishing, Motion Pictures, Broadcasting and Performing Arts
0311	Managers in Health Care
0414	Managers in Public Administration (other)
0314	Managers in Social, Community and Correctional Services
0911	Manufacturing Managers
2255	Mapping and Related Technologists and Technicians
2161	Mathematicians, Statisticians and Actuaries
2232	Mechanical Engineering Technologists and Technicians
2132	Mechanical Engineers
3212	Medical Laboratory Technicians
3211	Medical Laboratory Technologists and Pathologists' Assistants
3215	Medical Radiation Technologists
1243	Medical Secretaries
3216	Medical Sonographers
3219	Medical Technologists and Technicians (other - except Dental Health)
2142	Metallurgical and Materials Engineers
2213	Meteorological Technicians
2114	Meteorologists
3232	Midwives and Practitioners of Natural Healing
2143	Mining Engineers

4154	Ministers of Religion
5226	Motion Pictures, Broadcasting (other Technical and Co-ordinating Occupations)
7322	Motor Vehicle Body Repairers
7334	Motorcycle and Other Related Mechanics
5212	Museums and Art Galleries (related Technical Occupations)
5133	Musicians and Singers
Code	**N**
4161	Natural and Applied Science Policy Researchers, Consultants and Program Officers
2261	Nondestructive Testers and Inspectors
8254	Nursery and Greenhouse Operators and Managers
Code	**O**
3143	Occupational Therapists
8232	Oil and Gas Well Drillers, Servicers, Testers and Related Workers
7331	Oil and Solid Fuel Heating Mechanics
3231	Opticians
3121	Optometrists
Code	**P**
7294	Painters and Decorators
5136	Painters, Sculptors and Other Visual Artists
9234	Papermaking and Coating Control Operators
4211	Paralegal and Related Occupations
5245	Patternmakers - Textile, Leather and Fur Products
5232	Performers (other)
1223	Personnel and Recruitment Officers

2145	Petroleum Engineers
9232	Petroleum, Gas and Chemical Process Operators
3131	Pharmacists
5221	Photographers
2115	Physical Sciences (Other Professional Occupations)
3112	Physicians - General Practitioners and Family Physicians
3111	Physicians - Specialist
2111	Physicists and Astronomers
3142	Physiotherapists
7252	Pipefitters
7284	Plasterers, Drywall Installers and Finishers and Lathers
7251	Plumbers
6261	Police Officers (Except Commissioned)
0132	Postal and Courier Services Managers
4122	Post-Secondary Teaching and Research Assistants
7243	Power System Electricians
7352	Power Systems and Power Station Operators
0811	Primary Production Managers (Except Agriculture)
7381	Printing Press Operators
4155	Probation and Parole Officers and Related Occupations
5131	Producers, Directors, Choreographers and Related Occupations
2148	Professional Engineers, n.e.c. (other)
1122	Professional Occupations in Business Services to Management
5124	Professional Occupations in Public Relations and Communications

4121	Professors - University
5254	Program Leaders and Instructors in Recreation and Sport
4168	Program Officers Unique to Government
1224	Property Administrators
4151	Psychologists
9233	Pulping Control Operators
1225	Purchasing Agents and Officers
0113	Purchasing Managers
Code	**R**
7361	Railway and Yard Locomotive Engineers
7314	Railway Carmen/women
7362	Railway Conductors and Brakemen/women
2275	Railway Traffic Controllers and Marine Traffic Regulators
6232	Real Estate Agents and Salespersons
0513	Recreation and Sports Program and Service Directors
4167	Recreation, Sports and Fitness Program Supervisors Consultants
7313	Refrigeration and Air Conditioning Mechanics
3152	Registered Nurses
4217	Religious Occupations (other)
0712	Residential Home Builders and Renovators
3214	Respiratory Therapists, Clinical Perfusionists and Cardio-Pulmonary Technologists
0631	Restaurant and Food Service Managers
6233	Retail and Wholesale Buyers
0621	Retail Trade Managers

6211	Retail Trade Supervisors
7291	Roofers and Shinglers
Code	**S**
0611	Sales, Marketing and Advertising Managers
0313	School Principals and Administrators of Elementary and Secondary
1241	Secretaries (Except Legal and Medical)
1113	Securities Agents, Investment Dealers and Brokers
0012	Senior Government Managers and Officials
0013	Senior Managers - Financial, Communications and Other Business
0016	Senior Managers - Goods Production, Utilities, Transportation and Construction
0014	Senior Managers - Health, Education, Social and Community
0015	Senior Managers - Trade, Broadcasting and Other Services, n.e.c.
6216	Service Supervisors (other)
0651	Services Managers (other)
7261	Sheet Metal Workers
7343	Shoe Repairers and Shoemakers
7335	Small Engine and Equipment Mechanics (other)
4164	Social Policy Researchers, Consultants and Program Officers
4169	Social Science, n.e.c. (Other Professional Occupations)
4152	Social Workers
2173	Software Engineers
1121	Specialists in Human Resources
5253	Sports Officials and Referees
7252	Sprinkler System Installers

7351	Stationary Engineers and Auxiliary Equipment Operators
7252	Steamfitters, Pipefitters and Sprinkler System Installers
7263	Structural Metal and Platework Fabricators and Fitters
9223	Supervisors, Electrical Products Manufacturing
9222	Supervisors, Electronics Manufacturing
9225	Supervisors, Fabric, Fur and Leather Products Manufacturing
1212	Supervisors, Finance and Insurance Clerks
9213	Supervisors, Food, Beverage and Tobacco Processing
9215	Supervisors, Forest Products Processing
9224	Supervisors, Furniture and Fixtures Manufacturing
1211	Supervisors, General Office and Administrative Support Clerks
8256	Supervisors, Landscape and Horticulture
1213	Supervisors, Library, Correspondence and Related Information Clerks
8211	Supervisors, Logging and Forestry
7211	Supervisors, Machinists and Related Occupations
1214	Supervisors, Mail and Message Distribution Occupations
9211	Supervisors, Mineral and Metal Processing
8221	Supervisors, Mining and Quarrying
7222	Supervisors, Motor Transport and Other Ground Transit Operators
9221	Supervisors, Motor Vehicle Assembling
8222	Supervisors, Oil and Gas Drilling and Service
9226	Supervisors, Other Mechanical and Metal Products Manufacturing
9227	Supervisors, Other Products Manufacturing and Assembly
9212	Supervisors, Petroleum, Gas and Chemical Processing and Utilities

9214	Supervisors, Plastic and Rubber Products Manufacturing
7218	Supervisors, Printing and Related Occupations
7221	Supervisors, Railway Transport Operations
1215	Supervisors, Recording, Distributing and Scheduling Occupations
9216	Supervisors, Textile Processing
5227	Support Occupations in Motion Pictures, Broadcasting and the Performing Arts
2283	Systems Testing Technicians
Code	**T**
7342	Tailors, Dressmakers, Furriers and Milliners
4142	Teachers - Elementary School and Kindergarten
4141	Teachers - Secondary School
6221	Technical Sales Specialists - Wholesale Trade
0131	Telecommunication Carriers Managers
7246	Telecommunications Installation and Repair Workers
7245	Telecommunications Line and Cable Workers
7317	Textile Machinery Mechanics and Repairers
5243	Theatre, Fashion, Exhibit and Other Creative Designers
3144	Therapy and Assessment (Other Professional Occupations)
3235	Therapy and Assessment (other Technical Occupations)
7283	Tilesetters
7232	Tool and Die Makers
7383	Trades and Related Occupations (other)
5125	Translators, Terminologists and Interpreters
0713	Transportation Managers

Code	U
8231	Underground Production and Development Miners
7341	Upholsterers
2153	Urban and Land Use Planners
2282	User Support Technicians
0912	Utilities Managers
Code	**V**
3114	Veterinarians
3213	Veterinary and Animal Health Technologists and
Code	**W**
7373	Water Well Drillers
2175	Web Designers and Developers
7265	Welders and Related Machine Operators

Determine Your NOC Category

Follow these steps to see if your work experience meets the requirements to apply as a skilled worker.

1. Find the title of any full-time jobs you had in the past 10 years using above National Occupation Classification list. This is a list of all jobs that are in Skill Type 0, Skill Level A or B on the NOC. **Write down the four-digit code located to the left of your job's title.**

2. Go to the NOC Web site: (*http://cnp2001noc.worklogic.com/e/welcome.shtml*) and type your four-digit job-code in the "Quick Search" box. Make sure you press the "GO" button. A description of your occupation will appear. Make sure the description and "Main Duties" describe what you did at your last jobs.

Note: you do **not** have to meet the "Employment Requirements" listed in the description.

If the initial description and list of main duties **matches** what you did at your last jobs, you can count this experience as when you apply as a skilled worker. You can also earn points in Factor 3 of the Selection Factors.

If the description **does not match** your work experience then you might not have the experience you need to apply as a skilled worker. Look through the NOC list to see if another occupation matches your experience. Check all of the jobs you had in the past 10 years to see if you have at least one year of work experience in a job that will qualify you as a skilled worker.

Check the list of restricted occupations. If your work experience is in a restricted occupation then you **cannot** use it to qualify for the Skilled Worker category.

What are restricted occupations: To protect the Canadian labour market, Citizenship and Immigration Canada has to make sure that Canada does not have too many people with the same skills.

There are no restricted occupations at the time of this publication

You do not meet the minimum requirements if:

- none of your work experience is listed in the NOC list;
- your experience did **not** occur in the 10 years before you applied; or
- your only work experience is in a restricted occupation.

If you do not meet the minimum work experience requirements, your application as a Skilled Worker will be refused.

Few examples of NOC Listed professions

6271 Hairstylists and Barbers

Hairstylists and barbers cut and style hair and perform related services. They are employed in hairstyling or hairdressing salons, barber shops, vocational schools, health care establishments and theatre, film and television establishments.

Example Titles

barber
barber apprentice
hair colour technician
hairdresser
hairdresser apprentice
hairstylist
hairstylist apprentice
wig stylist

Main duties

Hairstylists perform some or all of the following duties:

- Suggest hair style compatible with client's physical features or determine style from client's instructions and preferences
- Cut, trim, taper, curl, wave, perm and style hair
- Apply bleach, tints, dyes or rinses to colour, frost or streak hair
- Analyze hair and scalp condition and provide basic treatment or advice on beauty care treatments for scalp and hair
- May shampoo and rinse hair
- May train or supervise other hairstylists, hairstylist apprentices and helpers.

Barbers perform some or all of the following duties:

- Cut and trim hair according to client's instructions or preferences
- Shave and trim beards and moustaches
- May shampoo hair and provide other hair treatment, such as waving, straightening and tinting and may also provide scalp conditioning massages
- May train and supervise other barbers and barber apprentices.

Employment requirements for Hair Stylists

Some secondary school education is required.

- Completion of a two- or three-year hairstyling apprenticeship program or completion of a college or other program in hairstyling combined with on-the-job training is usually required.

- Several years of experience may replace formal education and training.
- Employers may require applicants to provide a hairstyling demonstration before being hired.
- There are various provincial/territorial certification and licensing requirements for hairstylists, ranging from trade certification to licensing by a provincial/territorial association. Interprovincial trade certification (Red Seal) is also available for qualified hairstylists. Barbers
- Some secondary school education is required.
- Completion of a two-year apprenticeship or other barber program is usually required.
- On-the-job training may be substituted for formal education.
- There are various provincial/territorial certification and licensing requirements for barbers, ranging from trade certification to licensing by a provincial/territorial association. Barbers can also obtain interprovincial trade certification (Red Seal) as qualified hairstylists.

Additional information

- Red Seal trade certification allows for interprovincial mobility.

2232 Mechanical Engineering Technologists and Technicians

Mechanical engineering technologists and technicians provide technical support and services or may work independently in mechanical engineering fields such as the design, development, maintenance and testing of machines, components, tools, heating and ventilating systems, power generation and power conversion plants, manufacturing plants and equipment. They are employed by consulting engineering, manufacturing and processing companies, institutions and government departments.

Example Titles

aeronautical technologist
heating designer
HVAC (heating, ventilating & air conditioning) technologist
machine designer
marine engineering technologist mechanical engineering technician
mechanical engineering technologist
mechanical technologist
mould designer
thermal station technician
tool and die designer
tool designer

Main duties

Mechanical engineering technologists perform some or all of the following duties:

- Prepare and interpret conventional and computer-assisted design (CAD) engineering designs, drawings, and specifications for machines and components, power transmission systems, process piping, heating, ventilating and air-conditioning systems

- Prepare cost and material estimates, project schedules and reports
- Conduct tests and analyses of machines, components and materials to determine their performance, strength, response to stress and other characteristics
- Design moulds, tools, dies, jigs and fixtures for use in manufacturing processes
- Inspect mechanical installations and construction
- Prepare contract and tender documents
- Supervise, monitor and inspect mechanical installations and construction projects
- Prepare standards and schedules and supervise mechanical maintenance programs or operations of mechanical plants.

Mechanical engineering technicians perform some or all of the following duties:

- Assist in preparing conventional and computer assisted design (CAD) engineering designs, drawings and specifications
- Carry out a limited range of mechanical tests and analyses of machines, components and materials
- Assist in the design of moulds, tools, dies, jigs and fixtures for use in manufacturing processes
- Assist in inspection of mechanical installations and construction projects
- Participate in the installation, repair and maintenance of machinery and equipment.

Employment requirements

- Completion of a two- or three-year college program in mechanical engineering technology is usually required for mechanical engineering technologists.
- Completion of a one- or two-year college program in mechanical engineering technology is usually required for mechanical engineering technicians.

- Certification in mechanical engineering technology or in a related field is available through provincial associations of engineering/applied science technologists and technicians and may be required for some positions.
- A period of supervised work experience, usually two years, is required before certification.
- In Quebec, membership in the regulatory body is required to use the title of Professional Technologist.

Additional information

- There is mobility to other related occupations such as technical sales or drafting technologists and technicians.
- Progression to supervisory occupations such as mechanical construction supervisor, manufacturing supervisor or operations maintenance manager is possible with experience.

2133 Electrical and Electronics Engineers

Electrical and electronics engineers design, plan, research, evaluate and test electrical and electronic equipment and systems. They are employed by electrical utilities, communications companies, manufacturers of electrical and electronic equipment, consulting firms, and by a wide range of manufacturing, processing and transportation industries and government.

Example Titles

avionics engineer
control systems engineer
design engineer, electrical
distribution planning engineer, electrical engineer
electrical network engineer
electronics engineer
instrumentation and control engineer
planning engineer, electrical systems
process control engineer, electrical

roadway lighting design engineer
television systems engineer
test engineer, electronics

Main duties

Electrical and electronics engineers perform some or all of the following duties:

- Conduct research into the feasibility, design, operation and performance of electrical generation and distribution networks, electrical machinery and components and electronic communications, instrumentation and control systems, equipment, and components
- Prepare material cost and timing estimates, reports and design specifications for electrical and electronic systems and equipment
- Design electrical and electronic circuits, components, systems and equipment
- Supervise and inspect the installation, modification, testing and operation of electrical and electronic systems and equipment
- Develop maintenance and operating standards for electrical and electronic systems and equipment
- Investigate electrical or electronic failures
- Prepare contract documents and evaluate tenders for construction or maintenance
- Supervise technicians, technologists, programmers, analysts and other engineers.

Electrical and electronics engineers may specialize in a number of areas including electrical design for residential, commercial or industrial installations, electrical power generation and transmission, and instrumentation and control systems.

Employment requirements

- A bachelor's degree in electrical or electronics engineering or in an appropriate related engineering discipline is required.
- A master's or doctoral degree in a related engineering discipline may be required.
- Licensing by a provincial or territorial association of professional engineers is required to approve engineering drawings and reports and to practise as a Professional Engineer (P.Eng.).
- Engineers are eligible for registration following graduation from an accredited educational program, and after three or four years of supervised work experience in engineering and passing a professional practice examination.
- Supervisory and senior positions in this unit group require experience.

Funds Required to Settle in Canada

The Government of Canada provides no financial support to new skilled worker immigrants. You must prove that you have enough money unencumbered by debts or obligations to support yourself and your family members after you arrive in Canada.

The required funds are equal to or greater than the amount listed below for each family size:

Number of family members	Funds required*
1	$10,168
2	$12,659
3	$15,563
4	$18,895
5	$21,431
6	$24,170
7+	$26,910

***Exception:** If you have arranged employment as defined in Factor 5, you do not have to meet these financial requirements.

The minimum required funds may change at any time. Check CIC Web site to make sure you have the most recent information.

We strongly recommend that you research the cost of living in the region of Canada where you intend to live. Bring with you as much money as possible to make your establishment in Canada easier.

Disclosure of funds

You will have to tell a Canadian official if you carry more than $10,000 Canadian in cash funds upon your entry to Canada. This could be in the form of:

- money (coins or bank notes)
- securities in bearer form (stocks, bonds, debentures, treasury bills etc.)
- negotiable instruments in bearer form (bankers' drafts, cheques, travellers' cheques, money orders etc.)

Failure to disclose can result in fines and imprisonment

SIX SELECTION FACTORS AND PASS MARK

Self-Assessment Worksheet

This worksheet will help you to determine your chance of qualifying as a skilled worker. It explains the six factors on which points are awarded and helps you estimate how many points you may be awarded for each factor.

How to estimate your points

Read the explanation for each factor, then fill in your score on the worksheet.

If you have a spouse or common-law partner, you must decide which of you will be the principal applicant; the other person will be considered a family member. Use the self-assessment worksheet to determine which of you would score the most points. This person should be the principal applicant.

*Note: **A common-law partner** is a person of the same or opposite sex who has lived with you in a conjugal relationship for a period of at least one year.*

***A family member** is a spouse, common-law partner or dependent child included in your application.*

FACTOR 1: Education (maximum 25 points)

Points are awarded for earned educational credentials as well as the number of years of full-time or full-time equivalent study. To be awarded points, you must meet **both** stated criteria.

*Note: **Full-time studies:** At least 15 hours of instruction per week during the academic year. This includes any period of workplace training that forms part of the course*

***Full-time equivalent studies:** If you completed a program of study on a part-time or accelerated basis, count the length of time it would have taken to complete the program on a full-time basis.*

Instructions

Use the chart below to determine your points. If you have not completed the number of years of study that correspond to your highest educational credential, award yourself points based on the number of years of study.

Examples: If you have a Master's degree but have completed only 16 years of full-time study, award yourself 22 points. If you have a four-year Bachelor's degree and have completed 14 or more years of study, award yourself 20 points.

Master's or PhD **and** at least 17 years of full-time or full-time equivalent study	25
Two or more university degrees at the Bachelor's level and at least 15 years of full-time or full-time equivalent study; **or** A three-year diploma, trade certificate or apprenticeship and at least 15 years of full-time or full-time equivalent study	22
A university degree of two years or more at the Bachelor's level, and at least 14 years of full-time or full-time equivalent study; **or** A two-year diploma, trade certificate or apprenticeship and at least 14 years of full-time or full-time equivalent study	20
A one-year university degree at the Bachelor's level and at least 13 years of full-time or full-time equivalent study; **or** A one-year diploma, trade certificate or apprenticeship and at least 13 years of full-time or full-time equivalent study	15
A one-year diploma, trade certificate or apprenticeship and at least 12 years of full-time or full-time equivalent study	12
Secondary school (also called high school)	5
Your Score	

FACTOR 2: Language ability (maximum 24 points)

Points are awarded for proven ability in reading, writing, listening to and speaking English and/or French.

Instructions

STEP 1. If you have some abilities in both English and French, decide which of the two you are more comfortable using; this will be considered your **first official language**. The other will be your **second official language**.

STEP 2. Determine your points according to your ability to read, write, listen to, and speak these languages using the criteria in the Canadian Language Benchmarks.

Proficiency levels

The chart below contains basic descriptions of the proficiency levels you will be assessed against. These descriptions correspond to the Canadian Language Benchmarks and can be viewed in their entirety on CIC website by following the link to "How to Assess Your Language Skills".

Use this reference chart to find the Benchmark that best defines your language ability, or follow the link to "How to Assess Your Language Skills" on our Web site for direct links to each level.

Proficiency level	Ability			
	Speaking	**Listening**	**Reading**	**Writing**
HIGH: You communicate effectively in most social and work situations.	Benchmark 8: Pages 68-71	Benchmark 8: Pages 82-83	Benchmark 8: Pages 94-95	Benchmark 8: Pages 106-107
MODERATE: You communicate comfortably in familiar social and work situations.	Benchmark 6: Pages 60-63	Benchmark 6: Pages 78-79	Benchmark 6: Pages 90-91	Benchmark 6: Pages 102-103
BASIC: You can communicate in predictable contexts and on familiar topics.	Benchmark 4: Pages 12-13	Benchmark 4: Pages 24-25	Benchmark 4: Pages 36-37	Benchmark 4: Pages 48-49
NO: You do not meet the criteria for basic proficiency.	Do not meet Benchmark 4	Do not meet Benchmark 4	Do not meet Benchmark 4	Do not meet Benchmark 4

Calculating your language points

First official language	**Read**	**Write**	**Listen**	**Speak**
High proficiency	4	4	4	4
Moderate proficiency	2	2	2	2
Basic proficiency	1	1	1	1
No proficiency	0	0	0	0
Second official language	**Read**	**Write**	**Listen**	**Speak**
High proficiency	2	2	2	2
Moderate proficiency	2	2	2	2
Basic proficiency	1	1	1	1
No proficiency	0	0	0	0

Proof of Language Proficiency

The instructions above are meant to provide you with an informal self-assessment only. If you decide to apply to immigrate to Canada as a skilled worker, you must provide **conclusive proof** of your language abilities. There are two ways to provide this proof. Choose **one** of the options below to establish your proficiency in English and/or French.

OPTION 1: Take a language proficiency test from an approved organization

CIC strongly recommend that you take an official language test if you are claiming skills in a language that is not your native language.

Steps:	Results:
1. Make an arrangement for testing and pay test costs. A list of approved organizations can be found on our Web site. Follow the link to "How to Assess Your Language Skills". 2. Submit the assessment results with your immigration application.	• You test results must not be more than one year old at the time that you submit your immigration application. • Test results will be used as conclusive evidence of your language proficiency. • You will know **exactly** how many points you will receive for the language factor before you submit your application. To determine your points, see the test result equivalency charts that follow.

OPTION 2: Establish your proficiency levels through a written explanation and supporting documentation

Steps:	Results:
1. Gather material that supports your claim. This should include: • A submission written by you that details your training in, and use of, English and/or French • Official documentation of education in English and/or French • Official documentation of work experience in English and/or French 2. Determine what proficiency levels you wish to claim and indicate these levels clearly in your submission. 3. Submit these documents with your immigration application.	• CIC officers will **not** interview you to assess your proficiency levels. • Your submission must satisfy the officer that your language skills meet the benchmarks for the levels you are claiming. • A CIC officer will review the evidence you include with your application. • The officer will award points for your language ability based on what you send with your application. • You will not know in advance how many points the CIC officer will give you for your language skills.

Arranging A Language Test

If you choose Option 1, you must arrange a language test from any of the following approved organizations. For contact information, refer to our CIC Website and follow the link to "How to Assess Your Language Skills".

English language testing organizations	French language testing organizations
The University of Cambridge Local Examination Syndicate, Education Australia, and the British Council administer the **International English Language Testing System (IELTS).** **Note:** IELTS has "General Training" and "Academic" options for the reading and writing tests. If you choose to take an IELTS test, you must take the "General Training" option.	The Paris Chamber of Commerce and Industry administers the **Test d'Évaluation de Français (TEF).** **Note:** For immigration purposes, you must submit results for the following tests: - expression orale - compréhension orale - compréhension écrite - expression écrite
The University of British Columbia's Applied Research and Evaluation Services (ARES) administer the **Canadian International Language Proficiency Index Program (CELPIP).**	

Using your test results

Once you have taken a language test from an approved organization, you can determine how many points you will receive using one of the equivalency charts below:

International English Language Testing System (IELTS)

Level	**Points (per ability)**	**Test results for each ability**			
		Speaking	**Listening**	**Reading** (General Training)	**Writing** (General Training)
High	First official language: **4** Second official language: **2**	7.0 – 9.0	7.0 – 9.0	7.0 – 9.0	7.0 – 9.0
Moderate	Either official language: **2**	5.0 – 6.9	5.0 – 6.9	5.0 – 6.9	5.0 – 6.9
Basic	Either official language: **1** (maximum of 2)	4.0 – 4.9	4.0 – 4.9	4.0 – 4.9	4.0 – 4.9
No	**0**	Less than 4.0	Less than 4.0	Less than 4.0	Less than 4.0

Canadian English Language Proficiency Index Program (CELPIP)

Level	**Points (per ability)**	**Test results for each ability**			
		Speaking	**Listening**	**Reading**	**Writing**
High	First official language: **4** Second official language: **2**	4H 5 6	4H 5 6	4H 5 6	4H 5 6
Moderate	Either official language: **2**	3H 4L	3H 4L	3H 4L	3H 4L
Basic	Either official language: **1** (maximum of 2)	2H 3L	2H 3L	2H 3L	2H 3L
No	**0**	0 1 2L	0 1 2L	0 1 2L	0 1 2L

Test d'évaluation de français (TEF)

Level	Points (per ability)	Test results for each ability			
		Speaking (expression orale)	Listening (compréhension orale)	Reading (compréhension écrite)	Writing (expression écrite)
High	First official language: **4** Second official language: **2**	Level 5 Level 6 (349-450 pts)	Level 5 Level 6 (280-360 pts)	Level 5 Level 6 (233-300 pts)	Level 5 Level 6 (349-450 pts)
Moderate	Either official language: **2**	Level 4 (271-348 pts)	Level 4 (217-279 pts)	Level 4 (181-232 pts)	Level 4 (271-348 pts)
Basic	Either official language: **1** (maximum of 2)	Level 3 (181-270 pts)	Level 3 (145-216 pts)	Level 3 (121-180 pts)	Level 3 (181-270 pts)
No	**0**	Level 0 Level 1 Level 2 (0-180 pts)	Level 0 Level 1 Level 2 (0-144 pts)	Level 0 Level 1 Level 2 (0-120 pts)	Level 0 Level 1 Level 2 (0-180 pts)

Add your points: Total of speaking + listening + reading + writing = ______ (both languages)

Your Score	

What Happens Next:

An officer from Citizenship and Immigration Canada will look at the evidence you include with your application.

- Your submission must satisfy the officer that your language skills meet the benchmarks for the level you are claiming.
- The officer does not have to ask you for more evidence so include as much evidence and documentation with your application as you can.
- The officer will not interview you to assess your language skills.
- The officer will award points for your language ability based on what you send with your application. You will not know how many points the CIC Officer gives you for your language skills or if the CIC Officer is satisfied that you have **clearly** demonstrated the level of language skills you claim on your application.

Canadian Language Benchmark 8

Speaking: High Level

Global Performance Descriptor

- Learner can communicate effectively in most daily practical and social situations, and in familiar routine work situations.
- Can participate in conversations with confidence.
- Can speak on familiar topics at both concrete and abstract levels (10 to 15 minutes).
- Can provide descriptions, opinions and explanations; can synthesize abstract complex ideas, can hypothesize.
- In social interaction, learner demonstrates increased ability to respond appropriately to the formality level of the situation.
- Can use a variety of sentence structures, including embedded and report structures, and an expanded inventory of concrete, idiomatic and conceptual language.
- Grammar and pronunciation errors rarely impede communication.
- Discourse is reasonably fluent.
- Uses phone on less familiar and some non-routine matters.

Performance Conditions

- Interaction is with one or more people, face to face or on the phone. It is often at a normal rate.
- Speech is partly predictable and does not always support the utterance.
- Considerable level of stress affects performance when verbal interaction may result in personal consequences (e.g. on the job).

- Audience is small familiar and unfamiliar informal groups.
- Setting and context are familiar, clear and predictable.
- Topic is familiar, concrete and abstract.
- Pictures and other visuals are used.
- Length of presentation is 15 to 20 minutes.

Interaction one-on-one

- Interaction is face to face or on the phone.
- Interaction is formal or semi-formal.
- Learner can partially prepare the exchange.

Interaction in a group

- Interaction takes place in a familiar group of up to 10 people.
- The topic or issue is familiar, non-personal, concrete and abstract.
- Interaction is informal or semi-formal.

Listening: High Level

Global Performance Descriptor

- Learner can comprehend main points, details, speaker's purpose, attitudes, levels of formality and styles in oral discourse in moderately demanding contexts.
- Can follow most formal and informal conversations, and some technical work-related discourse in own field at a normal rate of speech.
- Can follow discourse about abstract and complex ideas on a familiar topic.
- Can comprehend an expanded range of concrete, abstract and conceptual language.

- Can determine mood, attitudes and feelings.
- Can understand sufficient vocabulary, idioms and colloquial expressions to follow detailed stories of general popular interest.
- Can follow clear and coherent extended instructional texts and directions.
- Can follow clear and coherent phone messages on unfamiliar and non-routine matters.
- Often has difficulty following rapid, colloquial/idiomatic or regionally accented speech between native speakers.

Performance Conditions

- Tasks are in a standard format, with items to circle, match, fill in a blank, and complete a chart.
- Learner is adequately briefed for focused listening.
- Communication is face to face, observed live, or video- and audio-mediated (e.g., tape, TV, radio).
- Speech is clear at a normal rate.
- Instructions are clear and coherent.
- Listening texts are monologues/presentations and dialogues (five to 10 minutes), within familiar general topics and technical discourse in own field.
- Topics are familiar.
- Presentation/lecture is informal or semi-formal with the use of pictures, visuals (10 to 15 minutes).
- Learner is briefed for focused listening.
- Speech is clear, at a normal rate.

Reading: High Level

Global Performance Descriptor

- Learner can follow main ideas, key words and important details in an authentic two to three-page text on a familiar topic, but within an only partially predictable context.
- May read popular newspaper and magazine articles and popular easy fiction as well as academic and business materials.
- Can extract relevant points, but often requires clarification of idioms and of various cultural references.
- Can locate and integrate several specific pieces of information in visually complex texts (e.g., tables, directories) or across paragraphs or sections of text.
- Text can be on abstract, conceptual or technical topics, containing facts, attitudes and opinions. Inference may be required to identify the writer's bias and the purpose/function of text.
- Learner reads in English for information, to learn the language, to develop reading skills.
- Uses a unilingual dictionary when reading for precision vocabulary building.

Performance Conditions

- Text is one page, five to 10 paragraphs long and is related to personal experience or familiar context.
- Text is legible, easy to read; is in print or neat handwriting.
- Instructions are clear and explicit, but not always presented step by step.
- Pictures may accompany text.
- Context is relevant, but not always familiar and predictable.

- Text has clear organization.
- Text content is relevant (e.g., commercials/advertising features, business/form letters, brochures.)
- Informational text is eight to 15 paragraphs long with clear organization in print or electronic form.
- Pictures often accompany text.
- Language is both concrete and abstract, conceptual and technical.
- Text types: news articles, stories, short articles, reports, editorials, opinion essays.

Writing: High Level

Global Performance Descriptor

- Learner demonstrates fluent ability in performing moderately complex writing tasks.
- Can link sentences and paragraphs (three or four) to form coherent texts to express ideas on familiar abstract topics, with some support for main ideas, and with an appropriate sense of audience.
- Can write routine business letters (e.g., letters of inquiry, cover letters for applications) and personal and formal social messages.
- Can write down a set of simple instructions, based on clear oral communication or simple written procedural text of greater length.
- Can fill out complex formatted documents.
- Can extract key information and relevant detail from a page-long text and write an outline or a one-paragraph summary.
- Demonstrates good control over common sentence patterns, coordination and subordination, and spelling and mechanics. Has occasional difficulty with complex structures (e.g., those

reflecting cause and reason, purpose, comment), naturalness of phrases and expressions, organization and style.

Performance Conditions

- Circumstances range from informal to more formal occasions.
- Addressees are familiar.
- Topics are of immediate everyday relevance.
- Text is one or two short paragraphs in length.
- Text to reproduce is one or two pages in legible handwriting or print, or may be a short oral text (10 to 15 minutes).
- Texts are varied and may be of a specialized or technical nature.
- Learner may fill out a teacher-prepared summary grid to aid note taking or summarizing.
- Forms have over 40 items/pieces of information.
- Messages are two or three paragraphs in length.
- Brief texts required in pre-set formats are one to several sentences, up to one paragraph long.
- Learner text is three or four paragraphs long, on non-personal, abstract but familiar topics and issues.
- Where necessary for the task, learners must include information presented to them from other sources (e.g., photographs, drawings, reference text/research information, diagrams).

FACTOR 3: Work Experience (maximum 21 points)

Calculate your points by adding all of the years of full-time, paid work experience you have that:

- occurred within the past 10 years
- is **not** listed as a restricted occupation (follow the link to "Will You Qualify?" on our Web site to check)
- occurred in occupations listed in Skill Type 0 or Skill Level A or B of the NOC

Years of experience	Points
1	15
2	17
3	19
4+	21

If your work experience does not meet all of the above conditions, you may not count this experience.

Your Score	

FACTOR 4: Age (maximum 10 points)

Points are given for your age at the time your application is received.

Age	Total Points
16 or under	0
17	2
18	4
19	6
20	8
21-49	10
50	8
51	6
52	4
53	2
54 and over	0

Your Score	

Factor 5: Arranged employment (maximum 10 points)

Determine your points based on the chart below:

If:	And:	Points
You are currently working in Canada on a temporary work permit (including sectoral confirmations).	Your work permit is valid for 12 or more months **after** the date you apply for a permanent resident visa; Your employer has made an offer to give you a permanent job if your application is successful.	10
You are currently working in Canada in a job that is HRDC confirmation-exempt under an international agreement or a significant benefit category (e.g. intra-company transferee).	Your work permit is valid for 12 or more months **after** the date you apply for a permanent resident visa; Your employer has made an offer to give you a permanent job if your application is successful.	10

If:	And:	Points
You do not currently have a work permit and you do not intend to work in Canada before you have been issued a permanent resident visa.	You have a full-time job offer that has been confirmed by Human Resources Development Canada (HRDC); Your employer has made an offer to give you a permanent job if your application is successful. You meet all required Canadian licensing or regulatory standards associated with the job. **Note**: - You cannot arrange for an HRDC confirmation. Your employer must do this. - HRDC will confirm job offers for occupations listed in Skill Type 0 or Skill Level A or B of the NOC.	10

	Points
A. Spouse or common-law partner's level of education - Secondary school (high school) diploma or less: **0 points** - A one-year diploma, trade certificate, apprenticeship, or university degree and at least 12 years of full-time or full-time equivalent studies: **3 points** - A diploma, trade certificate, apprenticeship, or university degree of two years or more and at least 14 years of full-time or full-time equivalent studies: **4 points** - A Master's or PhD and at least 17 years of full-time or full-time equivalent studies: **5 points**	3-5
B. Previous study in Canada: - You or your accompanying spouse or common-law partner studied at a post-secondary institution in Canada for at least two years on a full-time basis. This must have been done after the age of 17 and with a valid study permit.	5
C. Previous work in Canada: - You or your accompanying spouse or common-law partner completed a minimum of one year of full-time work in Canada on a valid work permit.	5
D. Arranged employment: - You earned points under Factor 5: Arranged Employment.	5
E. Relatives in Canada: - You or your accompanying spouse or common-law partner has a relative (parent, grandparent, child, grandchild, child of a parent, sibling, child of a grandparent, aunt/uncle, or grandchild of a parent, niece or nephew) who lives in Canada and is a Canadian citizen or permanent resident.	5

Your Score	

FACTOR 6: Adaptability (maximum 10 points)

Points are awarded for certain adaptability elements based on the experience of the principal applicant and/or his or her spouse or common-law partner.

Instructions:

Use the chart below to determine your points. If you have a spouse or common-law partner, points for each element can be awarded only once, either for you **or** your spouse or common-law partner.

Your Score	

Your Score

Use this worksheet to calculate your total score. A visa officer will assess your application and will make the final decision; if there is a difference between the points you give yourself and the points the officer awards you, the officer's assessment will prevail.

Factor		Maximum points	Your score
1	Education	**25**	
2	Language proficiency	**24**	
3	Work experience	**21**	
4	Age	**10**	
5	Arranged employment	**10**	
6	Adaptability	**10**	
	Total	**100**	

The pass mark

The pass mark was last set on September 18, 2003, at **67 points**. To learn the current pass mark, consult CIC website

If:	Then:
Your total score is equal to or greater than the pass mark...	- You may qualify for immigration to Canada as a skilled worker. Read the rest of this guide to decide if you wish to apply under the Federal Skilled Worker Class.
Your total score is less than the pass mark...	- You are not likely to qualify for immigration to Canada as a skilled worker. We recommend that you do not apply at this time; - However, you may apply if you believe there are other factors that would help you to become economically established in Canada. Send a detailed letter with your application explaining these factors. Include any documents that support your claim.

Principal Applicant

If you are married or living with a common-law partner, you and your spouse or common-law partner must decide who will be the principal applicant. The other person will be considered the dependant in the applications.

Note: A common-law partner is the person who has lived with you in a conjugal relationship for at least one year. Common-law partner refers to **both opposite-sex and same-sex couples.**

Use the self-assessment test to help you determine which person would earn the most points. The person who would earn the most points should apply as the principal applicant.

You can also take the on-line Self-Assessment at this site http://www.cic.gc.ca/english/skilled/assess/index.html to see how many points you would earn in the six selection factors explained above.

Application Fees

A number of cost recovery and administrative fees are payable by applicants for processing applications of various types and for certain citizenship and immigration procedures. However, all fees are subject to change without notice. In general, fees are payable at the time of application. Please check with your nearest Citizenship and Immigration Canada office or Canadian mission abroad for confirmation.

Fees

There are two fees: the **processing fee** and the **right of permanent residence fee**.

The processing fee:

- **is non**-refundable whether your application is approved or not;
- must be paid when you send your application to the visa office;
- must be paid by the principal applicant and each accompanying family member.

The right of permanent residence fee:

- **is refundable** if a permanent resident visa is not issued or used, or if you withdraw your application;
- can be paid at any time during the application process, but must be paid before a permanent resident visa can be issued. If you do not pay the fee when you submit your application, the visa office will contact you when it is time to pay;
- must be paid by principal applicant and his or her spouse or common-law partner (if applicable).

The tables below show you how to calculate the amount required in Canadian dollars. You may have the option of paying in another currency. For information on how to pay your fees, consult **Appendix A: Checklist**.

Immigration and right of permanent residence fees

A. PROCESSING FEE	Number of Persons	Amount per Person	Amount Due
Principal applicant	1	x $550	$550
Spouse or common-law partner		x $550	
Each dependent child 22 years and over		x $550	
Each dependent child under 22 years		x $150	
		Total A	

B. RIGHT OF PERMANENT RESIDENCE FEE	Number of Persons	Amount per Person	Amount Due
Principal applicant	1	x $490	$490
Spouse or common-law partner		x $490	
Applicant's dependent children		Not applicable	
		Total B	
		Total A+B	

Note: *All amounts are in Canadian dollars.*

Additional fees

You must also pay for the following for yourself and your family members (if applicable):

- medical examinations
- police certificates
- language assessments

Medical and Security Requirements

Medical requirements

You and your family members, whether accompanying you or not, must undergo and pass a medical examination in order to come to Canada. To pass the medical examination you or your family members must not have a condition that:

- is a danger to public health or safety
- would cause excessive demand on health or social services in Canada. Examples of "excessive demand" include ongoing hospitalization or institutional care for a physical or mental illness.

Instructions

Instructions on how to undergo the medical examination will normally be sent to you after you submit your application to the visa office. For further instruction, see **Appendix D.** (For information on printing the appendices, visit:

http://www.cic.gc.ca/english/applications/guides/EG78.html#wp655525

Exam validity

The medical examination results are valid for 12 months from the date of the first medical examination. If you are not admitted as a permanent resident during this time, you must undergo another complete medical examination.

Authorized doctors

Your own doctor cannot do the medical examination. You must see a physician on Canada's list of Designated Medical Practitioners. Note that the physician is only responsible for conducting a medical examination; he or she cannot give you any advice on the immigration process.

Security requirements

Police certificates and clearances

You and your family members must provide us with a police certificate issued by the authorities of each country in which you have lived for six (6) months or more since reaching the age of 18. Certificates must be originals and issued within the last three months.

If you have been convicted of a criminal offence in Canada, your application cannot be approved unless you receive a pardon. To avoid the unnecessary payment of processing fees for an immigration application that will be refused, you should first apply for a pardon to the:

Clemency and Pardons Division
National Parole Board
410 Laurier Avenue West
Ottawa, ON, Canada
K1A 0R1
Fax: 1-613-941-4981

Web site: www.npb-cnlc.gc.ca (application forms can be downloaded from the site)

Appendix B - Checklist. (included in application forms)

WHO MAY REPRESENT YOU

A representative may be a lawyer, a consultant or any other person, including a friend, whom you hire for a fee or ask to help you do any of the following at no charge: (1) apply for permanent residence or a temporary stay in Canada; (2) submit a refugee claim; (3) appear in front of an adjudicator; (4) appeal a decision; (5) apply for citizenship; or (6) request information on matters dealing with the *Immigration Act* or the *Citizenship Act.*

What you should know before seeking the services of someone to help with your application

Do you need a representative?

- Citizenship and Immigration Canada (CIC) **does not require** you to have a representative. CIC have tried to make the application kits as simple as possible so that you can complete them yourself. You can get additional information on how to complete an application from the CIC Web site at **http://www.cic.gc.ca/english/contacts/call.html** or from a CIC Call Centre
- If you decide to use the services of a representative, you are free to do so.
- **CIC treats all applicants equally and does not provide preferential service to applicants with representatives.**

Who can act as a representative?

- Anyone can act as a representative.
- Only lawyers licensed to practise in Canada can represent you at the Federal Court.

- CIC can provide information on your file only to people who are either (1) Canadian citizens, (2) permanent residents of Canada or (3) physically present in Canada. Representatives who live outside Canada and are neither Canadian citizens nor permanent residents might be unable to help you.

- Volunteer and non-governmental organizations that deal with immigrants may provide free services.

General points

- CIC cannot recommend representatives or vouch for their honesty or skills. It is your responsibility to make sure that the representative you choose is ethical and competent to perform the services required. You should not be afraid to ask the representative (whether a lawyer or a consultant) for references or for other proof that he or she has the necessary skills.

- **Beware of representatives who claim that you will get a visa, obtain citizenship or benefit from special treatment from the Canadian government by using their services. CIC is not associated with any representatives.**

- Be cautious when dealing with foreign-based representatives. Such companies or individuals may be outside the reach of Canadian law, and there may be no protection or remedy available in Canada to a dissatisfied client.

Lawyers

- Lawyers practising in Canada are regulated by provincial regulatory bodies. Only a lawyer who is a member in good standing of a provincial or territorial law society may practise law. The law societies regulate lawyers and can investigate complaints against members, impose discipline and provide financial compensation to clients who are victims of negligence or misconduct.

- If you live in Canada and you want to hire a lawyer, call the law society of the province or territory in which you live for the names of lawyers. In many cases, you can consult a lawyer free of charge for half an hour before deciding if you want to hire him or her. However, in some cases, a fee may be charged for the consultation.

Immigration Consultants

- Immigration consultants are not regulated by either the federal or provincial governments of Canada.

- Find out if the consultant (whether he or she is in Canada or overseas) belongs to a professional association in Canada and ask about his or her experience with immigration or citizenship matters.

- Call the Better Business Bureau (BBB) to find out if the consultant has a satisfactory rating. Business people who fail to respond to letters of complaint sent to the BBB receive an unsatisfactory rating.

Dealing with Representatives

- CIC requires your written authorization in order to release information to your representative.

- You may give your own mailing address or the mailing address of your representative as a point of contact for CIC. If you choose to give your representative's address, all correspondence from CIC, including notices for interviews, requests for information, medical forms and visas, will be sent to the representative.

- If you change representatives or stop using their services, you must cancel your authorization in writing to CIC or CIC will continue dealing with them. If you hire a new representative, you will have to provide a new authorization to CIC.

- Make sure that the representative who helps you with your application is willing to be identified as your representative.

Information given to CIC must be truthful

- Submitting false or misleading information to CIC can lead to the refusal of your application, the cancellation of your visa, the revocation of your citizenship, your deportation from Canada, and criminal charges being laid against you.

- You are responsible for any documents you submit to CIC or that your representative submits on your behalf.

Where to go for help if things go wrong

CIC cannot help you if you have a dispute with your representative as it is a private matter between the two of you. However, you may write to the CIC office dealing with your case or to the following address to inform CIC of the situation:

> Citizenship and Immigration Canada
> Social Policy and Programs
> Selection Branch
> Jean Edmonds Tower North, 7th Floor
> 300 Slater Street
> Ottawa, Ontario KIA 1L1

Note: You should file a complaint with the proper authorities as soon as possible if you encounter serious difficulties with your representative as limitation periods may apply.

If your representative is a lawyer practising in Canada

- Address your complaint to the law society of the province or territory where your lawyer practises. Law societies impose a code of conduct on their members to try to protect the public interest. They have rules for disciplining lawyers and compensating clients. You may be able to obtain financial compensation from the law society's insurance fund.

If your representative is a consultant practising in Canada

- If your consultant is a member of a professional association in Canada, file a complaint with that association.

- If your consultant is not a member of any association, you might ask the consumer protection office in your province or territory for advice. Some associations might offer to contact the consultant to seek a solution.

- You can report your problem to the Better Business Bureau in the province or territory where your representative works. The BBB might contact your representative to try to resolve the issue for you.

If your representative is either a lawyer or an immigration consultant practising in Canada

- If you believe your representative has committed an offense in the course of representing you, you should go to the local police or to the Royal Canadian Mounted Police.

- If you are in Canada and you wish to recover money you paid for services you did not get, you can file a lawsuit in small claims court. You do not need a lawyer to do so, but you will have to pay a small fee.

- Legal Aid services are available throughout Canada for people who cannot afford to pay for legal assistance. Contact them to see if you qualify for assistance.

If your representative's place of business is abroad

- If your representative is not a Canadian citizen or a permanent resident of Canada, you should present your complaint to the appropriate authorities overseas. The Canadian government cannot get involved in the dispute.

CIC Call Centre

In Montreal: (514) 496-1010

In Toronto: (416) 973-4444

In Vancouver: (604) 666-2171

For all other areas: 1-888-242-2100 (From Canada & U.S.A)

PERMANENT RESIDENT CARD

The Permanent Resident Card (also known as the Maple Leaf Card or the PR Card) is a new, wallet-sized, plastic card. People who have completed the Canadian immigration process and have obtained Permanent Resident status, but are not Canadian Citizens can apply for the card. The card replaces the IMM 1000 as the status document needed by Canadian Permanent Residents re-entering Canada on a commercial carrier (airplane, boat, train and bus) as of December 31, 2003.

Security features of the new PR Card will simplify the screening process of Permanent Residents when boarding a commercial carrier going to Canada. The card also increases Canada's border security and improves the integrity of Canada's immigration process.

Beginning on June 28, 2002, PR Cards will be mailed to new Permanent Residents of Canada as part of the landing process. People who are already in Canada as Permanent Residents can apply for the new PR Card beginning October 15, 2002.

About the Permanent Resident Card

Background

The Canadian government has understood the need for a Permanent Resident Card for quite some time. The events of September 11, 2001 raised the issue of border security and the safety of all Canadians to the forefront. This made the introduction of a PR Card a key government initiative.

Before June 28, 2002, a successful landing application process resulted in the issuing of an IMM 1000 form. This document showed the holder's Canadian entry history. It was a large, difficult-to-carry piece of paper with no photograph, few security features and little in the way of privacy for the Permanent Resident. Technological advancements have made it easy to change, copy or make fraudulent use of many documents, including the IMM 1000.

CIC was intent on finding a replacement for this form that would address convenience, safety, privacy and durability concerns. The new PR Card not only addresses these concerns, but also includes state-of-the-art security features, making it extremely resistant to forgery and alteration.

The new card is a wallet-sized, plastic card, which confirms the Permanent Resident status of the cardholder. It replaces the IMM 1000 Record of Landing Form for travel purposes.

Security Benefits

The new PR Card contains several security features that make it a safe proof of status document for the cardholder. As of December 31, 2003, the new card is a necessary document for every Permanent Resident re-entering Canada by commercial carrier (airplane, boat, train and bus) after international travel.

The card has a laser engraved photograph and signature, as well as a description of the physical characteristics (height, eye colour, gender) of the cardholder printed on the front.

The card's optical stripe will contain all the details from the cardholder's Confirmation of Permanent Resident form. This encrypted information will only be accessible to authorized official (such as immigration officers) as required to confirm the status of the cardholder. The card cannot be used to monitor the activities or track the movement of the cardholder; this will protect the cardholder's privacy.

The card's optical stripe is more advanced than a magnetic stripe (commonly used on bank cards) both in terms of information storage capacity and security of information. Much like a commercial compact disc (CD), it is impossible to change, erase or add to the information already encoded on the optical stripe.

New Immigrants

Beginning on June 28, 2002, all new Permanent Residents will automatically receive their PR Card in the mail following their arrival in Canada. At the point of entry in Canada, personal data will be confirmed as part of the landing process.

If you did not provide your mailing address to CIC at the point of entry, please do so as soon as possible. You can provide this information on-line **at http://www.cic.gc.ca/english/e-services/index.html** or you can contact the PR Card Call Centre at 1-800-255-4541. Please note that if CIC do not receive your address within 180 days of the date of your admission, you will need to re-apply for your PR Card and pay the applicable fee.

Please notify CIC of any change in your mailing address as soon as possible. You may send them your change of address by mail, or use the on-line Change of Address service.

If you do not receive your PR Card within 30 days after sending CIC your address, please contact CIC Call Centre.

You can obtain a PR Card Application kit from CIC website, or by contacting the PR Card Call Centre at 1-800-255-4541 (from Canada & USA).

Canadian Citizens

Permanent Resident Cards are not issued to Canadian Citizens. Citizens need a Canadian Passport for international travel.

New PR Card Fees

The PR Card costs $50.00 per applicant. Each person applying for Permanent Residence status in Canada will need a card (children included.) The Card is normally valid for five years. All Permanent Residents will need a valid PR Card for re-entry into Canada on a commercial carrier as of December 31, 2003. It will be the cardholder's responsibility to make sure their card will be valid at the time of their return to Canada. If a Permanent Resident with a PR Card has become a Canadian Citizen, the PR Card is automatically cancelled. This person would then need to obtain a Canadian passport for international travel purposes.

Apply for Canadian Citizenship

If you have been a Permanent Resident and have been living in Canada for three years or more, you are eligible to apply for Canadian Citizenship.

What does it mean to be a Canadian citizen?

Citizenship means working together with all other Canadians to build a stronger Canada, and making sure our values, dreams and goals are reflected in our institutions, laws and relations with one another.

After living in Canada for at least three years as a permanent resident, you have the right to apply for Canadian citizenship.

Canada is a country that:

- is free and democratic;
- is multicultural;
- has two official languages; and
- extends equal treatment to all its citizens.

What are the rights and responsibilities of a citizen?

The *Canadian Charter of Rights and Freedoms* sets out the democratic rights and fundamental freedoms of all Canadians. Some rights are essential for Canadian citizens:

- the right to vote or to be a candidate in federal and provincial elections;
- the right to enter, remain in or leave Canada;
- the right to earn a living and reside in any province or territory;

- minority language education rights (English or French); and
- the right to apply for a Canadian passport.

Canadian citizenship also implies the following responsibilities:

- to obey Canada's laws;
- to vote in the federal, provincial and municipal elections;
- to discourage discrimination and injustice;
- to respect the rights of others;
- to respect public and private property; and
- to support Canada's ideals in building the country we all share.

Who is entitled to apply for Canadian citizenship?

You can apply for Canadian citizenship if you:

- are at least 18 years of age;
- have been a legal permanent resident in Canada for three out of the previous four years;
- can communicate in English or French; and
- have knowledge of Canada, including the rights and responsibilities of citizenship.

Who cannot become a Canadian citizen?

You may not be eligible to become a Canadian citizen if you:

- are under a deportation order and are not currently allowed to be in Canada;
- are in prison, on parole or on probation; and
- have been charged or convicted of an indictable offence.

Could you be a Canadian citizen and not know it?

In most cases, you are a Canadian citizen if you were born:

- in Canada, or
- in another country, after February 15, 1977, and have one Canadian parent.

For more information, telephone the Call Centre.

How do you apply for Canadian citizenship?

If you meet the requirements for Canadian citizenship, you can get an "Application for Citizenship" form from the Call Centre, or download an application at http://www.cic.gc.ca.

Fill out the application form and follow the instructions provided. A non-refundable processing fee and a refundable Right of Citizenship fee must be paid at the time of the application. You must include the receipt of payment and necessary documents with your application form.

You will have to take a test to show that you meet the requirements for knowledge of Canada and of either English or French. Study the information in the booklet *A Look at Canada* which will be sent to you with the acknowledgment of your application.

If you meet the basic requirements for citizenship, you will be invited to a citizenship ceremony where you will take the oath and receive your citizenship certificate.

What is dual citizenship?

Dual or plural citizenship means holding citizenship in one or more countries in addition to Canada.

Canada has recognized dual citizenship since 1977. This means that, in some cases, you may become a Canadian citizen while remaining a citizen of another country.

Some countries will not allow their citizens to keep their citizenship if they become citizens of another country. You should check with the embassy or consulate of your country of origin to be sure of their rules and laws.

Where should you go for more information about Canadian citizenship?

If you are in Canada, telephone the Call Centre.

Outside Canada, contact a Canadian embassy or consulate.

HOW TO APPLY

Once you have decided that you want to bring your skills to Canada, make sure that you follow the correct steps to apply.

There are a number of steps to follow when you prepare your application as a Skilled Worker. It is important that you carefully read and follow the instructions for each step listed below to ensure that your application is complete and submitted correctly.

Before you start your application, you need the forms that are specific to the Visa Office in your country or region. You will need the forms from your Visa Office for some of the steps below. Look for the checklist in these documents. The checklist will help you make sure that you have completed your application.

Find the checklist and appendixes for the Canadian Visa Office in your country or region.

STEP 1. Gather Your Documents

Collect the documents you need to support your application. A full list of these documents is included in **Appendix A: Checklist** found in the Visa Office-specific instructions for your location. The Checklist will tell you how many copies of the application form you need, which documents must be originals and which should be photocopies, and whether a certified translation in English or French is required.

STEP 2. Prepare The Forms

If any of your family members are included in your application, you will need more than one copy of some forms. Photocopy the following forms, or download and print the appropriate number from www.cic.gc.ca/skilled:

Application for Permanent Residence in Canada (IMM 0008): Page two of the form asks for details of your family members. There is space for three family members on the form. If you have more than three family members, make enough copies for everyone.

Schedule 1: Background/Declaration and *Additional Family Information* (IMM 5406): You, your spouse or common-law partner and each dependent child aged 18 or over (whether accompanying you or not) must complete these forms. Make enough photocopies for everyone.

STEP 3. Complete The Forms

For specific instructions, see the **How to Complete the Forms**

STEP 4. Obtain Police Certificates

You need police certificates from every country in which you or your family members aged 18 years or over have lived for six months or longer since reaching the age of 18. You will find instructions in **Appendix B: Obtaining Police Certificates/Clearances**.

STEP 5. Calculate Your Fees

Use the instructions in the **Fees** section to calculate the fees you must send with your application. Pay the fees according to instructions in the Fee Payment section of **Appendix A: Checklist**. Do not mail cash.

STEP 6. Make Sure Your Application Is Complete

Use the **Checklist** to verify that you have all of the required documents. Note that we may request additional information at any time during the application process.

STEP 7. Submit Your Application

Submit your completed application to the address indicated in the Checklist. Print your name and address in the top left-hand corner of the envelope.

☻ **If you do not fully complete and sign the forms and pay all necessary fees, your application will be returned to you unprocessed.**

HOW TO COMPLETE THE FORMS

The following text does not contain instructions for all the boxes on the forms. Most questions are clear; instructions are provided only when necessary. Note the following:

- Print clearly with a black pen or use a typewriter.
- Attach a separate sheet of paper if you need more space and indicate the number of the question you are answering.
- You must answer all questions. If you leave any sections blank, your application will be returned to you and processing will be delayed. If any sections do not apply to you, answer "N/A" ("Not applicable").
- If your application is accepted and information you provide on the forms changes before you arrive in Canada, you must inform, in writing, the visa office to which you applied. You must do this even if your visa has already been issued.

WARNING! It is a serious offence to give false or misleading information on this form. We may check to verify your responses. Misrepresentation will result in a two-year ban from entering Canada.

Application for Permanent Residence in Canada (IMM 0008)

To be completed by:

- You, as the principal applicant

At the top of this form, you will find three boxes:

Box 1: Category under which you are applying.
Check the "Economic class" box.

Box 2: How many family members...
Write the total number of people included in your application, including yourself and any family members, whether they are accompanying you to Canada or not.

Family members include your:

- **Spouse:** A husband or wife of the opposite sex
- **Common-law partner:** A person of the opposite or same sex with whom you have lived in a conjugal relationship for at least one year
- **Dependent children:** Daughters and sons, including children adopted before the age of 18, who:
    - are under the age of 22 and do not have a spouse or common-law partner;
    - have been continuously enrolled as full-time students and financially supported by their parents since turning 22 (or from the date of becoming a spouse or common-law partner if this happened before the age of 22); or
    - have substantially depended on the financial support of their parents since before turning 22 and are

unable to support themselves due to a medical condition.

Box 3: Language you prefer for

Correspondence: Decide which of English or French you are more comfortable reading and writing, and check the appropriate box.

Interview: You may be selected for an interview. Interviews can be conducted in English or French. You may also be interviewed in another language of your choice; however, you will be responsible for the cost of hiring an interpreter.

Instructions for filling out the rest of the form are listed below:

1. Print your full **family name** (surname) as it appears on your passport or on the official documents that you will use to obtain your passport. Print all of your **given names** (first, second or more) as they appear on your passport or official documents. Do not use initials.

5. If you are a citizen of more than one country, give details on a separate page.
10. This section requires you to give details of your past marriages or common-law relationships. If you have never had a spouse or common-law partner other than your current one, check the "No" box and proceed to Question 11. If you have, check the "Yes" box and provide the details requested. If you have had more than two previous spouses or common-law partners, give details on a separate page.
12. Check the box that best describes the highest level of education you have completed. If you have not completed secondary school, check the "No secondary" box.

- **Secondary education:** the level of schooling after elementary and before college, university, or other formal training. Also called high school.
- **Trade/Apprenticeship**: completed training in an occupation, such as carpentry or auto mechanics.
- **Non-university certificate/diploma:** training in a profession that requires formal education but not at the university level (for example, dental technician or engineering technician).
- **Bachelor's degree:** An academic degree awarded by a college or university to those who complete the undergraduate curriculum; also called a baccalaureate. Examples include a Bachelor of Arts, Science or Education.
- **Master's degree:** An academic degree awarded by the graduate school of a college or university. Normally, you must have completed a Bachelor's degree before a Master's degree can be earned.
- **PhD**: the highest university degree, usually based on at least three years graduate study and a dissertation. Normally, you must have completed a Master's degree before a PhD can be earned.

14. This is the address we will use to mail correspondence regarding your application. Print your address in English and, if applicable, also in your own native script.

19. Identity cards issued by a foreign national, provincial, municipal or other government, as well as cards issued by a recognized international agency such as the Red Cross, can be used to identify yourself. If you have such a card, print the number in the space provided. Photocopy both sides of the card and attach the photocopy to your application. If you do not have an identity card, print "N/A".

Details of family members

There is space for three family members on this form. If you have more than three family members, photocopy this page before you start to fill it in so you have enough space for everyone.

Given name(s)

Print all of your family members' **given names** (first, second or more) as they appear on their passports or official documents. Do not use initials.

Country of citizenship

If your family member is a citizen of more than one country, give details on a separate page.

Relationship to you

Indicate whether the family member is your spouse, common-law partner, daughter or son.

Will accompany you to Canada

Tell us if your family member will come to Canada with you. He or she must immigrate before the visa expires, but may arrive in Canada after you.

Education

Indicate the level of education your family member has successfully completed. Use the categories listed in Question 12.

Photos

Ask a photographer to provide you with a set of photos of yourself and each of your family members included in your application, whether they will be accompanying you or not. The required number of photos for each individual is indicated in Appendix A, under **Photos**. (For information on printing the appendices, see **How to Apply to Immigrate to Canada**.)

Photos must comply with specifications given in Appendix C, Photo Specifications. Make sure you give a copy of these specifications to the photographer.

- On the back of one photo (and only one) in each set, write the name and date of birth of the person appearing in the photo as well as the date the photo was taken.
- Enclose each set of photos in separate envelopes. Write the family member's name, date of birth and relationship to you on the corresponding envelope and close the envelope with a paper clip.
- Photos must not be stapled, scratched, bent or bear any ink marks.

Background / Declaration (IMM 0008, Schedule 1)

To be completed by:

- You
- Your spouse or common-law partner (whether accompanying you to Canada or not)
- Your dependent children aged 18 or over (whether accompanying you to Canada or not)

1. Write all of your given names. Do not use initials.

6. Indicate your current status in the country where you now live (for example, citizen, permanent resident, visitor, refugee, no legal status, etc.).

10. Provide details of all secondary and post-secondary education. Begin with the most recent program completed.

11. You must account for every month since your 18th birthday. Under "Activity", print your occupation or job title if you were working. If you were not working, enter what you were doing (for example, unemployed, studying, travelling, etc.). Attach another sheet if necessary.

15. Give a complete address including the street, town or city, province or region, and country. If there was no street or street number, explain exactly the location of the house or building. You must account for every month during the past 10 years. Do not use post office (P.O.) box addresses.

Declaration

Read the statements carefully. Sign and date in the boxes provided. By signing, you certify that you fully understand the questions asked, and that the information you have provided is complete, truthful, and correct. If you do not sign, the application will be returned to you.

Economic Classes - Skilled Workers (IMM 0008, Schedule 3)

To be completed by:

- You, as the principal applicant

3. If you have an offer of employment that has been approved by Human Resources Development Canada, tick the "Yes" box and give the name of your potential employer. See Factor 5: Arranged Employment for more information.
5. Use the instructions under Factor 2: English and French Language Ability to help you determine your ability in English and French.
10. "Funds" refers to money in Canadian dollars, and includes the value of any property you own. It does not include jewellery, cars or other personal assets.
11. To Determine your National Occupational Code (NOC), refer to the instructions in the **Will You Qualify?** section of this guide.

Additional Family Information (IMM 5406)

To be completed by:

- You
- Your spouse or common-law partner (whether accompanying you to Canada or not)
- Your dependent children aged 18 or over (whether accompanying you to Canada or not)

It is very important that you list on this form any other children (even if they are already permanent residents or Canadian citizens) that you, your spouse or common-law partner or your dependent children might have who are not included in your Application for Permanent Residence. This includes

- married children
- adopted children
- step-children
- any of your children who have been adopted by others
- any of your children who are in the custody of an ex-spouse, common-law partner or other guardian

You must answer all questions. If any sections do not apply to you, answer "N/A".

Use of a Representative (IMM 5476)

Complete this form if you are appointing a representative.

If you have dependent children aged 18 years or older, they are required to complete their own copy of this form if a representative is also conducting business on their behalf.

A **representative** is someone who has your permission to conduct business on your behalf with Citizenship and Immigration Canada. When you appoint a representative, you also authorize CIC to share information from your case file to this person.

You are not obliged to hire a representative. We treat everyone equally, whether they use the services of a representative or not. If you choose to hire a representative, your application will not be given special attention nor can you expect faster processing or a more favourable outcome.

The representative you appoint is authorized to represent you only on matters related to the application you submit with this form. You can appoint only **one** representative for each application you submit.

There are two types of representatives:

Unpaid representatives

- friends and family members who do not charge a fee for their advice and services
- organizations that do not charge a fee for providing immigration advice or assistance (such as a non-governmental or religious organization)
- consultants, lawyers and Québec notaries who do not, and will not, charge a fee to represent you

Paid representatives

If you want us to conduct business with a representative who is, or will be charging a fee to represent you, he or she must be authorized. Authorized representatives are:

- immigration consultants who are members in good standing of the Canadian Society of Immigration Consultants (CSIC)
- lawyers who are members in good standing of a Canadian provincial or territorial law society and students-at-law under their supervision
- notaries who are members in good standing of the *Chambre des notaires du Québec* and students-at-law under their supervision

If you appoint a paid representative who is not a member of one of these designated bodies, your application will be returned. For more information on using a representative, visit our Web site.

Section B.

5. Your representative's full name

If your representative is a member of CSIC, a law society or the *Chambre des notaires du Québec*, print his or her name as it appears on the organization's membership list.

8. Your representative's declaration

Your representative must sign to accept responsibility for conducting business on your behalf.

Section D.

10. Your declaration

By signing, you authorize us to complete your request for yourself and your dependent children under 18 years of age. If your spouse or common-law partner is included in this request, he or she must sign in the box provided.

Release of information to other individuals

To authorize CIC to release information from your case file to someone other than a representative, you will need to complete form *Authority to Release Personal Information to a Designated Individual* (IMM 5475) which is available on our Web site and from Canadian embassies, high commissions and consulates abroad.

The person you designate will be able to obtain information on your case file, such as the status of your application. However, he or she will **not** be able to conduct business on your behalf with CIC.

You must notify cic if your representative's contact information changes or if you cancel the appointment of a representative.

Visa Office Specific Forms

These forms are part of the Skilled Worker application for permanent resident status in Canada. This is **step four** in your application. Make sure you complete steps one, two and three. Determine which Canadian visa office is responsible for:

- the country in which you are residing, provided you have been lawfully admitted to that country for at least one year; or
- your country of nationality.

Check the list of countries and Visa Offices (http://www.cic.gc.ca/english/offices/apply-where.html) to find out where you must send your application. Print out the forms and instructions specific to this office. Read the instructions carefully. You will find:

- a checklist of the documents you need to include with your application
- information about the medical examination;
- information about getting police certificates or clearances; and
- instructions about where to send your application.

Note: *Checklist and appendices are included in the application forms.*

The Application Assessment Process

A Visa Office will process your application. The Visa Office may process your application differently depending on your application and the Visa Office. Some processing steps are common to all Visa Offices.

After you submit your application, a Citizenship and Immigration Canada (CIC) officer will check to see that you submitted everything with your application. The officer will make sure that you:

- Completed your application form correctly;
- paid your application fee correctly; and
- included all supporting documentation.

If your application is not complete, CIC will return it to you without starting to process it.

Your Visa Office will send you a letter when they receive your completed application. The letter will tell you what you need to do and what happens next.

Processing Time

The length of time it takes to process your application can be different in each mission or Visa Office. Visit the mission Web site

http://www.cic.gc.ca/english/offices/missions.html (if available) where you submitted your application for more information on how long it might take to process your application.

You may be able to speed up the process by:

- making sure all the necessary information is included with your application;
- notifying the Visa Office of any changes to the information on your application;
- avoiding unnecessary enquiries to the Visa Office;
- making sure the photocopies and documents you provide are clear and readable;
- providing certified English or French translations of documents, where indicated; and
- applying from a country where you are a citizen or permanent resident.

Your application will be delayed if the Visa Office has to take extra steps to assess your case. Your application will take longer if:

- there are criminal or security problems with your application;
- your family situation is not clear because of a situation such as a divorce or adoption that is not yet complete or child custody issues that have not been resolved; or
- the local Visa Office has to consult with other CIC offices in Canada or abroad.

The Decision on Your Application

The CIC officer will make a decision on your application based on the points you accumulate in the six selection factors. The officer will also evaluate your ability to meet the Required Funds amount for the size of your family.

The Visa Office will contact you if they need more documentation or if you have to come in for a personal interview.

Confirmation of Permanent Residence

You will be given a *Confirmation of Permanent Residence* (COPR) if your application is successful. The COPR will have identification information as well as a photo and your signature. You **must** bring the COPR to the Port of Entry with your visa when you enter Canada.

Checking the Status of Your Application

Once you have received notice from our office that your application has been received, you can check the status of your application online at http://www.cic.gc.ca/english/e-services/index.html

Application for Permanent Residence

Guide for Provincial Nominees

OVERVIEW

The **Provincial Nominee Program** allows provincial governments to choose immigrants according to the economic needs of the province. Each province:

- establishes its own standards and processes by which it chooses its nominees
- tries to nominate those candidates who would be most likely to settle effectively into the economic and social life of the region.

Purpose

This guide is for people who have been or wish to be nominated by one of the following provinces:

- Alberta
- British Columbia
- Manitoba
- New Brunswick
- Newfoundland
- Nova Scotia
- Prince Edward Island
- Saskatchewan
- The Yukon Territory

It provides the following information:

- how to apply for permanent residence in Canada as a provincial nominee;
- all of the necessary instructions and forms to apply (federal government only).

Other classes

If you think you may qualify to apply under a different class, consult the chart below.

If:	Consult the guide:
You have been selected by the province of Quebec	Guide for Quebec-Selected Applicants
You are immigrating to Canada as a Federal Skilled Worker	Guide for Federal Skilled Workers
You are interested in immigrating to Canada as an investor, entrepreneur or self-employed person	Guide for Business Class Applicants
A relative such as a parent, spouse or common-law partner would like to sponsor your application for permanent residence	Guide for Family Class Applicants

Staying informed

Selection criteria and other information for skilled worker applicants can sometimes change. Note that:

- Applications will be processed according to the rules and regulations in effect at the time of assessment. These may change at any time.
- Our Web site contains the most up-to-date information and applications. Check periodically to make sure you have the most current information.

Provincial Contacts

Application procedures vary from province to province; however, Citizenship and Immigration Canada retains the authority to make the final decision on an application using existing selection and admissibility criteria, including security, criminal, and medical components for candidates who hold Provincial Nominee Certificates.

If you would like information on how to become nominated by a particular province, or if you require further details regarding the Provincial Nominee Program, contact the following provincial authorities:

Alberta Provincial Nominee Program Alberta Economic Development 4th Floor, Commerce Place 10155 102 St. Edmonton, Alberta Canada T5J 4L6 Web site: www.alberta-canada.com/pnp
British Columbia Ministry of Community, Aboriginal and Women's Services - Immigration Branch Provincial Nominee Program P.O. Box 9214, Victoria, BC Canada V8W 9J1 Tel: (250) 387-2190 Fax: (250) 387-3725 E-mail: PNPinfo@gems9.gov.bc.ca Web site: www.ecdev.gov.bc.ca/ProgramsAndServices/PNP

Manitoba Immigration Promotion and Recruitment Branch Citizenship and Multiculturalism Division 9th Floor - 213 Notre Dame Avenue Winnipeg, Manitoba Canada R3B 1N3 Phone: (204) 945-2806 Web site: www.gov.mb.ca/labour/immigrate
New Brunswick Provincial Nominee Program Training and Employment Development P.O. Box 6000 Fredericton, New Brunswick Canada E3B 5H1 E-mail: immigration@gnb.ca Web site: www.gnb.ca/immigration/english
Newfoundland Industry Trade and Technology Confederation Building West Block, 4th Floor P.O. Box 8700 St. John's, Newfoundland Canada A1B 4J6 Tel: (709) 729-2781 Fax: (709) 729-3208 Web site: www.nlbusiness.ca
Nova Scotia Provincial Nominee Program The Office of Economic Development 1800 Argyle Street P.O. Box 519 Halifax, Nova Scotia Canada B3J 2R7 Tel: (902) 424-8322 Web site: www.gov.ns.ca/econ/nsnp

Prince Edward Island Immigration and Investment Division 94 Euston Street, 2nd floor Charlottetown, PEI Canada C1A 7M8 E-mail: peinominee@gov.pe.ca Web site: www.gov.pe.ca/immigration
Saskatchewan Saskatchewan Immigrant Nominee Program 2nd Floor - 1919 Saskatchewan Drive Regina, Saskatchewan Canada S4P 3V7 E-mail: immigration@graa.gov.sk.ca Web site: www.immigrationsask.gov.sk.ca
Yukon Territory Business Development and Immigration Department of Economic Development P.O. Box 2703, Whitehorse Canada Y1A 2C6 Phone: (867) 667-3014 E-mail: bob.snyder@gov.yk.ca Web site: www.economicdevelopment.gov.yk.ca

Funds Required to Settle in Canada

The government of Canada provides no financial support to new immigrants. You must prove that you have enough money unencumbered by debts or obligations to support yourself and your family members after you arrive in Canada.

We strongly recommend that you research the cost of living in the region of Canada where you intend to live. Bring with you as much money as possible to make your establishment in Canada easier.

Disclosure of funds

You will have to tell a Canadian official if you carry more than $10,000 Canadian in cash funds upon your entry to Canada. This could be in the form of:

- money (coins or bank notes)
- securities in bearer form (stocks, bonds, debentures, treasury bills etc.)
- negotiable instruments in bearer form (bankers' drafts, cheques, travellers' cheques, money orders etc.)

Failure to disclose can result in fines and imprisonment.

Working in Canada

Finding employment in Canada requires planning. You should obtain as much information as possible before you apply to immigrate. There is no guarantee that you will be able to work in your preferred occupation.

Although credential assessment and licensing are not requirements of the skilled worker application, you need to be aware of these issues when considering immigrating to Canada.

Follow the Working in Canada link on our Web site for some helpful sites on regulated and non-regulated occupations.

Regulated occupations

Twenty percent of people working in Canada work in occupations that are regulated to protect the health and safety of Canadians. Examples include nurses, engineers, electricians and teachers.

Provincial and territorial regulatory bodies are responsible for establishing entry requirements for individual occupations; for recognizing prior credentials, training and experience; and for issuing licences required to practice. The recognition process varies between provinces and territories and between occupations. Recognition of qualifications and issuance of licenses can generally only be completed once in Canada. The process can take time. You may be asked to:

- provide documentation of qualifications
- undergo a language examination (which may differ from those required for immigration)
- complete a technical exam (with accompanying fee)
- do supervised work

Non-regulated occupations

For non-regulated occupations, there are no set requirements and there is no legal requirement to obtain a licence. The employer will set the standards and may very well request registration with a professional association.

Credential assessment

A credential assessment is advice on how qualifications from another country compare to Canadian qualifications. An assessment **does not** guarantee that:

- a regulatory body will issue you a licence to practice
- your credentials will be accepted by a Canadian employer

However, a credential assessment **will** help you understand the Canadian educational system and assist you with your job search.

You can have your credentials assessed by one of the provincial evaluation services. Follow the link to Credential assessment on our Web site for more information.

Labour market information

Job opportunities and labour market conditions are different in each region of Canada. It is important to research conditions in the area in which you want to live. Follow the Working in Canada link on our Web site for helpful sites on the Canadian labour market, job banks, and provincial and territorial labour market information.

Fees

The processing fee:

- **is non**-refundable whether your application is approved or not;
- must be paid when you send your application to the visa office;
- must be paid by the principal applicant and each accompanying family member.

Calculating your fees

Use the table below to calculate the amount required in Canadian dollars. You may have the option of paying in another currency. For information on how to pay your fees, consult **Appendix A: Checklist**.

(For information on printing the appendices, see **How to Apply to Immigrate to Canada**.)

PROCESSING FEES	Number of Persons	Amount per Person	Amount Due
Principal applicant	1	x $550	$550
Spouse or common-law partner		x $550	
Each dependent child who is 22 years of age or older or who is married or in a common-law relationship, regardless of age		x $550	
Each dependent child under 22 years of age and not married or in a common-law relationship		x $150	
Total			

Right of Permanent Residence Fee

- **$490 per person** for you (the principal applicant) and your spouse or common-law partner (if applicable). Dependent children are exempt.
- You will need to pay this fee before your application for permanent residence can be finalized. **We will send you a request to pay this fee** when we are ready to issue the permanent resident visa.

Additional fees

You must also pay the following additional fees for yourself and your family members (if applicable):

- fees required by the nominating province or territory (fees vary)
- medical examinations
- police certificates
- language assessments

Medical and Security Requirements

Medical requirements

You and your family members, whether accompanying you or not, must undergo and pass a medical examination in order to come to Canada. To pass the medical examination you or your family members must not have a condition that:

- is a danger to public health or safety
- would cause excessive demand on health or social services in Canada. Examples of "excessive demand" include ongoing hospitalization or institutional care for a physical or mental illness.

Instructions

Instructions on how to undergo the medical examination will normally be sent to you after you submit your application to the visa office. For further instructions, see **Appendix D.** (For information on printing the appendices, see **How to Apply to Immigrate to Canada**.)

Exam validity

The medical examination results are valid for 12 months from the date of the first medical examination. If you are not admitted as a permanent resident during this time, you must undergo another complete medical examination.

Authorized doctors

Your own doctor cannot do the medical examination. You must see a physician on Canada's list of Designated Medical Practitioners. Note that the physician is only responsible for conducting a medical examination; he or she cannot give you any advice on the immigration process.

Security requirements

Police certificates and clearances

You and your family members must provide us with a police certificate issued by the authorities of each country in which you have lived for six (6) months or more since reaching the age of 18. Certificates must be originals and issued within the last three months.

If you have been convicted of a criminal offence in Canada, your application cannot be approved unless you receive a pardon. To avoid the unnecessary payment of processing fees for an immigration application that will be refused, you should first apply for a pardon to the:

Clemency and Pardons Division
National Parole Board
410 Laurier Avenue West
Ottawa, ON, Canada
K1A 0R1
Fax: 1-613-941-4981

Web site: www.npb-cnlc.gc.ca (application forms can be downloaded from the site)

For more information on police certificates, see **Appendix B** and the police certificates section of the **Checklist**. (For information on printing the appendices, see **How to Apply to Immigrate to Canada**.)

How to Apply to Immigrate to Canada (Provincial Nominee)

STEP 1. Apply For Nomination

Before you can apply to immigrate to Canada as a provincial nominee, you must first be nominated by a province or territory. Each province or territory has its own nomination procedures. To learn more, consult the Provincial Contacts section.

STEP 2. Gather Your Documents

Collect the documents you need to support your application. A full list of these documents is included in **Appendix A: Checklist** found in the Visa Office-specific instructions for your location. The Checklist will tell you how many copies of the application form you need, which documents must be originals and which should be photocopies, and whether a certified translation in English or French is required.

STEP 3. Prepare The Forms

If any of your family members are included in your application, you will need more than one copy of some forms.

Application for Permanent Residence in Canada (IMM 0008): Page two of the form asks for details of your family members. There is space for three family members on the form. If you have more than three family members, make enough copies for everyone.

Schedule 1: Background/Declaration and *Additional Family Information* (IMM 5406): You, your spouse or common-law partner and each dependent child aged 18 or over (whether accompanying you or not) must complete these forms. Make enough photocopies for everyone.

STEP 4. Complete The Forms

For specific instructions, see the How to Complete the Forms section.

STEP 5. Obtain Police Certificates

You need police certificates from every country in which you or your family members aged 18 years or over have lived for six months or longer since reaching the age of 18. You will find instructions in **Appendix B: Obtaining Police Certificates/Clearances**.

STEP 6. Calculate Your Fees

Use the instructions in the Fees section to calculate the fees you must send with your application. Pay the fees according to instructions in the Fee Payment section of **Appendix A: Checklist**. Do not mail cash.

STEP 7. Make Sure Your Application Is Complete

Use the **Checklist** to verify that you have all of the required documents. Note that we may request additional information at any time during the application process.

STEP 8. Submit Your Application

Submit your completed application to the address indicated in the Checklist. Print your name and address in the top left-hand corner of the envelope.

If you do not fully complete and sign the forms and pay all necessary fees, your application will be returned to you unprocessed.

How to Complete the Forms

The following text does not contain instructions for all the boxes on the forms. Most questions are clear; instructions are provided only when necessary. Note the following:

- Print clearly with a black pen or use a typewriter.
- Attach a separate sheet of paper if you need more space and indicate the number of the question you are answering.
- You must answer all questions. If you leave any sections blank, your application will be returned to you and processing will be delayed. If any sections do not apply to you, answer "N/A" ("Not applicable").
- If your application is accepted and information you provide on the forms changes before you arrive in Canada, you must inform, in writing, the visa office to which you applied. You must do this even if your visa has already been issued.

*Note: To obtain these forms, refer to **How to Complete the Forms**.*

WARNING! It is a serious offence to give false or misleading information on this form. We may check to verify your responses. Misrepresentation will result in a two-year ban from entering Canada.

Application for Permanent Residence in Canada (IMM 0008)

To be completed by:

- You, as the principal applicant

At the top of this form, you will find three boxes:

Category under which you are applying...

Check the "Economic class" box.

How many family members...

Write the total number of people included in your application, including yourself and any family members, whether they are accompanying you to Canada or not.

Family members include your:

- **Spouse:** A husband or wife of the opposite sex
- **Common-law partner:** A person of the opposite or same sex with whom you have lived in a conjugal relationship for at least one year
- **Dependent children:** Daughters and sons, including children adopted before the age of 18, who:
    - are under the age of 22 and do not have a spouse or common-law partner;
    - have been continuously enrolled as full-time students and financially supported by their parents since turning 22 (or from the date of becoming a spouse or common-law partner if this happened before the age of 22); or
    - have substantially depended on the financial support of their parents since before turning 22 and are unable to support themselves due to a medical condition.

Language you prefer for...

Correspondence: Decide which of English or French you are more comfortable reading and writing, and check the appropriate box.

Interview: You may be selected for an interview. Interviews can be conducted in English or French. You may also be interviewed in another language of your choice; however, you will be responsible for the cost of hiring an interpreter.

Instructions for filling out the rest of the form are listed below:

1. Print your full **family name** (surname) as it appears on your passport or on the official documents that you will use to obtain your passport. Print all of your **given names** (first, second or more) as they appear on your passport or official documents. Do not use initials.

5. If you are a citizen of more than one country, give details on a separate page.

10. This section requires you to give details of your past marriages or common-law relationships. If you have never had a spouse or common-law partner other than your current one, check the "No" box and proceed to Question 11. If you have, check the "Yes" box and provide the details requested. If you have had more than two previous spouses or common-law partners, give details on a separate page.

12. Check the box that best describes the highest level of education you have completed. If you have not completed secondary school, check the "No secondary" box.

    Secondary education: the level of schooling after elementary and before college, university, or other formal training. Also called high school.

Trade/Apprenticeship: completed training in an occupation, such as carpentry or auto mechanics.

Non-university certificate/diploma: training in a profession that requires formal education but not at the university level (for example, dental technician or engineering technician).

Bachelor's degree: An academic degree awarded by a college or university to those who complete the undergraduate curriculum; also called a baccalaureate. Examples include a Bachelor of Arts, Science or Education.

Master's degree: An academic degree awarded by the graduate school of a college or university. Normally, you must have completed a Bachelor's degree before a Master's degree can be earned.

PhD: the highest university degree, usually based on at least three years graduate study and a dissertation. Normally, you must have completed a Master's degree before a PhD can be earned.

14. This is the address we will use to mail correspondence regarding your application. Print your address in English and, if applicable, also in your own native script.

19. Identity cards issued by a foreign national, provincial, municipal or other government, as well as cards issued by a recognized international agency such as the Red Cross, can be used to identify yourself. If you have such a card, print the number in the space provided. Photocopy both sides of the card and attach the photocopy to your application. If you do not have an identity card, print "N/A".

Details of family members

There is space for three family members on this form. If you have more than three family members, photocopy this page before you start to fill it in so you have enough space for everyone.

Given name(s)

Print all of your family members' **given names** (first, second or more) as they appear on their passports or official documents. Do not use initials.

Country of citizenship

If your family member is a citizen of more than one country, give details on a separate page.

Relationship to you

Indicate whether the family member is your spouse, common-law partner, daughter or son.

Will accompany you to Canada

Tell us if your family member will come to Canada with you. He or she must immigrate before the visa expires, but may arrive in Canada after you.

Education

Indicate the level of education your family member has successfully completed. Use the categories listed in Question 12.

Photos

Ask a photographer to provide you with a set of photos of yourself and each of your family members included in your application, whether they will be accompanying you or not. The required number of photos for each individual is indicated in Appendix A, under **Photos**. (For information on printing the appendices, see **How to Apply to Immigrate to Canada**.)

Photos must comply with specifications given in Appendix C, Photo Specifications. Make sure you give a copy of these specifications to the photographer.

- On the back of one photo (and only one) in each set, write the name and date of birth of the person appearing in the photo as well as the date the photo was taken.
- Enclose each set of photos in separate envelopes. Write the family member's name, date of birth and relationship to you on the corresponding envelope and close the envelope with a paper clip.
- Photos must not be stapled, scratched, bent or bear any ink marks.

Background / Declaration (IMM 0008, Schedule 1)

To be completed by:

- You
- Your spouse or common-law partner (whether accompanying you to Canada or not)
- Your dependent children aged 18 or over (whether accompanying you to Canada or not)

1. Write all of your given names. Do not use initials.

6. Indicate your current status in the country where you now live (for example, citizen, permanent resident, visitor, refugee, no legal status, etc.).

10. Provide details of all secondary and post-secondary education. Begin with the most recent program completed.

11. You must account for every month since your 18th birthday. Under "Activity", print your occupation or job title if you were working. If you were not working, enter what you were doing (for example, unemployed, studying, travelling, etc.). Attach another sheet if necessary.

15. Give a complete address including the street, town or city, province or region, and country. If there was no street or street number, explain exactly the location of the house or building. You must account for every month during the past 10 years. Do not use post office (P.O.) box addresses.

Declaration

Read the statements carefully. Sign and date in the boxes provided. By signing, you certify that you fully understand the questions asked, and that the information you have provided is complete, truthful, and correct. If you do not sign, the application will be returned to you.

Economic Classes - Skilled Workers (IMM 0008, Schedule 4)

To be completed by:

- You, as the principal applicant

4. "Funds" refers to money in Canadian dollars, and includes the value of any property you own. It does not include jewellery, cars or other personal assets.

Additional Family Information (IMM 5406)

To be completed by:

- You
- Your spouse or common-law partner (whether accompanying you to Canada or not)

- Your dependent children aged 18 or over (whether accompanying you to Canada or not)

It is very important that you list on this form any other children (even if they are already permanent residents or Canadian citizens) that you, your spouse or common-law partner or your dependent children might have who are not included in your Application for Permanent Residence. This includes:

- married children
- adopted children
- step-children
- any of your children who have been adopted by others
- any of your children who are in the custody of an ex-spouse, common-law partner or other guardian

You must answer all questions. If any sections do not apply to you, answer “N/A”.

Use of a Representative (IMM 5476)

Complete this form if you are appointing a representative.

If you have dependent children aged 18 years or older, they are required to complete their own copy of this form if a representative is also conducting business on their behalf.

A **representative** is someone who has your permission to conduct business on your behalf with Citizenship and Immigration Canada. When you appoint a representative, you also authorize CIC to share information from your case file with this person.

You are not obliged to hire a representative. We treat everyone equally, whether they use the services of a representative or not. If you choose to hire a representative, your application will not be given special attention nor can you expect faster processing or a more favourable outcome.

The representative you appoint is authorized to represent you only on matters related to the application you submit with this form. You can appoint only **one** representative for each application you submit.

There are two types of representatives:

Unpaid representatives

- friends and family members who do not charge a fee for their advice and services
- organizations that do not charge a fee for providing immigration advice or assistance (such as a non-governmental or religious organization)
- consultants, lawyers and Québec notaries who do not, and will not, charge a fee to represent you

Paid representatives

If you want us to conduct business with a representative who is, or will be charging a fee to represent you, he or she must be authorized. Authorized representatives are:

- immigration consultants who are members in good standing of the Canadian Society of Immigration Consultants (CSIC)
- lawyers who are members in good standing of a Canadian provincial or territorial law society and students-at-law under their supervision
- notaries who are members in good standing of the *Chambre des notaires du Québec* and students-at-law under their supervision

If you appoint a paid representative who is not a member of one of these designated bodies, your application will be returned. For more information on using a representative, visit our Web site.

Section B.

5. Your representative's full name

If your representative is a member of CSIC, a law society or the *Chambre des notaires du Québec*, print his or her name as it appears on the organization's membership list.

8. Your representative's declaration

Your representative must sign to accept responsibility for conducting business on your behalf.

Section D.

10. Your declaration

By signing, you authorize us to complete your request for yourself and your dependent children under 18 years of age. If your spouse or common-law partner is included in this request, he or she must sign in the box provided.

Release of information to other individuals

To authorize CIC to release information from your case file to someone other than a representative, you will need to complete form *Authority to Release Personal Information to a Designated Individual* (IMM 5475) which is available on our Web site and from Canadian embassies, high commissions and consulates abroad.

The person you designate will be able to obtain information on your case file, such as the status of your application. However, he or she will **not** be able to conduct business on your behalf with CIC.

You must notify us if your representative's contact information changes or if you cancel the appointment of a representative.

The Application Process

1. Submission

Each visa office has its own application process; however, there are two universal aspects of the process:

A. Completion check: Once you have submitted your application, we will check to determine that all required application forms have been properly completed and submitted, the application processing fee has been paid, and that all requested supporting documentation has been provided.

If your application package does not meet these requirements, we will return it to you. No file will be created or record kept until a complete application has been submitted.

B. Acknowledgment of receipt: If your application is complete, we will begin to process it. You will be sent a letter that:

- notifies you of this fact and provides you with your visa office file number
- sets out some basic instructions for contact with the visa office
- gives you a brief outline as to future processing steps

2. Processing

Review for decision

Your application will undergo a detailed review by a visa officer. The officer will consider all the information and documentation you have provided, and will assess it against current selection standards for skilled worker immigrants.

Factors that facilitate processing

There are certain things you can do to help ensure that your application is processed as promptly as possible:

- make sure that all the documentation and information requested is **provided at the time of initial application submission**
- make sure that you notify the visa office promptly of any and all changes to your mailing address, family situation, or any other information that is important to your application, such as additional education or work experience.
- refrain from making unnecessary inquiries to the Visa Office regarding the status of your case

Factors that may delay processing

The following factors may delay the processing of your application:

- unclear photocopies of documents
- documents not accompanied by a certified English or French translation
- verification of information and documents provided
- a medical condition that may require additional tests or consultations
- a criminal or security problem
- family situations such as impending divorce, or custody or maintenance issues
- completion of legal adoption
- consultation is required with other offices in Canada and abroad
- you are not a permanent resident of the country in which you currently live

Checking your application status

You can find out the current status of your application by logging on to e-Client Application Status. If you live in Canada, you may also call our Call Centre.

If you do not want your information available on-line, you can remove on-line information by logging on to e-Client Application Status. If you live in Canada, you may also call our Call Centre and ask an agent to do this for you.

Current processing times are updated weekly.

3. Decision

The officer will make a decision based on:

- the number of points that you accumulate in the six factors, based on the documentation you submit with your application
- your ability to meet the Required Funds amount for the size of your family

During the decision-making process, the officer may contact you if:

- further documentation is required
- a personal interview is required

Confirmation of permanent residence

If your application is successful, you will be issued a *Confirmation of Permanent Residence* (COPR) form that you and your accompanying family members must bring to the port of entry along with your visa. The COPR will contain all of your identification information, as well as a photo and your signature.

What Happens Next?

Employment and settlement services

Settlement services vary between regions and provinces. You can learn about them from:

- Citizenship and Immigration Canada Web site
- Human Resources Canada Centres
- Some provincial governments or provincial organizations

Permanent resident status

If your application is successful, you and your family members will receive status as permanent residents of Canada. Some conditions will apply:

- You will remain a permanent resident until you become a Canadian citizen, as long as you spend at least two years of each five year period in Canada
- You may leave and re-enter Canada as often as you wish
- If you spend more than two years of a five-year period outside Canada, you may lose your permanent resident status (certain conditions apply)

Rights

As permanent residents, you and your family members will have the right to:

- Live, study and work in Canada for as long as you remain permanent residents
- Access most social benefits accorded to Canadian citizens (see **Limitations**)
- Apply for Canadian citizenship and a Canadian passport (once you have been a legal permanent resident for three of the four previous years)

Limitations

There are a few limitations on permanent residents:

- You cannot vote in certain elections
- You may be ineligible for certain jobs requiring high-level security clearances
- If you or any of your family members commit a serious crime, you or your family members risk being deported from Canada

Obligations

As permanent residents, you will also have the same legal obligations as Canadians, such as paying taxes and respecting all federal, provincial, and municipal laws.

The Permanent Resident Card

All new permanent residents will be issued a card as part of the arrival process. Cards will be mailed to your home address soon after you become a permanent resident. For more information on the Permanent Resident Card, visit our Web site.

Application for Permanent Residence

FAMILY CLASS

Sponsorship Of Parents, Grandparents, Adopted Children And Other Relatives

The Sponsor's Guide

OVERVIEW

The Canadian government allows citizens and permanent residents of Canada to sponsor members of the family class, but it requires that arriving immigrants receive care and support from their sponsors. Members of the family class include a sponsor's spouse, common-law partner or conjugal partner; a dependent child of the sponsor; the sponsor's mother or father; a person the sponsor intends to adopt; and other relatives of the sponsor as defined by regulation.

Your application kit contains all the information you need to sponsor a person living outside Canada who is a member of the family class except if that person is:

- your spouse, common-law partner, conjugal partner or dependent child, including an adopted child whose adoption took place outside Canada and at the time of the adoption you were living exclusively outside Canada or had not yet become a permanent resident of Canada. Obtain the application package **Sponsorship of a spouse, common-law partner, conjugal partner or dependent child living outside Canada**;
- a spouse or common-law partner who lives with you in Canada. Obtain the application package **Spouse or common-law partner in Canada class**;
- a child born to you outside of Canada and you had Canadian citizenship at the time of his or her birth. This child is most likely a Canadian citizen and as such, cannot be sponsored. You should instead apply for a proof of citizenship for him or her. See relevant information on our Web site or obtain the package *Application for a Citizenship Certificate (Proof of Citizenship)*. To apply outside of Canada, contact a Canadian Embassy, High Commission or Consulate.

Before submitting an application

Read all the information in this application kit. It will help you decide if you should apply.

See **What Happens Next?** to find out about factors that can affect the processing of your application.

The forms you must complete are listed in the section How to apply to sponsor.

If you have any questions after reading this application package, visit our Web site or phone our Call Centre.

Note: If the person you want to sponsor or his or her family members became permanent residents of Canada sometime in the past but have subsequently left the country and have since been living outside Canada, they may not have lost their permanent resident status. If they have not lost their permanent resident status, you will not be able to sponsor them. For further information on re-entry of permanent residents to Canada, see the application kit *Applying for a Travel Document* on our Web site.

SPONSORSHIP

What does it mean to "sponsor?"

When you sponsor persons who are members of the family class, you must sign an **undertaking** with the Minister of Citizenship and Immigration (or with the *ministère de l'Immigration et des Communautés culturelles* (MICC) if you live in Quebec), promising to provide financial support for their basic requirements and those of their family members immigrating to Canada with them. Basic requirements are food, clothing, shelter and other basic requirements for everyday living. Dental care, eye care and other health needs not covered by public health services are also included. The undertaking ensures these persons and their family members do not have to apply for social assistance. Its length varies according to their age and their relationship to you.

Your obligations as a sponsor begin as soon as the person you are sponsoring and, if applicable, his or her family members arrive in Canada. The following table shows when your obligations end.

If that person or his or her family member is	Your obligations end
• your spouse or your common-law or conjugal partner,	• **three years** after that person becomes a permanent resident;
• your dependent child or a dependent child of your spouse, common-law or conjugal partner, who is under 22 years of age on the day he or she becomes a permanent resident,	• **ten years** after that child becomes a permanent resident or on the day that child reaches **age 25**, whichever comes first;
• your dependent child or a dependent child of your spouse, common-law or conjugal partner, who is 22 years of age or over on the day he or she becomes a permanent resident,	• **three years** after that child becomes a permanent resident;
• any other person (for example, your father, your mother, your grandparents or a dependent child of your parents).	• **ten years** after that person becomes a permanent resident.

Note: An immigrant who comes to Canada to live permanently does not become a permanent resident before having satisfied immigration officials that he or she meets all applicable requirements. The decision to grant permanent residence to an immigrant may coincide with that immigrant's arrival in Canada or may be reached at a later date.

If payments from a federal, provincial or municipal assistance program are made during the validity period of the undertaking to the person you are sponsoring or his or her family members, you

- will be considered to be in default of your obligations,
- may have to repay to the government concerned any benefits they received, and
- will not be allowed to sponsor other members of the family class until you have reimbursed the amount of these payments to the government concerned.

If you live in Quebec and the person you want to sponsor intends to live there upon arrival, make sure you read the information concerning **Sponsors Living in Quebec**.

Whom can you sponsor using this application package?

You can use this application package to sponsor

- your mother or father;
- your grandmother or grandfather;
- a child whom you adopted outside Canada and you were a Canadian citizen or permanent resident living in Canada at the time the adoption took place, or a child whom you intend to adopt in Canada;
  (See Appendix A for additional information on adoptions)
- your brother or sister, nephew or niece, grandson or granddaughter, if he or she is an orphan, under 18 years of age and not married or in a common-law relationship;

- any other person with whom you have a family relationship if you do not have a spouse, common-law partner, conjugal partner, son, daughter, mother, father, brother, sister, grandfather, grandmother, uncle, aunt, niece or nephew who is a Canadian citizen, registered Indian or permanent resident or whom you may sponsor. If you believe you are in this situation, contact our Call Centre.

If you want to sponsor your spouse, common-law partner or conjugal partner and your dependent children, you will have to use another application package. Contact our Call Centre, or visit our Web site for more information.

Who is a dependent child?

Your child or a child of the person you are sponsoring will be considered a dependent child if that child

A. is under the age of 22 and not married or in a common-law relationship; **or**

B. married or entered into a common-law relationship before the age 22 and, since becoming a spouse or a common-law partner, has

- been continuously enrolled and in attendance as a full-time student in a post secondary institution accredited by the relevant government authority and
- depended substantially on the financial support of a parent; **or**

is 22 years of age or older and, since before the age of 22, has

- been continuously enrolled and in attendance as a full-time student in a post secondary institution accredited by the relevant government authority and
- depended substantially on the financial support of a parent; **or**

C. is 22 years of age or older, has depended substantially on the financial support of a parent since before the age of 22 and is unable to provide for himself or herself due to a medical condition.

Dependent children must meet the above requirements both on the day the Case Processing Centre in Mississauga (CPC-M), Ontario, receives a complete application and, without taking into account whether they have attained 22 years of age, on the day a visa is issued to them.

All family members of a would-be immigrant, whether accompanying or not, must be examined. If you previously made an application for permanent residence and became a permanent resident of Canada, your family members who were not examined in accordance with Canadian Immigration Regulations at the time you made your application, are excluded from the family class and you may not sponsor them.

What special condition must be met by persons sponsoring an adopted child, a child to be adopted in Canada or an orphaned relative?

If you are sponsoring

- a child you have adopted or are in the process of adopting outside Canada and you were or are living in Canada at the time the adoption took/takes place, or
- a child you intend to adopt in Canada, or
- an orphaned brother, sister, nephew or niece described in Whom can you sponsor using this application package?,

you will have to satisfy the visa office that you have obtained good and reliable information about the child's health status before a permanent resident visa can be issued to that child. You may obtain this information from authorities in the country of adoption, through an independent medical examination or from the child's immigration medical record. Once you have obtained the information with respect to the child's medical condition, read the *Medical Condition Statement* provided in Appendix A, complete the bottom portion, sign it and send it to the visa office processing the permanent residence application submitted on behalf of the child.

Who can sponsor?

You may be eligible to sponsor if:

- the person you want to sponsor is a member of the family class;

  Note: If that person is not a member of the family class, you will not meet sponsorship requirements and, therefore, your application to sponsor will not be approved and the application for permanent residence of the person you want to sponsor will be refused, unless you decide to withdraw your sponsorship application. If you withdraw the sponsorship, you will have no appeal rights.

- you are 18 years of age or older;
- you are a Canadian citizen or permanent resident;
- you live in Canada;
- you sign an undertaking promising to provide for the basic requirements of the person being sponsored and, if applicable, his or her family members;
- you and the sponsored person sign an agreement that confirms that each of you understands your mutual obligations and responsibilities;

If you live in Quebec, see Step 2 of How to apply to sponsor for additional information on forms to complete.

- you have an income that is at least equal to the minimum necessary income, the amount of which is published yearly by the Canadian government. You will have to provide us with documents that show your financial resources for the past 12 months and prove you are financially able to sponsor members of the family class. You may solicit the help of a co-signer. If you live in Quebec, see also Sponsors living in Quebec.

Note: The minimum necessary income requirement does not apply if the person you are sponsoring is a child you adopted or intend to adopt in Canada and that child has no children of his or her own.

Who cannot sponsor?

You are not eligible to sponsor if you are in default of a previous sponsorship undertaking, of an immigration loan, of court ordered support payment obligations or of a performance bond (an amount you agreed to pay as a guarantee of performance of an obligation under the immigration legislation).

Default of a previous sponsorship undertaking means persons you sponsored in the past have received social assistance during the validity period of the undertaking.

Default of an immigration loan means you received a transportation, assistance or Right of Permanent Residence (previously Right of Landing) Fee loan and have not made a required payment or are in arrears with your loan payments.

Default of any court ordered support payment obligations means you were ordered by a court to make support payments to your spouse, common-law partner or child and have neglected to do so.

Default of a performance bond means you have not paid the sum of money that became payable to the Canadian government following a promise you made to pay this sum if the person specified in the performance bond that you signed or co-signed did not comply with the conditions imposed on him or her by immigration authorities.

If you are in default of a previous sponsorship, of an immigration loan, of court ordered support payment obligations or of a performance bond and you submit an application to sponsor, it will be refused even if you are sponsoring your spouse, common-law partner, conjugal partner, or child. Should you want to sponsor again, you will have to

- repay the full amount of any social assistance payment or repay the debt to the satisfaction of the provincial, territorial or municipal authorities that issued the benefit or ordered you to pay, if you are in default of a previous sponsorship,

  pay all arrears on your loan, if you are in default of an immigration loan,

  resolve the family support matter to the satisfaction of the provincial or territorial authorities who ordered the payment, or

  pay any outstanding bonds for which you are a signer or a co-signer and that became payable;

- submit a new sponsorship application;
- pay new processing fees; and
- meet all the eligibility requirements for sponsorship at that time.

For information on social assistance repayments, contact the appropriate provincial authorities (see Table 1).

For information on your loan account only, contact Collection Services at 1-800-667-7301 (this number may be accessed from within Canada and the United States only).

You cannot sponsor a person for whom you have submitted a previous sponsorship application and no final determination has been made with respect to that application.

You are ineligible to sponsor if:

- you are in prison;
- you are an undischarged bankrupt;
- you are in receipt of social assistance for a reason other than disability;
- you were convicted of a sexual offence or an offence against the person with respect to
  - one of your family members or relatives,
  - one of your spouse's or common-law partner's family members or relatives,
  - your conjugal partner or one of your conjugal partner's family members or relatives,

  if applicable, unless you were granted a pardon or five years have passed after the expiration of the sentence imposed on you;
- you were adopted outside Canada and subsequently obtained a revocation of your adoption for the purpose of sponsoring an application for permanent residence by your biological parent;
- you are subject to a removal order; or
- have been convicted of a serious criminal offence, have provided false information to Immigration, or have not met conditions of entry.

Under what circumstances may processing be suspended?

If any of the proceedings below apply to you and you send a sponsorship application, your application will not be processed until a final decision is rendered with respect to that proceeding.

- You have been charged with the commission of an offence that is punishable by a maximum term of imprisonment of at least 10 years.
- You are subject of a report that would render you inadmissible to Canada.

- You are the subject of an application to revoke your citizenship.
- You are the subject of a certificate signed by the Minister of Citizenship and Immigration and the Solicitor General of Canada stating you are inadmissible on grounds of security, human or international rights violation, serious criminality or organized criminality.
- You are appealing the loss of your permanent resident status.

Can someone co-sign your undertaking?

Your spouse or common-law partner may help you meet the income requirement by co-signing the sponsorship application. A common-law partner is a person who is living with you in a conjugal relationship and has done so for at least one year prior to the signing of the **undertaking**.

The co-signer must:

- meet the same eligibility requirements as the sponsor;
- agree to co-sign the undertaking; and
- agree to be responsible for the basic requirements of the person you want to sponsor and his or her family members for the validity period of the undertaking.

The co-signer will be equally liable if obligations are not performed.

Assets, potential earnings, or assistance from other family members will not be considered.

Sponsors Living in Quebec

An agreement reached between the federal and Quebec governments gives the province responsibility for determining whether or not sponsors living in Quebec have the financial ability to sponsor members of the family class.

Sponsors living in Quebec must read the information and follow the general instructions in this application kit. However, they only have to complete those forms specified in Step 1 of the section titled How to apply to sponsor. The Quebec government will send them other documents to complete, including an undertaking form (*Formulaire d'engagement*). Quebec residents will also have to pay the Quebec government the fees it charges to process the undertaking they submit to the *ministère de l'Immigration et des Communautés culturelles* (MICC).

If Quebec residents want to sponsor a member of the family class other than their spouse, common-law partner, conjugal partner or their dependent children who have no dependent children of their own, they and, if applicable, their co-signer will have to prove to the provincial immigration authorities (MICC) that they have sufficient income over the last 12 months to provide for the basic requirements of:

- themselves;
- their family members in Canada or elsewhere;
- the person they are sponsoring and his or her family members, whether or not they are coming to Canada; and,
- the persons for whom they and, if applicable, their co-signer have signed a previous undertaking that is still in effect.

The MICC may refuse Quebec residents as sponsors if:

- they or their co-signer, if applicable, have failed to fulfil the obligations of a previous undertaking because the person they sponsored received last-resort benefits (social assistance) or special benefits and they have not reimbursed the Quebec government all amounts owing;
- during the five years preceding the submission of their application to sponsor, they or their co-signer, if applicable, have failed to meet their support payment obligations;
- they cannot demonstrate their financial capability to sponsor;

- they do not meet other requirements imposed by the provincial authorities.

To help Quebec residents decide if they have the financial ability to meet sponsorship requirements, we are providing the Quebec Income Scale (see Table 2) at the end of this application kit.These amounts are indexed each year. Note that any calculation will only be an estimate since an MICC employee will make the official financial assessment.

For further information on Quebec's requirements, contact your nearest MICC regional office

Frequently Asked Questions (Family Class)

The information given here relates to questions most often asked by applicants on topics not covered elsewhere in this application kit. Share it with the person you want to sponsor as he or she could have similar concerns.

Can I cancel my undertaking once it has been approved?

If you change your mind about sponsoring your parents, grandparents, adopted children or other relatives, you must write a letter to the Case Processing Centre in Mississauga **before** they are issued permanent resident visas (see **What happens next** for information on the application process).

Once permanent resident visas are issued, the promise you, and if applicable, your co-signer, made to support your family is valid for the term of your undertaking.

> The undertaking is an unconditional promise of support. For example, the granting of Canadian citizenship, divorce, separation or relationship breakdown or moving to another province does not cancel the undertaking. The undertaking also remains in effect if your financial situation deteriorates.

When does default end?

If you are in default because a person you sponsored received social assistance during the validity period of the undertaking and you have not reimbursed the government concerned for the amount paid to the sponsored person or because you failed to meet an obligation in an undertaking, you remain in default, regardless of when the period of validity ends, until such time as you

- reimburse the government concerned, in full or in accordance with an agreement with that government, for amounts paid by it, or
- meet the obligations set out in the undertaking.

If I live outside Canada, can I sponsor?

If you are not a Canadian citizen, you cannot sponsor if you live outside Canada. If you are a Canadian citizen, you may sponsor a spouse, a common-law or conjugal partner, or a dependent child who has no dependent child of his or her own. If this is your situation, obtain the application package **Sponsorship of a spouse, common-law partner, conjugal partner or dependent child living outside Canada**. You must live in Canada when the sponsored person becomes a permanent resident.

What if I do not meet sponsorship requirements?

If it is your intent to withdraw your sponsorship application in the event we assess that you are ineligible to sponsor, you must notify the Case Processing Centre in Mississauga of your intent before the visa office begins to process the application for permanent residence of the person you want to sponsor. If you do not, you will not be eligible for a refund of your processing fees. You can notify us of your intent by checking the appropriate box on your application form (IMM 1344A). See instructions on how to complete the *Application to Sponsor and Undertaking* for additional details.

If you do not qualify as a sponsor and chose to withdraw your sponsorship application, you will be refunded the fees for processing the application for a permanent resident visa and any Right of Permanent Residence Fee you have paid. There will be no decision on the application for permanent residence of the person you are sponsoring and you will not have a right of appeal. You could then resolve the situation leading to your ineligibility and re-apply at a later date.

If you do not qualify as a sponsor and have not notified the Case Processing Centre in Mississauga of your intent to withdraw, the application of the person you are sponsoring will be processed. The visa office will likely refuse the application for permanent residence and inform you in writing of your right to appeal.

Why might the application for permanent residence of the person I want to sponsor be refused?

There are many possible reasons why an application for permanent residence might be refused. Some examples are:

- you may not meet the financial requirements where these are applicable;
- the person you want to sponsor or his or her family members may not have provided the required documents as requested;
- the relationship between you and the person you want to sponsor or his or her family members is not genuine or has been entered into for immigration purposes only; or
- the person you want to sponsor or his or her family members have a criminal record or serious illness.

See What happens next? for a list of factors that can slow down processing of applications.

What if the application of the person I want to sponsor is refused?

If the person you want to sponsor is not a member of the family class, his or her application for permanent residence will be refused.

If the person you want to sponsor does not meet the eligibility requirements or admissibility criteria for the family class, his or her application will be refused. The visa office will inform him or her of the reasons for the refusal and you will have the right to appeal the decision.

How to Apply to Sponsor

You must complete separate applications for each person you want to sponsor. Each application may include that person's family members. A family member, in relation to the person being sponsored, means the spouse or common-law partner of that person and the dependent child or grandchild of that person or of his or her spouse or common-law partner. For example, if you want to sponsor your two orphan brothers, you must complete a separate application for each of your brothers; if you want to sponsor your parents and your grandmother, you must complete one application for your parents and another for your grandmother. The application for your parents would identify one of your parents as the person being sponsored (principal applicant) and the other parent as his or her family member. The application for your grandmother or the application for each of your brothers would show each individual as the person being sponsored.

You must send your sponsorship application along with all required documentation to CPC-M (see Mailing your application), and pay the applicable fees. If the forms and supporting documents received are incomplete, they will be returned to you. If they are complete, we will assess your eligibility to sponsor and notify you of the results. We will also send you an application kit with forms to be completed by the person you want to sponsor and his or her family members. See What happens next? for more information.

If you think you are eligible to sponsor and wish to support the immigration application of your parent, grandparent, adopted child or of a relative who is a member of the family class, carefully read the following instructions.

STEP 1. There is only one copy of each of the forms included for the sponsorship application. Make enough photocopies of the blank forms for your needs.

If you live in a province or territory other than Quebec, you must complete the following forms:

- the *Application to Sponsor and Undertaking* (IMM 1344A);
- the *Sponsorship Agreement* (IMM 1344B; must also be signed by the person you want to sponsor). See instructions on how to complete the Sponsorship Agreement for more details;
- the *Financial Evaluation* (IMM 1283);
- the *Statutory Declaration of Common-law Union* (IMM 5409), to be completed only if you have a co-signer and he or she is your common-law partner;
- the *Receipt* (IMM 5401 – see section on fees);
- the *Checklist* (IMM 5287); and
- the *Use of a Representative* form (IMM 5476), if you choose to have a representative.

If you live in Quebec, you need only complete:

- the *Application to sponsor and Undertaking* (IMM 1344A);

> We will send a copy of your IMM 1344A to the MICC in Quebec, who will send you additional documents to complete, including a *Formulaire d'engagement* (a separate undertaking form). The MICC will provide you with all necessary instructions (for more information, see Sponsors living in Quebec).

- the *Receipt* (IMM 5401 – see section on fees);
- the *Checklist* (IMM 5287); and
- the *Use of a Representative* form (IMM 5476), if you choose to have a representative.

STEP 2. If you live in a province or territory other than Quebec, send to the person you want to sponsor the *Sponsorship Agreement* (IMM 1344B) signed by you and, if applicable, your co-signer (see instructions on how to complete the Agreement). That person must read the form, sign it and return it to you.

STEP 3. Complete the forms as instructed in the following pages.

STEP 4. Collect the documents you need to support your application. The *Checklist* will tell you which supporting documents must be originals and which should be photocopies. It will also tell you which require translation and certification (notarization).

Use the *Checklist* to make sure that you have included all of the required documents. We may request more information at any time during the process, even if the requested information is not listed on the *Checklist*.

> Sponsors must pay all processing fees associated with their case to submit an application. See section on fees.
>
> All information and documents are required to assess applications correctly and quickly. If the documents received are incomplete, applications will be returned to sponsors to be resubmitted with missing documentation.

Mailing Your Application

Put your forms along with your receipt and all the supporting documentation in an envelope and mail it to:

Case Processing Centre – Mississauga
P.O. Box 6100, Station A
Mississauga ON L5A 4H4

If you are sponsoring an adopted child, print "**ADOPTION**" immediately above Case Processing Centre on the envelope.

The envelope will require more postage than a normal letter. To avoid having your application returned to you, have the post office weigh it before mailing.

Should you require confirmation that your application arrived at destination, contact your local postal outlet for information on various mailing options available to you.

Unless notified otherwise, advise us immediately, by mail at the address above or facsimile (905 803-7392) if, following the submission of your application, there are any changes to your family status such as marriage, divorce, births, deaths, your address, telephone or fax number, or any other important information. When advising the office of such changes, you must clearly state your file number, which will be found at the top of any correspondence we will send you to acknowledge the receipt of your application.

If you move

If your address changes after you have submitted your application, let us know immediately.

- **by e-mail**, using CIC's on-line service. Just go to CIC's Web site and follow the instructions for filling out and submitting the electronic change of address form; or
- **by telephone**, by contacting our Call Centre.

Sponsors who signed an "engagement" with the province of Quebec and subsequently move from Quebec to another province in Canada while their sponsorship application is in process must sign a new undertaking and agreement. Conversely, sponsors who signed an undertaking with the Minister of Citizenship and Immigration and subsequently move to Quebec from another province in Canada while their sponsorship application is in process must sign an "engagement" with the province of Quebec.

Completing the Sponsorship Forms

The following will help you (and, if applicable, your co-signer) fill in the sponsorship forms included with your application kit. Most questions on the forms are clear; instructions are provided only when necessary.

You must answer all questions. If you leave any sections blank, your application will be returned to you unprocessed. If any sections do not apply, write "**Not Applicable**".

Complete the forms in block letters. Make sure all information is clear and easy to read. Your answers must be written in either the English or French language, unless instructed otherwise. If the space provided on the forms is insufficient to list any

information, use an additional sheet of paper. Make sure you indicate the form's title and the number or letter of the question you are answering. Write your name and the page number at the top left corner of each additional sheet.

WARNING! You (and, if applicable, your co-signer) must provide complete and accurate information. The information provided may be verified. If you give false or misleading information, you could be guilty of misrepresentation and have to pay a fine of up to $100,000 and face the risk of being imprisoned for a term of up to five years. It is a serious offence to make a false application.

Application to Sponsor and Undertaking (IMM 1344A)

A – Sponsor

1. Indicate whether you want to withdraw your sponsorship application or continue processing if you do not meet the sponsorship requirements. If your choice is to withdraw your sponsorship, the application for permanent residence of the person you want to sponsor will not be processed and you will have no right of appeal. All fees you will have paid, except the sponsorship fee of $75, will be repaid to you.

If you choose to continue processing or fail to notify the Case Processing Centre in Mississauga of your intent to withdraw, the application for permanent residence of the person you want to sponsor will be forwarded to the visa office, where it will be refused. You will have the right to appeal the decision. You will not be entitled to a refund of the processing fees.

Indicate also your preferred language for correspondence and complete the rest of the question.

5. This may be a post office box, rural route number, or another mailing address. Include your apartment number if you have one and your postal code.

10. Indicate whether you are a citizen or a permanent resident of Canada. If you are a naturalized Canadian (that is, you came to Canada as a permanent resident and were later granted Canadian citizenship), write the date you became a Canadian citizen. If you are a permanent resident, write the date you became a permanent resident of Canada. The date is found in Box 45 of your *Immigrant Visa and Record of Landing* (IMM 1000) or of your *Confirmation of Permanent Residence* (IMM 5292).

11. If you are a naturalized Canadian citizen and no longer have your *Immigrant Visa and Record of Landing* (IMM 1000) or Confirmation of Permanent Residence (IMM 5292), print the name you used at the time you became a permanent resident.

B – Co-signer

Your spouse or common-law partner should complete this section **only** if he or she is co-signing the application.

8 and 9: Follow the instructions for both **10** and **11** of Section A above.

C – Person being sponsored and his or her family members

(Attach a separate sheet if you need more space.)

Do not write in the boxes provided for length of undertaking and ID number. These are for official use only.

1. Give the details of the principal applicant (the person you want to sponsor).

Make sure that you enter the principal applicant's country of nationality if it is different from his or her country of birth. If the principal applicant has no country of nationality (stateless), enter his or her country of habitual residence.

2. Give details of the accompanying spouse or common-law partner of the principal applicant if applicable; give details of the non accompanying spouse or common-law partner of the principal applicant, if applicable, in **4**.

3. If the principal applicant and, if applicable, his or her accompanying spouse or common-law partner have dependent children who will be accompanying them to Canada, give the details of these dependent children.

4. Give details of the non accompanying spouse or common-law partner of the principal applicant, if applicable.

   If the principal applicant and, if applicable, his or her spouse or common-law partner, whether accompanying the principal applicant to Canada or not, have dependent children who will not be accompanying them to Canada, give the details of these dependent children.

   Note that if the principal applicant, or a family member referred to in **3** or **4** is a dependent child, you must check box A, B or C, as applicable. See **Who is a dependent child** in the section titled Sponsorship for additional information.

Note that the principal applicant must indicate on the application for permanent residence whether his or her family members will accompany him or her to Canada. The visa office will not issue permanent resident visas to family members who were identified as non-accompanying.

6. Print the **full** address where the principal applicant lives in **a)**. Information you provide in **b)** and **c)** will help us determine which visa office will process the application for a permanent resident visa. Under Canadian immigration legislation, an application for a permanent resident visa must be made at the visa office responsible for:

   - the country where the applicant is living, if the applicant has been lawfully admitted to that country for a period of at least one year, or
   - the applicant's country of nationality, or
   - the applicant's country of habitual residence, if the applicant is stateless and has legal status in that country.

   The person you are sponsoring will have to provide evidence of his or her status in the country where he or she is living. Should that status change or expire before the visa office has completed the processing of the application, processing of the application will be completed in the office where it was submitted unless circumstances dictate otherwise. The person concerned will be notified in the event his or her case is referred to another visa office. Consult our Web site for additional information on visa office jurisdiction.

If the principal applicant is a young child, include the name of the person who will be looking after his or her mail.

7. Print the mailing address where we can reach the principal applicant, if this address is different from the one in **6a)**.

It is important that you give us a complete and correct address for the principal applicant or the application will be delayed.

D – Adoption

If you are sponsoring a child you have adopted while you were living in Canada or intend to adopt in Canada

- check the appropriate box. If the child is already adopted, you must provide documentary evidence that you are the legal adoptive parent. See the *Document Checklist*;
- write the child's country of residence, or if the child is not yet identified, the country where you intend to adopt a child.

E – Eligibility Assessment

This section must be completed by the sponsor (and, if applicable, the co-signer.) It will help determine if you are eligible to sponsor and if your spouse or common-law partner is eligible to co-sign the application.

Note: If you find you are not eligible to sponsor, **do not** send in your application because it will be refused.

4. You must live in Canada and continue to do so when the person you want to sponsor and his or her family members become permanent residents.

6. If you have declared bankruptcy, do not submit this application unless you have been discharged from the bankruptcy.

9. If you have been ordered to leave Canada, you will have received a written notice from us. If you are unsure if an outstanding order is in place, contact our Call Centre to ask about your status. If you answer "yes," do not submit your application.

11. You may not sponsor anyone if you are in a jail, prison, penitentiary or reformatory. It may be possible to sponsor if you are on parole, probation, or are serving a suspended sentence.

16. If you have been charged with an offence under an Act of Parliament punishable by a maximum term of imprisonment of at least ten years, you may send in your application; however, we will not process it until the courts have made a decision on your case. If you are convicted of a serious offence, the application may be refused.

F – Residency Declaration

Write "**Not Applicable**" in this section.

G – Undertaking

Read this section carefully. Similar provisions apply to Quebec residents who sign an undertaking with the province.

H – Authority to disclose personal information

In addition to the information you are required to provide, we may ask government authorities in all countries where you have lived to share personal information they possess on your behalf.

I – Declaration

Read these sections carefully before signing Section J. Ask and obtain an explanation on every point that is not clear to you.

J – Signature(s)

You and, if applicable, your co-signer must sign this form. If you do not, your entire application will be returned to you and it will cause delays in processing. Once the form is signed, it is a legal contract between you, your co-signer (if applicable) and the Minister of Citizenship and Immigration.

Sponsorship Agreement (IMM 1344B)

Quebec residents need not complete this form.

Read the form carefully. This form needs to be signed by you, your co-signer (if applicable) and the person you are sponsoring (the principal applicant). Follow these steps:

1. Read and sign the form.
2. Have your co-signer (if applicable) read and sign this form.
3. Send the form to the person you are sponsoring to read and sign.

   Note: No one can sign the agreement on behalf of the person you are sponsoring.

4. The person you are sponsoring will send it back to you. When you receive it, make two photocopies.
5. Give one photocopy to the person you are sponsoring and send one to us at the time you submit your sponsorship forms. Retain the original for your records.

An agreement is not required if the person you are sponsoring **is under 22.**

A permanent resident visa will not be issued to the person you wish to sponsor and his or her family members unless there is a completed agreement. If you do not include the agreement with your application, you can expect delays in processing.

Statutory Declaration of Common-Law Union (IMM 5409)

If you have a co-signer, complete this form only if you and your co-signer are in a common-law relationship. A common-law partner is a person of the opposite or same sex who is living with you in a conjugal relationship and has done so for at least one year prior to the signing of the *Undertaking*.

A Commissioner for Oaths must certify this document. Provincial laws govern who can act in this position. In general, Members of Legislative Assemblies (MLAs), judges, justices of the peace, and lawyers are authorized to take oaths. Check your phone book for listings.

Financial Evaluation (IMM 1283)

Quebec residents need not complete this form.

The *Financial Evaluation* form will help you assess if you (and your spouse or common-law partner, if he or she is co-signing the undertaking) will have the financial ability to support the persons you are planning to sponsor and their family members.

You must prove that you have an annual income that is at least equal to the minimum necessary income to support the group of persons consisting of

- yourself and your family members, whether they are living with you or not;

- the person you are sponsoring and his or her family members;
- every other person you have sponsored in the past and their family members, where an undertaking is still in effect or not yet in effect;
- every other person for whom you have co-signed an undertaking that is still in effect; and
- every person not mentioned above for whom your spouse or common-law partner has given or co-signed an undertaking that is still in effect or not yet in effect, if your spouse or common-law partner is co-signing your current sponsorship undertaking.

If you declared bankruptcy and are required to meet settlement arrangements, income earned during the period of the bankruptcy cannot be considered.

Note: If you are sponsoring an adopted child or a child to be adopted in Canada, and that child has no dependent child of his or her own, the minimum necessary income requirement does not apply. However, the information you provide on the *Financial Evaluation* form will help us assess your ability to fulfil the obligations in your sponsorship undertaking.

Co-signer

If your spouse or common-law partner is co-signing your sponsorship undertaking, make sure you complete questions **1.B** and **15** to **19**.

Social assistance

Social assistance means any benefit, whether money, goods or services, provided to or on behalf of a person by a province under a program of social assistance. It includes assistance for food, shelter, clothing, fuel, utilities, household supplies, personal requirements and health care not provided by public health care.

Family members and persons included in undertakings in effect or not yet in effect

The minimum income you will need to meet the requirements of your sponsorship undertaking is determined in part by the number of persons described in questions **2** to **6**. For each group described in questions **3** and **4**, enter the number of persons included in that group and give details of each person in the group as instructed on the form. We have already entered 1 in the box in question **2**. to account for yourself. If you have a spouse or common-law partner and he or she is not included in **3**, complete question **5**; provide details as required. Enter in **6** the number of your other family members not included in **2**, **3**, **4** or **5**; give details of each person in the group as instructed on the form. Read each description carefully. Add the numbers entered in each of the boxes provided for the number of persons in questions **2**, **3**, **4** and, if applicable, **5** and **6**; enter the total in the box provided at question **7**. This total and the low income cut-off table will help you determine the minimum amount you will need to sponsor.

Minimum necessary income

Refer to the low income cut-off table (**Table 4**) and go down the column until you come to the line that matches the number of people as determined in box **7**. This is the amount of income you must have to sponsor your relatives. Enter that amount in box **8**.

Your available income

Make sure you provide all the required information regarding the income you earned over the twelve months preceding the mailing of your application (questions **10** to **14**) and, if you have a co-signer, the income he or she earned over that same period (questions **15** to **19**).

Your available income is the amount of money you have earned in the period of 12 months preceding the date of your application, excluding any allowance or benefit of the type described in **12.B** below.

To calculate your available income, you will need a document called an "Option-C Printout." It is the equivalent of the last notice of assessment you would have received in respect of the most recent taxation year and will serve as a basis for the calculation of your income. This printout is issued by the Canada Revenue Agency (CRA, formerly CCRA) and you can obtain it free of charge from CRA by calling 1 800 959-8281. Your spouse or common-law partner will also have to obtain an "Option-C Printout" if he or she is co-signing the undertaking.

If you are unable to obtain and produce an "Option-C Printout" or if your income reported in this document is less than your minimum necessary income, you will need to provide documentation establishing the amount of income you earned over the period of 12 months preceding the date of your application, such as pay stubs, if you are employed; a statement of business of activities, if you are self-employed; bank statements, if you have received interest income; statements or certificates, if you have other sources of income (investment, rental, pension, special benefits paid under the Employment Insurance Act, etc.). Your spouse or common-law partner will need to provide similar documentation if he or she is co-signing the undertaking and does not produce an "Option-C Printout." or if the income reported on your spouse or common-law partner's "Option-C Printout" combined with your available income is less than your minimum necessary income.

The office processing your application may ask you for additional information and documentation if it is not satisfied you have provided sufficient evidence to sustain your income calculation.

To calculate your earned income, complete question **12** (calculation based on the "Option-C Printout") on the *Financial Evaluation* form with the help of the instructions below. If you are not producing an "Option-C Printout" or if your total income calculated as per question **12** of the *Financial Evaluation* form is less than your minimum necessary income, complete question **13** (calculation based on the preceding 12 months) on the *Financial Evaluation* form. The greater of the two amounts entered at **12.C** and **13.C** is your available income; enter this amount in box **14**.

If your spouse or common-law partner is co-signing the undertaking, you will have to complete question **17** (calculation based on the "Option-C Printout") and/or question **18** (calculation based on the preceding 12 months) to calculate his or her earned income. The greater of the two amounts entered at **17.C** and **18.C** will be your co-signer's available income; enter this amount in box **19**.

The total of boxes **14** and **19** will be the total income that is available to you to support your application to sponsor. This total must at least be equal to the amount of the minimum necessary income (see box **8**) you need to sponsor.

11. Your situation over the last 12 months

In the table in question **11**, complete the sections (A, B and C) which apply to your situation during the 12 months preceding the date of your application. If your situation changed during that period, in the Period I column, enter information on the most recent period and, in the next columns, enter information on the previous period(s), which make(s) up the rest of the 12 months preceding your application.

For each of the employers you worked for during the period of 12 months preceding the date of your application and from which you have received or will receive a T-4 slip, give details about your employment in section B, including your **personal employment income**. Personal employment income is defined as the gross income earned from your job(s) as reported to CRA from a T4.

If you were self-employed, give details about your business in section C, including your **personal business income**. Personal business income is defined as the net income earned (or loss incurred) and reported to CRA from activities conducted for profit from a sole proprietorship, partnership or unincorporated business. This would include professions, trades and businesses such as small retail outlets and restaurants. **Income from other personal self-employment endeavours** such as farming, fishing, commission sales, consulting and child care that are conducted for profit should also be included.

Be careful to indicate clearly the reference period (first line at the beginning of each section you complete). For example, if the date of your application was June 5, 2004, and you were self-employed during the 12 months preceding your application, you would complete section C in the Period I column, providing on the first line of that section the start (June 6, 2003) and the end (June 5, 2004) of the 12-month period. However, if you had been working for an employer for only six months, were self-employed for the two months before you were hired and, before that, were unemployed, you would first complete section B in the Period I column, indicating your employment information and, on the first line of that section, the date you were hired (December 1, 2003, for the purpose of our example) and the date of your application (June 5, 2004). Then you would complete section C in the Period II column, providing information about your self-employment and, on the first line of that section, the date that your activities started (September 28, 2003 for the purpose of our example) and ended (November 30, 2003). Lastly, you would complete section A in the Period III column, indicating income you earned from sources other than employment (for example, pension income or special benefits paid under the *Employment Insurance Act* – see questions 12 and 13 for details) and, on the first line of that section, the period during which you were unemployed (June 6, 2003, to September 27, 2003).

If you need additional space, provide details on a separate sheet.

12. Calculation of income based on the "Option-C Printout"

12.A — Print the amount that appears at line 150 of the last notice of assessment ("Option-C Printout") issued to you by CRA for the most recent taxation year.

12.B — Enter all of the following payments that were included in line 150 of your notice of assessment, add them up and print the total:

- **Provincial instruction or training allowance**;
- **Social assistance** paid by a province;
- **Employment insurance**: only maternity, parental and sickness benefits paid under the *Employment Insurance Act* are considered income. Other payments such a employment insurance and federal training allowances are **not** considered as income; and
- **Guaranteed income supplement** paid under the *Old Age Security Act*.

12.C — Deduct the total entered at **12.B** (line 6) from the amount at **12.A** (line 1). The result **12.C** is your total income as per the simplified method of calculation.

13. Calculation of income based on the preceding 12 months

Complete question **13** if

- you cannot produce a notice of assessment ("Option-C Printout") for the most recent taxation year preceding the date of your application to sponsor, or
- you can produce a notice of assessment, but the amount at line 150 is less than the minimum necessary income (see definition above) and your financial circumstances have improved since you received the notice of assessment.

13.A — Personal income from employment, business and self-employment

Add all personal income from employment, business and other self-employment earned in the 12 months preceding the date of your application to sponsor, as instructed. Enter the result on line 5 in section **13.A**.

13.B — Other income

Calculate income that you received from other sources. Use the following definitions:

- **Net rental income:** net income earned (or loss incurred) and reported to CRA from rental property.
- **Investment and interest income:** income reported to and accepted by CRA from dividend payments, interest, stocks, bonds and other investments, and interest on savings deposits.
- **Pension income:** income from Old Age Security, Canada or Quebec Pension Plan, other pensions, superannuation and annuity payments from Canadian sources. Do not include Guaranteed Income Supplement (GIS) payments.
- **Maternity, parental and sickness benefits:** only maternity, parental and sickness benefits paid under the *Employment Insurance Act* are considered income. Other payments such as employment insurance and federal training allowances are not considered as income.

Other sources of income: include income you have received and will continue to receive on a regular basis that is not included above (for example, spousal, child support). Specify the source of the income on the form.

You cannot include provincial instruction and training allowances, social assistance, child tax benefits, guaranteed income supplement or employment insurance payments.

Add all income received from other sources and enter the result on line 11 in section **13.B**.

13.C — Add the totals entered at **13.A** (line 5) and **13.B** (line 11). The result **13.C** is your total income as per this method of calculation.

Your available income (box **14**) is the greater of the two amounts entered in boxes **12.C** and **13.C.**

Income available to your spouse or common-law partner, if he or she is a co-signer

Complete questions **15** and **16** if your spouse or common-law partner is co-signing the sponsorship undertaking. Print the required employer or, if self-employed, the business or professional information.You must also complete the calculation based on the "Option-C Printout" (question **17**) and/or the preceding 12 months (question **18**) to determine the income your co-signer earned and that can be added to your available income if you need help to meet the financial requirement.

16. Your co-signer's situation over the last 12 months

Complete the sections (A, B and C) which apply to your co-signer's situation during the 12 months preceding the date of your application. If your co-signer's situation changed during that period, in the Period I column, enter information on the most recent period and, in the next columns, enter information on the previous period(s), which make(s) up the rest of the 12 months preceding your application.

Refer to instructions for question 11 to help you complete question 16.

Note that if during any period in the 12 months preceding your application your co-signer was unemployed, the income he or she received from sources other than employment (for example, pension income or special benefits paid under the *Employment Insurance Act*) should be entered in section A.

If you need additional space, provide details on a separate sheet.

17. Calculation of income based on the "Option-C Printout"

17.A — Print the amount that appears at line 150 of the last notice of assessment ("Option-C Printout") issued to your spouse or common-law partner by CRA for the most recent taxation year.

17.B — Enter described payments that were included in line 150 of your spouse's or common-law partner's notice of assessment, add them up and print the total.

17.C — Deduct the total entered at **17.B** (line 6) from the amount at **17.A** (line 1). The result **17.C** is the total income your spouse or common-law partner can contribute as per this method of calculation.

18. Calculation of income based on the preceding 12 months

Complete question 18 if

- your co-signer cannot produce a notice of assessment ("Option-C Printout") for the most recent taxation year preceding the date of your application to sponsor, or
- his or her financial circumstances have improved since he or she received the notice of assessment.

18.A — Personal income from employment, business and self-employment
Add all personal income from employment, business and other self-employment your co-signer earned in the 12 months preceding the date of your application to sponsor, as instructed. Enter the result on line 5 in section **18.A**.

18.B — Other income
Calculate income that your co-signer received from other sources. Use definitions in question **13.B** to help you complete question **18.B**.

Add the totals entered at **18.A** (line 5) and **18.B** (line 11). The result **18.C** is the total income of your spouse or common-law partner as per this method of calculation.

The available income of your spouse or common-law partner (box **19**) is the greater of the two amounts entered in boxes **17.C** and **18.C**.

Total income available to sponsor

Add the amounts in boxes **14** and **19** and enter the total in box **9**, on page 1 of the form. This is the amount of money that you (and, if applicable, your co-signer) have available to sponsor.

Document Checklist (IMM 5287)

The *Document Checklist* is a reference list that helps ensure that you attach all required documents to your sponsorship application. If documentation is missing, your application will be returned to you.

Enclose the *Document Checklist* with your application.

Use of a Representative (IMM 5476)

Complete this form if you are appointing a representative.

If you have dependent children aged 18 years or older, they are required to complete their own copy of this form if a representative is also conducting business on their behalf.

A **representative** is someone who has your permission to conduct business on your behalf with Citizenship and Immigration Canada. When you appoint a representative, you also authorize CIC to share information from your case file with this person.

You are not obliged to hire a representative. We treat everyone equally, whether they use the services of a representative or not. If you choose to hire a representative, your application will not be given special attention nor can you expect faster processing or a more favourable outcome.

The representative you appoint is authorized to represent you only on matters related to the application you submit with this form. You can appoint only **one** representative for each application you submit.

There are two types of representatives:

Unpaid representatives

- friends and family members who do not charge a fee for their advice and services
- organizations that do not charge a fee for providing immigration advice or assistance (such as a non-governmental or religious organization)
- consultants, lawyers and Québec notaries who do not, and will not, charge a fee to represent you

Paid representatives

If you want us to conduct business with a representative who is, or will be charging a fee to represent you, he or she must be authorized. Authorized representatives are:

- immigration consultants who are members in good standing of the Canadian Society of Immigration Consultants (CSIC)
- lawyers who are members in good standing of a Canadian provincial or territorial law society and students-at-law under their supervision
- notaries who are members in good standing of the *Chambre des notaires du Québec* and students-at-law under their supervision

If you appoint a paid representative who is not a member of one of these designated bodies, your application will be returned. For more information on using a representative, visit our Web site.

Section B.

5. Your representative's full name

If your representative is a member of CSIC, a law society or the *Chambre des notaires du Québec*, print his or her name as it appears on the organization's membership list.

8. Your representative's declaration

Your representative must sign to accept responsibility for conducting business on your behalf.

Section D.

10. Your declaration

By signing, you authorize us to complete your request for yourself and your dependent children under 18 years of age. If your spouse or common-law partner is included in this request, he or she must sign in the box provided.

Release of information to other individuals

To authorize CIC to release information from your case file to someone other than a representative, you will need to complete form *Authority to Release Personal Information to a Designated Individual* (IMM 5475) which is available on our Web site and from Canadian embassies, high commissions and consulates abroad.

The person you designate will be able to obtain information on your case file, such as the status of your application. However, he or she will **not** be able to conduct business on your behalf with CIC.

You must notify us if your representative's contact information changes or if you cancel the appointment of a representative.

Fees

You must pay the following **processing fees** when you submit your sponsorship application:

- $75 for the sponsor;
- $475 for a principal applicant (the person being sponsored) who is 22 years of age or older, or who is married or in a common-law relationship, regardless of age;
- $75 for a principal applicant who is under 22 years of age and **not** married or in a common-law relationship;
- $550 for each accompanying family member who is 22 years of age or older, or who is married or in a common-law relationship, regardless of age; and
- $150 for each accompanying family member who is under 22 years of age and not married or in a common-law relationship.

Calculate your fees

Processing Fees	**Number of Persons**	**Amount per Person**	**Amount Due**
Sponsor, per application			$75
Principal applicant who is 22 years of age or older, or who is a spouse, common-law partner, regardless of his or her age. Number of persons must be 0 or 1.		x $475	
Principal applicant who is under 22 years of age and not a spouse, common-law partner partner. Number of persons must be 0 or 1.		x $75	
Accompanying family member of sponsored person, who is 22 years of age or older or a spouse or common-law partner, regardless of his/her age.		x $550	
Accompanying family member of sponsored person, who is under 22 years of age and not a spouse or common-law partner.		x$150	
Total right column			**$**

Right of Permanent Residence Fee

You will need to pay the **Right of Permanent Residence Fee** before the application for permanent residence of the person you want to sponsor can be finalized. **We will send you a request to pay this fee** when we are ready to issue the permanent resident visa. The fee is $490 per person for the principal applicant and each accompanying family member.

Exemptions

The following people are exempt from the Right of Permanent Residence Fee:

- your dependent children
- the dependent children of the principal applicant
- a child you are adopting
- your orphaned brother, sister, nephew, niece or grandchild

Do not send cash, personal cheques, bank drafts or money orders unless instructed otherwise.

How to pay your fees if you live in Canada

You have the option of paying your fees on our Web site or at a financial institution.

Option 1. **Payment of fees on our Web site**

To use this option, you need a credit card and access to a computer with a printer.

Go to our Web site at **www.cic.gc.ca** and select "**On-Line Services**" from the menu bar at the top, then "Payment of fees through the Internet".

Once you have paid the fees, you must print the official receipt and fill out by hand the "Payer Information" section. Attach the bottom portion (copy 2) of this receipt to your completed application.

Option 2. **Payment of fees at a financial institution**

STEP 1. Fill in the total

Enter the "Amount payable" you have calculated at the bottom of the *Receipt* (IMM 5401).

Photocopies of the receipt are not accepted. If you need an original receipt, order it from our Web site or contact the Call Centre.

STEP 2. Complete the "Payer Information" sections on the back of the receipt

If you already know the Client ID assigned to you, enter the number in the box provided. If you do not know your Client ID, leave that box empty.

STEP 3. Go to a financial institution and make the payment

Bring the receipt with you. A financial institution representative will tell you which forms of payment are acceptable. There is no charge for the service.

STEP 4. Send your receipt

Attach the middle portion (Copy 2) of the receipt to your completed application. Keep the top portion (Copy 1) for your files.

Do not include any other type of payment with your application.

Are the processing fees refundable?

Processing fees are fully refundable only if, before an officer starts assessing your eligibility to sponsor, you notify CPC-M in writing not to assess your sponsorship application. Processing fees are partially refundable if CPC-M determines you are ineligible to sponsor and you have notified the Case Processing Centre in Mississauga not to process the application for permanent residence of the person you want to sponsor (see **What if I do not meet sponsorship requirements?**). The amount refunded will be equal to the amount you have paid less $75. Once processing has started on the permanent residence application by the visa office, you will not be entitled to any refund of the processing fees.

After reading this application kit, you should be able to decide whether you are eligible to sponsor a member of the family class and what information and documentation is required for the application to be approved. Make sure that you are eligible before you pay your fees and that you provide all the information requested before you send the applications to CPC-M for processing.

What if you make an incorrect payment?

If you are required to pay additional fees and you live in Canada, CPC-M will send your application back to you and inform you of the amount outstanding. Pay the fees as instructed above and return the whole application to the Case Processing Centre in Mississauga.

The processing of your application will not begin before you have paid all applicable fees.

If the amount you have paid is greater than what you owe, your application will be processed and the overpayment will be refunded to you. If you are entitled to a refund, you should receive it four to six weeks after CPC-M has completed the refund request.

What Happens Next?

What happens with your application at the Case Processing Centre?

The application you send is verified for completeness. If it is complete, an officer will assess whether you meet the sponsorship requirements or not. If you need to provide additional documents or pay additional fees, your application will be returned to you with a letter asking you to provide the missing information or fees.

If you live in Quebec, we will inform the MICC of your application. The provincial authorities will send you additional information and instructions regarding the assessment of your financial situation, if applicable. After you have completed the required forms and provided the supporting documents, the MICC will let you and the visa office responsible for processing the application of the person you want to sponsor know whether your undertaking has been accepted or refused.

We will inform you of the results of its assessment of your sponsorship application and send you *The Immigrant's Guide* for sponsored parents, grandparents, adopted children and other relatives with the related forms. If your application to sponsor is approved, you will have to send the guide and forms to the person you want to sponsor.

If you fail to meet the sponsorship requirements, we will inform you of the results of the assessment and will refund part of the processing fees you paid, provided you have indicated that this is your wish on your application to sponsor (form IMM 1344A) and, if you are a Quebec resident and MICC refuses your undertaking, you follow the instructions CPC-M will give you. The application of the person you are sponsoring will not be processed. You will not have a right of appeal.

In the event you do not meet the sponsorship requirements, the application of the person you are sponsoring will be processed by a Canadian visa office when it is received if you have not indicated on the IMM 1344A your choice for a partial refund. You will not be entitled to a partial refund of the processing fees once processing of the application for permanent residence has begun.

What will the person you want to sponsor have to do?

He or she will have to:

- sign the *Agreement* (form IMM 1344B);
- complete the forms included with *The Immigrant's Guide* for sponsored parents, grandparents, adopted children and other relatives, and send them with the required documentation to the visa office that will be processing his or her application;
- go for an interview at a Canadian visa office;
- undergo a medical examination (results of the medical examination are valid for 12 months). The visa office will send the person you are sponsoring and his or her family members instructions on how to proceed;

  Note: It is the responsibility of the person being sponsored and of his or her family members to pay the costs of their medical examination.
- pass criminal and security checks; and
- obtain passports and, in some countries, exit visas.

The person you want to sponsor and his or her family members should not quit their jobs or sell their assets until they have their permanent resident visas.

What happens to the sponsorship and permanent residence applications if you submit an application for someone who is not sponsorable or is excluded as a member of the family class?

We will note that you fail to meet the requirements for a sponsorship as your sponsorship application has been submitted on behalf of someone who is not a member of the family class. If you have indicated that you wish to withdraw the sponsorship, all processing fees except the sponsorship fee ($75) will be returned to you. If you wish to have the application for permanent residence processed by a visa office, the visa office will refuse the family class application as there is no valid sponsorship and it was not submitted on behalf of someone who is a member of the family class. You will not be eligible for any refund of fees if the application is sent to the visa office.

Whether you choose to withdraw the sponsorship or have the application for permanent residence processed by the visa office, you will not have appeal rights as the application was not submitted on behalf of a member of the family class.

What happens with the application for permanent residence of the person you want to sponsor at the visa office?

The visa office will review the application and supporting documentation to assess the eligibility of the person you want to sponsor as a member of the family class and his or her admissibility as an immigrant to Canada. It will contact them to let them know if they need to provide additional supporting documents or be interviewed. The visa office will make a final decision to either approve or refuse the application for permanent residence.

If the application is refused, both the person you want to sponsor and yourself will be informed in writing of the reasons for the refusal. You will be notified of your rights to appeal and be provided with the instructions to commence an appeal, should you decide to do so.

What if you have a co-signer and he or she withdraws his or her financial support?

If your spouse or common-law partner withdraws support for the sponsorship application, you or your spouse or common-law partner must write a letter to CPC-M and the visa office **before** permanent resident visas are issued to the person you are sponsoring and his or her family members. You must include an amended copy of the sponsorship application and of the agreement, initialled by you and your co-signer, removing the co-signer's support. We will assess your financial situation to see if you have enough money to support your family without a co-signer. If you do not meet the financial requirements on your own, the application for permanent residence will be refused.

What factors can slow down processing?

Here is a list of common factors that can slow down the processing of your application.

- Incomplete or unsigned application forms
- Incorrect, incomplete address or failure to notify CPC-M of a change of address
- Missing documents
- Unclear photocopies of documents
- Documents not accompanied by a certified English or French translation
- Investigation of sponsors by CIC
- Verification of information and documents provided (for example, there may be lengthy procedures for background checks in the countries where the sponsored person and his or her family members have lived or need for a second interview for additional background screening)
- A medical condition that may require additional tests or consultations
- A criminal or security problem (for example, failure to declare family members or criminal charges pending)

- Family situations such as impending divorce, custody or maintenance issues
- Completion of legal adoption
- Consultation is required with other offices in Canada and abroad
- Inquiring about the status of your application before the standard processing time has elapsed
- The sponsored person is not a permanent resident of the country in which he or she currently lives
- The sponsored person or his or her family members require an interview and live in an area not regularly visited by Immigration officials
- Photos provided by the sponsored person and his or her family members do not comply with specifications set out in Appendix C accompanying the immigrant's guide

If your case is not routine, we may not be able to process your application within the regular service standards for routine cases. Consult our Web site for additional information on processing times.

Checking your application status

You can find out the current status of your application by logging on to e-Client Application Status. You may also phone our Call Centre.

If you do not want your information available on-line, you can remove on-line information by logging on to e-Client Application Status. You may also call our Call Centre and ask an agent to do this for you.

Current processing times are updated weekly.

Table -1 International Adoption Authorities in Canada

Provincial offices listed below will **only** provide information on how to repay money for DEFAULTS on previous sponsorships.

Sponsors wishing information about **other** immigration issues must contact our Call Centre.

Government of Canada
Human Resources Development Canada
Inter-country Adoption Services Unit
Child, Family and Community Division
Tel.: (819) 997-1562
Fax: (819) 953-1115
http://www.hrdc-drhc.gc.ca/hrib/sdd-dds/cfc/content/interAdopt.shtml

Alberta
Alberta Children's Services
Program Manager, Adoption Services
Tel.: (780) 422-5641
Fax: (780) 427-2048
http://www.child.gov.ab.ca/whatwedo/adoption

British Columbia
Ministry for Children and Families
Adoption Branch
Tel.: (250) 387-3660
Fax: (250) 356-1864
http://www.mcf.gov.bc.ca/adoption

Manitoba
Manitoba Family Services
Child and Family Services
Intercountry Adoptions Specialist
Tel.: (204) 945-6964
Fax: (204) 945-6717
http://www.gov.mb.ca

New Brunswick
Family and Community Services
Adoption Consultant
Tel.: (506) 444-5970
Fax: (506) 453-2082
http://www.gov.nb.ca

Newfoundland
Department of Health and Community Services
Director of Child, Youth Policy and Programs Services Branch
Tel.: (709) 729-6721
Fax: (709) 729-6382
http://www.gov.nf.ca/health

Nova Scotia
Department of Community Services
Manager of Adoption and Foster Care
Tel.: (902) 424-3205
Fax: (902) 424-0708
http://www.gov.ns.ca/coms/files/adopint.asp

Northwest Territories
Department of Health and Social Services
Coordinator, Child and Family Services Unit
Tel.: (867) 873-7943
Fax: (867) 873-7706
http://www.gov.nt.ca

Nunavut
Department of Health and Social Services
Tel.: (867) 975-5700
Fax: (867) 975-5705
http://www.gov.nu.ca

Ontario
Ministry of Community, Family and Children's Services
Adoption Unit, Central Services
Tel.: (416) 327-4742
Fax: (416) 212-6799
http://www.cfcs.gov.on.ca

Prince Edward Island
Department of Health and Social Services
Child, Family and Community Services Division
Tel.: (902) 368-6514
Fax: (902) 368-6136
http://www.gov.pe.ca

Saskatchewan
Saskatchewan Social Services
Adoption Program Consultant
Tel.: (306) 787-5698
Fax: (306) 787-0925
http://www.gov.sk.ca

Quebec
Ministère de la Santé et des Services sociaux
Secrétariat à l'adoption internationale
Tel.: (514) 873-5226 or 1 (800) 561-0246
Fax: (514) 873-1709
http://www.msss.gouv.qc.ca

Yukon
Family and Children's Services
Placement and Support Services
Tel.: (867) 667-3473
Fax: (867) 393-6204
http://www.gov.yk.ca

Table -2 Quebec Income Scale, 2006

As mentioned earlier (see Sponsors living in Quebec), Quebec is responsible for determining the financial capability of sponsors living in that province. We are providing the income scale in effect in Quebec from January 1 to December 31. These amounts are indexed each year. We encourage you to use the income scale to assess your ability to meet the provincial requirements. Note that your calculations will only be an estimate since the MICC will make the official financial assessment

Basic Needs of Sponsor and Dependent Persons	
Number of dependent persons	**Gross annual income of sponsor***
0	**$19,286**
1	**$26,036**
2	**$32,144**
3	**$36,968**
4	**$41,145**
Required gross annual income is increased by **$4,176** for each additional dependant.	

Basic Needs of Sponsored Persons		
Persons 18 and over	**Persons under 18**	**Annual gross amount required by sponsor***
0	1	**$6, 677**
0	2	**$10,581**
The annual gross amount required is increased by **$3,527** for each additional person under 18.		
1	0	**$14,108**
1	1	**$18,955**
1	2	**$21,402**
The annual gross amount required is increased by **$2,445** for each additional person under 18.		
2	0	**$20,687**
2	1	**$23,176**
2	2	**$25,017**
The annual gross amount required is increased by **$1,837** for each additional person under 18 and by **$6,577** for each additional person 18 or over.		

Example:	
Basic needs of a sponsor: (sponsor, spouse and 2 children under 18)	**$36,968**
Basic needs of sponsored person: (main sponsored person, spouse, 1 child 18 or over and 2 children under 18)	**$31,594**
Income necessary for acceptance of undertaking application	**$68,562**

* **Salaried worker**: gross annual before-tax income; **self-employed worker**: net before-tax business income

Table -3 Ministère de l'Immigration et des Communautés culturelles

Quebec City and Eastern Quebec **Direction régionale de Québec et de l'Est-du-Québec** 930, Chemin Ste-Foy, RC Québec QC G1S 2L4 Tél. : (418) 643-1435 ou 1 888 643-1435 Fax : (418) 646-0783
Bureau du Saguenay—Lac-Saint-Jean et de la Côte-Nord 3950, boulevard Harvey Jonquière QC G7X 8L6 Tél. : (418) 695-8144 Fax : (418) 695-7861
Estrie, Mauricie et Centre-du-Québec **Direction régionale de l'Estrie, de la Mauricie** et du Centre-du-Québec 202, rue Wellington Nord Sherbrooke QC J1H 5C6 Tél. : (819) 820-3606 ou 1 888 879-4288 Fax : (819) 820-3213

Bureau de Trois-Rivières 100, rue Laviolette, bureau RC 26 Trois-Rivières QC G9A 5S9 Tél. : (819) 371-6011 ou 1 888 879-4294 Fax : (819) 371-6120
Outaouais, Abitibi-Témiscamingue, Northern Quebec Direction régionale de l'Outaouais, de l'Abitibi-Témiscamingue et du Nord-du-Québec 430, boul. de l'Hôpital, 3e étage Gatineau QC J8V 1T7 Tél. : (819) 246-3345 ou 1 888 295-9095 Fax : (819) 246-3314
Laval, Laurentides and Lanaudière **Direction régionale de Laval, des Laurentides et de Lanaudière** Carrefour d'intégration de Laval 705, ch. du Trait-Carré, RC Laval QC H7N 1B3 Tél. : (450) 970-3225 ou 1 800 375-7426 Fax : (450) 972-3250
Montérégie **Carrefour d'intégration de Longueuil** 2, boulevard Desaulniers, 3e étage Saint-Lambert QC J4P 1L2 Tél. : (450) 466-4461 ou 1 888 287-5819 Fax : (450) 466-4481
Montreal Area By appointment only Tél. : (514) 864-9191

Table 4 – Low Income Cut-off (LICO)

Effective until February 1, 2007

Size of Family Unit	Minimum necessary income
1 person (the sponsor)	$20,337
2 persons	$25,319
3 persons	$31,126
4 persons	$37,791
5 persons	$42,862
6 persons	$48,341
7 persons	$53,821
For each additional person	$5,480

If you are using this application kit after February 1, 2007, contact our Call Centre for revised figures.

THE APPLICATION PROCESS

International Adoption

Canadian law allows you to adopt a child from another country if you are a Canadian citizen or permanent resident. To bring your adoptive child to Canada, you must sponsor the child for immigration. You can start sponsoring a child as soon as you decide to adopt or you can wait until after you have found a child and have started the adoption process.

There are two processes that you must go through when you adopt a child from another country: the adoption process and the immigration sponsorship process. **You need to know about both**.

The Adoption Process:

Adoptions are the responsibility of the provinces in Canada. You need to have a Home Study done, usually by your province, before Citizenship and Immigration Canada (CIC) processes your application for sponsorship.

You will have to comply with the adoption laws of the child's country of origin. You must also comply with the laws of your province. Make sure you are familiar with all of the legal requirements relevant to you before beginning the adoption process.

Find out what you must do to adopt a child from another country from your province.

The Hague Convention governs international adoptions in some cases. Before you begin your adoption process, find out if the Convention will apply to you.

The Immigration Process:

As an adoptive parent of a child from another country, you must apply to sponsor the child for permanent residence in Canada. You may apply for citizenship on the child's behalf after the child is in Canada and has permanent resident status.

CIC will request a letter of consent from your province showing that your province agrees to the adoption. The immigration visa will only be issued after the immigration mission in the child's country of origin receives this letter from your province.

For more information on bringing a child from another country to Canada, please see *International Adoption and the Immigration Process.*

Frustrated with time-consuming processes that seem bureaucratic?

These procedures help to protect children's best interests. The only way around this frustration is to please be patient.

International Adoption and the Immigration Process

- General Information
- Responsibility for the Adoption and Protection of Children
- Foreign Laws
- The Hague Convention
- The Sponsorship of Adopted Children under Canadian Laws
- Adoption and Immigration: General Steps
- Questions and Answers
- Provincial and Territorial Requirements

General Information

This section is designed to serve as a guide to the process of international adoption and the entry of adoptive children into Canada. It provides information on the basic steps and procedures that must be followed. The guide begins with an overview of adoption and immigration, and then focuses on the steps to be taken in the process.

It is an offence in certain provinces or territories to bring an adopted or a soon-to-be adopted child into Canada without the prior authorization of the province or territory.

Responsibility For The Adoption And Protection Of Children

International adoption can appear daunting at first. Its complexity stems from the various legislations involved in the process: social welfare laws, immigration laws and, not least, the laws of the child's country.

The responsibility for social welfare matters, including adoptions, lies with the provincial or territorial authorities. The ministry responsible for adoptions varies depending on the province or territory where the adoptive parents reside. For example, the authority might be the New Brunswick Department of Health and Community Services, Manitoba Family Services or Saskatchewan Social Services, to name a few. Each province or territory manages its own adoption legislation. If you are considering an international adoption, you should first contact the ministry or department in your province or territory to learn about its requirements (see list of provinces and territories).

Citizenship and Immigration Canada (CIC) is responsible for the immigration process that allows the child you have adopted or intend to adopt to come to Canada.

Although the process that leads to the issuance of immigrant visas in international adoption cases is a high priority for CIC, adoptive parents may encounter delays that might be perceived as nothing more than "red tape." The domestic and international procedures that exist, however, have been established to protect the safety and well-being of children.

Immigration and adoption standards are put in place to ensure the protection and best interests of the parties involved. Essentially, adoption is a process that ensures that the child is provided with a suitable family environment although, on occasion, abuse and fraud unfortunately occur.

About 2,000 foreign children are adopted by Canadian citizens or permanent residents every year. These children are given high priority in the immigration process.

Human Resources and Skills Development Canada (HRSDC) is a federal department whose programs and activities are designed to strengthen families and communities. Within HRSDC, the Intercountry Adoption Services (IAS), which is part of the Child, Family and Community Division, has responsibility for intercountry adoption issues. The IAS coordinates information among the provinces and territories, other federal departments, foreign authorities and non-governmental organizations . It also acts as the federal central authority under the Hague Convention on Intercountry Adoption.

Foreign Laws

Laws regarding adoption by foreigners vary from one country to another. It is the responsibility of the visa officer to ensure that the adoption is legal according to the laws of the country in question. If the adoption has already occurred, the onus is on the sponsor to provide the documentation needed to establish this fact. An adoption legally completed in a foreign country will be given automatic legal recognition under the laws of all jurisdictions in Canada except in Quebec, where such recognition must be granted by a Quebec court after the arrival of the child.

Not all countries allow the adoption of children by foreigners. Some allow only a guardianship while others forbid any international adoptions. Potential sponsors should consult their provincial or territorial adoption authorities or the appropriate foreign embassy in Canada before applying for sponsorship to determine if adoption is allowed. The sponsorship of children under guardianship is not currently allowed under Canadian immigration regulations. See the telephone numbers and addresses of foreign embassies or consulates in Canada.

The Hague Convention

In May 1993, 66 countries, including Canada, reached an agreement on the Hague Convention on Protection of Children and Co-operation in Respect of Intercountry Adoption (the Hague Convention on Intercountry Adoption). The Convention seeks to establish a cooperative framework between the countries of origin of children in need of adoption and their receiving countries to ensure that the child's best interests are safeguarded. The Convention's objective is to prevent abuses such as the abduction or sale of, or the trafficking in, children or any other improper financial gains. It also ensures proper consent to the adoption, allows for the child's transfer, and establishes the adopted child's status in the receiving country.

The Convention sets minimum international standards and procedures for adoptions that occur between signatory countries. Not every signatory country has yet ratified the Convention. In the case of adoptions taking place between countries that have ratified it, the Convention ensures greater protection from exploitation for children, birth parents and adoptive parents alike. Canada ratified the Convention in December 1996, and it came into force on April 1, 1997, in those provinces and territories that had taken the legislative steps required to conform to it.

Each country that is party to the Convention must designate a central authority to monitor requests for intercountry adoption. As adoption falls under provincial or territorial jurisdiction in Canada, each province and territory has its own central authority. The federal central authority coordinates matters between the federal departments and the provincial or territorial central authorities for adoption. It also assists the provincial and territorial authorities with the implementation of the Convention.

The central authorities of the receiving province or territory and the country of origin must agree to the child's placement. The immigration requirements must be met before the adoption can take place and before a visa officer can issue an immigrant visa for the child.

When Does the Hague Convention on Intercountry Adoption Apply in Canada?

The Hague Convention applies only when the child to be adopted resides in a country that has implemented the Convention, and when the prospective adoptive parents live in a province or territory that has also implemented the Convention. All provinces and territories have implemented the Hague Convention. The central authority of the province or territory determines if the Convention applies to a specific case.

Prospective adoptive parents must fill out an application for adoption and present it to the central authority of their province or territory. They are advised to contact their provincial or territorial authority to obtain information on the adoption process and the provincial or territorial requirements.

Note: Adoptions arranged privately without the involvement of any central authorities are not allowed if both the adoptive parents' province or territory of residence and the country where the child resides have implemented the Hague Convention.

THE SPONSORSHIP OF ADOPTED CHILDREN UNDER CANADIAN LAWS

Who Is Eligible to Sponsor?

Persons eligible to sponsor adopted children or children intended for adoption in Canada must be Canadian citizens or permanent residents, aged 18 or over, and living in Canada. Other eligibility criteria are outlined in the application kit Sponsoring a Family Class Relative.

Who May Be Sponsored?

There are two types of adoption cases:

- **Children Adopted Outside Canada**

  Children may be sponsored to come to Canada if they are under 22 years of age at the time of the sponsorship application and if they have been adopted outside Canada according to the laws of another country. A genuine parent-child relationship must be created as a result of the adoption.

- **Children Adopted in Canada**

  A child may also be sponsored as an intended adoptee to be adopted in Canada, if he or she is under 18 years of age at the time of the sponsorship application and:

  - the adoption is not primarily to obtain the child's permanent resident status in Canada; and;
  - the child has been placed for adoption in the country where the child resides or the child is otherwise legally available for adoption.

ADOPTION AND IMMIGRATION: GENERAL STEPS

To determine if an adoption will be processed under the Hague Convention, first consult the section on the Hague Convention.

1. Home Study

The home study is an essential component of the adoption process. Its objective is to assess the ability of the applicants to parent an adopted child. It can include references, medical reports and other personal information, and is usually done by a licensed social worker approved by the province or territory of residence of the applicants.

The adoption process may vary from one province or territory to another. However, all provinces and territories require that a home study be completed before approving the arrangements for the adoption.

A home study will assist prospective adoptive parents in dealing with international adoption and its implications. Bringing up an adoptive child sometimes requires special skills. Children may have had a difficult start in life, or may have been deprived of emotional support or physical stimuli in an orphanage, or may even have suffered some health ailments. Adoptive parents will have to be prepared for the reactions of their family, racial and cultural differences, and adjustment problems. All the possible implications for both the adoptive parents and the child will need to be well thought-out before proceeding. Applicants should contact the central authority responsible for adoptions in their province or territory to obtain all relevant information on home studies.

2. Sponsorship

Once a home study has been done, adoptive parents begin the immigration process by completing an Undertaking Form, available in the application kit Sponsoring a Family Class Relative.

The undertaking is a binding commitment from the sponsors to provide the necessary care and support for the child they wish to adopt or have already adopted. The agreement remains in force for 10 years or until the child reaches the age of 25 — whichever comes first.

3. Fees

There is a fee for the sponsorship to cover the cost of processing the sponsorship and the visa application. Instructions for the payment of the fee are provided in the sponsorship kit.

Consult the fee schedule for current fees.

4. Processing the Sponsorship

The sponsoring parents are to send the undertaking with the correct fee to the Case Processing Centre (CPC) in Mississauga, Ontario (address provided in the kit). The name of the child may be left blank in the undertaking if the child has not yet been identified.

The CPC in Mississauga will process the family class sponsorship application and inform the appropriate Canadian visa office abroad once the sponsorship has been approved. The CPC will also send an Application for Permanent Residence to the sponsoring parents.

Cases Subject to the Hague Convention

In these cases, the central authorities of the receiving province or territory and the country of origin must take place. Therefore, it is absolutely necessary to first contact the provincial or territorial authority where the child will reside.

Once a sponsorship application has been approved, the CPC in Mississauga will write to the provincial or territorial authority to request the issuance of a "Notification of Agreement" to the adoption proposal (see Questions and Answers). The province or territory is required to indicate in the letter of notification that the application is subject to the Hague Convention. The provincial or territorial notification will be sent directly to the visa office abroad to reduce delays.

Cases Not Subject to the Hague Convention

Once a sponsorship application has been approved, the CPC in Mississauga will write to the provincial or territorial authority to request the issuance of a "letter of no objection" or a "letter of no involvement" (see Questions and Answers). Where a home study and specific information on the child are required for the issuance of the letter, the central authority of the province or territory will review the home study and the information before issuing the appropriate letter and forwarding it to the Canadian visa office abroad.

5. Overseas

The child must meet a number of immigration requirements before an immigrant visa can be issued.

The Application for Permanent Residence Form sent by the CPC must be completed on the child's behalf. Sponsors can fill out the application form themselves and send it to the visa office, or they may send the form to the child's guardian, who will complete it and forward it to the visa office.

The child must undergo a medical examination conducted by a physician designated by CIC in the child's home country. This examination is crucial to the child's acceptance in Canada. It cannot be emphasized enough that the medical examination should be done **as early as possible** in the process and, in any case, prior to the adoption. The results of the medical examination may affect the decision of the adoptive parents to go ahead with a particular adoption, especially in the case of a complex or difficult medical history. If the child is medically inadmissible in Canada, he or she will normally be refused a visa.

The visa officer must be satisfied that the adoption is not one of convenience (that is, solely for the purpose of facilitating the entry of the child or that of his or her relatives into Canada). The application for permanent residence may be refused if the visa officer concludes that the real purpose of the adoption is for the child to gain admission to Canada as a permanent resident and not to give a family to the child.

The adoption, or the proposed adoption, must not contravene the adoption laws of the child's country of origin. If an adoption is subject to the Hague Convention on Intercountry Adoption, the terms of the Convention must be respected, otherwise the application will be refused.

A passport from the child's home country permitting travel to Canada must be obtained for the child once a visa has been issued.

Cases Subject to the Hague Convention

The visa office will notify the provincial or territorial authority when the child has met the immigration requirements and is ready to be issued a visa. Only

adoption takes place in the country of origin) or the child be entrusted to the adoptive parents (if the adoption will proceed in Canada).

Upon notification that the adoption and the transfer of the child to the adoptive parents has taken place, the visa office will verify the adoption or legal custody papers and the travel document, and issue an immigrant visa to the child.

Cases Not Subject to the Hague Convention

The visa office will process the case and ensure that the child meets the immigration requirements.

When this process is finalized, the visa office will verify the adoption or legal custody papers and the travel document, and issue an immigrant visa to the child.

Note: Sponsors should not go abroad intending to return to Canada with the child before they have been officially informed that the immigration process has been completed. They should not assume that Canada's immigration requirements will be waived when the adoption is completed.

While these procedures may seem complicated and lengthy, they are adhered to by all agencies involved in adoptions for the protection of the child. Sponsors are urged to be patient and to follow these procedures. Adoption is a happy moment in the lives of both the sponsor and the child. Citizenship and Immigration Canada tries to make it as easy as possible for sponsors to bring their child home while ensuring that the process is legal and that it protects the interests of all parties in the process.

QUESTIONS AND ANSWERS

What is a letter of no involvement or no objection?

A letter of no objection, required by Immigration Regulation R117(3), is a written statement from the child welfare authority of the province or territory in which the child is to reside, confirming that the authority has no objection to the adoption. However, where an adoption is finalized abroad prior to the child's immigration to Canada, some provinces or territories will issue a letter of no involvement which informs the visa office abroad that an adoption order that is legally granted in a foreign country will be recognized by the province or territory. It is important to note that no immigrant visa will be issued without either a letter of no involvement or a letter of no objection from the appropriate provincial or territorial authority.

What is a Notification of Agreement?

In cases where the Hague Convention applies, all adoptions must receive prior approval from the central authorities of the country of origin and the receiving province or territory before immigration procedures can begin. The province or territory where the child will reside must provide a Notification of Agreement instead of a letter of no objection. A Notification of Agreement is a written statement confirming that the province or territory agrees to the adoption.

What is an immigrant visa?

An immigrant visa is a document issued to the child which allows him or her to enter Canada to live permanently. When the child enters Canada, the immigrant visa must be presented to an immigration officer at the port of entry to complete the formal process of granting the child permanent residence in Canada. An immigrant visa expires one year after the medical examination of the child and must be used before that date.

Can I bring my adopted child to Canada before the immigrant visa is issued?

No. Before bringing their child back to Canada, adoptive parents must await notification that the child's immigrant visa has been issued. This will avoid unnecessary delays and costs.

How does adoption affect the child's relationship with his or her biological parents?

Adoption severs a child's legal relationship with its biological parents. This means that the child cannot later sponsor these relatives for entry into Canada. The sponsorship of children under guardianship is not currently possible under immigration legislation because guardianship does not sever the ties between the child and the biological parents.

How long will the adoption process take?

As a member of the family class, an adopted child, or one who will be adopted, receives priority processing. However, many factors affect the length of processing. The time required to process the sponsorship itself should not exceed two weeks. The CPC in Mississauga endeavours to process them as quickly as possible. The overseas portion of the processing depends on many factors, such as the time required to complete the medical examination, for instance. In addition, complications in the adoption process will result in delays in the immigration process.

How do I check on the status of my case?

The CIC Call Centre will be able to inform you on the status of your case. When the CPC acknowledges receipt of your undertaking, it will give you a client identification number which you should use in any future enquiries regarding your case.

You can also use CIC's e-Client Application Status tool to check your application status online.

Provincial And Territorial Requirements

As the requirements for international adoptions are subject to change and fall under provincial or territorial jurisdiction, we strongly recommend that you contact the province or territory where the child will reside for information, in particular regarding the home study requirements.

APPENDIX A
Sponsoring an Adopted Child or a Child You Intend to Adopt

This appendix provides only basic information. For more details contact our Call Centre.

As adoption is a provincial responsibility, people who wish to adopt a child from outside of Canada must first contact provincial or territorial adoption authorities (see **Provincial and Territorial Contacts**). Once you have initiated the adoption application through the provincial or territorial authorities and have obtained the appropriate approval, you may begin the sponsorship process for a child described below:

Adoptions completed abroad

The requirements that must be met for sponsorships of children adopted abroad are as follows:

- the child was under the age of 18 when the adoption took place;
- the adoption was in the best interests of the child, that is
  - a competent authority had conducted or approved a home study of the adoptive parents;
  - before the adoption, the child's parents gave their free and informed consent to the child's adoption;
  - the adoption created a genuine parent-child relationship;
  - the adoption was in accordance with the laws of the place where the adoption took place;
  - the adoption was in accordance with the laws of the sponsor's country of residence; If the sponsor lived in Canada at the time the adoption took place, the competent authority of the child's province of intended destination must have

stated in writing that it does not object to the adoption.
  - if the adoption was subject to the Hague Convention on Adoption, the competent authority of the country where the adoption took place and the province of destination have stated in writing that they approve the adoption as conforming to the Convention;
  - if the adoption was not subject to the Hague Convention on Adoption, there is no evidence that the adoption is for the purpose of child trafficking or undue gain within the meaning of the Convention.

Adoptions completed in Canada

The requirements that must be met for sponsorships of children adopted in Canada are as follows:

- the child is under the age of 18;
- there is no evidence that the adoption is for the purpose of acquiring any privileges or status under the *Immigration and Refugee Protection Act*;
- if the adoption was subject to the Hague Convention on Adoption, the competent authority of the country in which the child lives and the province of destination of that child have stated in writing that they approve the adoption as conforming to the Convention;
- if the adoption was not subject to the Hague Convention on Adoption,
  - the child has been placed for adoption in the country in which he or she lives or is legally available in that country for adoption and there is no evidence that the adoption is for the purpose of child trafficking or undue gain within the meaning of the Convention and
  - the competent authority of the child's province of intended destination must have stated in writing that it does not object to the adoption.

Sponsorships for children who are not yet identified are accepted; once the child is identified, it is the sponsor's responsibility to notify the appropriate visa office and provincial authority. For Quebec residents, contact the office of the *ministère de l'Immigration et des Communautés culturelles* for sponsorship requirements in Quebec (see Table 3 in the application guide for phone numbers).

If a sponsorship is approved, an application for permanent residence must be submitted. (Instructions will be given at the time of approval.) Generally, an application for permanent residence will be approved if the child passes an immigration medical examination and if a visa officer is satisfied that the adoption will create a genuine parent-child relationship. It will not be approved if a visa officer concludes that the purpose of the adoption is to gain admission for the child or the child's relatives.

For all adoption cases, there is an immigration requirement prior to visa issuance

- to obtain a letter from the provincial or territorial authorities stating that they have no objection to the adoption. Citizenship and Immigration Canada will make this request directly to the appropriate provincial or territorial authorities at the time of the sponsorship approval;
- to provide a written statement confirming that the sponsor of a child has obtained information about the medical condition of the child whom the sponsor has adopted or is in the process of adopting outside Canada, or intends to adopt in Canada. Read the *Medical Condition Statement* included with this appendix. If you are sponsoring a child adopted abroad or whom you intend to adopt in Canada, make sure you obtain the medical information. Then complete and sign the bottom portion of the *Medical Condition Statement* and return it to the visa office processing the permanent residence application you are submitting on behalf of the child.

The Hague Convention on Adoption

Many intercountry adoptions are now subject to the requirements of the Hague Convention on Adoption. These adoptions must be initiated through provincial or territorial adoption authorities and receive the appropriate approvals. Contact your provincial or territorial authorities (see below) for information on how the Convention may affect your adoption.

Provincial and Territorial Contacts

Alberta	Ontario
Alberta Children's Services Tel : (780) 422-5641 Fax : (780) 427-2048	Ministry of Children's Services Tel : (416) 327-4742 Fax : (416) 212-6799
British Columbia	**Quebec**
Ministry of Children and Family Development Tel : (250) 387-3660 Fax : (250) 356-1864	Ministère de la Santé et des Services sociaux Tel : (514) 873-4747 Fax : (514) 873-1709
Prince Edward Island	**Saskatchewan**
Department of Health and Social Services Tel : (902) 368-6514 Fax : (902) 368-6136	Saskatchewan Social Services Tel : (306) 787-0008 Fax : (306) 787-0925

Manitoba	Newfoundland
Family Services and Housing Tel : (204) 945-6964 Fax : (204) 945-6717	Health and Community Services Tel : (709) 729-5134 Fax : (709) 729-6382
New Brunswick	**Northwest Territories**
Department of Family and Community Services Tel : (506) 444-5970 Fax : (506) 453-2082	Health and Social Services Tel : (867) 873-7943 Fax : (867) 873-7706
Nova Scotia	**Yukon**
Nova Scotia Department of Community Services Tel : (902) 424-5367 Fax : (902) 424-0708	Family and Children's Services Tel : (867) 667-3473 Fax : (867) 393-6204
Nunavut	
Department of Health and Social Services Tel : (867) 975-5750 Fax : (867) 975-5705	

Residency Obligations for Permanent Residents

Permanent residence status gives a non-Canadian the right to live in Canada. You must meet certain residency obligations to maintain your status as a permanent resident.

Rights and Entitlements

As a permanent resident, you have a right to enter Canada. You also have most of the rights that Canadian citizens have under the *Canadian Charter of Rights and Freedoms*. You cannot, however, run for political office or vote until after you have been granted Canadian citizenship.

Get more information on the permanent resident card.

You can apply for Canadian citizenship after three years of residency in Canada. Find out more about how to become a Canadian citizen.

Permanent Residence Obligations

Here is what you must do to comply with your residency obligations.

You must accumulate **two years of physical presence** in Canada in every five-year period. You can also count Canadian residency days if you are outside Canada for an extended period of time for one of the following reasons:

- You are accompanying your Canadian-citizen spouse or common-law partner.
- You are a child accompanying a Canadian-citizen parent.

- You are employed on a full-time basis by a Canadian business, the Public Service of Canada or the public service of a Canadian province.
- You are accompanying your permanent resident spouse or common-law partner who is also outside Canada **and** who is employed on a full-time basis by a Canadian business, the Public Service of Canada or the public service of a Canadian province.
- You are a child accompanying a permanent resident parent who is outside Canada **and** employed on a full-time basis by a Canadian business, the Public Service of Canada or the public service of a Canadian province.

Please note that you are complying with your residency obligations only if:

- your accompanying permanent-resident spouse, common-law partner or parent is complying with their residency obligations; **and**
- you ordinarily reside with your accompanying Canadian-citizen or permanent-resident spouse, common-law partner or parent.

A **child** is someone under the age of 22 who has never been married or in a common-law relationship.

Returning Resident Permit

If you became a permanent resident of Canada before June 28, 2002, you may still be the holder of a returning resident permit issued to you under the previous legislation.

Under the transitional provisions, if you are a permanent resident who is in possession of a returning resident permit, you will be able to count time spent outside Canada toward satisfying your residency obligations. The time period covered by the returning resident permit must apply to the period being examined.

Failure to Comply with Residency Obligations

You may lose your permanent resident status if you fail to comply with your residency obligations.

It is up to you to provide all required information and to provide evidence of your compliance with these obligations.

Examinations and Appeals

If you have not been able to comply with your residency obligations, officers can take humanitarian and compassionate concerns into account when making residency determinations. Officers will consider the best interests of a child directly affected by the decision.

If you have been a permanent resident for more than five years, the assessment of your residency obligations will be limited to the five years immediately before your examination.

You may appeal determinations of non-compliance with your residency obligations to the Immigration Appeal Division (IAD) of the Immigration and Refugee Board.

In Canada

When a permanent resident fails to meet their residency obligations, officers may issue a departure order that requires that person to leave Canada. The decision to issue a departure order may be appealed to the IAD within 30 days of receiving the notification.

Permanent residence status will be lost if the decision is not appealed.

Abroad

When a permanent resident does not meet their residency obligations while abroad, officers may inform that person in writing that they have failed to meet their residency obligations. Information on appeal procedures will be provided at the same time.

Permanent residence status will be lost if an appeal of the determination is not received by the IAD within 60 days of receiving the written non-compliance notification.

For More Information

If you still have questions about your obligations as a permanent resident, please contact the Call Centre.

Few More Facts About Canada

ASIAN CANADIAN HISTORIC TIMELINE.

1788
John Meare arrives on Nootka Sound on Canada's Pacific cost, with two ships carrying 50 Chinese carpenters and craftsmen. They build a two-storied fort and a schooner, but are captured by the Spanish and taken to Mexico.

1858
The first Chinese gold-miners migrate to Barkerville, British Columbia from San Francisco. Chinese miners join thousands of other prospectors in the trek northward along the Fraser River.

Many Chinese people who came to Canada in the nineteenth century are from Guangdong province in southern China. Their historical arrival marks the establishment of a continuous Chinese community in Canada.

1861
Won Alexander Cumyow is born in Victoria. He is the first Chinese baby to be born in Canada.

1863
The first Chinese community organization is formed. The Hong Shun Tang, in Barkerville. A booming little town with a large Chinatown, including 300 Chinese residents.

1872
The British Columbia Qualifications of Voters Act denies the Chinese the right to vote.

1877
Arrival of Manzo Nagano, the first Japanese person known to land and settle in Canada.

1878
A British Columbia law is passed making it illegal for Chinese people to be employed on construction projects paid for by the provincial government.

1880-1886
The construction of the western section of the Canadian Pacific Railway employs thousands of Chinese workers. More than 4,000 died in the effort.

1884
The federal government sets up a Royal Commission to review Chinese immigration.

1885
Following the Royal Commission, the federal government introduces the Act to Restrict and Regulate Chinese immigration into Canada, which requires that Chinese people entering Canada to pay a head tax of $50 per person.

1886
With the completion of the Canadian Pacific Railway, Chinese start small service-oriented businesses. Many move east to centers such as Calgary, Toronto and Montreal in search of job opportunities and less discrimination.

1895
The British Columbian government denies citizens of Asian heritage the right to vote.

1900
The federal government raises the Chinese immigration head tax to $100, to take effect in 1902. The Royal Commission on Chinese and Japanese immigration holds hearings and concludes limiting Chinese and Japanese immigration will not damage trade between China and Canada.

1902
The Royal Commission on Chinese and Japanese Immigration declared all Asians, "unfit for full citizenship .. obnoxious to a free community and dangerous to the state".

1903
The federal government raises the head tax to $500. With only eight Chinese entering Canada, the government's increase in head tax had a drastic effect on Chinese immigration.

The first South Asians settle in the southwest section of British Columbia. Most of them were Sikhs who worked in the lumber industry.

1907
Though immigration was severely limited early in the century, a poor economy in Vancouver continued to produce strong discriminatory feelings by the unemployed whites toward Asians. This frustration lead to the creation of The Asiatic Exclusion League in British Columbia.

September 8, 1907.
Several thousand league-organized marchers met in downtown Vancouver to spread anti-Asian sentiment. The crowd had grown to about 15,000 supporters. The mob eventually moved to Chinatown and little Tokyo where they looted, burned and destroyed Chinese and Japanese businesses. Because the South Asians lived in a different part of the city, their community was spared the violence of the riot. The federal government paid the Chinese community $26,990 and the Japanese community $9175 for damage to their property.

1908
With the Hayashi-Lemieux Gentlemen's Agreement, Japan voluntarily agreed to restrict the number of passports issued to male laborers and domestic servants to an annual maximum of 400.

January 8, 1908.
An immigration policy was passed that only allowed entry to those traveling by "continuous passage" from their country of origin to Canada. Without direct passage to Canada, South Asians were not able to enter Canada.

1914
Gurdit Singh attempted to challenge the "continuous passage" legislation. He hired a ship, the Komagata Maru, and planned a non-stop voyage to Vancouver with 376 East Indian immigrants. Canadian officials did not allow the men to disembark. Negotiations carried on for two months after which the federal government expelled the ship and escorted the ship and all of its 376 passengers back out to sea.

1916-1917
200 Japanese Canadians volunteer for service with Canadian army in France for World War I. 54 are killed and 92 are wounded.

1917
Employers in British Columbia, Alberta, and Saskatchewan propose importing Chinese workers to relieve the labor shortage caused by World War I.

1917-1918
Ontarian, Manitoba, Saskatchewan, and British Columbia pass laws making it illegal to hire white women in Chinese-owned restaurants and laundries. The Chinese community challenges the law in the courts, but the ruling favors the provinces.

1919
Japanese fishermen control nearly half of the fishing licenses (3,267). The Department of Fisheries responded by reducing the number of licenses issued to "other than white residents, British subjects, and Canadian Indians". By 1925 close to 1000 licenses were stripped from the Japanese.

1920
A dozen Chinese veterans who saved in the Canadian Army during World War I are given the right to vote.

1921
The School Board of Victoria puts all Chinese students in one separate school. Parents remove their children from the school, which eventually turns into a boycott. It lasts a year until the Victoria school board permits the Chinese students to return.

1923
The Chinese immigration Act (the Exclusion Act) prohibits Chinese immigrants from entering Canada, with few exceptions. Many wives and children in China are unable to join their husbands and fathers in Canada. All Chinese people already living in Canada, even the native born, have to register with the government to receive a certificate of registration.

1931
Surviving Japanese veterans of World War are given the right to vote.

First Filipino immigrant recorded to enter Canada.

Vietnamese flee their native country. Many leaving on boats destined for the United States and Canada.

1976
Jean Lumb, becomes the first Chinese-Canadian to receive the Order of Canada Award.

1977
To mark the hundredth anniversary of the settling in Canada of the first Japanese, a mountain in British Columbia was named after the first settler, Manzo Nagano.

1979

Chinese Canadians organize nationally to protest the racist depiction of Chinese Canadians in a story called "Campus Giveaway" on CTV's nationally televised current events program, W5. The protect results in the creation of the Chinese Canadian National Council.

1983

Thirty-seven organizations take part in the First Conference of Filipinos held in Ontario.

1987

The Vietnamese Canadian Centre is founded in Ottawa.

1988

Prime Minister Brian Mulroney announces the Canadian Government's formal apology for the wrongful incarceration, seizure of property and the disenfranchisement of thousands of Canadians of Japanese ancestry. A redress settlement was also announced which included individual compensation for all survivors.

1989

The Chinese communities across Canada organize and join the worldwide call for democracy and human rights in response to the Tianamen Square Massacre in China.

1990

Influx of skilled immigrants from India, Pakistan and Philippines are on rise.

1993

Raymond Chan and Gary Mar become federal and provincial members of parliament.

1994
Toronto holds its first annual Asian Heritage Month in May – Edmonton, Halifax, Montreal, and Vancouver also soon followed by adopting May as Asian Heritage Month as well.

100 Vietnamese and Canadian human rights advocates hold a workshop addressing the ongoing human rights violations in Vietnam.

1995
Japanese Canadian National Museum & Archives Society is incorporated and begins planning for museum and archives facility in National Nikkei heritage Center.

1997
In Toronto, an "all Chinese language" radio station is established, with numerous television, and print media outlets.

Premier Ralph Klein strengthens ties with Korea. Recognizing Alberta is home to over 5,000 Korean Canadians and that Korean studies are offered at Alberta universities and colleges.

June 30, 1997
Hong Kong reverts back to China, prompting a steady flow of Hong Kong Chinese entrepreneurs to Canada.

1999
British Columbia proclaims May as Asian Heritage Month. This proclamation marks the 50th anniversary of the first Asian Canadian participation in British Columbian and Canadian elections.

2002
Canada has become the 99th country to ratify the Kyoto Protocol on reducing greenhouse gas emissions

2005

As of Feb-01, 2005 same-sex couples can now marry in seven out of the ten provinces of Canada, and in one out of the three territories. A court case is expected in Alberta in early 2005. If that case authorizes SSM in the province, then only 3% of Canadians will live in a jurisdiction that still prohibits SSM.

On Feb 01, 2005, the federal government introduced a bill (C-38) to legalize SSM from sea onto sea. The main result of the bill will be that 13% of same-sex couples who wish to get married will be able to do it more conveniently -- without leaving their province or territory of residence

Bill C-38 came about because of court rulings that found the traditional definition of marriage violated the equality rights of gays and lesbians under the Charter of Rights and Freedoms.

Same-sex marriage is now the law in seven provinces and one territory. Bill C-38 would harmonize the definition of marriage across Canada.

Canadian Economy in Brief
March 2006 Overview

- In the fourth quarter of 2005 real gross domestic product (GDP) grew 2.5%, following a 3.5% gain in the third quarter. For 2005 as a whole, GDP increased 2.9%, the same rate as in 2004.

- Final domestic demand climbed 4.3% in the fourth quarter, reflecting healthy employment, income and profit growth. Non-residential investment in plant and equipment led the way.

- Net trade retarded growth. Real imports climbed 11.4%, satisfying increased domestic demand, notably the need for machinery and equipment. Real exports rose a solid but more modest 9.6%.

- With its 26th consecutive quarterly surplus, the current account balance jumped $22.1 billion to a record level of $53.1 billion, or 3.8% of nominal GDP. For 2005 as a whole, the current account surplus stood at a record level of $30.2 billion, or 2.2% of nominal GDP, the same share as in 2004.

- Since the end of 2004 the Canadian economy has created 305,700 net new jobs, close to 90 per cent of which are full-time. The 6.4% unemployment rate in February matched the lowest level in over 30 years.

Real GDP grows 2.5%

Real GDP rose 2.5% in the fourth quarter. Final domestic demand growth remained solid (Chart 1), but imports increased more than exports, moderating output growth.

Chart 1
Growth in real GDP and real final domestic demand
per cent (annual rate)

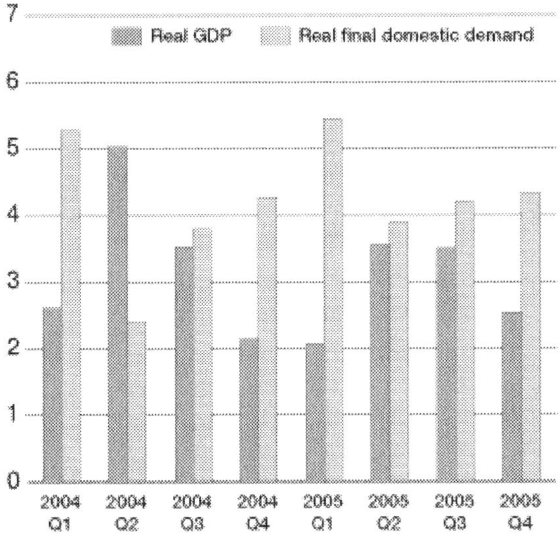

Consumer spending growth picks up

Real consumer spending grew 2.9% in the fourth quarter, a modestly stronger pace than in the third quarter. Spending on non-durables, semi-durables and services grew faster than in the third quarter while purchases of durables actually declined as sales of motor vehicles and automotive parts dropped sharply.

Main Economic Indicators
(per cent change at annual rates unless otherwise indicated)

	2004	2005	2005:Q2	2005:Q3	2005:Q4		Most recent
Real gross domestic product	2.9	2.9	3.6	3.5	2.5		–
Final domestic demand	3.9	4.3	3.9	4.2	4.3		–
Government expenditure							–
Goods and services	2.7	2.8	3.2	4.4	3.6		–
Gross fixed capital	4.9	4.2	1.8	5.0	11.1		–
Consumer expenditure	3.4	4.0	3.8	2.4	2.9		–
Residential investment	8.3	3.3	6.7	2.5	1.4		–
Business fixed investment	6.1	9.1	4.4	13.8	12.9		–
Non-residential construction	0.8	6.8	6.5	11.7	12.3		–
Machinery and equipment	9.8	10.7	2.9	15.3	13.3		–
Business inventory investment ($ billion)	11.5	14.3	12.9	14.4	11.9		–
Exports	5.0	2.3	-0.5	7.4	9.6		–
Imports	8.1	7.0	-3.2	10.2	11.4		–
Current account balance							
(nominal $ billion)	28.8	30.2	20.2	31.0	53.1		–
(percentage of GDP)	2.2	2.2	1.5	2.2	3.8		–
Nominal personal income	4.3	4.9	6.2	6.3	5.8		–
Nominal personal disposable income	3.9	4.0	4.9	7.0	5.3		–
Real personal disposable income	2.5	2.4	2.8	4.5	5.0		–
Profits before taxes	18.7	10.7	12.3	20.0	16.4		–
Costs and prices (%, y/y)							
GDP price deflator	3.0	3.1	2.3	3.1	4.1		–
Consumer Price Index	1.9	2.2	1.9	2.6	2.3	2.8	Jan-2006
CPI excluding eight most volatile items	1.5	1.6	1.6	1.6	1.6	1.7	Jan-2006
Unit labour costs	1.1	2.3	1.9	2.7	3.4		
Wage settlements (total)	1.7	2.3	2.6	2.8	1.7	1.7	Dec-2005
Labour market							
Unemployment rate (%)	7.2	6.8	6.8	6.8	6.5	6.4	Feb-2006
Employment growth	1.8	1.4	1.7	1.5	2.4	1.5	Feb-2006
Financial markets (average)							
Exchange rate (cents U.S.)	77.0	82.6	80.4	83.3	85.2	86.10	10-Mar-06
Prime interest rate (%)	4.0	4.4	4.3	4.3	4.8	5.50	09-Mar-06

Note: Real values are in chained 1997 dollars.
Sources: Statistics Canada, the Bank of Canada and Human Resources and Social Development.

The 5.8% increase in personal income in the fourth quarter followed a 6.3% gain in the third. While employment rose more than in the third quarter, average hours worked per employee inched lower. Real personal disposable income climbed for the ninth consecutive quarter, up 5.0%. Per capita real personal disposable income increased 3.6%. The personal savings rate was 0.3% in the fourth quarter, the only quarter in 2005 in which consumers spent less than their disposable income.

Residential investment increases

Residential investment increased 1.4% in the fourth quarter after gaining 2.5% in the third. Rising interest rates likely slowed the housing market, but low rates still supported a high level of activity. While renovations jumped 11.2%, a dip in housing starts fostered a modest decrease in new construction activity, the fourth consecutive quarterly decline. Housing resale activity dropped.

Business fixed investment climbs

Supported by record profits, high capacity utilization, and lower import prices due to the appreciating dollar, business spending on plant and equipment registered a 12th consecutive increase in the fourth quarter, growing 12.9%. Investment in machinery and equipment jumped 13.3%. Except for motor vehicles, all types of investment showed significant gains, with spending on other transportation equipment soaring in the quarter.

Non-residential construction increased a robust 12.3% after a slightly smaller third-quarter gain. For the fourth consecutive quarter, both building construction, such as office towers and shopping malls, and engineering projects contributed to growth. Higher energy prices have boosted investment in the oil and gas extraction industry, increasing engineering projects.

Business inventory accumulation slows

Businesses increased inventories by $11.9 billion, down from $14.4 billion in the third quarter. The slowdown was concentrated in durable goods and wholesale trade industries. The inventory-to-sales ratio edged lower.

Exports rise

Real exports increased 9.6% in the fourth quarter (Chart 2). As in the third quarter, exports of cars jumped as strong U.S. sales in the second and third quarters reduced U.S. inventories. Exports of machinery and equipment and forest products both rebounded from previous declines. Machinery and equipment exports have benefited from strong U.S. machinery and equipment investment since 2003. Exports of forest products rose with U.S. residential investment plus demand from rebuilding projects in the U.S. following Hurricane Katrina. Exports of services increased 2.9%.

Chart 2
Growth in real exports and real imports

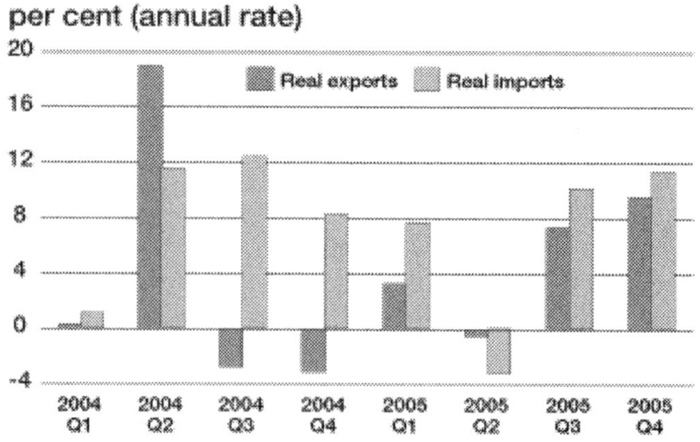

Imports increase more than exports

Real imports rose 11.4%, the second consecutive double-digit increase. Most major categories saw solid gains. Boosted by robust investment growth, imported machinery and equipment climbed 19.2%, an 11th consecutive increase. Non-automotive consumer products also registered a second consecutive double-digit increase. Imported services increased 3.9%.

Current account surplus mounts to record

In the fourth quarter, the terms of trade rose. Export prices jumped with the price of exported energy products while import prices fell, in part because of an appreciating dollar. Thus, despite the negative contribution of real trade, the nominal trade surplus soared $16.0 billion. Further, increased dividends from abroad received by Canadians and decreased income paid to non-residents from Canadian profits improved the investment income deficit by $6.6 billion. The current account surplus climbed $22.1 billion to a record level of $53.1 billion and at 3.8% sat a fraction below its record share of nominal GDP (Chart 3). For 2005 as a whole, the current account surplus stood at a record level of $30.2 billion, or 2.2% of nominal GDP.

Chart 3
Current account as a percentage of nominal GDP

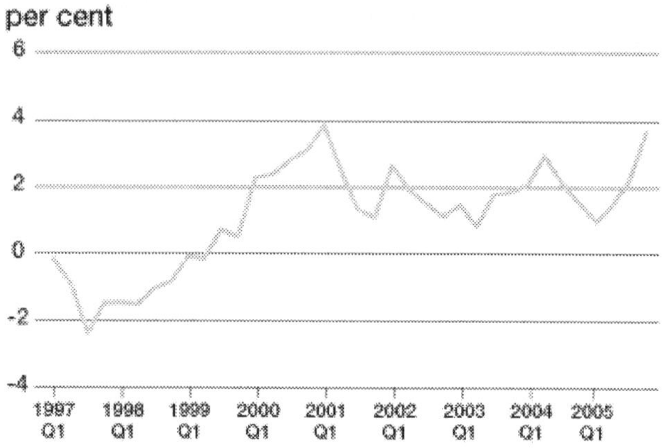

Corporate profits grow again

Corporate profits rose 16.4% in the fourth quarter following a 20.0% third-quarter gain. A strong upward trend in profits has raised their share of GDP to a record 14.6%, well above the 10.2% historical average since 1961 (Chart 4). Financial enterprises reported significant gains and mining companies other than those involved in oil and gas extraction benefited from rising metal prices.

Chart 4
Profits before taxes as a share of nominal GDP

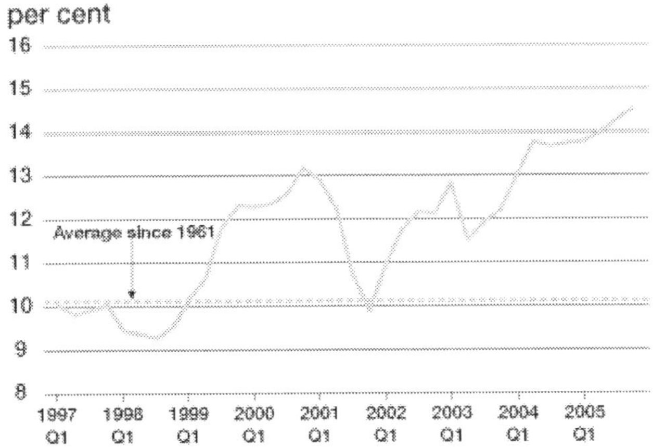

Consumer price inflation remains subdued

Reflecting higher world commodity prices, the GDP deflator, a comprehensive measure of prices, rose over 5% in the fourth quarter to stand 4.1% higher than a year earlier.

Year-over-year consumer price inflation stood at 2.8% in January, up from 2.2% in December, as prices for gasoline, natural gas and fresh vegetables rose. At 1.7% in January, core CPI inflation, which excludes the eight most volatile items, sat below the mid-point of the 1% to 3% target band.

Unemployment rate remains near low

Employment grew 2.4% in the fourth quarter, and another 51,000 jobs were added in January and February. Since the end of 2004 the Canadian economy has created 305,700 net new jobs, the majority of them full-time. The participation rate stood at 67.0% in February, down slightly from January and from its record high of 67.7% set in the second quarter of 2004.

The unemployment rate declined 0.2 percentage points in February and sat at 6.4%, matching the lowest level in over 30 years last reached in November 2005.

Hourly labour productivity increased 0.7% in the fourth quarter and was 1.3% higher than a year earlier. Labour costs per unit of output rose 4.8% in the fourth quarter to stand 3.4% higher than a year earlier.

Bank of Canada raises policy rate

On March 7, the Bank of Canada raised its key policy rate—the target for the overnight rate—by one quarter of a percentage point to 3.75 per cent, the fifth increase in a six-month period. The Bank stated that "some modest further increase in the policy interest rate may be required to keep aggregate supply and demand in balance and inflation on target over the medium term." The U.S. Federal Reserve raised its target rate 14 times from 1.25% in June 2004 to 4.50% in January 2006. U.S. interest rates are higher than rates in Canada at all maturities.

The Canadian dollar climbed to close at a 14-year high of 88.39 cents U.S. on March 2. It then eased to 86.10 cents U.S. on March 10.

Note: Unless otherwise noted, data and per cent changes are quoted at annual rates. The cut-off date for data is end of day, March 10, 2006.

The Budget in Brief 2006

The Budget in Brief 2006

Budget 2006—Focusing on Priorities

Introduction

Budget 2006 is about focusing on priorities. It delivers real results for people in a focused and fiscally responsible way.

As the measures outlined in this plan make clear, this budget makes federal spending more transparent, accountable and disciplined, while creating greater opportunity for Canadians, investing in our families and communities, and making our streets safer and our borders more secure.

It also delivers more tax relief than the last four federal budgets combined—putting more than twice as much into tax relief than new spending.

Budget 2006 also provides a framework for discussion to restore fiscal balance in Canada, based on fundamental principles all Canadians can support.

By addressing clear priorities in accountability, opportunity, families and communities, and security—while laying the foundation for budgets to come—Budget 2006 charts a new course for building a better Canada.

Highlights

Economic Developments and Prospects

- The Canadian economy recorded solid growth in 2005, largely supported by healthy increases in final domestic demand.

- Looking ahead, forecasters expect slightly stronger near-term growth than estimated at the time of the November 2005 *Economic and Fiscal Update.*

- Private sector forecasters have raised their forecasts for gross domestic product (GDP) inflation in 2006, largely because of unexpectedly strong growth in commodity prices in late 2005. As a result, the forecast level of nominal GDP in 2006 and 2007 is now over $20 billion higher than projected at the time of the Update.

- The risks to the Canadian economic outlook remain largely external, and include uncertainty about commodity prices, the risk of a sudden correction in U.S. house prices, and the risk that the Canadian dollar may appreciate further in response to adjustments to global imbalances.

Building a Better Canada

Accountability

A core priority of the Government is to improve the accountability and transparency of government operations to Canadians. The *Federal Accountability Action Plan,* released on April 11, introduced a wide-ranging set of reforms, including establishing the position of a Parliamentary Budget Officer and a commitment to provide quarterly updates of the fiscal outlook for the current fiscal year.

Budget 2006 announces a more transparent framework for budget planning, consisting of the following elements:

- The Government will make decisions in the budget over a two-year planning horizon. Measures will be introduced when they are affordable and ready to be implemented.

- The Government will restrain the rate of spending growth. The Government will introduce a new approach to managing overall spending to ensure that government programs focus on results and value for money, and are consistent with government priorities and responsibilities. The President of the Treasury Board will identify savings of $1 billion in 2006–07 and 2007–08.

- The Government will plan on reducing the federal debt by $3 billion annually. The Government is advancing by one year, to 2013–14, the goal of lowering the debt-to-GDP ratio to 25 per cent.

- The Government will examine the possibility of allocating a portion of any surplus at year-end larger than $3 billion to the Canada Pension Plan and Quebec Pension Plan, in order to make them more equitable for young Canadians and improve economic competitiveness.

- Financial reporting will be improved, in keeping with recommendations from the Auditor General of Canada.

Opportunity

- This budget proposes comprehensive tax relief for individuals, valued at almost $20 billion over the next two years—more than the last four budgets combined.

    - As a result, about 655,000 low-income Canadians will be removed from the tax rolls altogether.

- Overall, this budget delivers more than twice as much tax relief as new spending.

- The goods and services tax (GST) will be reduced by 1 percentage point as of July 1, 2006.

- In addition to reducing the GST, Budget 2006 proposes to reduce personal income taxes for all taxpayers through:

    - The new Canada Employment Credit—a tax credit on employment income of up to $500, effective July 1, 2006, to help working Canadians. The eligible amount will double to $1,000 as of January 1, 2007.

    - A permanent legislated reduction in the lowest tax rate to 15.5 per cent from 16 per cent as of July 1, 2006. The budget also confirms that the lowest tax rate will be 15 per cent from January 1, 2005 until June 30, 2006.

    - Increases in the basic personal amount—the amount that all Canadians can earn without paying federal income tax—above its currently legislated level for 2005, 2006 and 2007.

    - As a result of these personal income tax and GST reductions, families earning between $15,000 and $30,000 a year will be better off by almost $300 in 2007. Families earning between $45,000 and $60,000 will save almost $650.

- To create an environment for jobs and growth, Budget 2006 proposes to make Canada's tax system more internationally competitive by:

    - Reducing the general corporate income tax rate to 19 per cent from 21 per cent by 2010.

  - Eliminating the corporate surtax for all corporations as of January 1, 2008.

  - Eliminating the federal capital tax as of January 1, 2006, two years ahead of schedule.

- To support the growth of small business, Budget 2006 proposes to:

  - Increase the amount of small business income eligible for the 12-per-cent tax rate to $400,000 from $300,000 as of January 1, 2007.

  - Reduce the 12-per-cent tax rate applying to qualifying small business income to 11.5 per cent in 2008 and 11 per cent in 2009.

- Budget 2006 takes action in support of a more skilled and educated workforce by proposing:

  - A new tax credit of up to $2,000 for employers who hire apprentices.

  - A new $1,000 grant for first- and second-year apprentices.

  - A new $500 tax deduction for tradespeople for costs in excess of $1,000 for tools they must acquire as a condition of employment. Also, the $200 limit on the cost of tools eligible for the 100-per-cent capital cost allowance will be increased to $500.

  - A new tax credit for the cost of textbooks, which will provide a tax reduction of about $80 per year for a typical full-time post-secondary student.

  - The elimination of the current $3,000 limit on the amount of scholarship, bursary and fellowship income a post-secondary student can receive without paying federal income tax.

  - Confirming up to $1 billion to provinces and territories to support urgent investments in post-secondary education infrastructure.

  - Expanded eligibility for Canada Student Loans through a reduction in the expected parental contribution, starting in August 2007.

- Budget 2006 affirms this government's strong commitment to agriculture by providing an additional $2 billion over two years to the farming sector.

  - $1.5 billion will be provided this year. This includes $500 million for farm support, plus a one-time investment of $1 billion to assist farmers in the transition to more effective programming for farm income stabilization and disaster relief.

- Budget 2006 provides $400 million over two years to combat the pine beetle infestation, strengthen the long-term competitiveness of the forestry sector and support worker adjustment.

- Looking forward, the Government will develop a broad-based agenda to promote a more competitive, productive Canada.

Families and Communities

Budget 2006 provides $5.2 billion over two years in increased support for Canadians and their families.

Canada's Universal Child Care Plan

- $3.7 billion over two years for the Universal Child Care Benefit (UCCB), which will provide all families with $100 per month for each child under age 6. The UCCB will not affect federal income-tested benefits and will be provided as of July 1, 2006.

- $250 million to support the creation of new child care spaces. The goal is to create 25,000 additional spaces each year.

Other Family Measures

- A children's fitness tax credit for up to $500 in eligible fees for physical fitness programs for each child under age 16.

- Assistance for persons with disabilities will be enhanced by:

    - Increasing the maximum annual Child Disability Benefit (CDB) to $2,300 from $2,044, effective July 2006.

    - Extending eligibility for the CDB to middle- and higher-income families caring for a child who is eligible for the disability tax credit, effective July 2006.

    - Boosting the maximum amount of the refundable medical expense supplement to $1,000 from $767, effective 2006.

- $52 million per year for the Canadian Strategy for Cancer Control.

- Increasing to $2,000 the maximum amount eligible for the pension income credit, effective 2006. This will benefit nearly 2.7 million taxpayers with pension income and will remove approximately 85,000 pensioners from the tax rolls.

Budget 2006 provides almost $3 billion over two years to help make our communities better places to live.

Immigration Measures

- Reducing the Right of Permanent Residence Fee from $975 to $490, effective immediately.

- Increasing immigration settlement funding by $307 million and taking steps towards the establishment of a Canadian agency for the assessment and recognition of foreign credentials.

Affordable Housing

- Confirming up to $800 million to provinces and territories to address immediate pressures in affordable housing.

Aboriginal Communities

- $450 million for improving water supply and housing on reserve, education outcomes, and socio-economic conditions for Aboriginal women, children and families.

- Confirming up to $300 million to provinces to address immediate pressures in off-reserve Aboriginal housing, and up to $300 million to territories for affordable housing in the North.

Environment

- A tax credit for the purchase of monthly public transit passes, effective July 1, 2006.
- Accelerating the capital cost allowance for forestry bioenergy.

Infrastructure

- $5.5 billion over four years for a new Highways and Border Infrastructure Fund, Canada's Pacific Gateway Initiative, the Canada Strategic Infrastructure Fund, the Municipal Rural Infrastructure Fund and a Public Transit Capital Trust.

Other Measures

- Exempting donations of publicly listed securities to public charities from capital gains tax, effective immediately.
- Exempting donations of ecologically sensitive land made under the Ecogift program from capital gains tax, also effective immediately.
- $50 million to the Canada Council for the Arts.
- Providing temporary solvency funding relief to help re-establish full funding of federally regulated defined benefit pension plans in an orderly fashion, with safeguards for promised pension benefits.

Security

Budget 2006 provides $1.4 billion over two years to protect Canadian families and communities, to secure our borders and to increase our preparedness to address public health threats. Over the same period, this budget provides $73 million to better secure our financial system. The Government is also committed to strengthening Canada's role in the world by investing an additional $1.1 billion over two years in Canada's armed forces and by working to ensure the effectiveness of international assistance.

Cracking Down on Crime

- $161 million for 1,000 more RCMP officers and federal prosecutors to focus on such law-enforcement priorities as drugs, corruption and border security (including gun smuggling).

- $37 million for the RCMP to expand its National Training Academy (Depot) to accommodate these new officers and build the capacity to train more officers in the future.

- Set aside funds to expand Canada's correctional facilities to house the expected increase in inmates as a result of changes in sentencing rules.

- $20 million for communities to prevent youth crime with a focus on guns, gangs and drugs.

- $26 million to give victims a more effective voice in the federal corrections and justice system, and to give victims greater access to services (such as travel to appear at parole hearings).

Securing Safe and Open Borders

- $101 million to begin arming border officers and eliminating "work-alone" posts.

- $303 million to implement a border strategy to promote the movement of low-risk trade and travellers within North America while protecting Canadians from security threats.

Preparing for Emergencies

- $460 million ($1 billion over five years) to further improve Canada's pandemic preparedness.
- $19 million per year to Public Safety and Emergency Preparedness Canada to enhance our capacity to deal with catastrophes and emergencies.

Transportation Security

- $133 million to support Canadian Air Transport Security Authority operations.
- $95 million for new measures to enhance the security of passenger rail and urban transit.

Strengthening Canada's Role in the World

- $1.1 billion ($5.3 billion over five years) to strengthen the Canadian Forces' capacity to defend our national sovereignty and security.
- Up to $320 million in 2005–06 to fight polio, tuberculosis, malaria and HIV/AIDS and to help low-income countries cope with natural disasters or sharp rises in commodity prices.

Enhancing Security in the Financial System

- $64 million to enhance Canada's anti-money laundering and anti-terrorist financing regime.
- $9 million to fund integrated enforcement teams to combat currency counterfeiting.

Restoring Fiscal Balance in Canada

In Budget 2006, the Government is committing to take immediate action to restore fiscal balance. This government will address concerns over fiscal imbalance through:

- Implementation of the 10-Year Plan to Strengthen Health Care.
- A Patient Wait Times Guarantee for medically necessary services, developed with provincial and territorial governments.
- Certainty for equalization and Territorial Formula Financing payments for 2006–07 through reliance on more current economic and fiscal data, as well as one-time adjustments of $255.4 million to offset declines.
- Additional funding of up to $3.3 billion for provinces and territories to help address immediate pressures in post-secondary education, affordable housing (including Northern and off-reserve Aboriginal housing) and public transit, contingent on sufficient funds being available from the 2005–06 surplus.
- A commitment to work with provinces and territories toward a common securities regulator.

The Government is also committing to further action over the next year, working toward more open, transparent and collaborative fiscal relations in Canada. It proposes:

- A principle-based framework on fiscal arrangements, outlined in the companion document *Restoring Fiscal Balance in Canada*, which will lead to:
    - A new approach for allocating unplanned federal surpluses.

- Renewed, transparent and principle-based Equalization and Territorial Formula Financing programs.
- A new approach to long-term and predictable support for post-secondary education and training.
- A new framework for long-term funding support for infrastructure programs.

The Government is looking forward to a rich dialogue on fiscal relations, engaging Canadians, provincial and territorial governments, academics and experts, concluding with further action to improve fiscal relations in Canada.

Fiscal Outlook

- For 2005–06, the federal surplus is currently estimated at $8 billion, based on monthly financial information through February 2006. The final result will reflect developments in March and year-end accrual adjustments.

- Starting this fiscal year, the Government is planning on achieving annual debt reduction of $3 billion.

- The Government is directing higher than expected surpluses over the planning period to the priorities of Canadians, largely to reducing taxes. As a result, revenues as a share of gross domestic product (GDP) are projected to decline from 16.4 per cent in 2004–05 to 15.5 per cent in 2007–08.

- The Government is committed to reducing growth in spending to a rate that is sustainable. Program expenses as a share of GDP are projected to decline from 13.7 per cent in 2004–05 to 13.0 per cent in 2007–08.

- The debt-to-GDP ratio is projected to fall to 31.7 per cent by 2007–08, on track to meet the new medium-term objective of reducing the debt-to-GDP ratio to 25 per cent by 2013–14.

Table 1
Summary Statement of Transactions (Including May 2006 Budget Measures)

	Actual[1]	Estimate	Projection	
	2004–05	2005–06	2006–07	2007–08
		(billions of dollars)		
Budgetary revenues	211.9	220.9	227.1	235.8
Program expenses	176.3	179.2	188.8	196.5
Public debt charges	34.1	33.7	34.8	34.8
Total expenses	210.5	212.9	223.6	231.4
Planned debt reduction	1.5	8.0	3.0	3.0
Remaining surplus			0.6	1.4
Federal debt	494.4	486.4	483.4	480.4
Per cent of GDP				
Budgetary revenues	16.4	16.1	15.7	15.5
Program expenses	13.7	13.1	13.0	13.0
Public debt charges	2.6	2.5	2.4	2.3
Total expenses	16.3	15.6	15.4	15.2
Debt reduction	0.1	0.6	0.2	0.2
Federal debt	38.3	35.5	33.3	31.7
Nominal GDP (billions of dollars, calendar year)	1,290	1,369	1,451	1,517

Note: Totals may not add due to rounding.
[1] Revised to reflect the impact of consolidating found

Budget 2006 New Initiatives- Table 2

	2005–06	2006–07	2007–08	Total
		(millions of dollars)		
Accountability		57	60	117
Opportunity				
Reducing the GST rate to 6 per cent		3,520	5,170	8,690
Other tax relief for all Canadians	4,965	3,640	3,685	12,290
Creating jobs and growing Canada's economy		1,405	735	2,140
Promoting education, training and research		575	665	1,240
Support for opportunity in primary economic sectors	755	1,700	700	3,155
Other actions to support opportunity		3	3	6
Subtotal	5,720	10,843	10,958	27,521
Families and communities				
Families				
Canada's Universal Child Care Plan		1,610	2,335	3,945
Other family measures		632	672	1,304
Subtotal		2,242	3,007	5,249
Communities				
Immigration measures		251	298	549
Aboriginal communities		150	300	450
Environment		160	240	400
Infrastructure		464	925	1,389
Other community measures		75	85	160
Subtotal		1,100	1,848	2,948
Subtotal		3,342	4,855	8,197
Security				
Protecting Canadian families and communities		193	331	524
Securing our borders		188	216	404
Defence		401	725	1,126
Pandemic preparedness		170	290	460
Financial security		40	33	73
Subtotal		992	1,596	2,588
Equalization and Territorial Formula Financing		255		255
Expenditure reallocations		(1,200)	(2,420)	(3,620)
Total net budget 2006 initiatives	5,720	14,290	15,049	35,058

Note: This table does not include initiatives announced before the November 2005 *Economic and Fiscal Update* and confirmed by the Government.

PART THREE

WELCOME TO CANADA

WHAT YOU SHOULD KNOW

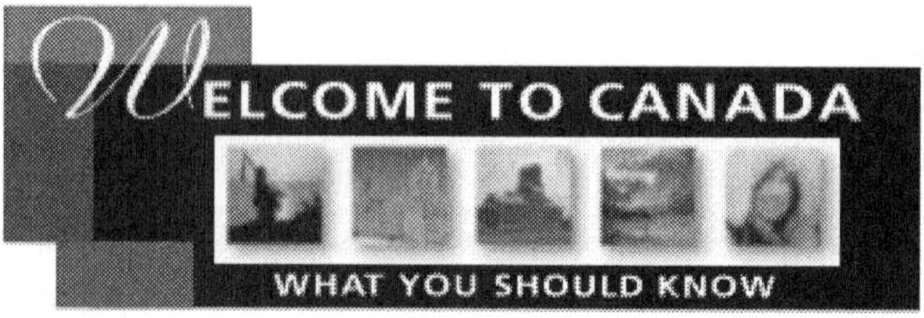

Table of Contents

WELCOME TO CANADA!

Congratulations! You have taken a big step. Moving to a new country takes courage. It also creates exciting opportunities and new beginnings. Taking the time to learn what to expect -- and what is expected of you -- will help you succeed. This guide tells you a little about what it's like to live in Canada. It also lets you know who can help if you need more information. We hope it will help you adapt to your new life. Be assured that those who already live in Canada add their wishes for your happiness and success in your new country.

Your first year in Canada will be emotional and full of change. You may be looking for a place to live, a job, and schools for your children. You will probably make many new friends. Some of them will know how it feels to move to a new community or new country.

Regardless of your situation, being a newcomer may mean giving up some familiar things for a new way of life. As a result, you may feel anxious or afraid, especially during the first few days and weeks. Almost all newcomers experience these emotions as they settle in. Feeling at home in a new country takes time.

The best way to adjust to your new community is to become involved! Do not hesitate to speak English or French, even if you make mistakes. Understanding and speaking one of Canada's official languages will help you adapt more easily. As you talk with the people you meet, you will feel more in control of your new life. Use each day as an opportunity to learn. Ask questions whenever you need to. Most people are pleased to help. Canadians believe in the spirit of community. No matter which city or town you choose to live in, you will find people who can help you adapt to your new life, and fit into Canadian society.

In the weeks, months and years ahead, you will have many opportunities to participate fully in Canadian life. Take them. You and your family can grow together, side by side with other Canadians, and make a better life for everyone. This is your new home. Welcome to Canada!

Sources of information

- How to find information
- Getting around
- Using the telephone
- The telephone book
- Call centres and touch-tone telephones
- Emergency 911
- Voice mail
- Pay phones
- Directory assistance
- Toll-free numbers
- Telephone services for people with special needs
- Using computers
- Public libraries

How to find information

The Government of Canada has designed this guide for you -- the new resident in Canada. It includes some basic information about living in Canada. The guide also contains many telephone numbers and addresses, which should be helpful in the next few days, and during the next few years. It can refer you to the help you need, or tell you how to find it.

You may have already received general information about your new country. But what you'll need to know now is more specific. Where can you take language classes? What about housing? How do you go about finding a job in Canada? Whom do you call to find out about schools for your children?

The *Welcome to Canada* guidebook and pamphlets can help you find the answers to these questions. Canada is a huge country, and every province is different. While we can't provide you with all the information you need, we may be able to refer you to the departments, agencies, and organizations, which can help you. Some may be able to help you directly; others may refer you to another source of information.

Immigrant-serving organizations can help you to settle into Canadian society, and many of their services are free. Contact an immigrant-serving organization to find what services are provided. You may find the addresses and telephone numbers of some of these organizations in the pamphlet called *Finding Help in Your Community,* which is in the back pocket of this guide. Many of these organizations represent a number of different immigrant services and groups, so they are a great place to start.

Canada's three levels of government -- federal, provincial and municipal -- also offer a variety of helpful programs and services for newcomers. Who offers these programs and services may vary across Canada, since different provinces have different immigration agreements with the federal government. You will find commonly used government telephone numbers listed in the pamphlet called *Key Information Sources,* which is in the back pocket of this guide. To find out about free language training in your area, please refer to the pamphlet called *Language Training,* also in the back pocket of this guide.

Since the province of Quebec looks after many important aspects of its immigration program, this guide does not attempt to cover services in this province. If you are planning to move to Quebec, you may wish to pick up their guide for newcomers, entitled: *Vivre au QUÉBEC!* You can obtain this booklet from the *ministère des Relations avec les citoyens et de l'Immigration (MRCI).* You will find the MRCI telephone numbers for your area listed in the pamphlets called *Key Information Sources* and *Finding Help in Your Community,* which are in the back pocket of this guide.

Religious institutions, community groups, ethnic associations and newcomer clubs, which can give you a hand are probably located right in your neighbourhood. Their telephone numbers can be found in the local telephone book.

Remember, the information and services provided may vary from one place to another. To get the most out of this guide and the pamphlets that go with it, we suggest that you:

- **get a map of your community;**
- **get a copy of the local telephone book; and**

- **contact the immigrant-serving organizations in your community.**

This guide, along with an immigrant-serving organization, can help you through the steps you need to take to settle. It can help you sort out the information you are missing and what services you need. The *Welcome to Canada* guide also includes a checklist to help you with the things you need to do first.

Getting around

It is useful to have a map of the area where you will be living. It will help you to get around and find the services you need. Most bookstores, gas stations and convenience stores sell maps at a reasonable price. You may also be able to get a map of your community free through your local Chamber of Commerce or municipal office. You can also look at maps in the library, at no cost. However, you can't take maps out of the library.

Using the telephone

Canadians like to use the telephone for communicating. They talk on the telephone everywhere -- at home, in their cars, on the street, in telephone booths. You will find that telephone books are great sources of information. Most of the important telephone numbers you need can be found in alphabetical order in the telephone book. You will receive one from the company, which installs a telephone in your home. You may also be able to pick one up from a phone centre. Phone centres are often located in large shopping malls. There are also telephone books at the library, and where you find pay phones.

At home: You pay a basic rate each month for telephone service. This pays for all local calls. You will be charged extra for each long distance call you make. Long distance calls are made to telephone numbers outside your local area.

Away from home: Pay phones in most provinces cost 25 cents per local call, and you can find them in most public places. If you do not know a telephone number, dial 411 and ask the operator. There is a charge for using this number. You may also purchase telephone cards, which can be used to call anywhere from any telephone, including public telephones.

The telephone book

Telephone books in Canada include white, blue, and yellow pages. The white pages list home telephone numbers in and around your area, as well as some businesses. The blue pages list government numbers. The yellow pages list business numbers -- restaurants, services, stores, and so on. These are listed by subject or product.

In the front part of the telephone book you will find emergency numbers like fire departments and ambulance services. The most important number listed here is an emergency number, 911 in many provinces, which you can call for help in life-threatening emergencies.

The white pages of the telephone book list home and business numbers in alphabetical order, from A to Z, using the last name of the person listed. So look up John Smith under S, for Smith.

The blue pages of the telephone book list telephone numbers for Canadian government departments, including the federal, provincial, municipal and regional governments. For frequently used government telephone numbers, see the pamphlet called *Key Information Sources,* in the back pocket of this guide.

The yellow pages are found in a separate telephone book in some of the larger cities in Canada.

Call centres and touch-tone telephones

Many businesses and government departments receive so many calls that they have set up "call centres" to help them answer the most commonly asked questions. Call centres use a series of messages, which have already been recorded to answer your questions. You find these messages by using the numbers, letters and symbols on the keys of your touch-tone telephone. The call centre message will tell you which keys on your telephone to press for the information you need. If you miss it the first time around, the message will usually tell you which key to press to hear it again. The list of messages is usually called a "menu." You choose and order the information you want.

You can also enter information into some call centres, using the keys on the telephone.

Remember: the "pound" key is the one that looks like this [#]. The "star" key looks like this [*].

Emergency 911

If you fear for your safety, or the safety of someone in your family, you should call your local emergency number for help. In many Canadian cities this number is 911. This connects you immediately to ambulances, fire departments, the police, and other emergency services. In other communities not equipped with 911 services, dial 0 and ask the operator for help. Other medical emergency numbers are listed in the first few white pages of the telephone book. These may include a poison information number, a distress or sexual assault help line, and a number to call if you or someone in your family is being abused.

Voice mail

Many Canadians, and most Canadian businesses and departments, have some form of answering machine or service to take messages for them when they are away from their phones. The telephone may ring several times, and then a recorded message will ask you to leave your name and number and a short message. You will usually hear a beeping sound followed by a silence. At this point leave your spoken message and remember to speak clearly and slowly. You may want to repeat your telephone number twice.

Pay phones

You may want to use a public telephone when you are out, or before you get your telephone installed. There are many pay telephone booths set up on city streets, in shopping malls, in airports -- anywhere there are lots of people. You pay for these telephone calls as you use the telephone. For local calls, you put in 25 cents (this charge may vary in some provinces) and make your call. You should have the right number of coins to put in the slot. If the call is long distance, you will need to put in more money (coins) as you go along, and an operator, or the message across the screen on the pay telephone, will tell you how much. Make sure you have lots of coins with you! Eventually, you may want to get a calling card from a telephone company. This card allows you to dial in a special code and make calls on public phones without putting in any money. These calls are then billed on your regular telephone bill at home.

Directory assistance

If you need help finding a telephone number, you may call for assistance. Call 411 for local numbers, and 0 for overseas numbers. All telephone numbers have an area code, which refers to the location of the number. You can look up these codes in your local telephone book. If the call you wish to make is outside the local area code, it is probably going to be long distance. ***Call 1+AREA CODE+555-1212*** if you need help to find the number. Remember, there is a charge for using this service.

Toll-free numbers

Canada is a very large country, and it can be expensive to make calls from one city to another. Many businesses and government departments use telephone numbers that start with **1-800, 1-888, or 1-877**. This lets you call them for free, within a province, or within Canada. These are known as toll-free numbers. Simply dial the 1-800, 1-888, or 1-877 number exactly as listed.

Telephone services for people with special needs

Many telephone companies in Canada can provide special telephone equipment for people with a hearing, speech, visual or physical disability. Contact your local telephone company to get more information on these kinds of services and equipment. You can find the name of the telephone company in your area by looking at a telephone book in a pay telephone. The Customer Service number is usually in the first few pages of the book. In areas served by Bell Canada, you can also visit a Bell Phone centre. These are usually found in large shopping malls.

Using computers

A great deal of helpful information is now available through the Internet, a worldwide resource and information system. You don't need to own a computer or have Internet access at home to use it. You can often use the Internet (or "surf the web," as Canadians like to say), free of charge at your local public library (you must reserve a time slot), community centre, school, immigrant-serving organization or Human Resources Development Canada office. Useful information can be found on various "web sites," which are like codes or addresses on the Internet.

Public libraries

In most communities across Canada, there are public libraries which can be used free of charge. Libraries are a resource which many newcomers make use of to read the daily newspapers, use the internet and borrow books.

- ☑ **Do you have a map of the area where you will be living?**
- ☑ **Do you know how to use a telephone book?**

GETTING TO KNOW CANADA

- The Canadian way of life

The Canadian way of life

Canada is an immense country. It is very diverse in its people, its landscape, its climate and its way of life. However, Canadians do share the same important values. These values guide and influence much of our everyday life. These are values of pride, a belief in equality and diversity and respect for all individuals in society. Women, men, children and seniors are all equally respected in Canada. Canadians may be different from each other but it is these shared values that make Canada a friendly, caring, peace loving and secure society in which to live.

Fairness, tolerance and respect. Canadians want fairness and justice for themselves, their children and their families. And most are fair and just to others, no matter who they are or where they come from.

Diversity and cooperation. Canadians understand the value of cooperation. In a country as large and diverse as Canada, people must be able to learn to resolve or ignore small conflicts in order to live happily and peacefully.

Equal opportunity. Canadians believe in equality. Each person is equal before the law and is treated equally by the law. Women and men have the same opportunity for success. Canadians let people live as they wish, as long as they do not limit how others live.

Civil responsibility. Canadians appreciate their rights and freedoms, which are the same without regard to gender, race, or ethnicity. Most also want to contribute to our society. As a newcomer, you should be aware of your rights and responsibilities. The right to participate in Canadian society implies an obligation to help it succeed. Canadian citizenship is about caring enough to want to get involved and make Canada even better.

Environmental responsibility. Canadians are especially conscious of their natural environment and the need to both respect and protect it for the future. For example, individual Canadians participate in recycling programs that help convert "garbage" into usable materials. Canadians also like to keep their parks and streets clean, by putting their garbage into garbage cans and cleaning up after their pets. In many public places, smoking is not permitted.

BASIC SERVICES

- Citizenship and Immigration Canada (CIC) Call Centres
- Immigrant-serving organizations
- Host Program
- Immigrant Settlement and Adaptation Program (ISAP)
- LINC (Language Instruction for Newcomers)
- Government services

Citizenship and Immigration Canada (CIC) Call Centres

You can get general information about immigration and citizenship by calling the CIC Call Centre. Recorded information is available 24 hours a day, seven days a week, in English or French. If you have access to the Internet, you can also view the CIC Web site (http://www.cic.gc.ca) for recent announcements, publications, and application kits and guides. (See the section on "Using computers" for further information on Internet web sites.)

The CIC Call Centre can provide:

- **general information about immigration and citizenship programs and services;**
- **general information about your application;**
- **application and information kits;**
- **help with fee calculations.**

Remember: If you have an immigration client identification (ID) number, you will need it to obtain information about your application.

Here's how it works:

1. **A recorded message will tell you to press 1 or 2 to select English or French.**
2. **The recorded message will list a "menu" from which to choose the information you need. Press the star [*] key to repeat the message.**
3. **Press 9 to return to the main menu and make your choice.**
4. **During normal business hours (8 a.m. to 4 p.m.) across Canada, you can press 0 to speak directly to a program assistant. If all the assistants are busy, stay on the line until one becomes free.**

How to contact the Call Centre:

If you are in the local calling area of:

Montreal, call: 514-496-1010

Toronto, call: 416-973-4444

Vancouver, call: 604-666-2171

If you are anywhere else in Canada, call toll-free: 1-888-242-2100. If you wish to use the Internet, the address is http://www.cic.gc.ca.

Remember: One of the most frequent reasons for calling the Call Centre is to obtain application kits for Citizenship and Immigration services. These include sponsorship or citizenship applications. You don't need to speak to an assistant to order these kits -- simply follow the recorded instructions and leave your name and mailing address, including the postal code.

Immigrant-serving organizations

Canada has hundreds of organizations, which help newcomers settle into life in Canada. Many of them represent a number of different multicultural agencies and associations, so they can help you in several ways. They may provide language training, or help you find housing, or look for a job. They may also provide support for women, children, and families who are dealing with domestic violence. Some of these organizations can provide these services in your first language, which may be helpful in the first few months. The addresses and telephone numbers of many of these organizations are listed in the pamphlet *Finding Help in Your Community,* found in the back pocket of this brochure.

Host Program

The Host program is a federal government program, designed to:

- **Match you with a friend familiar with Canadian ways,**
- **Help you overcome the stress of moving to a new country,**
- **Help you learn about available services and how to use them,**
- **Help you practice English or French,**
- **Help you develop contacts in your employment field,**
- **And help you participate in community activities.**

In return, the host volunteer will have you as a new friend, learn about your culture and strengthen community life.

Immigrant Settlement and Adaptation Program (ISAP)

ISAP is a federal government program, designed to:

- **Help you with immediate needs,**
- **Refer you to economic, social, health, cultural, educational and recreational facilities,**
- **Provide you with information and orientation on banking, shopping, managing a household and so on,**
- **Provide you with interpretation or translation services when necessary,**
- **Provide you with short-term counseling,**
- **And provide you with employment-related services.**

LINC (Language Instruction for Newcomers)

LINC is a federal government program for adults that is designed to:

- **Assess your level of English or French through the LINC Assessment Centres,**
- **Refer you to an appropriate LINC Provider through the Assessment Centres,**

- **Provide you, through School boards, Colleges and Community Organizations, with full-time, part-time, evening, weekend and other classes based on your needs,**
- **Provide you with transportation and child minding when necessary.**

Government services

The main telephone numbers for federal, provincial, and municipal or regional government departments are listed in the blue pages of your local telephone book. Some are listed by department, or by service. Frequently called numbers are often listed at the beginning of each section, including a central information number.

If you need help to find a federal government program or service, call Information on the Government of Canada at 1-800-622-6232 or if you wish to use the Internet, the address is:

If you wish to use the Internet, the address is:
http://www.canada.gc.ca

WHERE TO BEGIN

- Papers and other identity documents
- Using public transportation
- Where to stay
- Canadian money
- Shopping
- Going out of town

Papers and other identity documents

Official papers, which relate to who you are and where you come from are extremely important. They can be hard to replace if you lose them. These include health records, birth certificates, and Records of Landing (IMM 1000). If you are living in Quebec, you will have a *Certificat de selection du Québec* (CSQ). You will need these papers to apply for important government services and benefits, and to obtain a Social Insurance Number card and Health Insurance Card. So it is very important to keep them in a safe place at all times, and not to lend them to your friends or let someone else use them. You could lose your benefits if you give your cards to someone else.

It is not necessary to carry your passport or visa around with you, but it is important to have a couple of pieces of ID (identification) with you at all times. Any two of the following would be good: a driver's licence, a photocopy of your permanent resident papers (the original should be kept in a safe place or in a safety deposit box at the bank), a Social Insurance Number card, a Health Insurance Card, and a credit card.

Using public transportation

Getting around in Canada is fairly easy. Most cities have urban transportation systems, including buses, streetcars, and trains, and some of the larger cities also have subways.

You can board these systems at regular stops along their routes. Some let you pay with cash; others require tickets. If you don't have a ticket for the bus, you must pay with the right amount of money (exact fare). This is because the driver does not carry any change. Once you get settled, you may want to buy a monthly pass or a package of tickets to save money. You can buy subway tickets at the subway station.

If you have to take several buses or the subway for a single trip, you do not need to pay each time. Simply ask the driver for a transfer, or pick one up from the machines on the subway platform.

If you are not sure where to board the bus or the streetcar, just ask someone, or follow the crowd. It's usually at the front of the bus, where you show your pass to the driver. When using public transportation, Canadians line up. First come, first served, is a common approach to many activities in Canada.

Maps of routes and schedules are usually available from the public transit company in your area, and there may also be a telephone information line. You may want to ask someone for the name of the transit company where you live, and then look it up in the white pages of your telephone book.

Where to stay

For the first few weeks or months, you will probably want to find some temporary housing while you look for a more permanent place to live. Hotels can be quite expensive, so you may want to rent a furnished room or apartment at first.

To help you in your search, you could check the classified ads in the daily newspaper in your area. Look under Apartments or Houses for Rent. You should also talk to the immigrant-serving organizations in your community. They might be able to help.

Canadian money

Canada's currency is the dollar. There are 100 cents in a dollar. Canadian coins include the penny (1 cent), nickel (5 cents), dime (10 cents), quarter (25 cents), a one-dollar coin known as the "loonie," and a two-dollar coin called a "toonie". The most common paper bills are $5, $10, $20 and $50.

Chances are that when you get to Canada you will have some Canadian money with you. If you don't, you may wish to exchange a small amount of your native currency for some Canadian money as soon as you arrive. Most airports have foreign exchange offices, which can do this for you. Try not to exchange too much, however, since the rate of exchange (how much your money will buy) may not be as good as at a local bank.

Shopping

In the first few days you may need a few supplies, like food and extra clothing. Stores in Canada may be set up a little differently than what you have experienced in other countries.

Most Canadian stores have central cashiers where you pay for your goods, but they can be hard to find. Grocery stores usually have rows of cashiers at the entrance to the store, and you bring your goods to the cash, line up and pay. Department stores, which sell a variety of products, are sometimes set up this way too. Other stores have cashiers set up in different places around the store, and you pay at the nearest cashier. You will receive a paper receipt for whatever you buy, and this is your "proof of payment."

Many stores in Canada have metal shopping carts where you can put your purchases as you make your way through the store to the cashier.

Many Canadian stores are grouped together in large shopping malls, so you can do all your shopping in one place. Remember that each store has its own cash register where you pay for your purchases.

Many places in Canada also have large open-air markets, where you can buy fresh fruits and vegetables from local farmers. You pay for your purchases as you go along, from the farmers at each "stand."

Going out of town

Buses, trains and planes travel throughout Canada. For out-of town trips, contact travel agencies, airline companies or bus lines. For information about train travel, contact Via Rail. The telephone numbers are listed in the yellow pages.

☑ **Have you got any Canadian money?**

☑ **Are your identity papers in a safe place?**

☑ **Do you have some form of identification with you?**

HEALTH SERVICES

- Applying for a Health Insurance Card
- Finding doctors and clinics
- Emergency help
- Immunization for children
- Immunization for adults
- Medical surveillance
- Pregnancy
- To find out more...

Applying for a Health Insurance Card

Canada has one of the finest health insurance programs in the world. Health insurance means that you don't have to "pay" directly for most health care services. They are paid for through your taxes. When you use these services, you simply present your Health Insurance Card.

While health insurance is a national service, each province administers its own program. There may be some variations for eligibility from province to province. In some provinces you will have to pay a small monthly fee for this insurance. It is important to apply for your Health Insurance Card as soon as possible. You will receive your Health Insurance Card from the province where you live. You can get an application form at a doctor's office, a hospital, a pharmacy or an immigrant-serving organization. You can also get forms from the provincial ministry responsible for health, listed in the blue pages of your telephone book. You will need to show some identification, such as your birth certificate or passport and/or Record of Landing (IMM 1000).

Permanent residents in British Columbia, Ontario, Quebec and New Brunswick have a three-month eligibility-waiting period. During this time, you should apply for temporary private, health insurance coverage. Private insurance companies are listed in the yellow pages of the telephone book, usually under "Insurance." Private health insurance is also available for services, which are not covered under the government health insurance plan. These might include dental costs or private hospital rooms. Some employers also offer additional health insurance for a monthly deduction from your pay cheque. In most provinces, health insurance does not cover the cost of prescription drugs, dental care, ambulance services and prescription eyeglasses.

Needy refugee claimants and refugees living in the provinces, which have the three-month eligibility-waiting period, can receive emergency and essential health services. The cost of these services is covered by the Interim Federal Health Program.

Remember: Each member of your family needs his or her own Health Insurance Card. Always bring your card with you when you go to the doctor or the hospital.

A Health Insurance Card must not be exchanged with anyone else. It is for your use only and you could lose the benefits it provides by letting other people use it. You could also face criminal charges and be removed from Canada.

Finding doctors and clinics

Most Canadians have a family doctor and dentist. Ask an immigrant service organization or someone you know to recommend one. You can also look them up in the yellow pages of the telephone book under "Physicians and Surgeons," or "Dentists." Canada also has a large number of medical clinics, which can offer a variety of health services without an appointment, or in a minor emergency. These are listed under "Clinics" or "Clinics-Medical" in the yellow pages.

Emergency help

If you need urgent medical help, quickly go to the emergency department of your nearest hospital or call the emergency number "911."

If you have a serious medical condition, such as diabetes, high blood pressure or allergies to medications, ask your doctor or hospital about Medic Alert tags and bracelets. These can provide useful information in an emergency.

Immunization for children

Immunization or vaccination for children is one of the most effective ways we protect all Canadians, young and old, from getting serious infectious diseases. These diseases include diphtheria, polio and tetanus. Your child gets a small dose of vaccine to help him or her build up "immunity" to these diseases. You can arrange to have your child inoculated through your doctor or pediatrician, or through a public health clinic. You will receive an immunization or vaccination record, which you may have to provide to your child's school.

In Canada there is a "schedule" for these immunizations. For example, some shots are given when your child is two months old, at four months, at six months, and so on. Ask your doctor or pediatrician for a copy of this schedule, or look up the municipal department responsible for school immunization in the blue pages of your telephone book. You may also find a central help line listed under "Immunization" in the white pages of the telephone book. The schedule varies slightly from province to province.

Immunization for adults

If you were not immunized against preventable diseases before coming to Canada, you should contact your doctor or local public health clinic immediately.

Medical surveillance

During the medical exam you underwent before becoming a Canadian resident, you may have been told that you needed a follow-up medical exam once you got to Canada. This is known as medical surveillance for those who have an inactive infectious disease. You must report, by telephone, to the public health authority of the province or territory where you live within 30 days of entering Canada. You will find this number in the blue pages of your telephone book. This is very important for your health, and for the health of your fellow Canadians.

Pregnancy

Maternity leave is the right of all working mothers in Canada. If you are pregnant and have to stop working for a while, you can take leave, from your employer for a set period of time. You may also be entitled to paid leave, or maternity benefits. You can get more information from the provincial ministry responsible for labour or from a Human Resources Development Canada office.

For help and information before and after your baby is born, contact your local community service centre or hospital. They offer prenatal courses, medical help, nursing care, and a way to meet other new mothers. They can also give you information on registering the birth with the province, so that you receive an official birth certificate. They can also advise you about birth control and abortion.

☑ **Have you applied for your Health Insurance Card?**

To find out more...

Key medical emergency numbers are listed in the front section of the white pages of your telephone book. Look up doctors and clinics in the yellow pages. There is also printed health information available from provincial ministries of health and from Citizenship and Immigration Canada. Free pamphlets are also available on a variety of topics from Health Canada (found in the federal listings in the blue pages of your telephone book), or from doctor's offices and drug stores.

ESTABLISHING YOURSELF

- Applying for a Social Insurance Number card
- Applying for the Canada Child Tax Benefit

Applying for a Social Insurance Number card

Applying for a Social Insurance Number (SIN) card is one of the most important things you will do after coming to Canada. You will need one to work here, to open a bank account or to obtain your tax credit. This number tells the government who is earning money, paying taxes, paying into pension plans, and using government services. Your employers will ask you for this number.

To apply for one, simply go to your nearest Human Resources Development Canada office (listed in the blue pages of your telephone book). As a new immigrant, you will need to provide the original of your Record of Landing (IMM 1000). If the name you are using to apply for your SIN card is different than the one found on the document you are providing, you must also provide either a marriage certificate or a change of name document.

Remember: You must make sure that the name on all documents is the same name. This name must always belong to the same person, and it must be spelled correctly.

Applying for the Canada Child Tax Benefit

If you have children under 18, the Government of Canada may be able to help you with some of the costs of raising them. This monthly tax-free payment is called the Canada Child Tax Benefit. The amount of the benefit is based on several factors, such as: your family income, the number of children you have and their ages, and your province or territory of residence. When you apply, you must provide proof of your Canadian immigration status, and proof of birth for any of your children born outside of Canada.

To apply for the Canada Child Tax Benefit, you must have filed an Income Tax and Benefit Return. If you were not residents of Canada in time to fill out a return, you will need to complete a separate form to declare your world income. You can get these forms and more information on the Canada Child Tax Benefit by calling the Canada Customs and Revenue Agency at (613) 941-9300 or the toll-free number: 1-800-387-1193, or visit http://www.ccra-adrc.gc.ca

If you live in Quebec, Canada Customs and Revenue Agency will automatically send the Régie des rentes du Québec all information needed to register your children for the Quebec family allowance.

FINDING A PLACE TO LIVE

- Renting
- Your rights as a tenant
- Buying
- Heat and hydro
- Getting a telephone
- Furnishing
- To find out more...

Renting

Many Canadians rent housing, and so do most newcomers, at least for the first few years. Apartments and houses for rent are usually listed in the classified advertising section of the newspaper. It is also a good idea to walk around an area you would like to live in, and see if there are any signs posted on or by the buildings. Do not take the first place you see -- try to shop around a little, see what's available. Prices often vary considerably.

Some apartments can be rented by the month, but with most rented housing you sign a lease for a year. This is a legally binding contract between you and the landlord. Make sure you understand exactly what you have to pay for, and what is included in your rent. For example, do you pay for the heating costs or are they included? Canada is a cold country in the winter, and heating can be expensive. Are you allowed to have pets? Are the fridge and stove included? Do you have to pay municipal taxes? Also, you may have to pay a security deposit (such as the first month's rent) to rent the apartment you have chosen. Read the lease over carefully before you sign it.

You should also purchase tenant's insurance to cover the costs of replacing the household contents of your apartment. It is probably a good idea to ask someone in your local community group or immigrant-serving organization for information about housing. They can also explain the legal terms used in leases.

Remember: Avoid signing a lease if you plan to move again soon.

Your rights as a tenant

Both tenants (someone who rents a room, an apartment or house) and landlords both have legal rights. There are laws, which protect you from sudden rent increases or being forced to leave your apartment. You have the right to live anywhere you choose. Discrimination on the basis of colour, creed, sex, age or disability is not allowed by the *Canadian Charter of Rights and Freedoms.* Provincial landlord and tenant laws also protect against such discrimination. You also have responsibilities. It is important to keep the house or apartment you are renting in the same condition you found it. Call the provincial or municipal government department responsible for housing, sometimes called a rental board, if you need information or help, or look up the provincial Landlord and Tenant Regulations. You will find the numbers in the blue pages of the telephone book. You can also ask community groups for information or help.

Buying

Buying a home is a big step, and you might want to wait until you are settled before you do so. Most homes in Canada are sold through real estate agents, although some owners do it themselves. You may see "For Sale" signs posted in front of homes, and you can also read the classified advertising section of the daily newspaper.

When buying a house, it's important to remember that there are many hidden costs. These may include the agent's fee, in some provinces, as well as lawyer's or notary's fees, yearly property tax, house insurance, registration fees, various home buyer taxes, and the cost of maintaining the house -- heat, hydro, water, sewer, and so on. Make sure you know exactly what your costs will be before you buy.

You may want to find out about the First Home Loan Insurance Program, run by Canada Mortgage and Housing Corporation. It enables you to buy a home with a smaller down payment. The Corporation's fee is rolled into the total mortgage in the form of a small percentage.

Heat and hydro

Whether you rent or buy, you will need to sign up for various basic services, such as heat and hydro (electricity). In Canada, some homes are heated by gas, others by oil, and others by electricity. Frequently, there are one or two main companies, which provide these services in an area, and you can find these in the yellow pages of the telephone book. Try looking under "Gas," "Heating Companies," "Oils/Fuel," and "Hydro-Electric."

Getting a telephone

You will want to get a telephone installed quickly, so that you can reach the people and the services you need from the comfort of your home. Bell Canada operates most of the telephone service across Canada, but you can find out the name of the telephone company in your area in a telephone book. The Customer Service number should be in the first few pages of the book. The telephone company in your area normally has phone centres in large shopping malls. You can visit them to get your service set up.

You can either rent a telephone from your telephone company and pay month by month or buy one. The cost of making local calls is covered by the monthly service fee, which is added to the cost of renting the telephone. Long distance and overseas calls are not covered by this monthly fee, and can be quite expensive. Many telephone companies offer special plans, which can reduce the costs of long distance calls. Phone cards, which can be used to call anywhere from any phone including public telephones, are a cost-effective way to reduce long-distance charges.

Remember: Canada is a very large country, so even when you're calling within the same province or city, long distance charges may apply.

Furnishing

Chances are you're going to need some basic furniture and household appliances. You can buy new, which can be costly, or wait for stores to have sales and buy things gradually. You can also buy used furniture and appliances, which is what many Canadians do. Articles or furniture for sale listings are found in the classified advertising section of the newspaper. You can also try used furniture stores, church and local rummage or garage sales, or community organizations. Your local community immigrant service organization should be able to help you with names and addresses.

To find out more...

Probably one of the best sources of information is your local immigrant-serving organization. You might also want to consult the provincial or municipal department responsible for housing, listed in the blue pages of your telephone book. They may have a central information number.

The Canada Mortgage and Housing Corporation (CMHC) has a free pamphlet entitled *Home buying, Step by Step.* They also run the Canada Housing Information Centre, and can provide information on the rental and housing markets across Canada. Call their toll-free number for more information: 1-800-668-2642 or visit their website at http://www.cmhc-schl.gc.ca

---

- ☑ **Have you contacted your telephone company?**
- ☑ **Do you have your address and telephone number with you?**
- ☑ **Do you know how to get heat and light?**

PROTECTING YOUR MONEY

- Banks and other financial institutions
- Opening an account
- Using banking machines
- Direct deposit
- Sending money
- Applying for credit
- Telemarketing
- To find out more...

Banks and other financial institutions

Most Canadians keep their money in the bank. A bank account is a safe place to keep your money. Banks let you write cheques, earn interest, apply for credit, and pay your bills. These kinds of financial services are also offered by credit unions, caisses populaires and trust companies.

Opening an account

Most banks have various kinds of accounts, and you can discuss which kind you need with them. To open one, you should be prepared to provide certain kinds of personal information, as well as various forms of identification, such as your passport, or your Social Insurance Number. The bank will need your Social Insurance Number for income tax purposes. This is the same for anyone, at any bank. If you have not received your SIN card when you go to open your account, you should present proof that you have applied for one.

Remember: Post Office savings accounts do not exist in Canada.

Using banking machines

Many Canadians now use Automated Banking Machines, known as ATMs, to do most of their banking. It's like a self-service bank, one that's "open" 24 hours a day, seven days a week. With a bankcard, you can use these machines to get cash from your accounts, to pay bills, to deposit cheques, and so on. You will likely pay a small fee for this service.

You can apply for a card at your bank. You will need to create a Personal Identification Number (PIN) for yourself to access your accounts. Don't lend your bankcard to anyone, or tell anyone your PIN. Don't even let anyone see your PIN number when you enter it in the banking machine. This will keep your account (and your money) safe.

Bankcards can also be used to buy things at many stores. The money is taken directly from your account when you use your card. This is known as Interac Direct Payment.

While all of these services are useful, keeping track of all your bank transactions can get complicated. Remember to record everything and take note of your balance and the fees charged by your financial institution.

Direct deposit

Direct deposit has become very popular with Canadians. It means that money owed to you, such as a paycheque or a government payment, is put electronically into your account. You have access to the money immediately, and you don't have to wait for the cheque to come in the mail or line up at the bank to deposit it. You can request this service if you expect to receive regular payments. Most government departments offer this service, as well as many companies.

Sending money

If you send money outside Canada, don't send cash. Use a certified cheque or money order. Ask your bank about these options. You can also buy a money order at the post office or wire money through private money order/transfer services (which are listed in the yellow pages of the telephone book).

Applying for credit

Getting credit means that you borrow money to buy something now and pay it back later, with interest. Interest is the fee charged for using the money. Interest rates can be quite high, so you should be very careful how you use credit.

Credit comes in many forms -- credit cards, lines of credit, mortgages, or loans. You can apply for credit cards at banks and trust companies. These cards allow you to buy items on credit and be billed for them within a month. If you pay the full amount back by the due date, you won't be charged any interest.

If you borrow any money on credit, make sure you understand exactly when you have to pay it back and how much it will cost. This includes monthly payments if you are borrowing money on an installment plan.

Many department stores now advertise special sales which claim that you can buy something now and pay for it in a year, or in six months with no interest, and so on. Make sure you understand exactly what you must pay and when, before you sign anything. If any information is hard to understand, ask someone you trust for a clear explanation.

Telemarketing

You may get calls from people who are trying to sell you something. They may be honest; but then again, they might be dishonest. The best way to protect yourself is never to give out any personal or financial information to anyone over the telephone. If you feel uneasy about the caller, just hang up.

To find out more...

There is a great deal of free information available to you from your bank, including financial advice. The Canadian Bankers Association also offers a free series of publications, ranging from how to open an account, how to manage your money, how to use bank machines, and how to save for your children's education. You can call their toll-free number to obtain copies: 1-800-263-0231 or you can visit their website at http://www.cba.ca

---

☑ **Have you opened a bank account?**

FINDING A JOB

- Immigrant-Serving Organizations can help
- Human Resources Development Canada offices
- Using the newspaper and other resources
- Documents and foreign credentials
- Getting paid
- Working for yourself
- Business and travel
- Daycare
- Labour laws and human rights
- Volunteering

At first you may find it difficult to get work that matches your skills. It may also be difficult to find a job that pays as much as you want until you get Canadian experience. Try not to be discouraged. When the right job does come along, you will have the benefit of that previous experience.

When you apply for a job in Canada, the employer will want some information about you. Bring a list of your education and work experience (a résumé). Also bring letters of reference from your former employers, your professional degrees and trade certificates. You may be asked to provide English or French copies of these documents.

Remember that certain trades or professions are regulated, which means that you must be licensed, registered or certified to practice them. In other words, you must meet certain standards, which are set by the organization responsible for your profession in the province where you plan to work. The standards vary from province to province. So even though you may be qualified in another country, your qualifications must meet Canadian standards for you to be licensed to practice.

Immigrant-Serving Organizations can help

If you cannot speak the language used by the employer, ask a friend to interpret for you, or get a translator through an immigrant-serving organization. You might also want to ask about job finding clubs, about workshops, and about getting help with preparing a résumé or writing a letter. These services are often provided by immigrant-serving organizations themselves or by the province. Refer to the pamphlet *Finding Help in Your Community* in the back pocket of this book.

Human Resources Development Canada offices

Many jobs are posted either on billboards or on self-serve computers at your local Human Resources Development Canada (HRDC) office. The Canadian government runs HRDC offices throughout Canada. They provide information and services for people looking for work. Some offer free use of computers, printers, the Internet, telephones, fax service, and resource libraries. They may offer workshops on how to prepare a résumé or look for work, as well as computer training and other courses.

HRDC also runs the Job Bank, and the Electronic Labour Exchange (ELE), an Internet site that matches jobs to people and people to jobs. Employers use the exchange to advertise a job and you can use it to advertise your skills to thousands of potential employers. The Internet address for the Electronic Labour Exchange is http://www.ele-spe.org

Another Internet site, which may be useful, is "Work search." This is an easy-to-use site, which can help you with all aspects of looking for work. The Internet address for this site is www.worksearch.gc.ca. The HRDC youth InfoLine is 1-800-935-5555.

You can find the nearest Human Resources Development Canada office listed in the blue pages of the telephone book, under Human Resources Development Canada.

Using the newspaper and other resources

Many jobs are listed in newspapers. Look in the classified advertisements section under "Help Wanted" and "Careers". There may also be a separate career section in the weekend paper.

Libraries are also helpful. They have books on how to find a job or write a résumé, and they often keep directories of businesses across Canada or in your area. These publications can help you to find information about potential employers. Their "periodical" section will also have copies of various weekly magazines, which provide new listings of jobs across Canada. You can also access the Internet at most public libraries. Ask for more information at the reference desk.

"Networking" is also a popular way of finding a job in Canada. This means contacting all the people you know, including your friends and relatives, and letting them know you are looking for work. This may help you to find a job, which is not actually advertised anywhere. Job-finding clubs run by immigrant-serving organizations may also be useful.

There are also private job placement agencies, which may be able to help you find permanent, temporary or contract work. Remember that since employers pay a fee to use these agencies, your salary may be somewhat lower than it would be if you found the job by yourself. These agencies are listed in the yellow pages of the telephone book. Look under "Employment Agencies."

Documents and foreign credentials

You may need Canadian qualifications to work at a licensed trade or profession. You may have to write an examination or work as a trainee to qualify. The requirements vary from province to province and from profession to profession. You might want to contact the national and/or provincial association, which looks after accreditation in your profession or trade. You can also contact the Canadian Information Centre for International Credentials, or other international credentials evaluations services. These are listed in the pamphlet *Key Information Sources* in the pocket at the back of this brochure.

Getting paid

Employers have the choice to pay their workers every week, every two weeks or once a month. You can be paid in cash, by cheque or by direct deposit to your bank account. Your pay stub (the piece of paper attached to your pay cheque) shows how much you earned. It also lists any money taken off (deductions) for federal and provincial taxes, pension plans, employment insurance, and any other items.

Working for yourself

More and more Canadians are working for themselves and running home-based businesses. You too might want to join this fast-growing group of entrepreneurs and go into business for yourself, or with a partner. Numerous information resources are available to you.

The Canadian Bankers Association offers a free publication entitled: *Starting a Small Business.* This contains most of the information you will need at the beginning. You can order this by calling their toll-free number: 1-800-263-0231.

The Business Development Bank of Canada also provides a book for newcomers interested in working for themselves, called *Starting a Business in Canada: A Guide for New Canadians.* They also offer management training, counseling and planning services for entrepreneurs. Call their toll-free number for more information: 1-888-463-6232 or visit their website at http://www.bdc.ca

Canada Business Service Centres provide a central resource for Canadian business information, especially government information. You can find them in every province, and territory. They offer service on the Internet, or you can speak directly to a business information officer. To find the Canada Business Service Centre nearest you, look in the blue pages of your telephone book under the federal government.

The *Small Business Loans Act* helps small businesses get loans from banks and other lenders. Contact Industry Canada in the federal government listings in the blue pages of your telephone book for more information.

Business and travel

Although the Canadian government realizes that travel is often part of doing business, you may lose your permanent resident status if you stay outside of the country for more than 183 days in a year. Before you leave for business, you should check with the CIC Call Centre.

If you are an entrepreneur who has been admitted to Canada on certain conditions, Citizenship and Immigration Canada will check to see how your business is doing. The Department will also provide special counseling services to help you. If after two years you have not fulfilled the conditions under which you were admitted, you and your dependants might be asked to leave. Remember, this only applies to those who come in as entrepreneurs under certain terms and conditions.

Daycare

When you do find work, you must remember that it is illegal in Canada to leave children under the age of 12 at home by themselves. You may need to pay someone to look after your children while you work. There are several options you can look into, such as licensed day care centres, home-based day care, nursery schools, and "drop-in" day care centres. You can also hire someone to come into your home and look after your children. Look in the yellow pages under "Day Nurseries" or "Day Care." Also check the classified advertisements section of the newspaper under "Employment Wanted" to find a caregiver in your area. Government-subsidized daycare exists for low-income families.

Labour laws and human rights

In Canada there are provincial and federal labour laws designed to protect employees and employers. These laws set minimum wage levels, health and safety standards, hours of work, maternity leave, annual paid vacations and provide protection for children. There are also human rights laws, which protect employees from unfair treatment by employers based on sex, age, race, religion or disability.

You also have the right to join a labour union in Canada. Unions negotiate wages, hours of work and working conditions. Union fees will be deducted from your salary.

If you feel you are being treated unfairly by your employer, you may seek advice and/or assistance from an officer of the Ministry of Labour in the province where you work. You can also contact the Canadian Human Rights Commission or a Human Resources Development Canada office, where you can talk to a federal government labour affairs officer.

Volunteering

You might wish to help out in an agency or community organization as a volunteer. This means that you volunteer your time but you do not get paid. However, volunteering can help you develop Canadian job experience, get a practical knowledge of the Canadian workplace, practice your English or French and make new friends, as well as help others. You can find volunteer centres in the yellow pages of your telephone book, or contact your local community agency.

An example of volunteering is the Host Program. The Canadian government funds the Host Program to help newcomers adapt, settle and integrate into Canadian life. Host volunteers are Canadians who offer their time to be with newcomers and introduce them to the Canadian way of life.

For more information on the Host Program, contact one of the local immigrant-serving organizations listed in the pamphlet called *Finding Help in Your Community,* in the back pocket of this guide.

- ☑ **Do you know that it is illegal to leave children under 12 at home alone?**
- ☑ **Have you applied for a Social Insurance Number card at the Human Resources Development Canada office?**

LEARNING ENGLISH OR FRENCH

- Language Instruction for Newcomers to Canada (LINC)
- To find out more...

There are two official languages in Canada -- English and French. Almost everyone in Canada speaks at least one of these languages and millions of Canadians speak both. There are anglophone and francophone communities in every province and territory. English is the language of the majority everywhere in Canada, except in the province of Quebec where French is the official language. French is spoken in many communities in other provinces, especially New Brunswick, Ontario and Manitoba. New Brunswick is an officially bilingual province.

One of the most important skills you will need to adapt to life here in Canada is to speak English or French. Once you learn one or both of these languages, you will find it easier to get a job, to understand Canada, and to communicate with your children, who will be busy learning English or French at school. You will also need to know English or French to become a Canadian citizen.

There are many language courses available, and many of them are free. Sometimes these courses are called "ESL" for English as a Second Language courses, or "FSL," for French as a Second Language courses.

Language Instruction for Newcomers to Canada (LINC)

The Government of Canada, in cooperation with provincial governments, school boards, community colleges, and immigrant-serving organizations, offers free language training across the country to adult permanent residents. In most provinces, the name of the program is LINC. (In French this program is known as CLIC, for

Cours de langue pour les immigrants au Canada.) LINC can also assess your current language skills, to find out which training program would be best for you.

LINC offers both full- and part-time classes, to suit your needs. Most LINC centres can also refer you to other non-LINC classes in your area, and some offer free childcare while you attend classes.

Remember, language classes are available for all the adults in your family, not just the person who may be looking for work.

To find out more...

To find out where you can get LINC classes in your area, you will find a listing of LINC assessment centres in the pamphlet called *Language Training,* in the back pocket of this guide. You could also contact your local immigrant-serving organization. They will likely refer you to a LINC assessment centre, which will then refer you to organizations offering LINC classes. You might also want to telephone your local school board directly to find out about classes in your community.

Most universities and community colleges also offer language classes, as well as some private language schools and community organizations. You can contact these groups directly for more information. Remember to ask about fees, since these courses may not be free.

☑ **Do you know where the LINC assessment centre is in your community?**

EDUCATION

- Finding schools
- Enrolling your children
- Adult education
- To find out more...

Children between 6 and 16 must attend school, and most of them go to public schools. Classes usually start in early September and end in late June. There is a two-week vacation at Christmas and one-week vacation in either February or March. Children attend school Monday to Friday, for about six hours per day. They usually bring their lunch with them.

There are also private schools, but these can be quite expensive. Public and separate (Catholic) schools are paid for through your taxes.

Finding schools

The best way to find out which schools your children should attend is by phoning the school boards in your area. These are listed under "Schools" in the yellow pages of your telephone book. This choice is usually based on where you live and which system you prefer.

Many schools are not within walking distance, and children often take school buses (provided by the school at minimal or no cost to you) or public transportation to get there. This is something to consider when choosing either a school or a place to live.

Enrolling your children

When you enroll your children, take their birth certificates or other identity documents to the school. If the originals of the documents are in languages other than English or French, you should have them translated into English or French. Also bring their Record of

Landing (IMM 1000), passport and any former school and health records. You could also be asked for immunization records.

Adult education

Learning is a lifelong activity in Canada, and many Canadians continue to study as adults. Adult education is not free. Student loans are available through the universities and colleges. You may wish to train for a new job, or to improve the skills you already have. You may also wish to apprentice for a trade. The qualifications for many trades are different from province to province, and you must obtain a license before you can practice. Remember that some Canadian schools will not give credit for a course or diploma obtained outside Canada.

If you want information on continuing education, contact the school board, college or university in your community. Look these up in the yellow pages of the telephone book under "Schools," "Colleges," and "Universities." You can also get a list of the educational institutions in your area from an immigrant-serving organization.

You might also want to look up professional or trade associations in the province where you live for information on qualifications.

To find out more...

Other sources of information are:

- **provincial departments of education;**
- **school boards;**
- **universities and community colleges;**
- **professional or trade associations;**
- **immigrant-serving organizations.**

☑ **Are your children registered in school?**

☑ **Have your educational credentials been translated into English or French?**

TAXATION

- Income tax
- Other taxes
- To find out more...

Canadian residents can benefit from programs that have been paid for from their taxes and payroll contributions. These programs include social assistance for people in need; employment insurance for workers who have lost their jobs; worker's compensation for workers injured on the job; old-age pensions for citizens 65 years of age and older.

Income tax

Canadians pay a variety of taxes. Income tax is used by governments to provide services, such as roads, schools and health care. All residents of Canada are subject to income tax. Each year you must submit an Income Tax and Benefit Return to tell the government how much money you earned and how much tax you paid. Taxes are deducted automatically from most income you receive. If you paid too much, you will get a refund. If you paid too little, you will have to pay more.

Filing an income tax return is extremely important. You will need to file one each year to qualify for various government benefits, such as the Canada Child Tax Benefit. You can get the forms for the federal income tax from any post office or Canada Customs and Revenue Agency tax services office. Canada Customs and Revenue Agency has several publications for newcomers, which should be helpful. (Call 1-800 959-2221 or visit http://www.ccra-adrc.gc.ca) They also have volunteers who can help you fill out your tax forms, under the Community Volunteer Income Tax Program. This is a free service. The deadline for completing your tax return is April 30 of each year. Remember, if you lived in Quebec during the year you will also have to file a separate provincial tax return.

Other taxes

Whenever you buy something, a Goods and Services Tax (GST) will be added to the price. This includes everything from socks to a new house. You may also pay a provincial sales tax (PST), which varies from province to province. If you own your own home, you will also pay property and school taxes. For more information on these taxes, contact either your local school board or your municipal government.

To find out more...

Contact

- **Canada Customs and Revenue Agency,**
- **the provincial Ministry of Revenue, or**
- **your local school boards, all of which are listed in the telephone book.**

CANADIAN LAW

- Police
- Legal services
- Children's rights
- Women's rights
- Domestic violence
- Seniors' rights

Canada is governed by an organized system of laws. These laws are created by governments, which are chosen freely by the people. The law in Canada applies to everyone, including the police, judges, politicians, and members of the government. The main purposes of our laws are to provide order in society, to provide a peaceful way to settle disputes, and to express the values and beliefs of Canadian society. Everyone in Canada whether a citizen, or a permanent resident has equal access to the justice system.

Police

The police are there to keep people safe and enforce the law. You can ask the police for help in all kinds of situations -- if there's been an accident, if someone has stolen something from you, if you are a victim of assault, if you see a crime taking place, if someone you know has gone missing, etc.

There are different types of police in Canada, including provincial police departments and the Royal Canadian Mounted Police, who enforce federal laws. Remember, the police are there to help you. Don't hesitate to call 911 or 0 for the operator to contact your local police force in an emergency.

If for some reason you are questioned by the police or arrested, do not resist. Remember, in Canada, you are presumed innocent until proven guilty. Communicate as clearly as possible and look directly at the officer. Be ready to show some kind of identification. If you are taken into custody you have the right to know why and to have a lawyer and a translator, if needed. Under Canadian law, it is a serious crime to try to bribe the police by offering money, gifts or services in exchange for special treatment.

Legal services

If you need a lawyer to protect your interests in court, then you can hire one, for a fee. You may also be entitled to free legal services, or "legal aid," depending on your income. You will find the numbers for provincial legal aid in the booklet called *Key Information Sources* in the back pocket of this guide. An immigrant-serving organization will also be able to tell you where and how to obtain these services.

Children's rights

Parents in Canada have a legal duty to provide their children with the necessities of life until they reach age 16. It is illegal in Canada to abuse your children either physically, psychologically, or sexually. All forms of child abuse are serious crimes. Abuse can include spanking children enough to cause bruises, terrorizing or humiliating them, any kind of sexual contact, and neglect. Police, doctors, teachers and children's aid workers will take action if they think children are being harmed. In serious cases, children can be taken away from their parents. Some cultural practices are not acceptable in Canada. For instance, all forms of female genital mutilation (FGM) are prohibited under Canadian law.

In Canada, men and women are equal. They have the same rights, as outlined in the *Canadian Charter of Rights and Freedoms.* Discrimination against women and violence towards women are both against the law. Women who are abused by their husbands can seek help for themselves and their children in community shelters. They are also entitled to legal protection to keep them safe.

There are a number of organizations in Canada, which work to safeguard and promote the rights of women, and some of these organizations work to help immigrant women in particular. Your local immigrant-serving agency will be able to provide you with the names of these organizations. Information on legal rights and shelters can be found near the front of your telephone book under "Distress Centres," "Child Abuse," or "Sexual Assault."

Domestic violence

Violence towards any person -- man, woman or child -- is against the law in Canada. No one has the right to hit or threaten people or to force them into sexual activities. The law applies no matter who it is -- wife/husband, partner, girlfriend/boyfriend, parent, or another relative.

If you or your children are being abused, call the police at 911 or your local emergency number. They can help you find medical help or drive you to a safe place, if you wish. Emergency shelters, counseling and free legal advice are available for adults and children who are being abused. There are also Rape Crisis and Sexual Assault Support Centres listed in the first few pages of the telephone book. They are there to help you. In many Canadian cities there are also 24-hour-a-day telephone help lines, if you just need someone to talk to. They can also refer you to the help you need.

Many community centres also offer counseling for abusive partners who are seeking help, for families who wish to stay together, and for children.

Seniors' rights

A senior citizen is someone 65 years of age or older. If you are a senior, you may be entitled to certain government benefits, such as the Old Age Security pension (OAS) and the Guaranteed Income Supplement (GIS). In order to qualify, you must meet certain residence requirements. You may also be eligible for old age security benefits from your former country. Some provinces supplement these plans, and offer extra benefits such as prescription drug plans. For information, call 1-800 277-9914 (toll-free). If you have a hearing or speech impairment and you use a TDD/TTY device, please call 1-800 255-4786. The French toll-free number is 1-800 277-9915.

Many businesses also offer special rates for senior citizens, or special areas where seniors can be served more comfortably.

☑ **Do you know that violence towards any person -- man, woman or child -- is against the law in Canada?**

☑ **Do you know that the practice of female genital mutilation (FGM) is against the law?**

TRANSPORTATION

- Getting a driver's licence
- Buying a car
- Use of seat belts
- Car seats for children
- In case of an accident
- To find out more...

Getting a driver's licence

You need a valid driver's licence to drive a car in Canada, and these are issued by the province or territory where you live. Your foreign driver's licence may be valid for a short time after you arrive in Canada, but eventually you will need to take a Canadian driving test to remain licensed. This will help you to learn about the rules of the road in Canada. You may also want to obtain an International Driving Permit. Find out more from your provincial ministry of transportation or from your provincial motor vehicle licensing agency.

Driving lessons are available from private companies, for a fee. You may want to have a few lessons before you take your test. Look in the yellow pages under "Driving Instruction."

Remember: It is a legal requirement to carry your driver's licence with you whenever you drive. You should also carry your car registration and vehicle permit with you. It is good advice to carry a copy of your car insurance certificate.

Buying a car

Cars can cost a lot of money, whether they are used or new. Make sure you can afford the upkeep, the gas, the monthly payments and the costs of registering and insuring it. Some Canadians opt to lease cars. Leasing can be handy, but there are a number of hidden costs involved, such as administrative fees or handling taxes. Whichever option you choose make sure you understand exactly what your financial obligations are.

Car insurance is another major expense. All cars must be registered with the provincial motor vehicle licensing agency where you live, and must be insured. This is the law. Car insurance can be expensive, but it protects you and other drivers in case of an accident. You buy insurance through private insurance companies, listed in the yellow pages under "Insurance". Some provinces also sell insurance through provincial corporations. Shop around for the best rates. An accident-free record will help you get a better insurance rate. In most provinces, you can obtain more information by calling the Insurance Bureau of Canada or visiting their website at http://www.ibc.ca

Use of seat belts

You and your passengers must wear seat belts at all times when you are driving in Canada. This is the law. The use of a seat belt can save your life in an accident, and you can be fined for not wearing one.

Car seats for children

Babies and children who are too small to wear seat belts safely must be placed in car seats whenever you drive. These can also help to save lives in case of an accident. There are different types of car seats for different ages and weights. For example, infants must be placed in special seats that face the back of the car. Children over 18 kg need a booster seat.

In case of an accident

Call 911 or your local emergency number right away if you need medical help. Stay where you are, and get someone to call the police. You should also report the accident immediately to your car insurance company. It is also important to exchange your name, address, and telephone number, as well as your insurance and driver's licence numbers with the other driver. Never leave the scene of an accident, especially if you have hit someone. This is a serious offence known as "hit-and-run."

- ☑ **Do you have a valid driver's licence?**
- ☑ **Do you have car insurance?**
- ☑ **Do you have a car seat for your child?**

Contact the public transit organizations, provincial ministries of transportation, provincial motor vehicle licensing offices or insurance associations listed in the telephone book.

KEEPING IN TOUCH

- Canada Post
- Returning Resident Permits

Canada Post

Canada's mail is handled by the Canada Post Corporation. To send mail, use a postage stamp. You can buy postage stamps at any post office. They are also sold in many drug stores, hotel lobbies, airports, railway stations, bus terminals and some newsstands. The cost of the stamp is based on the weight and size of the letter or package, and where your mail is going. When you send something to an address in Canada, remember to include the six-digit postal code for that address, and also a return address. This will speed up delivery. If you are sending something overseas, you must use the special code for that country. You can find these at a post office.

Mail your letter or small package either at a post office or in the red Canada Post mailboxes you will find on streets and in shopping malls all across Canada. Take large parcels to a post office.

Canada Post offers many other services too, such as express delivery, postal money orders and insurance for very important mail. This insurance can protect your mail against loss or damage. Express delivery is more expensive than regular letter mail. Check the rates at the nearest Canada Post office. There are also private special delivery or courier services. Look these up under "Courier" in the yellow pages of the telephone book. Mail is distributed daily from Monday to Friday, except on official holidays. This includes home delivery, to post office boxes, or to community mailboxes. If you want to send a telegram, look up "Telegram Services" in the yellow pages for more information.

Returning Resident Permits

From time to time you may wish to leave Canada to visit your relatives. If you are not a Canadian citizen, and you plan to be outside Canada for more than 183 days in a year, you will need to apply for a Returning Resident Permit. If you don't have one, you could be refused entry into Canada when you return. You could lose your permanent resident status. Before you go you should telephone the CIC Call Centre for information and an application form. Remember there is a processing fee for this service.

BECOMING A CANADIAN

- The rights and responsibilities of citizenship
- How to apply

Although you can't apply for Canadian citizenship until you have lived in Canada for at least three years, you can be thinking about what it means from the moment you arrive. Canadians believe that Canada is a special place. Most Canadians agree with the United Nations that "Canada is the best country in the world in which to live."

To obtain Canadian citizenship, you will have to demonstrate a deep commitment to this country.

- **You will need to meet the physical residence requirements. You must live in Canada for at least three years before applying to become a citizen.**
- **You will need to have sufficient knowledge of either English or French.**
- **You will need to demonstrate your knowledge of Canada and the responsibilities and privileges of citizenship.**
- **You must be 18 years of age or older to apply as an individual.**

The rights and responsibilities of citizenship

For many newcomers, this gift of citizenship, this special sense of belonging, is a goal that guides much of what they do every day. It involves pride. A belief in equality and diversity. Respect for others. It means accepting the shared values that make Canadians who they are, and respecting both the rights and the privileges of being Canadian.

Canadian citizenship is precious and respected. Citizenship is a contract between you and your country, to share in the rights and privileges citizenship offers, and to fully carry out the responsibilities that go with it.

How to apply

To obtain information and an application kit to become a Canadian citizen visit http://www.cic.gc.ca or contact the CIC Call Centre. For the telephone number, refer to the section **Basic Services:** Citizenship and Immigration Canada (CIC) Call Centre

A Few last words

We hope this guide has given you some understanding of what it means to live in Canada. We've tried to combine practical information with an idea of the values and beliefs, which keep us together as Canadians, and as a country. As you journey towards Canadian citizenship, we sincerely hope this information helps you feel at home, feel that special sense of belonging. We are a nation of newcomers, and we welcome you to our family.

> ***"I've become a Canadian citizen and feel proud, happy and lucky. I was so grateful to Canada. I had missed my childhood and now was starting another period of my life. I think every Canadian should be proud. Even if I am a different colour, I have my rights. I am a Canadian."***

Channa Som, Survivor, Cambodian "killing fields."

> ***"To me, Canada is a unique combination of many things and many people from many places. It's a creation that the world -- and we -- should cherish and nourish.***

Serge Radchuk, originally from Ukraine.

> ***"I'll never forget the immigration officer I met at Dorval. He had an enormous, long ginger handlebar moustache that looked like a flaming sword. This man turned to me and spontaneously said, 'Welcome to Canada.' I was so touched that he knew I needed some reassurance and that he would understand my feeling of nervousness."***

Hubert de Santana, originally from Kenya.

Please Note

This guide contains information that was current at the time of publication. It features information from many sources, and should not be confused with official statements of policy or programming. The Government of Canada is not responsible for information that changes between printings.

Living in Canada: Your checklist

With so much to remember, we decided to create a checklist to help you to get the important things done first. We hope you find it useful.

In Your First Few Weeks

You will need to...

- **Exchange your money for Canadian currency**
- **Find temporary accommodation**
- **Have some identification (ID) with you**
- **Apply for private Health Insurance**
- **Get a map of the area and find out about transportation in your area**
- **Get your own telephone book**
- **Contact an immigrant-serving organization in your community**
- **Fill out the forms for a Social Insurance Number card and a Health Insurance card**

In Your First Few Months

You will need to...

- **Find permanent housing**
- **Get a telephone installed**
- **Register your children in school**
- **Get a family doctor**
- **Have your children immunized**
- **Open a bank account**
- **Look for a job**
- **Carry your address and telephone number with you**
- **Try to make friends -- join the Host Program**
- **Know where the Language Instruction for Newcomers (LINC) assessment centre is in your community and register for language classes**
- **Apply for the Canada Child Tax Benefit; call 1-800 387-1193**

In Your First Year

You will need to...

- **Get a valid driver's licence**
- **Practice and improve your language skills**

- **Register for adult continuing education classes**
- **Take time to relax and participate in community activities**
- **Understand your rights and responsibilities under Canadian law**
- **Know that you can apply for Canadian citizenship after living in Canada for three years**
-

Finding Help in Your Community

There are many organizations, which provide services designed for newcomers to Canada. In fact, your local immigrant serving organization should be your first point of contact. Many of these organizations across the country are listed in this directory, organized by province.

Since Quebec looks after many aspects of its immigration program, this pamphlet does not attempt to cover services in that province. However, it does list the phone numbers for the *ministère des Relations avec les citoyens et de l'Immigration,* which offers many services to newcomers in Quebec. If you are living in, or planning to move to Quebec, you may wish to pick up their guide for newcomers, entitled: *Vivre au QUÉBEC!*

You may also wish to refer to the other two pamphlets in the back pocket of your guide: *Key Information Sources,* and *Language Training.*

Remember when you use the telephone, speak slowly and clearly, and have a pen or pencil and some paper to write down information. You may be referred to another phone number, or be given other useful information.

KEY IMMIGRANT SERVING ORGANIZATIONS ACROSS CANADA

Association for New Canadians
P.O. Box 2031, Station C
St. John's, Nfld. A1C 5R6
Tel: 709-722-9680

New Brunswick

Multicultural Association of Greater Moncton Area
1299A Mountain Road, Suite 2
Moncton, N.B. E1C 2T9
506-858-9659

Multicultural Association of Fredericton
123 York Street, Suite 201
Fredericton, N.B. E3B 3N6
Tel: 506-457-4038

Saint John YM/YWCA
19-25 Hazen Avenue
Saint John, N.B. E2L 3G6
506-646-2389

Nova Scotia

YMCA Newcomer's Centre
3663 Dutch Village Road
Halifax, N.S. B3K 3B7
Tel: 902-457-9622

Metropolitan Immigrant Settlement Association
2131 Gottingen Street, Suite 200
Halifax, N.S. B3K 5Z7
Tel: 902-423-3607

Prince Edward Island

PEI Association for Newcomers to Canada
179 Queen Street
Mailing address: P.O. Box 2846,
Charlottetown, PEI C1A 8C4
Tel: 902-628-6009

To contact immigrant serving organizations in the province of Quebec, contact the *ministère des Relations avec les citoyens et de l'Immigration* (MRCI). MRCI is organized by region:

Carrefours d'intégration - Island of Montréal
East Island
8000, boulevard Langelier
6e et 7e étages
Saint-Léonard (Québec) H1P 3K2
(514) 864-9191

West Island
181, boulevard Hymus
2e et 3e étages
Point-Claire (Québec) H9R 5P4
(514) 864-9191

South Island
800, boulevard de Maisonneuve Est
(Place Dupuis), rez-de-chaussée)
Montréal (Québec) H2L 4L8
(514) 864-9191

Direction régionale de l'Estrie, de la Mauricie et du Centre-du-Québec
740, rue Galt Ouest, bureau 400
Sherbrooke, Québec J1H 1Z3
819-820-3606 or 1-888-879-4288

Direction régionale de l'Outaouais,
de l'Abitibi-Témiscamingue et du Nord-du-Québec
4 rue Taschereau, suite 430
Hull, Québec J8Y 2V5
819-772-3021 or
1-888-295-9095

Direction régionale de Laval, des Laurentides, et de Lanaudière
800, boulevard Chomedey
Tour C, bureau 200
Laval, Québec H7V 3Y4
450-681-2593 or
1-800-375-7426

Direction régionale de la Capitale-Nationale et l'Est du Québec
930, chemin Ste-Foy
Québec, Québec G1S 2L4
418-643-1435 or
1-888-643-1435

Bureau de Trois-Rivières
100, rue Laviolette, R.C. 26
Trois-Rivières, Québec G9A 5S9
819-371-6011 or 1-888-879-4294

Direction régionale de la Montérégie
3e étage
2, blvd Désaulniers
St-Lambert, Québec J4P 1L2
450-466-4461 or 1-888-287-5819

Bureau de Jonquière
3950 boulevard Harvey
Jonquière, Québec G7X 8L6
418-695-8144

Ontario

Quinte United Immigrant Services
32 Bridge Street East
Belleville, Ontario K8N 5N9
613-968-7723

Newcomer Information Centre, Centre for Language
Training and Assessment Brampton Civic Centre
150 Central Park Drive, Suite 200
Brampton, Ontario L6T 1B4
905-270-6000

Brampton Neighbourhood Resource Centre
168 Kennedy Road South
Units 3 and 4
Brampton, Ontario L6W 3G6
905-452-1262

Catholic Cross-Cultural Services
37 George Street North, Suite 403
Brampton, Ontario L6X 1R5
905-457-7740

Immigrant Settlement and Counseling Services of Brantford
320 North Park Street, Unit 2
Brantford, Ontario N3R 4L4
519-753-9830

YMCA of Cambridge
250 Hespeler Road
Cambridge, Ontario N1R 3H3
519-621-3250

Arab Community Centre
5468 Dundas Street West, Suite 324
Etobicoke, Ontario M9B 6E3
416-231-7746

Dejinta Beesha
8 Taber Road
Etobicoke, Ontario M9W 3A4
416-743-1286

Rexdale Women's Centre
8 Taber Road, 2nd Floor
Etobicoke, Ontario M9W 3A4
416-745-0062

Polycultural Immigrant and Community Services
3363 Bloor Street West
Etobicoke, Ontario M8X 1G2
416-233-0055

Guelph and District Multicultural Centre
214 Speedvale Avenue West, Unit 7
Guelph, Ontario N1H 1C4
519-836-2222

Settlement and Integration Services Organization of Hamilton
360 James Street North
Hamilton, Ontario L8L 1H5
905-521-9917

Kingston and District Immigrant Services
322 Brock Street
Kingston, Ontario K7L 1S9
613-548-3302

Mennonite Central Committee of Ontario
50 Kent Avenue
Kitchener, Ontario N2G 3R1
519-745-8458

Kitchener-Waterloo YMCA
301-276 King Street West
Kitchener, Ontario N2G 1B6
519-579-9622

London Cross-Cultural Learner Centre
717 Dundas Street East
London, Ontario N5W 2Z5
519-432-1133

Catholic Cross-Cultural Services
90 Dundas Street West, site 204
Mississauga , Ontario L5B 2T5
905-273-4140

Dixie-Bloor Neighbourhood Resource Centre
3439 Fieldgate Drive
Mississauga, Ontario L4X 2J4
905-629-1873

India Rainbow Community Services of Peel
3038 Hurontario Street, Suite 206
Mississauga, Ontario L5B 3B9
905-275-2369

Malton Neighbourhood Services
7200 Goreway Drive
Mississauga, Ontario L4T 2T7
905-677-6270
905-672-3660

Inter-Cultural Neighbourhood Social Services
3050 Confederation Parkway
Mississauga, Ontario L5B 3Z6
905-273-4884

Northwood Neighbourhood Services (C.S.)
2528A Jane Street
Wycliffe Jane Plaza
North York, Ontario
416-748-0788

Catholic Immigration Centre
219 Argyle Avenue
Ottawa, Ontario K2P 2H4
613-232-9634

Lebanese and Arab Social Services Agency of Ottawa-Carleton
151 Slater Street, Suite 707
Ottawa, Ontario K1P 5H3
613-236-0003

Ottawa Chinese Community Service Centre
391 Bank Street, 2nd Floor
Ottawa, Ontario K2P 1Y3
613-235-4875

Catholic Community Services of York Region
21 Dunlop Street
Richmond Hill, Ontario L4C 2M6
905-770-7040

New Canadians' Centre
Windsor Essex County Family YMCA
511 Pelisser Street
Windsor, Ontario N9A 4L2
519-256-7330

South Asian Family Support Services (SAFS)
1200 Markham Road, Suite 214
Scarborough, Ontario M1H 3C3
416-431-4847

Centre for Information and Community Services of Ontario (CICS)
3852 Finch Avenue East, Suite 310
Scarborough, Ontario M1T 3T9
416-292-7510

Thunder Bay Multicultural Association
17 North Court Street
Thunder Bay, Ontario P7A 4T4
807-345-0551

Bloor Information and Life Skills Centre
672 Dupont Street, Suite 314
Toronto, Ontario M6G 1Z6
416-531-4613

Canadian Ukrainian Immigrant Aid Services
2150 Bloor Street West, Suite 96
Toronto, Ontario M6S 1M8
416-767-0036

Jewish Immigrant Aid Services of Canada
4600 Bathurst Street, Suite 325
North York, Ontario M2R 3V3
416-630-6481

Halton Multicultural Association
635 4th Line, Unit 48
Oakville, Ontario L6L 5W4
905-842-2486

Jewish Family Services of Ottawa-Carleton
1774 Kerr Avenue, Suite 230
Ottawa, Ontario K2A 1R9
613-722-2225

Ottawa Carleton Immigrant Services Organization
959 Wellington Street
Ottawa, Ontario KIY 4W1
613-725-0202

New Canadians Centre - Peterborough
205 Sherbrooke Street, Unit D
Peterborough, Ontario K9J 2N2
705-743-0882

Folk Arts Council of St. Catharines
85 Church Street
St. Catharines, Ontario L2R 3C7
905-685-6589

Tropicana Community Services Organization
670 Progress Avenue, Unit 14
Scarborough, Ontario M1H 3A4
416-439-9009

Catholic Cross-Cultural Services
780 Birchmount Road, Unit 3
Scarborough, Ontario M1K 5H4
416-757-7010

Sudbury Multicultural Folk Arts Association
196 Van Horne Street
Sudbury, Ontario P3E 1E5
705-674-0795

Afghan Women's Counseling and Integration
Community Support Organization
2333 Dundas Street West, Suite 205A
Toronto, Ontario M6R 3A6
416-588-3585

Canadian Centre for Victims of Torture
192-194 Jarvis Street, 2nd Floor
Toronto, Ontario M5B 2B7
416-363-1066

Catholic Cross-Cultural Services
10 St. Mary Street, Suite 410
Toronto, Ontario M4Y 1P9
416-324-8225

Harriet Tubman Community Organization Inc.
2975 Don Mills Road
Toronto, Ontario M2J 3B7
416-496-2044

Centre for Spanish-Speaking Peoples
1004 Bathurst Street
Toronto, Ontario M5R 3G7
416-533-8545

COFTM Centre Francophone
20 Lower Spadina Avenue
Toronto, Ontario M5V 2Z1
416-203-1220

COSTI-IIAS Immigrant Services
1710 Dufferin Street
Toronto, Ontario M6E 3P2
416-658-1600

CultureLink
160 Springhurst Avenue, Suite 300
Toronto, Ontario M6K 1C2
416-588-6288

Ethiopian Association in Toronto, Inc.
2057 Danforth Avenue, 3rd Floor
Toronto, Ontario M4C 1J8
416-694-1522

Jamaican Canadian Association
995 Arrow Road
Toronto, Ontario M9M 2Z5
416-746-5772

Kababayan Community Service Centre
1313 Queen Street West, Suite 133
Toronto, Ontario M6K 1L8
416-532-3888

Mennonite New Life Centre
1774 Queen Street East
Toronto, Ontario M4L 1G7
416-699-4527

Newcomer Information Centre,
YMCA of Greater Toronto
42 Charles Street East, 3rd Floor
Toronto, Ontario M4Y 1T4
416-928-3362

MIDAYNTA
1992 Yonge Street, Suite 203
Toronto, Ontario M4S 1Z8
416-544-1992
416-440-0520

Tropicana Community Services Organization
670 Progress Avenue, Unit 14
Scarborough, Ontario M1H 3A4
(416) 439-9009

Riverdale Immigrant Women's Centre
1326 Gerrard Street East, Suite 100
Toronto, Ontario M4L 1Z1
416-465-6021

Scadding Court Community Centre
707 Dundas Street West
Toronto, Ontario M5T 2W6
416-392-0335

South Asian Women's Centre
1332 Bloor Street West
Toronto, Ontario M6H 1P2
416-537-2276

Barrie YMCA Immigrant Services
22 Grove Street West
Barrie, Ontario L4N 1M7
705-726-6421 ext. 264

Afghan Association of Ontario
29 Pemican Court, #6
Weston, Ontario M9M 2Z3
416-744-9289

Tamil Eelam Society of Canada
861 Broadview Avenue
Toronto, Ontario M4K 2P9
416-463-7647

Thorncliffe Park Neighbourhood Services
18 Thorncliffe Park Drive
Toronto, Ontario M4H 1N7
416-421-3054

Toronto Chinese Community Services Association
310 Spadina Avenue, Suite 301
Toronto, Ontario M5T 2E8
416-977-4026

Toronto Organization for Domestic Workers' Rights (INTERCEDE)
234 Eglinton Avenue East, Suite 205
Toronto, Ontario M4P 1K5
416-483-4554

Vietnamese Association of Toronto
1364 Dundas Street West
Toronto, Ontario M6J 1Y2
416-536-3611

Woodgreen Community Centre of Toronto
835 Queen Street East
Toronto, Ontario M4M 1H9
416-469-5211

Working Women Community Centre
533A Gladstone Avenue
Toronto, Ontario M6H 3J1
416-532-2824

Lakeshore Area Multi-Service
Project Inc.
185 Fifth Street
Toronto, Ontario M8V 2Z5
416-252-6471

Multicultural Council of Windsor
and Essex County
245 Janette Avenue
Windsor, Ontario N9A 4Z2
519-255-1127

Youth Assisting Youth
1992 Yonge Street, Suite 300
Toronto, Ontario M4S 1Z7
416-932-1919

Social Development Council Ajax, Pickering
134 Commercial Avenue
Ajax, Ontario L1S 2H5
905-686-2661

YMCA of Metro Toronto
(Korean Community Services)
721 Bloor Street West, Suite 303
Toronto, Ontario M6G 1L5
416-538-9412

Afghan Association of Ontario
29 Pemican Court, #6
Weston, Ontario M9M 2Z3
416-744-9289

The Job Search Workshops in Ontario
1-800-813-2614

Manitoba

Jewish Child and Family Services
Suite C200-123 Doncaster Street
Winnipeg, Manitoba R3N 2B2
204-477-7430

Indochina Chinese Association of Manitoba
648 McGee Street
Winnipeg, Manitoba R3E 1W8
204-772-3107

Philippine Association of Manitoba
88 Juno Street
Winnipeg, Manitoba
204-772-7210

Success Skills Centre
616-1661 Portage Avenue
Winnipeg, Manitoba R3J 3T7
204-786-3200

Black Youth Helpline
P.O. Box 11
1631 St-Mary's Road
Winnipeg, Manitoba R2M 4A5
204-339-2769

Manitoba Interfaith
406 Edmonton Street, 2nd floor
Winnipeg, Manitoba R3B 2M2
204-943-9158

Lao Association of Manitoba
7-983 Arlington Street
Winnipeg, Manitoba R3E 2E6
204-774-1115

Immigrant Women Association of Manitoba
200-323 Portage Avenue
Winnipeg, Manitoba R3B 2C1
204-989-5800

Employment Projects for Women
990-167 Lombard Avenue
Winnipeg, Manitoba R3B 0V3
204-949-5300

Ukrainian Canadian Congress
456 Main Street
Winnipeg, Manitoba R3B 1B6
204-942-4627

Citizenship Council of Manitoba
406 Edmonton Street, 2nd Floor
Winnipeg, Manitoba R3B 2M2
204-943-9158

International Centre of Winnipeg
406 Edmonton Street, 2nd floor
Winnipeg, Manitoba R3B 2M2
204-943-9158

Saskatchewan

Prince Albert Multicultural Council
17 11th Street West
Prince Albert, Saskatchewan S6V 3A8
306-922-0405

Regina Open Door Society
1855 Smith Street
Regina, Saskatchewan S4P 2N5
306-352-3500

Saskatoon Open Door Society
311 4th Avenue North
Saskatoon, Saskatchewan S7K 2L8
306-653-4464

Moose Jaw Multicultural Council
60 Athabasca Street East
Moose Jaw, Saskatchewan S6H 0L2
306-693-4677

Alberta

Calgary Immigrant Aid Society
12th Floor, 910-7 Avenue SW
Calgary, Alberta T2P 3N8
403-265-1120

Central Alberta Refugee Effort (C.A.R.E.) Committee
202-5000 Gaetz Avenue
Red Deer, Alberta T4N 6C2
403-346-8818

Calgary Immigrant Development and
Educational Advancement Society
203-4310 17th Avenue SE
Calgary, Alberta T2A 0T4
403-235-3666

The Calgary Bridge Foundation for Youth
4112-4 Street NW
Calgary, Alberta T2K 1A2
403-230-7745

Changing Together - A Centre for Immigrant Women
#103, 10010 - 107A Avenue
Edmonton, Alberta T5H 4H8
780-421-0175

Edmonton Catholic Schools
10915-110 Street
Edmonton, Alberta T5H 3E3
780-426-4375

Edmonton Immigrant Services Association
11240 - 79 Street
Edmonton, Alberta T5B 2K1
780-474-8445

Edmonton Public School Board
6703-112 Street
Edmonton, Alberta T6H 3J9
780-431-5479

New Home Immigration and Settlement
572 Hermitage Road
Edmonton, Alberta T5A 4N2
780-456-4663

The Reading Network - Grande Prairie Regional College
Lower Level, 9920 - 100 Avenue
Grande Prairie, Alberta T8V 0T9
780-538-4363

Calgary Catholic Immigration Society
3rd Floor, 120-17 Avenue SW
Calgary, Alberta T2S 2T2
403-262-2006

Calgary Immigrant Women's Association
300, 750 - 11 Street SW
Calgary, Alberta T2P 3N7
403-263-4414

Calgary Mennonite Centre for Newcomers
201, 3517 - 17 Avenue SE
Calgary, Alberta T2A 0R5
403-569-0409

Catholic Social Services
10709-105 Street
Edmonton, Alberta T5H 2X3
780-424-3545

Indo-Canadian Women's Association
335 Tower II, Millbourne Mall
Edmonton, Alberta T6K 3L2
780-490-0477

Edmonton Chinese Community Services Centre
9540 - 102 Avenue
Edmonton, Alberta T5H 0E3
780-429-3111

Edmonton Mennonite Centre for Newcomers
#101, 10010 - 107A Avenue
Edmonton, Alberta T5H 4H8
780-424-7709

Millwoods Welcome Centre for Immigrants
335 Tower II, Millbourne Mall
Edmonton, Alberta T6K 3L2
780-462-6924

YMCA of Wood Buffalo
#200, 9913 Biggs Avenue
Fort McMurray, Alberta T9H 1S2
780-743-2970

Lethbridge Family Services - Immigrant Services
508-6th Street South
Lethbridge, Alberta T1J 2E2
403-320-1589
403-317-7654 (FAX)

SAAMIS Immigration Services
177 12 Street NE
Medicine Hat, Alberta T1A 5T6
403-504-1188
Fax 403-504-1211

Catholic Social Services - Red Deer
5104-48th Avenue
Red Deer, Alberta T4N 3T8
403-347-8844

Catholic Social Services
202-5000 Gaetz Avenue
Red Deer, Alberta T4N 6C2
403-346-8818

British Columbia

Burnaby Family Life Institute
32-250 Willingdon Avenue
Burnaby, BC V5C 5E9
604-659-2200

Burnaby Multicultural Society
6255 Nelson Avenue
Burnaby, BC V5H 4T5
604-431-4131

Campbell River and Area Multicultural and Immigrant Services Association
43-1480 Dogwood Street
Campbell River, BC V9W 3A6
250-830-0171

Chilliwack Community Services
45938 Wellington Avenue
Chilliwack, BC V2P 2C7
604-792-4267

Comox Valley Family Service Association
1415 Cliffe Avenue
Courtenay, BC V9N 2K6
250-338-7575

Cowichan Valley Intercultural and Immigrant Aid Society
3-83 Trunk Road
Duncan, BC V9L 2N7
250-748-3112

Kamloops Cariboo Regional Immigrant Services Society
110-206 Seymour Street
Kamloops, BC V2C 2E5
250-372-0855

Multicultural Society of Kelowna
100-1875 Spall Road
Kelowna, BC V1Y 4R2
250-762-2155

Langley Family Services Association
5339-207th Street
Langley, BC V3A 2E6
604-534-7921

Central Vancouver Island Multicultural Society
114-285 Prideaux Street
Nanaimo, BC V9R 2N2
250-753-6911

Lower Mainland Purpose Society for Youth and Families
40 Begbie Street
New Westminster, BC V3M 3L9
604-526-2522

North Shore Multicultural Society
102-123 East 15th Street
North Vancouver, BC V7L 2P7
604-988-2931

Penticton and District Multicultural Society
508 Main Street
Penticton, BC V2A 5C7
250-492-6299

Immigrant and Multicultural Services Society of Prince George
1633 Victoria Street
Prince George, BC V2L 2L4
250-562-2900

Richmond Multicultural Concerns Society
210-7000 Minorou Boulevard
Richmond, BC V6Y 3Z5
604-279-7160

Family Services of Greater Vancouver
250-7000 Minorou Boulevard
Richmond, BC V6Y 3Z5
604-279-7100

Richmond Connections
190-7000 Minorou Boulevard
Richmond, BC V6Y 3Z5
604-279-7020

Surrey Delta Immigrant Services Society
1107-7330 137th Street
Surrey, BC V3W 1A3
604-597-0205

Options: Services to Community
100-6846 King George Highway
Surrey, BC V3W 4Z9
604-596-4321

Progressive Intercultural Community Services Society
109-12414-82nd Street
Surrey, BC V3W 3E9
604-596-7722

Family Services of the North Shore
101-255 West 1st Street
Vancouver, BC V7M 3G8
604-988-5281

Collingwood Neighbourhood House
5288 Joyce Street
Vancouver, BC V5R 6C9
604-435-0323

Kiwassa Neighbourhood House
2425 Oxford Street
Vancouver, BC V5K 1M7
604-254-5401

MOSAIC
1522 Commercial Drive, 2nd Floor
Vancouver, BC V5L 3Y2
604-254-9626

Ray-Cam Cooperative Centre
920 East Hastings Street
Vancouver, BC V6A 3T1
604-257-6949

South Vancouver Neighbourhood House
6470 Victoria Drive
Vancouver, BC V5P 3X7
604-324-6212

Frog Hollow Neighbourhood House
2131 Renfrew Street
Vancouver, BC V5M 4M5
604-251-1225

Pacific Immigrant Resources Society
385 South Boundary Road
Vancouver, BC V5K 4S1
604-298-4560

West End Community Centre Association
870 Denman Street
Vancouver, B.C. V6G 2L8
604-257-8333

Victoria Immigrant and Refugee Centre
305-535 Yates Street
Victoria, BC V8W 2Z6
250-361-9433

Mennonite Central Committee of BC
31414 Marshall Road, Box 2038
Abbotsford, BC V2T 3T8
604-850-663

Immigrant Services Society
530 Drake Street
Vancouver, BC V6B 2H3
604-684-7498

Jewish Family Service Agency
300-950 West 41st Avenue
Vancouver BC V5Z 2N7
604-257-5151

Little Mountain Neighbourhood House
3981 Main Street
Vancouver, BC V5V 3P3
604-879-7104

The People's Law School
150-900 Howe Street
Vancouver, BC V6Z 2M4
604-688-2565

Riley Park Community Association
50 East 30th Avenue
Vancouver, BC V5V 2T9
604-257-8641

SUCCESS
28 West Pender Street
Vancouver, BC V6B 1R6
604-684-1628

Hispanic Community Centre
Society of BC
4824 Commercial Street
Vancouver, BC V5N 4H1
604-872-4431

Vancouver Association for the Survivors of Torture (VAST)
3-3664 East Hastings Street
Vancouver, BC V5K 2A9
Tel: 604-299-3539

Vernon and District Immigrant Services
100-3003 30th Street
Vernon, BC V1T 9J5
250-542-4177

Intercultural Association of Victoria
930 Balmoral Road
Victoria, BC V8T 1A8
250-388-4728

Abbotsford Community Services
2420 Montrose Avenue
Abbotsford, BC V2S 3S9
604-859-7681

PART FOUR

WORKING IN CANADA

STRATIGIZING FOR EMPLOYMENT

WHY STRATEGIZE?

The Canadian Workplace Reality

Job search in Canada is no longer a matter of completing an application form and hoping for a job offer. Canadian businesses involved in technological innovation, corporate restructuring and unpredictable fluctuations in the recent global economy can no longer guarantee a job for life for you.

How people work is changing and so are occupational titles. Individuals are encouraged to look for work that matches their personal values and talents. The term "job" has transformed into "meaningful work" which is planned and has personal value in addition to the monetary compensation.

The onus is on the job seeker to research, to track and to secure employment options. These job opportunities may materialize as contract jobs, part-time jobs, "work-from-home" jobs, job sharing arrangements, casual assignments and long-term arrangements – or any combination thereof. To ensure your financial security, you need to constantly market your expertise to potential consumers of service.

Many internationally educated professionals in Canada have described barriers to enter their career after their arrival in Canada. The acculturation process may create such scenarios as:

- You may not necessarily achieve your career goals immediately
- You may have to take the time to gain Canadian accreditation for your professional credentials
- You may have to settle for alternative employment in the short-term to accommodate your life style and to upgrade your English language skills

- You may have to upgrade your technical skills on your own time to become employable in your field of interest.

Personal career management has become the responsibility of the individual worker who is expected to continuously create employment opportunities in keeping with a focused and planned career path.

Become a Career Strategist

In order to successfully manage your career and financial security, it is not enough to be a "job seeker" who depends on advertised vacancies as was done in traditional job search. The career strategist knows him/herself, knows the world of work, is a lifelong learner and creates his/her own work opportunities on an ongoing basis. Career planning has evolved into work/life planning –an entrepreneurial process which involves more creative thinking and risk-taking on the part of the individual.

To gain personal control and confidence in an unpredictable workplace, the following concepts are important to keep in mind:

Essential Concepts to Remember in Work Search*

- Employment opportunities depend on the current supply of work and demand for workers in the Canadian labour market
- There is an abundance of information on the changing Canadian labour market to chart your work search campaign
- Technology impacts all occupations most of which require skilled workers
- Ongoing research of labour market information is a vital skill to be learned for career planning and employment search

Due to the necessity of constant change and the demands of the Canadian economy, many new work opportunities are being created. Be prepared to work differently: to contribute your ideas, to take initiative

The key tasks to become a career strategist may include:

1. Identify and diversify your career vision to give you purpose and direction in securing employment
2. Consistently re-assess and upgrade your technical and employability skills to help you to remain employable in the short-term and the long range
3. Networking and researching labour market information to keep you updated on trends in Canadian industries and occupations so that you can align your opportunities to the requirements of the job market.
4. Conduct a personal job search campaign by developing strategic job search documents and self-marketing techniques
5. Access Canadian on-line career resources and free community-based employment services to benefit from free information and support in your search for employment
6. Adopt a customer service philosophy in order to present your skills as a solution to current business demands.

---

*O'Reilly, Elaine. *Making Career Sense of Labour Market Information.* Canadian Career Development Foundation. HRDC British Columbia Ministry of Advanced Education. 2001. www.workinfornet.bc.ca

THE STRATEGY to discover work opportunities……

As a career strategist, you first need to answer the following questions:

- What skills do I have to offer the Canadian labour market?
- Where will the jobs be?
- What competencies do Canadian employers look for in a worker?
- How do I market myself effectively to potential employers?
- Which free employment services may assist me in the community?

The next steps will be to formulate and maintain a Plan of Action:

- people to contact
- places to go to
- things to do
- questions to ask regarding your work search in Canada.

Your success in the workplace will be determined by the initiative, time and effort you invest in your professional and personal vision.

SOME WEBSITES to strategize your research.....

The following websites have been organized and categorized in order to present options for you in your work research and career strategizing efforts.

1. Assess what skills and strengths YOU as a unique individual have to offer to the Canadian labour market?

Know your Skills, Values, Interests and Personality Preferences

http://www.cdm.uwaterloo.ca Career Development eManual, University of Waterloo, Ontario

http://www.jobhuntersbible.com Online supplement to Richard Bolles "What Color is Your Parachute?" → Tests & Advice

2. Discover the current Canadian Labour Market Trends

Which industries are growing? Where are the jobs?

www.labourmarketinformation.ca Government of Canada

http://www24.hrdc-drhc.gc.ca HRDC Sector Studies & Partnerships → Canadian Industry profiles

www.jobsetc.ca Government of Canada → Jobs, Workers, Training & Careers

http://www.canadaprospects.com Canadian Career Consortium, Career awareness, career planning and work search programs

http://www.strategis.gc.ca Industry Canada, Canada's business & consumer site

http://www.canadainternational.gc.ca Government of Canada, services for non-Canadians

www.councils.org The Alliance of Sectoral Councils → Directory of products & services related to growth industries in Canada. Funded by Human Resources Development Canada.

www.skillscanada.com Resources for careers in the skilled trades in Canada

www.statcan.ca Statistics Canada → The Daily, Labour Force Survey

www.tradesway.com HRDC & Centre for Education and Training→Search Newcomers

3. Find out about Canadian COMPANIES

Service/Product, corporate culture, networking contacts, job postings & career resources.

www.sedar.com Canadian public company profiles

www.ctidirectory.com Canadian Trade Index, Canadian Manufacturers & Exporters

www.cdnbusinessdirectory.com Canada Business Directory
www.cbr.ca Canadian Business Resource, Database of Canadian corporate profiles

www.newswire.ca Canadian database of news releases

www.yellowpages.ca National & local business directory

http://vts.ic.gc.ca Industry Canada, Virtual Trade Show on Information & Communication technologies and company profiles

www.corporateinformation.com International corporate profiles

www.infomart.ca Canadian news & business information on-line, Industry Profiles & Corporate Data

4. Learn more about Canadian OCCUPATIONS

Job requirements & descriptions, projected growth & related occupations

http://www23.hrdc-drhc.gc.ca/2001/e/generic/welcome.shtml HRDC, National Occupational Classification

http://jobfutures.ca Human Resources Development Canada, Job Futures 2002 → Occupations and Want to Immigrate?

http://www.careerccc.org/careerdirections/eng/e_ho_set.htm Canada Career Consortium, Canadian occupations not requiring university education

www.cicic.ca Canadian Information Centre for International Credentials →Information on Specific Occupations and Trades

http://www.equalopportunity.on.ca/eng_g/apt/index.asp Government of Ontario, Gateway to Diversity, Internationally Trained Workers, Access to Professions & Trades

www.madewiththetrades.com Careers in the construction industry

http://www.red-seal.ca HRDC, Interprovincial Standards Red Seal Program for trades, apprenticeships and skilled workers

5. Know the SKILLS, WHICH may make you more employable

What are the interpersonal skills that Canadian employers are expecting from all job seekers in addition to technical skills?

http://www.careerccc.org/destination2020 Canada Career Consortium, Build your Work Skills

http://www.conferenceboard.ca/education/learning-tools/esp20 The Conference Board of Canada, Employability Skills 2000+

http://www15.hrdc-drhc.gc.ca HRDC, Essential Skills for Life Learning and Work

http://www.psc-cfp.gc.ca/research/personnel/ei_e.htm Emotional Intelligence in the Workplace, Human Resource Management Trends & Issues, Public Service Commission of Canada

http://www.canadaone.com/magazine/eq080498.html Emotional Intelligence and the New Workplace, CanadaOne Magazine, free on-line magazine for small business in Canada

6. Prepare to MARKET YOUR SKILLS to Canadian employers

Effective job search documents & self-marketing techniques

http://www.workinfonet.ca – Jobs, work & recruiting. Canada WorkInfonet Partnership.

http://www.worksearch.gc.ca Human Resources Development Canada, work search strategies

www.monster.ca Canada's career management portal

www.rileyguide.com Online resource for employment & career information

www.quintcareers.com Career & job portal

7. Identify which Free Community Services are available to assist you to live and work in the Canadian workplace?

Employment & settlement services

http://www.hrdc-drhc.gc.ca/dept/guide/jwtc.shtml Human Resources Development Canada Offices – Jobs, Workers, Training & Careers

www.SEECanada.Org Gateway to Settlement, Employment & Education for skills professionals & Tradespersons planning to immigrate to Canada

www.poss.ca Human Resources Development Canada, Toronto's Virtual Employment Resource Centre

www.settlement.org Information & resources for immig**rants** to Ontario. Citizenship & Immigration Canada Employment

8. Prepare for PROFESSIONAL DEVELOPMENT

Standards of Practice, networking & career resources

www.careerkey.com Career networking resource on-line – Links – Associations

www.cicic.ca/profess-enphp Canadian Information Centre for International Credentials – national professional organizations

http://www.charityvillage.com/charityvillage/profas.asp Professional associations in the non-profit sector

http://circ.micromedia.on.ca/hotlinks/associations/main.htm Associations Canada

http://info.asaenet.org/gateway/OnlineassocSlist.html American Society of Association Executives, directory of associations

9. If you need SOME ADDITIONAL INFORMATION, try 0consulting with an on-line career resource person :

Free on-line career consultation & information

www.workopolis.com – Career Resources – Immigrate to Canada – New Canadian Advisor

www.CanadaInfoNet.org Canadian mentors for professionals, business & skilled trades people considering immigrating to

TOP INTERVIEW QUESTIONS ASKED BY CANADIAN EMPLOYERS

1. Tell me about yourself?
2. Tell me about any of your weakness?
3. What are some of your strengths?
4. Where do you see yourself in 5 years?
5. What work experience have you had that prepares you for this position?
6. Why should we hire you?
7. Do you consider yourself a creative problem solver? Give me an example.
8. Why did you leave your last position?
9. Your resume shows you have moved around a lot. How can I be sure you will stay at this company?
10. What did you think of your last supervisor/manager?
11. Describe your ideal position.
12. What did you like about your last job?
13. What did you dislike about your last job?
14. Describe how you work under pressure.
15. Describe your ideal boss.
16. What do you have to offer this company that others may not?
17. What kind of salary are you looking for?
18. What was your annual salary at your last position?
19. What have you gained from working at your last job?
20. What were your responsibilities and duties?
21. What motivates you?
22. Do you consider yourself successful?
23. What traits or qualities do you most admire in someone?
24. What are your hobbies?
25. Are you willing to relocate?
26. Tell me about your proudest accomplishment?
27. What has been your most meaningful educational experience?

28. Can you tell me something about our company.
29. Describe how you perform in a high stress position?
30. How do you feel about routine work?
31. What steps are you taking to improve yourself?
32. Do you have a personal goal that you still want to achieve?
33. Tell me about what you would do to get organized for a project.
34. Have you ever been responsible for financial management?
35. There is a period of time on your resume when you were not employed. Can you tell me what you did in that time period?
36. Would it be appropriate to contact your most recent employer?
37. What do you think will be the most difficult aspect of this job?
38. What special skills / talents do you have?
39. Do you have any questions for me? (usually at the end of interview)

Note: When you will visit your nearest Human Resource Centre or an HRDC sponsored agency in Canada, you will find many books on interview questions with their answers and some with professions specific answers. You will also find many books on resume writing.

INTERVIEW QUESTIONS BY DIFFERENT GROUPS

Your Past

1. Why did you leave your last job?
2. What aspects of your responsibilities did you consider most critical?
3. What type of management did you have in your last job?
4. Which job, of all the ones you have had, did you like the best? Why?
5. Which job did you like the least? Why?
6. What did you accomplish which benefited the company? The job?
7. Where does this job fit in to your overall career plan?
8. How do you organize for major projects?

What You Learned

1. What special aspects of your education/training have prepared you for this job?
2. In what area would you most like additional training if you do get this job?

Why you Learned

1. What are your career goals?
2. What kid of job do you see yourself holding in five years time? Why?
3. What would you most like to accomplish if you get this job?
4. What do you consider your biggest career success to date?

Type of Jobs & Your Style

1. Tell me about one of your favourite work experiences. What did you like best about it.
2. How do you know when you have done a good job.
3. How did your past supervisor evaluate your performance? What areas of improvement were suggested?
4. Why do you feel that you are qualified for this position?

Stress Management

1. Tell me about a work situation that gave you difficulty?
2. Define co-operation.

Strengths

1. What key factors have accounted for your career success to date?
2. In what areas have others been particularly complimentary about your abilities?

Weakness

1. What do you think your co-workers would view as your greatest weakness?

Interpersonal Skills.

1. What sorts of people do you have difficulty working with?
2. With which of your past work groups did you most enjoy working?
3. What factors most influenced your positive feelings.

4. With which of your past work groups did you least enjoy working? What accounted for that, what did you do about it and what was the outcome?

5. What aspects of your interpersonal skills would you like most to improve?

6. Tell me about a confrontational situation at work. How did you handle it?

Type of Work you Like

1. What type of work do you find most stimulating and rewarding? Why? Least stimulating? Why?
2. In which of your last positions were you most motivated and productive?
3. What has your experience taught you about the type of work you least enjoy?
4. What factors contributed the most to your job dissatisfaction?

Your Preferred work Environment

1. In which of your past work environments (team, independent) were you the happiest? Why?
2. In which of your past work environments did you feel you had the greatest amount of influence and impact?
3. How would you describe the ideal work environment? Which things would be present? Which things would be absent?

Traits and Characteristics

1. What word best describes your personal style?
2. Which of your personal traits has been most helpful in your career?
3. If 3 of your close associates were here, what would they say about you?

Business Philosophy

1. How do you think successful businesses manage their employees.

Your Operating Style

1. How would you categorize your operating style (the way you go about your business/work?)
2. What are the basic work principles by which you operate?

Overcoming Rejections & Objections

1. You're overqualified!
2. We're looking for someone a little younger/older!
3. All hiring is done by personnel/we're supposed to go through personnel with these things!
4. We're cutting back right now. Why don't you call in three months/we're actually laying people off right now!
5. I'd love to see you, but I'm tied up in a meeting!

INTERVIEW PRACTICE - AN EXAMPLE

Practicing for the interview means practicing several behaviours – not just answering questions. You must dress well, watch your body language and posture, practice your manners and eye contact, as well as practice answering questions correctly, smoothly and with confidence.

The practice questions below, in one form or another, account for a large percentage of interview questions. With each question, you are given a series of choices as to how you might answer the question. When you select an answer, you will learn to whether your answer is correct or not - and why. Answering these questions will help you polish your interviewing techniques. The questions and answers in this exercise are generic and in many cases, must be tailored to your individual situation. Still, the logic behind the answer remains essentially the same.

1. Why are you the best person for the job?

(a) "I've held a lot of positions like this one and that experience will help me here."
(b) "Because I am good at what I do."
(c) "Our discussion here leads me to believe this is a good place to work."
(d) "You need someone who can produce results and my background and experience are proof of my ability. For example…"

2. If asked a point blank question such as : Are you creative? Are you analytical? Can you work under pressure? Etc. what is the best way to answer?

(a) Answer yes or no.
(b) Answer yes and give a specific example.
(c) Answer yes and give an explanation.

3. Describe yourself.

(a) Outline personal data, hobbies and interests.
(b) Give an overview of your personality and work habits.
(c) Give three specific examples of your personality traits and accomplishments.

4. Why are you in the job market?

(a) "I have invested a great deal of time with my company and become disenchanted with the ways things are done".
(b) "I have a solid plan for my career. Within that plan I am looking for additional responsibility and more room for growth."
(c) "I have been passed over for promotions when I know I am capable of doing
more. I want to move on to a company that will not stunt my growth."

5. What are you looking for in a position?

(a) "I'm looking for an opportunity to apply my skills and contribute to the growth of the company while helping create some advancement opportunities for myself ".

(b) "I'm looking for an organization that will appreciate my

contributions and reward my efforts."

(c) "I'm looking for a position that will allow me to make enough money to support my lifestyle. I am a hard worker and will give a concerted effort to earn the money I need."

6. What do you know about our organization?

(a) "I've done a little homework and here is what I know about your organization... (cite examples)."

(b) "Everything I've seen and heard makes me want to be a part of this organization. I understand your industry is ________ and your primary customer is ______. A particularly exciting part of your business appears to be_____

(c) "I know enough to know this is an exciting place to work. It appears to be fit for my career goals."

7. What are your strengths?

(a) "I am good at giving constructive criticism to my co-workers. This honesty is something I'm very proud of and have found essential to having open working relationships."

(b) "I consider myself to be very consistent. I have proven myself to be someone who can be counted upon to do what is expected."

(c) "I would have to choose between two skills. I am very proud of my determination and ability to get things done. At the same time I am very proud of my analytical abilities and problem solving skills These skills combine to give me a unique ability to solve problems and then implement the solutions."

8. Why haven't you taken a job yet?

(a) "I've talked to a number of people, but it is very difficult to find an organization that is the right fit."

(b) "I've come across a few attractive opportunities but, so far. I haven't found a position that pays what I feel I am worth."

(c) "I have done some careful planning because this decision is very important to me. I have been offered positions but, to date, I have not been able to find a position that meets my criteria and this is important because the match must be good for me as well as the company. The position we are discussing today appears to be a good fit."

9. Where do you see yourself in five years?

(a) "In five years, I will have either been promoted to your job or have started my own business."

(b) "This is a very volatile market. I find it difficult to project out five years."

(c) "That really depends on the firm I join. I would like to take a position with some responsibility and room for growth. The key is with the right challenge, I intend to continually contribute and grow with the firm."

10. Before we go any further, what kind of money do you need to make?

(a) "I was making 50K at my last job and I feel I am worth at least 10 % more."

(b) "The current job market shows a salary range of $____ to $____ for this type of position. However, my salary requirements are negotiable. Your firm has a reputation of compensating employees fairly and I trust you would do the same in my case. I am very interested in finding the right opportunity and will be open to any fair offer when I do so."

(c) "Money is not very important to me. I need to be able to pay the bills, but the work environment is far more important to me."

Questions To Ask From Hiring Managers

- What is the organization structure of your department?
- How would you describe your company culture?
- What is your vision for your department over the next two to three years?
- What major challenges are you currently facing as a manager?
- What is your competitive advantage in the marketplace?
- What makes your company better than your competitors?
- What are the areas where your competitors are better than your company?
- What would you consider to be exceptional performance from someone performing in this position in the first 90 days?
- What is the internal perception of pursuing further education, such as a Master's degree?
- What is your management style?
- What is your preferred method of communicating with your team?
- How are you measured as a manager?
- What can I do to make you successful?
- How long have you been with the organization?
- What has been your career path within the organization?
- What will be the measurements of my success in this position?
- What are the organizational goals?
- What are the metrics used to measure whether or not you are achieving your goals?
- How far out into the future is the organization planning?
- How are new strategic initiatives communicated to the organization?
- Do you have control over your own budget? How is the initial budget amount determined?
- What is your approach with regard to the use of technology?
- What is the next step in the interviewing process?

TIPS FOR YOUR INTERVIEW

Some "Dos" and "Don't"

1. Do plan to arrive on time or a few minutes early. Late arrival for a job interview is never excusable.

2. If presented with an application, do fill it out neatly and completely. Don't rely on your application or resume to do the selling for you. Interviewers will want you to speak for yourself.

3. Do greet the interviewer by last name if you are sure of the pronunciation. If not, ask the employer to repeat it. Give the appearance of energy as you walk. Smile! Shake hands firmly. Be genuinely glad to meet the interviewer.

4. Do wait until you are offered a chair before sitting. Sit upright, look alert and interested at all times. Be a good listener as well as a good communicator.

5. Do look a prospective employer in the eye while speaking.

6. Do follow the interviewer's leads, but try to get the interviewer to describe the position and the duties to you early in the interview so that you can apply your background, skills and accomplishments to the position.

7. Do make sure that your good points come across to the interviewer in a factual, sincere manner. Stress achievements. For example: sales records, processes developed, savings achieved, systems installed, etc.

8. Do always conduct yourself as if you are determined to get the job you are discussing. Never close the door on opportunity.

9. Do show enthusiasm. If you are interested in the opportunity, enthusiastic feedback can enhance your chances of being further considered. If you are not interested, your responsiveness will still demonstrate your professionalism.

10. Don't forget to bring a copy of your resume! Keep several copies in your briefcase if you are afraid you will forget.

11. Don't smoke, even if the interviewer does and offers you a cigarette. Do not chew gum.

12. Don't answer with a simple "yes" or "no." Explain whenever possible. Describe those things about yourself which relate to the situation.

13. Don't lie. Answer questions truthfully, frankly and succinctly.

14. Don't make unnecessary derogatory remarks about your present or former employers. Obviously, there were issues or else you would not have left a prior company or be looking to leave a present employer. However, when explaining your reasons for leaving, limit your comments to those necessary to adequately communicate your rationale.

15. Don't over-answer questions. And if the interviewer steers the conversation into politics or controversial issues, try to do more listening than speaking since this could be a sensitive situation.

16. Don't inquire about salary, vacations, bonuses, retirement, etc., on the initial interview unless you are sure the employer is interested in hiring you. If the interviewer asks what salary you want, indicate what you've earned but that you're more interested in opportunity than in a specific salary.

Negative Factors Evaluated by An Interviewer

Personal appearance which is less than professional.
Overbearing, overaggressive or egotistical behavior.
No positive purpose.
Lack of interest and enthusiasm -- passive and indifferent.
Lack of confidence and poise; nervousness.
Overemphasis on compensation.
Evasiveness; making excuses for unfavorable factors in work history.
Lack of tact, maturity and courtesy.
Condemnation of past employers, managers, projects or technologies.
Inability to maintain a conversation.
Lack of commitment to fill the position at hand.
Failure to ask questions about the position.
Persistent attitude of "What can you do for me?"
Lack of preparation for interview -- failure to get information about the company, resulting in inability to ask intelligent questions.

Closing the Interview

1. If you are interested in the position, let the interviewer know. If you feel the position is attractive and you want it, be a good salesperson and say something like: "I'm very impressed with what I've seen here today; your company, its products and the people I've met. I am confident I could do an excellent job in the position you've described to me." The interviewer will be impressed with your enthusiasm.

2. Don't be too discouraged if no immediate commitment is made. The interviewer will probably want to communicate with

other people in the company or possibly interview more candidates before making a decision.

3. If you get the impression that the interview is not going well and that you have already been rejected, don't let your discouragement show. Once in a while an interviewer who is genuinely interested in you may seem to discourage you as a way of testing your reaction.

4. Thank the interviewer for his or her time and consideration. If you have answered the two questions-- "Why are you interested in this position?" and "What can you offer?"-- you have done all you can.

Do You Have International Experience?

Do you have International Experience? That is the question employers should be asking candidates. However more realistically the question many job seekers are hearing is - do you have Canadian Experience?

International experience is an asset. This means companies can tap into different cultural groups, understand cultural differences and employ people that can communicate effectively with other groups of people. You can bring new and innovative ideas to the table – things that worked in your country. Also international experience gives companies that competitive edge globally.

So, when you are asked if you have Canadian Experience – How do you answer that question? Do you simply say 'no' and believe that all employers are looking for Canadian Experience. Or do you tell employers how your experience can benefit that company. Researching companies and looking at their websites will give you an idea about how your experience can benefit the company.

I know that it's hard to keep hope when you have been rejected so many times. However hope and staying positive is the key to being successful. If you assume you will be rejected when you meet with an employer, you probably will be rejected.

I met one individual last week that was so negative about everything. She had lost hope – for her everything was impossible. When you have so much negativity it is hard to see the possibilities out there – and they are out there, trust me!

A survival job is one you can take to pay the bills, which is not in your field of interest. Take a survival job, but don't get too comfortable in that position. An interesting fact is if you stay in your survival job for over 2 years you will never leave. When I am doing jobs that are not challenging me or of interest, this affects my entire attitude and self-esteem. You are professionals and for some of you have many years experience in your field from another country. Don't loose that experience. Don't stop job searching and trying to find a job that will make you happy. Coming to a new country might be a difficult ride and you may have to do jobs that you don't want to. However when you finally do get a job in your field, everything that you experienced will be worthwhile and you will be a stronger person.

A long time ago, one of my clients shocked me. He knew that the terminology in his profession was different in Canada then in his native country. Every time I saw him he reported that he had done tons of research and was learning everything about his profession in Canada.

Some occupations in Canada require you to have a license in order to practice your profession. For example engineering is a regulated profession and you need a license. However you can still work in an engineering related position, as long as your work under a licensed engineer. The first step is to find out if your field is regulated. If so what steps do you need to take to work in your profession. There is a great website that will give you all this information: – http://www.equalopportunity.on.ca/eng_g/apt/index.asp

It is also important to have your education assessed in Canada to see if it matches the Canadian standards. Employers are sometimes not sure of the quality of education people received. So if you write on your resume that your education equals a Masters degree in Canada, employers will be more willing to call you for an interview. To get your education assessed goto: www.wes.org

Once again I will say that it is a struggle to settle in a new country and find work in your field. There are a lot of non-profit agencies that provide employment services for free. Many of these agencies will give you the tools to be successful in your job search. Take advantage of these resources.

Good luck and remember nothing is impossible, unless you think it is.

Top 10 Ways To Get Canadian Experience

Are you Internationally Educated? If so you should congratulate yourself, you are brave and courageous. It' takes a very special person who can leave their country and start over in Canada. The following are the top ten ways to find work in Canada:

1. A good way to learn about your occupation in Canada is to have information interviews with people who are working in your field, associations and licensing bodies. An information interview is when you meet with someone and ask them questions about what they like about their job, dislike and the future potential to name a few. This will help you become better informed about the industry. There are other ways to find out about your field such as: websites and printed reports. However talking to an expert or someone already employed will give you a greater insight.

2. Certain terminology in your occupation may be different in Canada. You may want to go to the library and the Internet to learn the language your industry uses.

3. Start to reform at your resume to a Canadian style. Information that may have been relevant in your own country may not be relevant in Canada. In some other countries it's normal to write your marital status, age and religion. In Canada we have the Ontario Human Rights Code, which protects us against discrimination. Also have someone look over your resume before you send it out. You can go to a non-profit employment service and have your resume critiqued for free.

4. 80% of the jobs are unadvertised and in the 'Hidden Job Market'. Tapping into the 'Hidden Job Market' involves a lot of networking and making cold calls. These two methods

may seem a little intimidating but they are worth trying. 20% of the job market consists of jobs that are advertised on the Internet, Newspapers and Trade Magazine. I recommend using these methods a little bit during your job search. However focus on the 'Hidden Job Market', there's less competition.

5. In your own country you probably had a big network of contacts, however in Canada your network may be small. I have a challenge for you it's time to re-build your network in Canada. Socialize with people, attend job search workshops offered by your community, volunteer, attend job fairs and join associations. Talk to everyone! Your family doctor may be able to help connect you to people, your children's teacher or a priest. Remember that people like to help other people.

6. Unfortunately you may not be able to have the same job in Canada right away. Try to find a job that's related to your field of expertise. If you are an engineer find a job as a technician or technologist. Research the positions that are related to your occupation and apply to them. Getting your foot in the door of a company is a great start, once in you will probably be able to apply to internal openings.

7. Through volunteering, co-op, on-the-job programs and job trials you will be able to prove your skills and abilities to a Canadian employer, learn about the Canadian workplace culture, gain 'Canadian Experience' and build your network. I would use my availability to volunteer as a marketing strategy. For example if an employer doesn't have current openings say "I understand that you do not have current openings, I would love to volunteer for you company."

8. When asked 'Do you have Canadian Experience?' don't just say no and feel that you have been rejected and that all employers are looking for this so called 'Canadian Experience'. Tell the employer how your skills are similar

to the skills that they are looking for. Also tell them how your international experience will help to benefit the company.

9. In an interview prepare yourself by researching the company, position and yourself. Sell your skills to the employer by telling them stories of your accomplishments and achievements. You are a small company selling your most valuable product yourself.

10. Stay positive, be persistent, proactive, follow-up with all contacts and maintain your motivation level. You will do it and you can do it. Good Luck.

MANAGE YOUR IMPRESSION

How Stereotypical Associations Form Your Future in Canada

How to manage your impression in Canada? I'm going to provide you an alternate strategy that really works most of the time to minimize the negative impact of your foreign credentials, international experience or fit for an employment in Canadian labour market.. This information can help you to smoothly integrate into Canadian society and to secure a job in your field within a shorter period of time if you cannot afford to upgrade your education with a Canadian college or university. In fact this alternate strategy is just the universal principles of managing your impressions.

Canadians are highly productive nation. With only 32 million of population and being the world's 2nd largest country in size, in 2003–04, Canada's federal government has collected about $186 billion in taxes (http://www.fin.gc.ca/taxdollar). But according to conference board Canada, they can add another $4 billion a year in revenue if Canadian employers can utilize the skilled immigrants to their full potential.

If you analyze the international statistics about Canadian presence at global level you will observe that most of the Canadian employers and many professional bodies may not be as visionaries as their Americans and Europeans counterparts in terms of capitalizing on international manpower out of Canadian geography. To me the one significant factor for missing the opportunity is their negligible presence on international level as compared to Americans, British, Europeans and Scandinavians. In other words, they rarely compete for international contracts or business opportunities aggressively other than offered by United States, subsequently Canadians had fewer chances of working with Chinese, Indians, Pakistanis, Filipinos and other professionals out of Canadian geography who are rapidly becoming the main source of supply for skilled professionals for Canadian labour market. Thus human resource managers are unable to reach on a true or fair judgment about their competence or talents with international credentials and experience. As most of interviewers make their decisions based on outwardly obvious within half an hour interview. So the Canadian HR managers or generalist who shortlist resumes for interviews, do not reflect their faith or comfort on international education and experience. The resume of an internationally educated and experienced professional could be quickly pitched off compare to a locally less educated or less experienced candidate. Thousands of internationally educated and experienced professionals like doctors, engineers, lawyers, school teachers technologists and many more who are driving cabs and delivering pizza's are the proof of that vision. To Canadian employers and businesses, the whole world is just the U.S.A as it absorbs 85% of Canadian exports (see statcan table imports & exports in part-1 page 32). That is why there are so many derogatory stereotypical associations that are harbored by many Canadian employers and professional bodies that affects the lives of internationally trained professionals and having negative impact on Canadian society and economy at large. But in spite of all disadvantages you can still be successful in Canadian Labour market by capitalizing on positive stereotype associations. So what is a "stereotype" and how can you capitalize on positive stereotype associations and tackle the negative ones?

Lets understand what is a "stereotype". A "stereotype" is defined in Merriam Webster's Dictionary as a : "standardized mental picture that is held in common by members of a group or nation and that represents an oversimplified opinion, prejudice attitude, or uncritical judgment," The Encyclopedia Britannica describes " prejudiced" as , an "attitude", usually emotional, acquired without prior or adequate evidence or experiences." When we think of stereotypes and prejudices, we usually think of race, national origin or gender. Many people will harbor stereotypes and prejudices toward you if you wear black or pink, speak quickly or slowly, are rich or poor, tall or short, thin or fat, dowdy or fashionable, are good or poor listener, articulate or inarticulate, courteous or rude, clean or dirty, organized or disorganized – the list is endless.

Every, person you meet size you up within the first few seconds. They form impression about you who you are, what you think and how you are likely to act. And once those impressions are set in their minds, they are difficult to change.

The impression others form of you are seldom based on rational thought or independent investigation. They are the product of hundreds of associations we all make between outwardly obvious characteristics and the invisible inner qualities we believe they reflect. These stereotypes and prejudices, some positive and some negative, are an intellectual and emotional shorthand. They arises from our past experiences, social biases, promoted or perpetuated in the media and the literature we read, and from the instinctive and emotional hardwiring within our brains.

If it is a respected brand name product on a supermarket shelf, we take for granted that it is higher in both quality and price then the generic brand. If the package is attractive and inviting, we conclude the product inside must share those qualities. People make the assumptions because from past experience they believe such assumptions are warranted, and they don't have the time, energy or inclination to test their validity each time they reach for an item on the shelf.

In this article, I examined that how stereotypes and prejudices are formed and how they influence impression formation. A clear understanding of this process is critical if you hope to present yourself in the best possible light by capitalizing on positive stereotypes and nullifying unflattering ones during your job search and settlement process in Canada.

People seldom have the time or inclination to make fully informed decisions about other people. So they rely on sources that do not require case-by-case analysis and often no rational thought whatsoever. Those sources are :

Myth
Personal experience
Emotion-based stereotypes

Myth: In the Middle Ages, many Christians were told that Jews had horns and tails like the Devil. As absurd as this is, some of those who never actually met a Jew believed it to be true. Today we like to think we are more enlightened, but we continue to accept a wide assortment of myths about members of certain groups, nationalities or race. Some of these stereotypes are based on fact, but researchers find little support for many others.

Personal Experience: The most entrenched stereotypes and prejudices are those that are based on the actual experiences of the person who harbor them.

Almost everyone recognizes that all individuals who fall within a particular group do not embody the characteristics they attach generally to that group. Even the most abused young African – American males knows that all white cops aren't bad, and whites who have had consistently favorable exposure to the police recognize that there are some bad cops. But we all play the odds. If we had have consistent experiences with those who fit a particular stereotype, we conclude that others in that group are likely to think and act in the same way.

Jesse Jackson, for example, once said: " There is nothing more painful for me than to walk down the street and hear footsteps and start to think about robbery, and then see it's somebody white and feel relieved." African American Scholar Johnnetta Cole acknowledged that among black women, " one of the most painful admission I hear is :"I am afraid of my own people" .

Studies also have demonstrated that those who are themselves victims of stereotyping and prejudice are no more charitable toward members of other groups than the rest of us. In a report from the

National Conference of Christians and Jews, minority groups expressed stronger prejudices then those harbored by whites toward other minority groups, as reflected in this sampling from the report cited by Dinesh D'Souza in The End of Racism: 49% of the African American and 68% percent of the Asians surveyed thought Hispanics " tend to have bigger families than they can support; 46% of the Hispanics and 42% of the African American viewed Asian American as "unscrupulous, crafty and devious in business"; and 53% of the Asians and 51% of the Hispanics thought African Americans " are most likely to commit crimes and violence."

Keep this in mind as you evaluate the probable stereotypes and prejudices that others might harbor toward you. Don't assume that other professional women won't harbor gender-based biases against you because you too are a professional women, or that the beautiful women who obsesses about her appearance won't think you are shallow if you do likewise. Some won't but many will. Until you have gathered enough information about a person to conclude reliably that he or she has not adopted generally prevalent stereotypes, assume that he or she has.

Emotion-Based Stereotypes: Many of the schemas we form of others are based neither on myth nor conscious recall of past experience. Often the impression we form is attributed to emotion or intuition.

Intuition arises when years of experience stored behind the curtain of our subconscious percolates from those deep recesses when our memory is triggered by similar experiences. All of us stored an extraordinary amount of data in our brains about how other's behaviors relate to their beliefs and values. We know that those who smile sincerely are most often friendly; those who are great listeners are usually compassionate; and those who won't look us in the eye are frequently lying. When we see those behaviors, we seldom consciously think to ourselves: She is smiling so she must be friendly" or "She is listening so she must be compassionate," or "She is looking away so she must be lying". We just "get a feeling, which is a message from our subconscious as it taps into our stored memory of prior experiences.

Intuition usually can be explained rationally. But we make many associations that cannot. For example, dozens of studies have equated the color of clothing with people's assumptions as to someone's professionalism or honesty. Navy blue consistently scores higher than bright flashy colors, and solids receive higher ratings than plaids or dramatic patterns. In part, this can be explained rationally. Through years of experience we have found that those who are more professional and honest tend to dress more conservatively, and those who dress in flashy cloths tend to be less professional and less honest. But the same rational process can't explain why we find pastel colors more soothing, black depressing, or bright colors more invigorating and red is the color of choice to show sexuality, anger and other passions. Yet those reactions are so consistent that colors has often come to symbolize the emotions they represents. But remember, stereotypes and prejudices lie at the foundation of impression formation, whether based on myth, experience or emotional responses. They don't need to make sense to have an effect on how you are perceived.

With the above mentioned information, I hope you would have developed an idea or understanding of stereotype but "what's in it for me"? Since the last few years the influx of immigrants to Canada is from China, India, Philippines and Pakistan (top four) in independent or economic class and they are skilled workers. Considerable research indicates that even highly trained and educated skilled immigrants have a problem accessing occupations for which they have been trained in their country of origin. There are many studies that indicate a gap between wages of immigrants and native-born Canadians. Overall foreign-trained immigrants earn less than native-born residents with the same level of education they do. Recent studies show that North American and European immigrants fare better than immigrants from such countries as Asia and Central America do. Being a skilled worker professional one of the major derogatory stereotypical association that I observed and harbored by most of Canadian employers towards Asian candidates is based on their English language accent. Lets find out how you are being sized up by the Canadian employer or HR generalist during an interview and why accent is so important in impression formation. You must improve your accent and capitalize on this stereotypical association.

ACCENTS

The single most important factor during your job search or settlement in Canada that will have significant affect on your life will be your English language accent. This factor has the potential to make you employed or unemployed regardless of how qualified you are and subsequently rich or poor within short time-frame.

Canada's diverse, multicultural and multilingual population is affected constantly by the stereotypical associations made regarding accents and regional dialects. The stereotypes associated with particular accents are usually offshoots of the stereotypes that are directed toward race and ethnicity, although other factors also influence the extent to which accents affect impression formation.

In a study conducted by Dr. Lillian Glass and published in her book *"Talk to Win'* forty-one participants between the ages of twelve and seventy-two were asked if they like each of thirty different accents *"a lot", "a little", or "not at all"*. Dr. Glass's findings reflect that over a third of the accents listed were disliked by a majority of the respondents.

The accents that were favored were generally those incorporating sounds that are typical of English and other "romance languages." Those accents that were most disliked incorporate sounds that are not prevalent in English phonics, such as the comparatively choppy sound of Asian languages, throaty guttural sounds common to Middle Eastern languages, or the harsh sound of Germanic and Slavic languages.

This is not surprising if we consider that our emotional brains don't feel as comfortable when they process foreign data as they do when they receive familiar stimuli. *Studies showed that, with a few exceptions, the more different an accent sounds from our own, the more likely we are to equate it with lower socioeconomic class, less competence and lower intelligence. Not surprisingly, people with such accents on average receive lower pay and attain less success in the work environment. Those with non-standard accents often judge others with different nonstandard accents just as harshly as any one else.*

Those with accents that are the standard in the community, on the other hand, are perceived as more competent, confident, intelligent, friendly, ambitious and successful. They also are assumed to have a higher socioeconomic status, and what they say is thought to convey more substance. Studies also show that teachers with "standard" accents are better understood by their students, who remember what they say longer. They are also considered more dynamic.

Studies have identified three elements that most frequently trigger negative accent-related stereotypes.

The first characteristic of a poorly received accent is that it is difficult to understand. Just as others will make a broad range of negative associations if you mumble, talk too fast or otherwise make them too hard to understand what you say, so too, if your accent makes it difficult for others to understand you, they will become impatient, irritated and form derogatory associations with regard to your intelligence, capability, friendliness and competence. If you have a distinct accent that is still easy to understand, much less bias will arise.

The second factor that influences negative accent related associations is directly tied to the ever-important concept of expectations. If we meet a person from a foreign country, who has been in Canada for a relatively short period of time, and as a result, struggle with the English language and speak with a heavy and sometimes incomprehensible accent, we seldom judge the person harshly because of his accent. We expect someone who is learning a language to have difficulties. But when we encounter someone we know to have been in Canada for an extended period of time, or who has a job that requires him to be able to communicate in English without his accent presenting a barrier. The typical reaction is to assume that if he has had a reason and opportunity to learn to speak without a heavy accent, but has not, it is either because of he is not intelligent enough, industrious enough or friendly and thoughtful enough to have done so. These are strong negative associations, and perhaps even unfair, but they exist as a function of our expectations.

The final cause of negative associations with accents is that they accentuate whatever racial or ethnic biases and prejudices people otherwise harbor. Many people have significant racial and ethnic prejudice and bias, and tend to make strong stereotypical association with any members of the group who are the victims of those biases. We w'll know that there are no longer such biases when at the end of a racial joke everyone looks puzzled and say, " I don't get it, what's the guy's race got to do with the joke anyway?" Until then, racial and ethnic biases will be a reality that can be addressed with impression management.

Studies also shows that the biases often are the product of associations made at an emotional level. Heavy accents accentuate this emotional brain response. When someone has no identifiable accent, his or her race or ethnicity is much less frequently even considered. Test researchers experience against your own.

Think of individuals you know who come from particular ethnic or racial background. Focus on one or two of them who have perfect English accents, whether they are Asian, Middle Eastern, African Americans or of some other race or nationality. If you're like most people, you seldom think about their background. Then consider a few individuals you know who have heavy accents, and you probable will find that you think much more frequently about their race or ethnicity. Those who have other's minds, and with it the lingering biases other may harbor.

If you have an accent that is (1) so heavy that its difficult to understand, (2) heavier then one would expect who has had the opportunity and practical need to acquire standard English accent, or (3) reflects a racial, ethnic, regional or other background towards which strong stereotypes apply, your accent will effect the impression you make on many people.

I am not suggesting that people abandoned their cultural heritage, or that standard English accent is in any way superior to others. But we do want to impress upon those who have accents that a heavy accent will affect impression formation, particularly if the accent is associated with the racial or ethnic group toward which significant prejudice exists. If you eliminate your accent, you will decrease many of the negative stereotypes to which you are subjected. If you choose to retain your accent, you should recognize that your impression management plan should incorporate traits to offset the negative stereotypes that your accent may trigger.

With regards to stereotypical associations and other impression management techniques, I just touched the topic and showed you the tip of an iceberg that can change your life in Canada. So you must buy and read a good book on impression management several times before you migrate to Canada.

DO YOU KNOW YOUR AUDIENCE ?

Positive impression formation always requires a transmitter and a receiver that are in sync. What may impress one audience may be unimpressive to another. Think of yourself as radio station that must clearly identify its target market before it decides on a content and format of its broadcast. It is wants to appeal to a talk show audience, it emphasize lively chat. If it hopes to reach listeners at work, it adopts an easy listening music format. If its audience consists of eighteen-to-twenty-five-year – old, it plays the contemporary top forty.

Unlike radio stations, you don't have just a single audience. You have many. One moment you may want to appeal to a conservative businessman, the next to your co-workers, and a few hours later to your friends or family. To be successful in each relationship, you cant always present the same content and format. You should project the different qualities in every encounter, but how best to achieve that objective will vary from situation to situation.

The first step to knowing your audience is to identify their expectations and probable stereotypical associations. If you want to meet a client for a business lunch, you could anticipate that he would expect that you would dress and act professionally. He might also expect that you would take him to an upscale restaurant, pick up the bill and be solicitous if you were trying to curry his favour. If you dressed or acted too casually, you would disappoint those expectations, which would tend to create a negative impression.

On the other hand, if you were to make a lunch date with a high school classmate, her expectations would be very different. She would not expect you to take her to an expensive restaurant, or pick-up the cheque. She would expect a more casual, free-flowing conversation, and less formal dress and behavior. If you shown up in your new Brioni suite and kept it buttoned at the waist throughout lunch. Designer tie cinched tight, and posture as erect and formal as your speech, you disappoint her expectations. She would probably think you were full of yourself, nervous, unfriendly and boring.

There are many ways to gather information about the person or people you want to impress. Whenever possible, this information-gathering process should begin in advance of your first meeting and continue as the relationship grows.

Before a job interview, for example, you should learn as much as possible about the company. Company broachers, newspapers and the Internet provide invaluable information. If you know someone at the company, take her out to lunch and pick her brain. You may discovered that a distinctive corporate environment exist in which emphasis is placed more on one quality in its employees then on others. Stop by and visit the company before the interview. See how it's furnished. Is it stark and efficient, or luxurious and opulent? Watch the employees. All they all business, or is there a friendly patter that reflects a casual environment is usually a casual environment? Notice the working conditions. Are people cramped in small cubicles, or do they have large, private offices? Is there a staff room with plenty of space for employees to relax during breaks and lunch, or does everyone grab a quick bite at his or her desk? The corporate environment is usually a reliable reflection of the values of its decision makers. Your awareness of those values will help determine how can appeal to them if you choose to..

A friend of yours, an avid fly fisherman, put it best: "If you want to catch a trout, the first thing you have to do is to find out what they are biting. Sit on the riverbank and watch. If they are eating mosquitoes, use a fly that looks like a mosquito. If they are eating wasps, use a fly that looks like a wasp. The important think is to use whatever bait is attractive to them. You have to think like a fish, not a fisherman".

ARE YOU A PROFESSIONAL ?

You don't need to hold a graduate degree to be "professional"; nor are you "professional" just because you do. The bank teller who greets each customer with a friendly "hello, may I help you?" is professional. The telephone operator who tells the caller: " Hold your horses, I'll get you when I can" isn't. The cab driver, who keeps his car clean and neat, and seat belts readily accessible, is professional. The housekeeper who leaves the windows streaky isn't. The policeman who asks politely, "May I see your license, please?" is professional. The doctor's receptionist who asks in front of a crowed waiting room, "Are you here to see the doctor about that discharge again?" absolutely, positively isn't.

In a most recent survey respondents were asked to identify what traits most influenced their impression of someone's professionalism.

The way someone "dressed" was identified by 29.1% of the respondents as a first trait they considered. Another 6.4% listed "appearance" or "grooming". More then 35% of the respondents, therefore, identified appearance-related traits first. By comparison, body language and vocal traits tied for second place, each accounting for 14.6 % of the total responses. Only 8.2% of the respondents identified someone's job or educational level as a first characteristic they considered as they evaluated whether someone is "professional".

In the narrative portion of the participants' responses to the questionnaires, it was found that there are three themes arose most frequently as people discussed what impresses them as professional.

Appearance: The first criterion is whether you are neat, clean and appropriately dressed for your position. Whether you are a school teacher, postal worker, appliance repairman or jet pilot; whether you wear a required uniform or have complete discretion in your choice of wardrobe, don't take your decision about grooming or what to wear lightly.

Graciousness: If you are loud, pushy or discourteous, or if you embarrass, interrupt, ignore or are otherwise insensitive to other's need, you will not be viewed as professional, regardless of your academic qualifications or job status. On the other hand, if you display dignity, good manners, courtesy, respect for privacy and graciousness, you will be well on your way.

Dedication: Julius Erving described what it means to be professional as " Doing all the things you love to do on the day when you don't feel like doing them". If you have a nine-to-five attitude and just go through the motions, you won't be seen as professional. If you skip your breaks to get your job done well, or come in before nine and stay after five if that is what is required, you will. Professionalism means letting your boss, coworkers, and customers know that they can count on you to get the job done right, no matter what. It requires an outward display of commitment, responsibility and dedication.

ARE YOU A LEADER ?

What makes us turn to certain men and women for direction and inspiration? Leadership. By "leadership" we do not mean "authority". We have all known those in positions of authority may be high achievers, but they aren't leaders in the true sense of the word, they are just bosses. When we speak of leaders, we also are not referring to politicians or CEO's alone, but also to the millions of parents, teachers, little league coaches, small business owners and partners of all types.

Leadership is an invisible strand as mysterious as it is powerful, it pulls and it bonds. It is a catalyst that creates unity out of disorder. Yet, it defies definition. No combination of talents can guarantee it. No process or training can create it where the spark does not exist.

The qualities of leadership are universal: they are found in the poor and the rich, the humble and the proud, the common man, and the brilliant thinker; they are qualities that suggest paradox rather than pattern. But wherever they are found leadership makes things happen.

Researchers discovered and repeatedly identified following characteristic in true leaders.

Leaders are doers: Leaders take charge. They are proactive. They are outspoken. They volunteer. They don't wait for things to happen. They make them happen. They are willing to take risks and responsibility. They contemplate, but they don't obsess.

Leaders are confidents: Leadership requires confidence, not swaggering cockiness, but a calm, natural, effortless control.

Leaders lead, they don't push: True leaders don't force anyone to follow them; they make others want to follow them. They don't abuse their authority for ego gratification, but exercise it purposely, to benefit not just themselves but also those they lead.

Leaders watch their flock: Leaders makes others feel important and cared for. They are sensitive to their needs and desires. They do not expect their followers to respond to their own needs, but are sensitive to the needs of those who follow them.

Leaders are open-minded: Opinionated, head strong, know-it-alls are seldom successful leaders. Effective leaders recognize that the knowledge required for leadership is enhanced by a willing ear and an open mind .

Leaders support and empower others: leaders bring out the best in there followers with there support and encouragement.

Leaders appreciate others: Leaders give praise and credit freely. They are not stingy with accolades, and do not steal other's thunder.

Leaders trust others to succeed: Leaders knows when and whom to trust, and with what to trust them. They encourage other's success, and give them the incentive to strive for it.

Leaders show respect for others: Leaders don't act superior to those they lead. They recognize it is human nature to like those who like us, trust those who trust us, and respect those who respect us.

Leaders show true personal character: True leadership is not acquired by authority, but by influence. Such influence is obtained by trust in the fundamental character of a leader.

Leaders are enthusiastic: Enthusiasm energizes those who follow a leader, and injects them with the leader's commitment and dedication to his or her cause.

Leaders Inspire: Leaders inspire others with their vision, creativity, innovation and imagination. They engender a belief in a positive future, which their followers hope to achieve for their benefit, not just the leader's.

Leaders are capable: Successful leadership requires performance. Capability, in the form of intelligence, competence, confidence and professionalism, is required to instill trust that a leader will be able to create order from chaos and to guide his or her followers through both calm and tumultuous times.

Leaders lead by example: Leaders asks no more from their followers then they are willing to give themselves.

Leaders build partnership: Leaders do not sit atop the wagon pulled by others, but join them side by side to pull together toward a common goal.

DARE

Dare to try. Dare to love. Dare to make a commitment.
Dare to take a risk.

To laugh is to risk appearing the fool.
To weep is to risk appearing sentimental.
To reach for another is to risk involvement.
To expose your feelings is to risk exposing your true self.
To place your ideas, dreams before a crowd is to risk their loss.
To love is to risk not being loved in return.
To live is to risk dying.
To believe is to risk despair.
To try is to risk failure.
But risks must be taken, because the greatest hazard in life is to risk nothing.
The people who risk nothing, do nothing, have nothing, are nothing.
They may avoid suffering and sorrow, but they cannot learn, feel, change, grow, love, live.
Chained by their attitudes they are slaves; they have forfeited their freedom.

Only a person who risks is free.

from
The President's Newsletter, November 1982
Phi Delta Kappa
Bloomington, Indiana

NEWS RELEASES

Off-Campus Work Permit Program Launched

Ottawa, April 27, 2006 — Foreign students studying in Canada can apply for off-campus work permits effective immediately, the Honourable Monte Solberg, Minister of Citizenship and Immigration, announced today.

"Foreign students make a significant contribution to Canada," said the Minister. "They enrich campus and community life with new ideas and new cultures, and they are an important pool of potential future skilled workers that Canadian businesses need to remain competitive."

Foreign students contribute approximately $4 billion a year to Canada's economy. There are about 100,000 foreign students in Canada who could be eligible for work permits under the Off-Campus Work Permit Program.

The program is not intended to take jobs away from Canadian students. Each applicant will be required to compete for employment on an equal basis with Canadians.

Citizenship and Immigration Canada (CIC) has signed agreements with most provinces to implement the program, and agreements with New Brunswick and the Yukon are currently being finalized. The agreements allow eligible foreign students at public post-secondary institutions to work off-campus for up to 20 hours a week during the school year and full-time during study breaks.

Eligible foreign students can apply for an off-campus work permit immediately, and may be able to work off-campus as early as this summer. The work permit is valid for the duration of their study permit.

"CIC is working in cooperation with the provinces and territories to make Canada a destination of choice by making it easier for foreign students to work in Canada during and after their studies," said Minister Solberg. "Off-campus work agreements will make it easier for students to gain work experience in the Canadian labour market and earn extra income while studying," he said.

The Canadian Federation of Students, the Fédération étudiante universitaire du Québec, the Association of Universities and Colleges of Canada and the Association of Canadian Community Colleges, who have all been consulted on the initiative, support efforts to make it easier for foreign students to work in Canada.

"With Canadian work experience, foreign students will be able to integrate into the Canadian labour force more quickly. This will help address skilled labour shortages in Canada," said Minister Solberg.

For more information (media only):

Lesley Harmer
Director of Communications
Minister's Office
Citizenship and Immigration Canada
(613) 954-1064

Marina Wilson
Media relations spokesperson
Communications Branch
Citizenship and Immigration Canada
(613) 941-7021

Note: Spokespeople for the following organizations are aware of the initiative, and are prepared to comment on the announcement:

Canadian Federation of Students
George Soule
National Chair
(613) 232-7394

Fédération étudiante universitaire du Québec
Véronique Martel
Press Secretary
(514) 396-3380

Association of Canadian Community Colleges
Nejat Gorica
Vice-President, Business Development and Technical Cooperation
(613) 746-2222, ext. 3872

Association of Universities and Colleges of Canada
Jeff Pappone
Media Relations Officer
(613) 563-3961, ext. 330

Backgrounder
Work Programs for Foreign Students

Citizenship and Immigration Canada (CIC) is helping eligible foreign students gain valuable Canadian work experience by giving them the same opportunity to work as Canadian students.

In 2005, more than 50,000 new foreign students came to Canada to study in post-secondary institutions. On December 1, 2005, there were more than 152,000 foreign students studying in Canada.

Off-Campus Work Permit Program

CIC implemented a pilot Off-Campus Work Permit Program in Manitoba in 2003. Pilots programs were added in Quebec and New Brunswick in 2004. Before these programs were in place, students were restricted to holding jobs on the campus at which they were studying. Following the success of the pilots, the program is now being implemented nationally.

In order to be eligible for the program, foreign students must have a valid study permit, and they must have studied full-time at an eligible public, post-secondary institution for at least six months out of the 12 months preceding their application. Institutions must sign an agreement with the province or territory in which they are located in order to participate in the program. The agreement includes monitoring and reporting requirements to ensure that students retain their eligibility for the program.

Under agreements with the provinces, eligible full-time students who retain satisfactory academic standing can apply to work for a maximum of 20 hours a week off-campus while classes are in session and full-time during scheduled breaks (including summer or winter holidays and reading weeks).

Exchange students, students enrolled in English- or French-as-a-second-language programs, and students who have received awards from the Canadian Commonwealth Scholarship Program, the

Government of Canada Awards Program or the Canadian International Development Agency are not eligible for work permits under the Off-Campus Work Permit Program.

About 100,000 foreign students who are studying in Canada could be eligible to apply for work permits under the Off-Campus Work Permit Program.

Post-Graduation Work Program

Until 2003, foreign students who graduated from a post-secondary institution in Canada could receive a one-year permit to work in Canada in their field of study if they met the eligibility criteria.

Between 2003 and 2005, CIC implemented post-graduation work permit extension pilot projects in New Brunswick, Alberta, Saskatchewan, Nova Scotia, and Newfoundland and Labrador.

Under the pilot projects, students could renew their work permits for an additional year, which allowed them to work for a total of two years in Canada after they graduated. The pilots were replaced by a national post-graduation work program in May 2005.

The Post-Graduation Work Program is available to all eligible foreign students who would like to gain Canadian work experience in their field of study after graduation. In 2005, CIC added a "bonus" year for graduates outside Montréal, Toronto and Vancouver who intend to work outside these three major centres. This helps spread the benefits of immigration to more of Canada's regions since nearly 80 percent of Canada's foreign students are enrolled in institutions in Toronto, Montréal or Vancouver.

Other Work Opportunities for Foreign Students

Spouses and common-law partners of foreign students can also apply for work permits if they meet the eligibility criteria (for more information, see the link to the CIC Web site below).

While CIC encourages recent graduates to remain in Canada to help address the shortage of skilled workers and to increase our global competitiveness, many choose to return to their home country after completing their studies. When they enter the work force, they act as ambassadors for Canada and help increase international understanding and cooperation. In addition, they provide good business contacts for Canada and Canadians abroad.

For more information on work opportunities for students, please visit www.cic.gc.ca/english/study/work-opps.html.

FAQ'S

Q1: Are all foreign students in Canada eligible for the program?

A: If you are a foreign student studying in Canada, you must meet the following criteria in order to be eligible for a work permit under the Off-Campus Work Permit Program:

- you must have a valid study permit;
- you must have studied full time at an eligible institution for at least six months out of the 12 months before you apply;
- you must maintain satisfactory academic standing (as defined by your academic institution);
- you must be enrolled in an academic program of study; and
- you must comply with the conditions of your study permit and your work permit, if applicable. If you fail to do so, you will be found to be in non-compliance and will not be able to re-apply for the program.

Q2: Are there any students who are not eligible?

A : a) Foreign students who are not studying at publicly funded post-secondary educational institutions are not eligible.

Publicly funded post-secondary educational institutions are:

- public post-secondary institutions that have signed an off-campus work agreement with their provincial government; or
- private post-secondary institutions that operate under the same rules and regulations as public institutions, receive at least 50% of their financing for their overall operations from government grants, and have signed an off-campus work

agreement with their provincial government. Currently, *établissements privés subventionnés d'enseignement collégial* (private subsidized college institutions) in Quebec qualify.

b) If you are not enrolled at a participating institution you are not eligible.

c) All exchange students, guest students, students enrolled in English or French second language programs, and students who have received awards from the Canadian Commonwealth Scholarship Program, the Government of Canada Awards Program or the Canadian International Development Agency, or students who in the past did not comply with the conditions of their study or work permit, are not eligible for work permits under the Off-Campus Work Permit Program.

Q3: How do I apply?

A: You can find everything you need to apply on the CIC Web site. You can download the application form and guide for work permits, as well as the other forms that must be submitted with your application (www.cic.gc.ca/english/applications/work-students.html).

Q4: How do I find out if the institution where I study is participating in the Off-Campus Work Permit Program?

A: Contact the institution where you are studying and ask if it has signed an agreement for the purpose of this program with the province or territory in which it is located. You can also visit the CIC Web site to see if your institution is participating (www.cic.gc.ca/english/study/guide-list.html) or contact the department responsible for education in your province or territory for more information.

Q5: If I receive a work permit, how long is it valid for?

A: Your work permit will allow you to work off campus until you complete your studies, as long as you remain in satisfactory academic standing and comply with the conditions of your work permit and your study permit.

Q6: Is there a fee to apply for the work permit?

A: Yes. The fee is $150.

Q7: Once I apply for the work permit, how long will it take to process my application?

A: Generally, it will take from one month to six weeks. Please visit our Web site to see the current processing times for work permits at www.cic.gc.ca/english/department/times/process-in.html#temp_res. However, your individual circumstances may affect the processing time. They include:

- whether you are eligible for the program;
- whether your application is complete; and
- whether the institution you attend has signed an agreement with the province or territory in which it is located.

Q8: If I meet the eligibility criteria, and the institution where I study is participating in the program, can I apply for a job off campus right away, or do I have to wait until I receive my work permit?

A: You can apply for a job right away, but you cannot legally work off campus in Canada until you receive a work permit. If you begin to work off campus before you receive a work permit, you could lose your eligibility to participate in the Off-Campus Work Permit Program.

Q9: Will my application be processed in time for me to work during the summer of 2006?

A: It is anticipated that some foreign students will be able to commence working off campus this summer; however, it depends on your individual circumstances. There are several factors that may affect how long it takes to process your application. They include:

- whether you are eligible for the program;
- whether your application is complete;
- whether the institution you attend has signed an agreement with the province or territory in which it is located; and
- when you submit your application.

Q10: Are there any restrictions on where I can work or the type of job that I can apply for?

A: You will be able to work anywhere in Canada as long as you remain a full-time student in satisfactory academic standing while classes are in session and you comply with the conditions of your work permit.

In some cases, there may be restrictions on the type of job you can hold. For example, you may be required to undergo a medical examination for some occupations. If you have questions, contact the CIC Call Centre for more information at 1-888-242-2100.

Q11: Are there any restrictions on how many hours I can work once I receive my work permit?

A: Once you receive your work permit, you can work up to 20 hours per week off campus while classes are in session. You can work full time during scheduled breaks, including summer or winter holidays and reading weeks.

While classes are in session, you must be studying full time and retain satisfactory academic standing in order to keep your work permit.

Q12: Why is this program not available to foreign students when they start their studies?

A: The likelihood of a student quitting his or her program is increased during the first months. CIC wants to ensure that work permits are issued to students who are legitimate students. When they apply, these students will be required to prove that they have been studying full time for six of the last 12 months at a participating institution.

Q13: I am considering studying in Canada. Can I apply for a work permit at the same time as I apply for my study permit?

A: You cannot apply for a study permit and a work permit at the same time under the Off-Campus Work Permit Program. In order to qualify for the program, you must already hold a valid study permit, and have been a full-time student at a participating institution for at least six months out of the last 12 months before you apply.

Citizenship for Adopted Children

Ottawa, May 15, 2006 — On this International Day of Families, the Honourable Monte Solberg, Minister of Citizenship and Immigration, introduced a new bill in the House of Commons to amend the *Citizenship Act*. The proposed legislation will allow children adopted abroad by Canadian citizens to obtain Canadian citizenship without first having to become permanent residents. As a result, the difference in treatment between children adopted abroad and children born abroad of a Canadian parent will be minimized.

"We are supporting Canadian families who adopt foreign-born children by helping them get citizenship without having to go through the immigration process," Minister Solberg said. "It is fitting that the introduction of this important bill occurs on the International Day of Families."

In order for the adopted child to be granted citizenship, the adoption must conform to the laws of the province or the territory of residence of the adoptive parents. Adopted children will be able to acquire Canadian citizenship as soon as the adoption process is completed, providing that an application for citizenship is submitted in their name.

"This is a major step forward for foreign-born adopted children and their adoptive families," said Sandra Scarth, President of the Adoption Council of Canada.

"The Government of Canada is committed to working to welcome these young new Canadians and enhance fairness," said Minister Solberg.

For more information (media only):

Lesley Harmer
Director of Communications
Minister's Office
Citizenship and Immigration Canada
(613) 954-1064

Marina Wilson
Spokesperson
Media Relations
Citizenship and Immigration Canada
(613) 941-7021

Ida-Mae Tracey
Office Manager
Adoption Council of Canada
1 888 542-3678

Patricia Fenton
Executive Director
Adoption Council of Ontario
(416) 482-0021

Karen Madeiros
Executive Director
Adoptive Families Association of BC
(604) 320-7330

Notice

Simplified Application Process

Citizenship and Immigration Canada has introduced a new simplified application process for federal skilled workers and business immigrants.

Beginning ***September 1, 2006,*** most Federal Economic Class applicants are only required to provide the modified application form (IMM 0008SW or IMM 0008BU) and processing fees at the time of application. Supporting documents will need to be provided only when the visa office is ready to assess the application.

Q1: Why has CIC introduced the simplified application process for Federal Economic Class applications?

CIC is committed to client-focused service delivery. CIC recognized that procedural changes could be made to simplify the initial application requirements for Federal Economic Class applicants waiting to have their applications assessed.

Q2: When did the simplified application process come into effect?

The simplified application process came into effect on September 1, 2006.

Q3: What does the new simplified application process entail?

Simplified kits and forms have been developed to guide applicants through the new process. Applicants are required to fill out and submit a three-page form plus the processing fees, which secures them a place in the queue. All supporting documents are requested later, approximately four months before the visa office is ready to assess the application. A letter of receipt provides advice to the applicant on labour-market preparation encouraging prospective immigrants to make maximum use of the waiting period by, for example, enrolling in courses to upgrade their language skills.

Q4: What does the supporting documentation to be provided later include?

Supporting documentation would include education documents or other certificates attesting to the educational level, employment letters confirming work experience, language test results, police certificates, birth and marriage certificates, and bank statements confirming the applicant's funds.

Q5: Will this new simplified application process be used at all visa offices?

Beginning September 1, 2006, the simplified application process is the norm at all visa offices except Buffalo, U.S.A. For applicants who submit their applications in Buffalo for processing by Buffalo and the other U.S. offices, the regular application process (supporting documents submitted at the same time as the application form) continues to apply.

Q6: Why will the new simplified application process not be used by Buffalo and other U.S. offices?

Buffalo and other U.S. offices mainly process applicants who currently meet Canadian labour market needs. This means that most applicants are already in Canada and have some type of arranged employment. The regular application process continues to apply since, by policy, these applicants are processed on a priority basis.

Q7: Can a foreigner living in the United States who has legal status submit a simplified application?

No. Since Buffalo continues to use the regular application process, American citizens and other residents of the United States must submit a full application to our visa office in Buffalo, which will then forward it to the visa office closest to the applicant's residence.

Q8: If I am using the Simplified Application Process, do I have to notify the visa office if I change jobs?

No. You only have to notify us if you get a new address (postal or e-mail) or hire a new immigration representative, or if you want to withdraw your application. You do not have to notify us of any other changes until the visa office contacts you (about four months before the office is ready to assess your application).

Q9: I have already submitted my application. Do I have to start over?

No. Applications that were already submitted will be processed as usual. Full applications received after the September 1 implementation date are accepted, but the supporting documents will be returned to the applicant until the visa office requests them.

Q10: Why do you return the supporting documents?

The simplified application process is intended to help clients by eliminating the burden of continuously having to submit documents while in the queue. It also allows CIC to save duplication of work as well as storage space. In addition, given application processing times, most documents will have to be updated if the applicant's situation changes (e.g. marital status, job, education, and financial situation).

Q11: I have been nominated under a province's immigration program. Do I submit a simplified application?

No. Individuals applying under a Provincial Nomination Program do not submit a simplified application since these applications are processed on a priority basis.

Q12: Will my processing fees be reimbursed if I decide to withdraw my application?

Yes. If you contact the visa office before they contact you (i.e. before the assessment of your application begins), you will be reimbursed.

Q13: Will this initiative reduce processing times?

No. The simplified application process however reduces the amount of information applicants need to submit when they apply while still securing them a place in the queue, and they do not have to send supporting documents twice.

Q14: I have just taken a language proficiency test at a designated organization (such as the International English Language Testing System (IELTS), Canadian English Language Proficiency Index Program (CELPIP) or the Test d'évaluation de français (TEF)). Can I submit the results now?

If you apply after September 1, 2006, (under the simplified application process) no supporting documents are accepted at the outset. Please only submit your language test results once you have been asked by the visa office to submit supporting documentation. Any documents submitted prior to this will be returned. If you take the language test within one year of submitting your simplified application, those results remain valid and will be accepted as supporting documentation by the visa office.

News Release

New Agreement on Immigration Attracts Entrepreneurs To B.C.

Burnaby, August 22, 2006 — The Honourable Monte Solberg, Minister of Citizenship and Immigration, and the Honourable Colin Hansen, Economic Development Minister, British Columbia, announced today the signing of a memorandum of understanding (MOU) that will help speed up the process for immigrant entrepreneurs to get to British Columbia.

"It is a pleasure to announce this new memorandum of understanding between Canada's government and the Province of British Columbia," said Minister Solberg. "This pilot project will help British Columbia get the entrepreneurs it needs faster, and is another important step toward our goal of making immigration work for Canadians."

The pilot project outlined in the MOU will allow B.C. and Citizenship and Immigration Canada (CIC) to identify people who have applied to come to Canada as entrepreneurs. CIC will then contact applicants who have indicated an intention to settle in B.C. and steer them toward the Provincial Nominee Program (PNP). This step will speed up the application process significantly since PNP processing can fast track applicants with specific skills that could benefit the province's economic development.

"As B.C.'s economy keeps gaining strength, we need to attract more skilled workers and business people," said Minister Hansen. "Since creating the business skills category in 2002, business immigrants have invested over $351 million in our province, creating more than 1,300 new jobs.Today's agreement will help us to attract more applicants who are looking to invest in our province, create new jobs and contribute to economic growth."

B.C. business owners are equally supportive of the new MOU. Allen Born, Chairman of Tekion, a North American fuel cell company, stated: " British Columbia is considered to be the fuel cell capital of the world. The B.C. PNP played an instrumental role in our decision to start a company here. As a result, we have created Tekion, a micro fuel cell company now employing 75 people."

Since 2001, more than 2,000 skilled and business immigrants and their dependants have made British Columbia their home through the B.C. PNP. Last year, through the PNP, over 800 skilled workers and entrepreneurs moved to B.C. from around the world.

To learn more about immigration to Canada, visit the CIC Web site at www.cic.gc.ca.

For more information on B.C. government services, visit the province's Web site at www.gov.bc.ca.

News Release

Surging Resource Prices Stimulate Growth in Western Provinces

OTTAWA, May 3, 2005 – Elevated primary resource prices, combined with healthy fiscal situations, are making Alberta and British Columbia two of the fastest growing provincial economies in Canada, according to the Conference Board's *Provincial Outlook – Spring 2005.*

"Sizzling global demand for mining resources is driving economic growth across western Canadian provinces," said Marie-Christine Bernard, Associate Director, Provincial Outlook. "With oilsands investments and strong energy exploration activity, Alberta's economy is firing on all cylinders. B.C. is enjoying healthy gains in most sectors, as well as strong construction activity leading toward the 2010 Winter Olympics. Saskatchewan will ride high commodity prices to a second consecutive year of strong growth."

Saskatchewan and British Columbia enjoyed strong GDP growth in 2004. They are expected to match each other in 2005, achieving growth of three per cent.

Alberta's real gross domestic product (GDP) growth of 3.5 per cent in 2005 will lead all provinces. The province's growth is expected to ease to three per cent in 2006, second only to Newfoundland and Labrador. The provincial budget showcased an admirable fiscal situation, as soaring energy royalties helped eliminate Alberta's accumulated debt.

Manitoba's real GDP is expected to increase by 2.3 per cent in 2005. The province's goods sector is solid, led by non-residential investment in energy projects—and future prospects look bright with hydroelectric power generation being promoted under the federal government's Kyoto implementation plan.

Even with strong consumer spending, real GDP growth (at market prices) of 2.1 per cent is expected in Ontario this year. After navigating a turbulent period in which the stronger dollar punished exports, a rebound is in sight for later this year and into 2006.

Weakening housing starts and more moderate retail sales growth will dampen domestic demand in Quebec. As a result, real GDP growth (at market prices) will fall to two per cent in 2005. Stronger construction activity in 2006 is expected to lead to growth of almost three per cent.

Together, the Atlantic provinces will grow by two per cent in 2005. Stronger mining production and an expansionary provincial budget will boost Newfoundland and Labrador's 2005 real GDP growth to 2.3 per cent. With a full year of production at White Rose and Voisey's Bay in 2006, real GDP growth is expected to soar to 5.4 per cent, the highest in Canada.

At 1.8 per cent growth, Nova Scotia's economy is expected to be the country's weakest in 2005, but manufacturing and the service sector have better prospects for next year. New Brunswick will experience broad-based gains this year, with construction and manufacturing doing well. For Prince Edward Island, sizzling construction activity will help the economy, but budget cuts will erode some of those gains.

The *Provincial Outlook* provides a quarterly economic outlook for all 10 Canadian provinces.

News Release

Government of Canada Announces Internationally Trained Workers Initiative

OTTAWA, April 25, 2005 — The Government of Canada today launched the Internationally Trained Workers Initiative, delivering on the commitment made in the Speech from the Throne to improve the integration of immigrants and internationally trained Canadians into the work force. The launch was held simultaneously in Toronto and Vancouver.

"For Canada to succeed in the 21st century economy and ensure our quality of life, we must continually improve the quality of our work force," said the Honourable Lucienne Robillard, President of the Queen's Privy Council for Canada, Minister of Intergovernmental Affairs, and Minister of Human Resources and Skills Development, in announcing the comprehensive strategy in Toronto. "We look forward to working with partners to ensure that everyone can use their skills and abilities, no matter where they received their training, so that they—and Canada—can benefit to the fullest."

Today's announcement includes the following:

- The launch of the Government of Canada's initiative to help address shortages of health-care professionals by providing $75 million over the next five years to improve the integration of internationally trained doctors, nurses and other health-care professionals into the Canadian system;
- The launch of the Government of Canada's Foreign Credential Recognition program, with $68 million in funding over six years to facilitate the assessment and recognition of foreign qualifications for both regulated and non-regulated occupations;
- The launch of the Government of Canada's on-line Going to Canada Immigration Internet Portal, to be implemented in

cooperation with the provinces and territories. This is part of a $100 million commitment to an improved and integrated service delivery strategy. The portal will help prospective immigrants make informed decisions about coming to Canada and prepare for the Canadian labour market and society before they arrive;

- A commitment to provide $20 million a year in ongoing funding to the Enhanced Language Training initiative, which helps immigrants acquire the language skills necessary to obtain and retain jobs commensurate with their level of skill and experience. This initiative complements the $140 million a year being spent to provide basic language training to immigrants outside of Quebec; and
- The government's recently launched Action Plan Against Racism, with $56 million over five years for a series of measures to combat the discrimination Canadians sometimes face, including in the workplace, and to help realize Canada's vision of an inclusive and equitable society.

"With this initiative, we are addressing many of the challenges that immigrants and internationally trained Canadians face when starting a career in Canada," said the Honourable Hedy Fry, Parliamentary Secretary to the Minister of Citizenship and Immigration, in Vancouver. "When the Prime Minister asked me to lead this comprehensive and integrated interdepartmental initiative, it became clear that the Government of Canada could not accomplish this alone. We need to build on partnerships with stakeholders who have jurisdiction in many of the areas that require intervention if we are to achieve common success."

These actions are part of a coordinated strategy to bring the skills and experience of internationally trained professionals into the Canadian labour market. Provincial and territorial governments are essential partners. The Government of Canada will also work with cities and communities, service providers, employers, labour, professional and regulatory bodies, post-secondary educational institutions, the business community itself, and other stakeholders to find national, coherent solutions to this challenge.

"Immigration is vital to our economic and social development, but for a variety of reasons some immigrants face difficulties integrating into the work force and society," the Honourable Joe Volpe, Minister of Citizenship and Immigration, told representatives of professional associations, regulators, employers, educators and immigrants in Toronto. "The Internationally Trained Workers Initiative reflects this government's commitment to equality of opportunity and our understanding that Canada's diversity is a source of strength and innovation."

"We are taking direct action to fulfill the commitment we made last September when the First Ministers unanimously agreed on the Ten-Year Plan to Strengthen Health Care," said the Honourable Ujjal Dosanjh, Minister of Health, in Vancouver. "This initiative will help address shortages of health-care professionals and improve Canadians' access to high-quality care. It supports our efforts with the provinces and territories to renew the health system and ensure it is sustainable."

On March 21, the Minister of State (Multiculturalism), Raymond Chan, launched Canada's first-ever Action Plan Against Racism. "We have just unveiled, as part of our Action Plan Against Racism, the Racism-Free Workplace Strategy," said the Honourable Raymond Chan, in Vancouver. "The goal of this strategy is to eliminate all discriminatory barriers to employment and to ensure full inclusion in the workplace. To this end, we have also initiated projects through the multiculturalism program that actively involve internationally trained workers in overcoming barriers based on foreign credential recognition. Only by working together can we ensure that everyone has the opportunity to achieve their potential and contribute fully to Canadian society."

The Internationally Trained Workers Initiative has been developed in partnership with a broad variety of stakeholders, who have been consulted in a series of roundtables across Canada by the

Honourable Hedy Fry. Some 14 federal departments and agencies are working on the initiative in close collaboration with provincial and territorial governments, regulators and various stakeholders.

News Release

Investment in Enhanced Language Training Pays off

TORONTO, April 25, 2005 — As part of the Internationally Trained Workers Initiative, Citizenship and Immigration Canada is helping newcomers acquire the language skills they need to reach their full potential in the Canadian labour market, Citizenship and Immigration Minister Joe Volpe announced today.

"Language is one of the main barriers to integration into the workplace for many immigrants to Canada," said Minister Volpe. "This investment will help engineers, trades people, doctors, nurses and workers in many other fields who received their training outside of Canada to find and keep good jobs that match the skills and experience they bring to Canada."

While most newcomers have adequate conversational language skills upon arrival in Canada, many employers report gaps in the specialized workplace language skills and vocabulary that are required in many trades and professions. The Enhanced Language Training (ELT) initiative will provide job-specific language training to enable immigrants to gain the language skills they need to flourish in the workplace.

"I am pleased to report the progress we have made to date on this important initiative and share with you the list of projects that have been implemented across the country in 2004–2005," added the Minister. "This would not have been possible without the successful partnership we established with Ontario, Saskatchewan, Manitoba, Nova Scotia and British Columbia on the delivery of ELT projects in these provinces."

The government currently spends about $140 million a year on basic language training for about 50,000 adult immigrants outside of Quebec. The Enhanced Language Training initiative accounts for an additional $20 million annually, and provides bridge-to-work assistance, including mentoring, work placement and other assistance in accessing the labour market.

The ELT initiative is an important component of the Government of Canada's efforts to attract highly skilled workers and ensure more successful integration of immigrants into the economy and communities. Other measures include working with regulatory bodies and sector councils to facilitate the development of effective processes for the recognition of foreign credentials and prior work experience, and the development of the Going to Canada Immigration Portal to provide better information to immigrants before they come to Canada.

News Release

Health Minister Dosanjh Announces $75 Million Initiative To Bring More Internationally Educated Professionals into Health Care System

VANCOUVER - Health Minister Ujjal Dosanjh today announced a $75 million federal initiative that is expected to assist more than 2,000 internationally educated health care professionals to put their skills to work in Canada's health care system.

"The whole country benefits when immigrants and internationally educated Canadians are able to make full use of their knowledge and experience," said Minister Dosanjh. "This initiative will strengthen our health system by helping to increase the supply of health care professionals, which will improve access to quality health care and reduce wait times."

The $75 million, which was included in Budget 2005, will be provided over five years. During this period, it is estimated the funding will assist in the assessment and integration into the workforce of up to 1,000 physicians, 800 nurses and 500 other regulated health care professionals. The numbers will vary, however, according to the priorities of provincial and territorial governments.

"This fulfils the Government of Canada's commitment at the First Ministers Meeting last September to accelerate and expand the assessment and integration of internationally educated health care professionals," said Minister Dosanjh. "This complements a series of other measures we are taking in collaboration with provinces and territories and the health care community to provide cities and rural areas across this country with the health care workers they need."

Strengthening the health care workforce is a key objective of the Ten-Year Plan to Strengthen Health Care, which all First Ministers signed in September 2004. The Government of Canada is supporting the training and hiring of more health care professionals through the $5.5-billion Wait Times Reduction Fund. In addition, the Pan-

Canadian Health Human Resource Strategy provides $20 million per year to improve health care workforce planning, promote the use of interdisciplinary health care teams and increase recruitment and retention of needed health care professionals.

Minister Dosanjh also noted that today's $75 million announcement is part of a wider Internationally Trained Workers Initiative, involving 14 federal departments and agencies.

"The Initiative will improve the integration of immigrants and internationally trained Canadians into the labour force so they can contribute their full potential to Canada and share in its prosperity," said Minister Dosanjh.

The $75 million initiative on internationally educated health care graduates will build on work that is already underway. As part of that work, which received $8.5 million in earlier funding from the Government of Canada, Minister Dosanjh today announced:

- The launch of a national website that will help international medical graduates prepare to become licensed to practice in Canada. The Association of International Physicians and Surgeons of Ontario, with funding of $126,356 from Health Canada, took the lead in preparing the online Canadian Information Centre for International Medical Graduates (www.IMG-Canada.ca). The site is a central point of information for international medical graduates, providing comprehensive information on the Canadian health care system and medical licensure requirements, education and training services in different provinces and territories. It also provides information on alternative health care careers. The Website will enable international medical graduates to assess their options and opportunities even before they come to Canada and will be linked to Citizenship and Immigration's "Going to Canada" immigration portal. Minister Dosanjh officially launched the site Monday with Dr. Dale Dauphinee, executive director of the Medical Council of Canada.

- A National Credential Verification Agency will be established by the Medical Council of Canada to provide a streamlined process for verifying the credentials of international medical graduates. After this verification, these graduates can then take an evaluation exam or other steps toward becoming licensed to practice in Canada. The single-source verification service will prevent these graduates from having to get their credentials verified in each province or territory in which they seek licensure. This $1.86 million project is funded by Human Resources and Skills Development Canada.
- The Medical Council of Canada will make its evaluation exam more readily accessible to international medical graduates in a $1.34 million project funded by Human Resources and Skills Development Canada. This exam is the first stage in the licensing process for international medical graduates in Canada. The exam will be put into an electronic format to enhance its availability.
- The Canadian Post M.D. Education Registry is receiving $834,625 from Human Resources and Skills Development Canada to create a pan-Canadian database with information about international medical graduates that will improve planning for the assessment, training and integration of these graduates.

News Release

AN IMMIGRATION SYSTEM FOR THE 21st CENTURY

OTTAWA, April 18, 2005 — The Honourable Joe Volpe, Minister of Citizenship and Immigration, today announced a series of measures aimed at improving service delivery and the efficiency of Canada's immigration and citizenship programs.

"Canada's immigration system is a model for the world and today's measures allow us to maintain and enhance our position. We will do this by reducing application processing times for permanent residents who want to become Canadian citizens and sponsored parents and grandparents who want to be reunited with their family in Canada. International competition for talented international students is fierce and today's announcement moves Canada even further ahead," said Minister Volpe.

Today's measures include an investment of $69 million over two years to restore, by 2007–2008, processing times to an average of 12 months for a grant of citizenship and four months for a proof of citizenship. Citizenship and Immigration Canada (CIC) is also exempting citizenship applicants from undergoing language ability and knowledge-of-Canada tests at 55 rather than 60 years of age, while in no way reducing the rigorous security screening requirements that all applicants for Canadian citizenship must go through before becoming citizens of Canada.

The measures to speed up the processing of sponsorship applications for parents and grandparents coming to Canada as family class immigrants include tripling the number of parents and grandparents who can immigrate to Canada from 6,000 to 18,000 a year in 2005 and in 2006. Also, the issuance of multiple-entry visitor visas will be facilitated so that parents and grandparents can visit their families in Canada while their applications are in process. The Government of Canada will invest $36 million a year for two years to cover the costs of processing and integrating parents and grandparents.

CIC is expanding two pilot initiatives for international students to enhance the competitiveness of Canada's education industry. The first will allow international students across Canada to work off-campus while completing their studies and the second will allow them to work for a second year after graduation. This second initiative will apply outside of Montreal, Toronto and Vancouver to help spread the benefits of immigration to more regions in Canada. The Government of Canada is investing $10 million a year for five years to support this strategy.

The measures announced today demonstrate action on commitments laid out by by Minister Volpe in his January 2005 six-point plan for addressing critical issues in the citizenship and immigration programs.

For more information on today's announcements, please visit CIC's Web site at www.cic.gc.ca.

New Initiatives: Off-campus Work and Post-Graduation Employment

Off-Campus Work

MAY 13, 2005: The off-campus work program allows foreign students at public post-secondary institutions to work off-campus while completing their studies.

Off-campus work is an option for students studying at institutions in provinces that have signed agreements with CIC. These provinces are as follows:

- Manitoba
- New Brunswick
- Quebec. The census metropolitan areas of Montréal and Québec are currently excluded. The agreement will soon be amended to include them.

As new agreements are reached, more provinces and territories will be added to the list. Watch the CIC Web site for updates.

Students who come to Canada under the Canadian Commonwealth Scholarship and Fellowship Plan or under the Government of Canada Awards Program funded by Foreign Affairs Canada or by the Canadian International Development Agency are not eligible for off-campus work.

Post-Graduation Employment

As of May 16, 2005, the post-graduation work program will allow certain students to work for up to two years after their graduation. Previously, students were only allowed to work for one year.

Foreign students are eligible for a post-graduation work permit only for employment in their field of study. They must still have a valid study permit and apply for the work permit within 90 days of receiving written confirmation (transcript, letter, etc.) from their institution indicating that they have met the requirements of their program.

Once students have one of these documents, they can apply for a work permit. Post-graduation work permits are only available to graduates of a program at a Canadian university, a community college, a CEGEP, a publicly funded trade or technical school or a Canadian private institution authorized by provincial statute to confer degrees.

To be eligible for a two-year work permit (rather than just a one-year permit), foreign students must have

- successfully completed a program of at least two years of full-time studies;
- received written confirmation (transcript, letter, etc.) from the educational institution indicating that they have met the requirements of the program of study;
- studied at and graduated from an institution located outside of the Communauté métropolitaine de Montréal (CMM), the Greater Toronto Area (GTA) or the Greater Vancouver Regional District GVRD);

http://www.cic.gc.ca/english/study/work-locations.html

Note: If you complete your studies at a campus located inside the **CMM,** the **GTA** or the **GVRD,** but at an institution whose headquarters for that campus are located outside those areas, you are not eligible for a two-year work permit under this program.

- found employment outside of the **CMM, GTA** or **GVRD.**
- **Note:** Foreign students who graduate from an institution located inside one of those areas are not eligible for a second year of work, even if the employment is located outside of those areas.

Foreign students who currently hold a one-year post-graduation work permit and who meet the eligibility criteria for a two-year permit can apply for a one-year extension of their work permit.

Important Information About Work Permits For Students:

Do not work without being authorized to do so. If you do, you will be in contravention of the law and may be asked to leave Canada. Students who qualify for the new initiatives still require a work permit, but they will be able to apply for one without having to obtain a labour market opinion from Human Resources and Skills Development Canada. Students must not begin to work until they have received their work permit.

Find out about work opportunities for foreign students at
http://www.cic.gc.ca/english/study/work-opps.html

Guru's Knowledge

I think there is a world market for maybe five computers.
(Thomas Watson, chairman of IBM, 1943)

Computers in the future may weigh no more than 1.5 tons.
(Popular Mechanics, forecasting the relentless march of science, 1949)

I have traveled the length and breadth of this country and talked with the best people, and I can assure you that data processing is a fad that won't last out the year. (The editor in charge of business books for Prentice Hall, 1957)

There is no reason anyone would want a computer in their home.
(Ken Olson, president, chairman and founder of Digital Equipment Corp., 1977)

This 'telephone' has too many shortcomings to be seriously considered as a means of communication. The device is inherently of no value to us.
(Western Union internal memo, 1876.)

The wireless music box has no imaginable commercial value. Who would pay for a message sent to nobody in particular?
(David Sarnoff's associates in response to his urgings for investment in the radio in the 1920s.)

The concept is interesting and well-formed, but in order to earn better than a 'C,' the idea must be feasible."
(A Yale University management professor in response to Fred Smith's paper proposing reliable overnight delivery service. (Smith went on to found Federal Express Corp.))

Who the hell wants to hear actors talk?
(H.M. Warner, Warner Brothers, 1927.)

I'm just glad it'll be Clark Gable who's falling on his face and not Gary Cooper. (Gary Cooper on his decision not to take the leading role in "Gone With The Wind.")

A cookie store is a bad idea. Besides, the market research reports say America likes crispy cookies, not soft and chewy cookies like you make.
(Response to Debbi Fields' idea of starting Mrs. Fields' Cookies.)

We don't like their sound, and guitar music is on the way out.
(Decca Recording Co. rejecting the Beatles, 1962.)

Heavier-than-air flying machines are impossible.
(Lord Kelvin, president, Royal Society, 1895.)

Professor Goddard does not know the relation between action and reaction and the need to have something better than a vacuum against which to react. He seems to lack the basic knowledge ladled out daily in high schools. (1921 New York Times editorial about Robert Goddard's revolutionary rocket work.)

Drill for oil? You mean drill into the ground to try and find oil? You're crazy. (Drillers who Edwin L. Drake tried to enlist to his project to drill for oil in 1859.)

Stocks have reached what looks like a permanently high plateau. (Irving Fisher, Professor of Economics, Yale University, 1929.)

Airplanes are interesting toys but of no military value. (Marechal Ferdinand Foch, Professor of Strategy, Ecole Superieure de Guerre).

Everything that can be invented has been invented. (Charles H. Duell, Commissioner, U.S. Office of Patents, 1899.)

Louis Pasteur's theory of germs is ridiculous fiction. (Pierre Pachet, Professor of Physiology at Toulouse, 1872)

The abdomen, the chest, and the brain will forever be shut from the intrusion of the wise and humane surgeon." (Sir John Eric Ericksen, British surgeon, appointed Surgeon-Extraordinary to Queen Victoria 1873.)

640K ought to be enough for anybody." (Bill Gates, 1981)

The level of human knowledge in every known field to them whether it is science, technology or culture have not yet reached to its embryonic stage. (Tariq Nadeem - Author, 2005)

One day, we all will be the citizens of planet Earth governed by a UN like federal government. Eventually we will be heading towards the realization of "one planet one country dream".

(Tariq Nadeem - Author, 2005)

GLOBAL CAREER & EMPLOYMENT WEBSITES

Following websites has been compiled for the benefit of professionals and students who are interested in work or a career overseas. It aims to serve as a quick and easy guide to some of the most useful employment websites on the Internet. However, due to the extremely fast rate of change on the web, the accuracy of all websites cannot be guaranteed. Please let us know if you are aware of any additional sites which merit inclusion.

Generic employment websites

Bilingual Jobs	http://www.bilingual-jobs.com/
Career Builder	http://www.careerbuilder.com
Career Magazine	http://www.careermag.com
Escape Artist	http://www.escapeartist.com
Employment Resources on the Net	http://www.noncon.org/insight/jobs
Hobsons Global Careers & Education	http://www.hobsons.com
Idealist.Org	http://www.idealist.org
J-Hunter	http://www.j-hunter.com
Job Hunt	http://www.job-hunt.org
Jobnet	http://www.jobnet.com.au
Jobs Abroad	http://www.jobsabroad.com
Monster Work Abroad	http://workabroad.monster.com
Monster Worldwide	http://www.monsterworldwide.com
News Directory	http://www.newsdirectory.com
Newspapers Online	http://www.newspapers.com/
Overseas Jobs	http://www.overseasjobs.com/
Quintessential Careers	http://www.quintcareers.com/
TMP Hudson Global Resources	http://www.hudsonresourcing.com
The Riley Guide	http://www.rileyguide.com/
What you need to know about International Resources	http://jobsearch.about.com/cs/internationaljobs1/

Africa

African Development Bank	http://www.afdb.org/
Africa Online	http://www.africaonline.com/
Career Junction	http://www.careerjunction.co.za/
Careers.Org - South Africa	http://www.careers.org/reg/cint-safrica.html
Find a Job in Africa	http://www.findajobinafrica.com/
I-Africa Careers	http://careers.iafrica.com/
Job Navigator	http://www.jobs.co.za/

Asia

Adecco Asia	http://www.adecco-asia.com/
Asia Business Daily	http://www.asiabusinessdaily.com/
Asian Development Bank	http://www.adb.org/
Asia Employment Centre	http://jobs.asiaco.com/jobbank/
Asia Inc Online	http://www.asia-inc.com/
Asia Job Search Resources	http://www.escapeartist.com/jobs7/asia.htm
Asia Net	http://www.asia-net.com/
Asia Pacific Economic Cooperation	http://www.apec.org/
Asia Partnership	http://www.asiapartnership.com/
Asia Times	http://www.asiatimes.com/
Asiaweek	http://www.asiaweek.com/asiaweek//
Careerbuilder.com	http://www.careerbuilder.com/
Far Eastern Economic Review	http://www.feer.com/
J-Hunter	http://www.j-hunter.com/
Job Asia	http://www.jobasia.com/
Job Culture	http://www.jobculture.com/
Jobs Database	http://www.jobsdb.com/
Job Street Australasia	http://www.jobstreet.com/
Recruit Asia	http://www.recruitasia.com/
Wang & Li Asia Resource Online	http://www.wang-li.com/

Australia

Austrade	http://www.austrade.gov.au/
Australian Business Limited	http://www.australianbusiness.com.au/
Australian Federal Government	http://www.fed.gov.au/
Australian Job Search	http://www.jobsearch.gov.au/
Australian Financial Review	http://afr.com/
Australian Stock Exchange	http://www.asx.com.au/
Australian Universities	http://www.avcc.edu.au/
Career Guide	http://www.yourcareerguide.com/
Career One	http://www.careerone.com.au/
CPA Australia	http://www.cpaaustralia.com.au/
Dep't of Foreign Affairs & Trade	http://www.dfat.gov.au/
Fairfax Classifieds	http://www.market.fairfax.com.au/
Gradlink	http://www.gradlink.com.au/
Graduate Opportunities	http://www.graduateopportunities.com/
Institute of Chartered Accountants	http://www.icaa.org.au/
Job Watch	http://home.vicnet.net.au/
Monster	http://www.monster.com.au/
My Career	http://www.mycareer.com.au/editorial/graduate/
My Future	http://www.myfuture.edu.au/
SEEK	http://www.seek.com.au/
SEEK Campus	http://campus.seek.com.au/
The Age	http://www.theage.com.au/
The Australian	http://www.theaustralian.com.au/
Victorian Government	http://www.vic.gov.au/
Visa Requirements	http://www.immi.gov.au/
WageNet	http://www.wagenet.gov.au/

Austria

Adecco Austria (German)	http://www.adecco.at/
Hill Woltron Recruitment (German)	http://www.hill-woltron.com/

Job Direct (German)	http://www.job-direct.co.at/
Jobnet Austria (German)	http://jobnet.uibk.ac.at/
Job Pilot Austria (German)	http://www.jobpilot.at/
Manpower Austria (German)	http://www.manpower.at/
Trenkwalder	http://www.trenkwalder.at/

Bangladesh

Bangladesh Internet Resources	http://www.bdcenter.com/
The Independent	http://independent-bangladesh.com/

Belgium

Belgian job directory (Dutch)	http://www.info123.be/
Job@ (Dutch)	http://www.jobat.be/
Jobs and Careers Belgium	http://www.jobs-career.be/
Jobs today	http://www.jobstoday.be/
Vacature (Dutch & French)	http://www.vacature.be/
VDAB	http://www.vdab.be/

Brunei

Brunei Government Site	http://www.brunei.gov.bn/
Brunei News	http://www.bruneinews.net/

Cambodia

Business in Cambodia	http://www.business-in-cambodia.com/
Cambodia News	http://www.cambodia-web.net/

Canada

Monster	http://monstor.ca
BC Workinfo Net	http://workinfonet.bc.ca/
CACEE	http://www.cacee.com/
Canada Careers	http://www.canadiancareers.com/
Canada Employment Weekly	http://www.mediacorp2.com/
Canadian Public Service	http://www.psc-cfp.gc.ca/index_e.htm
Career & Immigration Tips	http://www.careertips.com
Dep't of Foreign Affairs & Trade	http://www.dfait-maeci.gc.ca/
Work Site Canada	http://www.worksitecanada.com/
Workapolis	http://www.workapolis.com/

Caribbean

Caribbean Hello	http://www.caribbeandaily.com/
The Daily Herald	http://www.thedailyherald.com/

China

Beijing Review	http://www.bjreview.com.cn/
Business Directory of China	http://www.china-business-directory.com/
Career Agent China	http://china.career-agent.net/

China Daily	http://chinadaily.com.cn/
China News Digest	http://www.cnd.org/
China Vista	http://www.chinavista.com/
China HR	http://www.chinahr.com/
China Window	http://www.china-window.com.cn/
Chinese Newspapers Online	http://www.lib.duke.edu/ias/eac/chnsp.htm
Fujian	http://www.fz.fj.cn/
Guangzhou Ribao	http://www.gmw.com.cn/
Inside China Today	http://www.einnews.com/china/
People's Daily	http://www.snweb.com/
South China Morning Post	http://www.scmp.com/
Wen Hui Daily	http://www.whb.com.cn/
Zhaopin	http://www.zhaopin.com.cn/

Czech Republic

CV Online (Czech)	http://www.cvonline.cz/
Czech Jobs (Czech)	http://www.jobs.cz/
Department of Foreign Affairs	http://www.czech.cz/
Hot Jobs (Czech)	http://www.hotjobs.cz/
Job European Job Sites	http://1job.net/
Jobmaster (English and Czech)	http://www.jobmaster.cz/

Denmark

EURES (English & Danish)	http://www.eures.dk/
Job Bank (Danish)	http://www.jobbank.dk/
Job Denmark (Danish)	http://www.jobdanmark.dk/
Job guide (Danish)	http://www.job-guide.dk/
Job Index (Danish)	http://www.jobindex.dk/

Europe

Career Builder	http://www.careerbuilder.com/
Careers Europe	http://www.careers.co.uk/
EURES	http://www.europa.eu.int/jobs/eures/
Euro-graduate	http://www.eurograduate.com/
European Union	http://europa.eu.int/
IAgora - iWork	http://www.iagora.com/
Job Pilot	http://www.jobpilot.com/
Job Site	http://www.jobsite.co.uk/
Step Stone	http://www.stepstone.com/

Fiji

Fiji Online	http://www.fiji-online.com.fj/
Fiji Trade Contacts	http://www.fiji-online.com.fj/business/

Finland

Aamulehti Newspaper (Finnish)	http://www.aamulehti.fi/tyopaikat/
Academic Career Services in Finland	http://www.minedu.fi/
Academic Careers Service	http://www.aarresaari.net/english/

Ministry of Labour	http://www.mol.fi/tyopaikat/
PIB	http://www.pib.fi/

France

ANPE (French)	http://www.anpe.fr/
Experian en France	http://www.experian.fr/carriere/job.htm
French-Aust. Chamber of Commerce	http://www.facci.com.au/
French Employment Directory	http://www.jobpilot.fr/
French News and Employment	http://wanadoo.fr/

Germany

Berlitz (Teaching English)	http://www.berlitz.com/
Die Zeit Jobs	http://www.jobs.zeit.de/
Job Exchange	http://www.hueber.de/german/jobs/index.asp
Stellen Market (German)	http://www.stellenmarkt.de/
Student Employment in Germany	http://www.careernet.de/

Greece

Athens News	http://athensnews.gr/
OAED	http://www.oaed.gr/mainenglish.htm
Skywalker Job Search	http://www.skywalker.gr/

Hong Kong

Career Times Hong Kong	http://www.careertimes.com.hk/
Chinese University of Hong Kong	http://www.cuhk.edu.hk/
Classified Post	http://www.classifiedpost.com.hk/
Gemini Personnel Ltd	http://www.gemini.com.hk/
HKU Careers Service	http://www.hku.hk/cepc/
Hong Kong Jobs	http://www.hkjobs.com/
Hong Kong Polytechnic University	http://www.polyu.edu.hk/
Hong Kong Trade Dev't Council	http://www.tdctrade.com/
Hong Kong Uni Employers	http://www.hku.hk/cepc/service/com_name.htm
Ming Pao Daily News	http://www.mingpaonews.com/
Recruit Online with Panda Planet	http://www.pandaplanet.com/
Sing Tao	http://www.singtao.com/
South China Morning Post Careers	http://careers.scmp.com/
Ta Kung Pao	http://www.takungpao.com.hk/

Africa Iceland

Jobs Iceland	http://www.job.is/atvinnutorg/

India

Jagran	http://www.jagran.com/
Deccan Chronicle	http://www.deccan.com/
Deccan Herald	http://www.deccanherald.com/
Economic Times	http://www.economictimes.com/
Express India	http://expressindia.com/

India Connect	http://www.indiaconnect.com/
India Government Homepage	http://alfa.nic.in/
India Server	http://www.indiaserver.com/
India World	http://www.indiaworld.com/
INDOlink	http://www.indolink.com/
Jobs Ahead	http://www.jobsahead.com/
Kerala Home Page	http://www.keral.com/
Naidunia	http://www.naidunia.com/
Net Guru India	http://www.netguruindia.com/
News India-Times	http://www.newsindia-times.com/
Sanjevani	http://www.sanjevani.com/
The Hindu	http://www.hinduonline.com/
The Statesman	http://www.thestatesman.net/
The Telegraph	http://www.telegraphindia.com/
Times of India Jobs and Careers	http://www.timesjobsandcareers.com/

Indonesia

Australia Indonesia Business Council	http://www.aibc.net.au/
Bali Post Online	http://www.balipost.co.id/
Bisnis Indonesia	http://www.bisnis.com/
Bernas	http://www.indomedia.com/bernas/
Indobiz	http://www.indobiz.com/
IndoWEB	http://www.indoweb.com/
Dep't of Foreign Affairs Indonesia	http://www.dfa-deplu.go.id/
Indonesia Government Homepage	http://www.ri.go.id/
Indonesia Professional Associations	http://www.dnet.net.id/ipa/
Kompas Cyber Media	http://www.kompas.com/
Living in Indonesia – for Expatriates	http://www.expat.or.id/
Media Indonesia Online	http://www.mediaindo.co.id/
Pikiran Rakyat	http://www.pikiran-rakyat.com/
Republika Online	http://www.republika.co.id/
Suara Merdeka	http://www.suaramerdeka.com/

Ireland

AA Ireland	http://www.aaireland.ie/jobs/
Irish Jobs	http://www.irishjobs.ie/
NI Jobs	http://www.nijobs.com/
Nixers	http://www.nixers.com/
Recruit Ireland	http://www.recruitireland.com/
The Irish Times	http://www.ireland.com/

Israel

Marksman International Personnel	http://www.marksman.co.il/
The Jerusalem Post Daily	http://www.jpost.co.il/

Italy

Adecco Italia	http://www.adecco.it/
Corriere della Sera (Rome)	http://www.corriere.it/
Italian and international jobs	http://www.joblinks.f2s.com/

Job Pilot (Italian)	http://www.jobpilot.it/
Job Online	http://www.jobonline.it/
Talent Manager	http://www.talentmanager.it/

Japan

Agara	http://www.agara.co.jp/
Asahi Shimbun (Tokyo)	http://www.asahi.com/
Chugoku Shimbun (Hiroshima)	http://www.chugoku-np.co.jp/
Gaijinpot	http://www.gaijinpot.com/
Hokkoku Shimbun	http://www.hokkoku.co.jp/
Ingenium	http://www.ingeniumgroup.com/indexe.asp
InterCareer Net Japan	http://www.intercareer.com/japan/
Japan Newspapers & Media Online http://www.sabotenweb.com/bookmarks/newspapers.html	
Japan Times (Tokyo)	http://www.japantimes.co.jp/
Job Dragon	http://www.jobdragon.com/index_e.asp
Mainichi Interactive	http://www.mainichi.co.jp/
Nara Shimbun	http://www.nara-shimbun.com/
Nikkei	http://www.nikkei.co.jp/
Nikkan Koyko Shimbun	http://www.nikkan.co.jp/
Nishinippon Shimbun	http://www.nishinippon.co.jp/
O Hayo Sensei (Teaching)	http://www.ohayosensei.com/
Okinawa Times	http://www.okinawatimes.co.jp/
Pacific Stars and Stripes	http://www.estripes.com/
Ryukyu Shimpo	http://www.ryukyushimpo.co.jp/
Tokyo Stock Exchange	http://www.tse.or.jp/
Yomiuri Online	http://www.yomiuri.co.jp/

Latin America

Jobs in Latin America	http://www.latpro.com/

Luxembourg

HVB Luxembourg	http://www.hvb.lu/en/jobs/
ADEM	http://www.etat.lu/adem/

Malaysia

Graduan	http://www.graduan.com.my/
Daily Express	http://www.infosabah.com.my/
JARING	http://www.jaring.my/
Jobstreet	http://www.jobs.com.my/
Kuala Lumpur Stock Exchange	http://www.klse.com.my/
Malaysia Online	http://www.mol.net.my/
Manfield in Malaysia & Singapore	http://www.manfield.com.sg/
Sarawak Tribune	http://www.sarawaktribune.com.my/
Star Jobs	http://star-jobs.com/
Wencom Career Guide	http://www.jaring.my/wencom/career.htm

Mauritias

L'Express	http://www.lexpress.mu/
Le Mauricien	http://www.lemauricien.com/mauricien/

Middle East

Bayt	http://www.bayt.com/
Careers Emirates	http://careeremirates.com/
Gulf Job Sites	http://www.gulfjobsites.com/

Nepal

Nepalese Newspapers	http://www.south-asia.com/

Netherlands

Dambusters Recruitment	http://www.dambustersrecruitment.com/
English Language jobs in Holland	http://www.englishlanguagejobs.com/
Jobs Today Directory (Dutch)	http://www.jobstoday.nl/
Jobnews (Dutch)	http://www.jobnews.nl/
JobTrack (Dutch)	http://www.jobtrack.nl/
Van Zoelen Recruitment	http://www.vz-recruitment.nl/

New Zealand

Best Jobs New Zealand	http://www.bestjobsnz.com/
Kiwi Careers	http://www.careers.co.nz/

Norway

EMB Net	http://www.no.embnet.org/Jobs/index.php3
FINN	http://www.finn.no/
Norge Jobbguiden	http://www.jobbguiden.no/
RekrutteringssystemerAS	http://www.rekrutteringssystemer.no/

Pakistan

Business Recorder	http://www.brecorder.com/
News International	http://www.jang-group.com/thenews/
The Dawn	http://dawn.com/

Philippines

Business World	http://bworld.com.ph/
Chinese Commercial News	http://www.siongpo.com/
Filipino Express	http://www.filipinoexpress.com/
Filipino Online Job Hunting	http://www.trabaho.com/
Manila Bulletin	http://www.mb.com.ph/
Philippines Times	http://www.philippinespost.com/
Philippine Star	http://www.philstar.com/
Visayan Daily Star	http://www.visayandailystar.com/

Portugal

Emprego (Jobs) (Portuguese)	http://emprego.aeiou.pt/
IEFP	http://www.iefp.pt/
Jobs Express (Portuguese)	http://www.expressoemprego.pt/
Portugal Jobs	http://portugal-info.net/jobs/deletejob.htm
Talent 4 Europe	http://www.talent4europe.com/Portugal/jobs.htm

Poland

Job Pilot (Polish)	http://www.jobpilot.com.pl/
Polandjobs.com	http://www.polandjobs.com/
Top Jobs (Polish)	http://www.topjobs.pl/

Romania

Best Jobs Romania	http://bestjobs.neogen.ro/
Jobsearch Romania (Romanian)	http://www.jobsearch.ro/index.cfm
Romania jobsearch portal	http://addbusiness.hypermart.net/employment/

Russia

Human Resources Online Russia	http://www.hro.ru/
Russia Today	http://www.russiatoday.com/
St Petersburg Times	http://www.sptimes.ru/

Singapore

Asia One	http://www.asia1.com.sg/
Alpha Maps	http://www.alpha-maps.com/
Business Times	http://business-times.asia1.com.sg/
Career Zone – Jobs in Singapore	http://www.careerzone.com.sg/
Contact Singapore	http://www.contactsingapore.org.sg/
Job Bank	http://www.adpost.com/sg/job_bank/
Lianhe Zaobao	http://www.asia1.com.sg/zaobao/
Manpower Singapore	http://www.manpower.com.sg/
Nanyang Polytechnic	http://www.nyp.edu.sg/
National University of Singapore	http://www.nus.edu.sg/
Singtao Times	http://www.singtao.com/
Shipping Times	http://business-times.asia1.com.sg/shippingtimes/
Singapore Chamber of Commerce	http://www.sicc.com.sg/
Singapore Government	http://www.gov.sg/
Singapore Information Map	http://www.sg/
Singapore Stock Exchange	http://www.ses.com.sg/
The Straits Times	http://straitstimes.asia1.com.sg/
9to5 Asia	http://coldfusion.9to5asia.com/

South Korea

Chosun Daily News	http://www.chosun.com/
Chungang Ilbo	http://www.joins.com/
Dong A Ilbo	http://www.donga.com/
Han-Kyoreh Shinmum	http://www.hani.co.kr/
Korean News Service	http://www.nowcom.co.kr/
Korea Post	http://www.koreapost.com/
Korea Times	http://www.korealink.co.kr/times/times.htm
Maeil Shinmun	http://www.m2000.co.kr/
Munhwa Ilbo	http://www.munhwa.co.kr/
The Korea Herald	http://www.koreaherald.co.kr/

Spain

Terra (Spanish)	http://www.terra.es/
Trabajos (Spanish)	http://www.trabajos.com/
Todo Trabajo (Spaish)	http://www.todotrabajo.com/
Trabajo.org (Spanish)	http://www.trabajo.org/

Sri Lanka

Daily News	http://www.dailynews.lk/
Lanka Academic Network	http://www.lacnet.org/
Sri Lanka Server	http://www.lanka.net/
Tamil Eelam News (Tamil)	http://www.eelam.com/news/tamil/

Sweden

AMS	http://www.ams.se/englishfs.asp?
I see Head hunting & Consulting	http://www.isee.se/
Jobline	http://www.jobline.se/
Manpower Sweden (Swedish)	http://www.manpower.se/
Proffice (Swedish)	http://www.proffice.se/
Swednet Job Search	http://www.swednet.org.uk/
Temporary Office Work in Sweden	http://www.proffice.com/

Switzerland

Emploi Switzerland	http://emploi.ch/
Job Engine	http://www.jobengine.ch/
Swiss Info	http://www.swissinfo.org/
Swiss Jobs	http://www.swissjobs.ch/
Swiss Web Jobs	http://www.jobs.ch/
Top Jobs Switzerland	http://www.topjobs.ch/

Taiwan

China Economic News Service	http://cens.com/
China Times	http://www.chinatimes.com.tw/
JobsDB.com	http://www.jobsdb.com.tw/
SinaNet Taiwan News	http://sinanet.com/
Taiwan Jobs Center	http://jobs.asiaco.com/taiwan/
Taiwan Stock Exchange	http://www.tse.com.tw/
Taiwan Tribune	http://www.taiwanese.com/

Thailand

Bangkok Post Jobs	http://www.bangkokpostjobs.com/
Business Day	http://bday.net/
Phuket Gazette	http://www.phuketgazette.net/
Siam Jobs - resume/jobs database	http://www.siam.net/jobs/
Thai Aust. Chamber of Commerce	http://www.austchamthailand.com/
Thailand Business	http://www.accessasia.com/xroad/xrthbus.html

United Kingdom

Academic Jobs	http://www.jobs.ac.uk/
ASA Education (Teaching in UK)	http://www.asaeducation.com/
BBC News Online	http://news.bbc.co.uk/
Celsian Group	http://www.celsiangroup.com/
Daily Record	http://www.dailyrecord.co.uk/
Financial Times	http://www.ft.com/
Fish 4 - Jobs	http://www.fish4.co.uk/
IC Resources	http://www.ic-resources.co.uk/
Job Mall	http://www.jobmall.co.uk/
Jobsearch	http://www.jobsearch.co.uk/
JobServe	http://www.jobserve.co.uk/
Microscape Recruitment Ltd	http://www.microscape.co.uk/welcome.asp
Net Job	http://www.netjobs.co.uk/
Planet Recruit	http://www.planetrecruit.com/
Prospects	http://www.prospects.ac.uk/
SEEK UK	http://www.seek.com.au/if.asp?loc=ukjobs
Technojobs UK	http://www.technojobs.co.uk/
Telegraph Newspaper Online	http://www.telegraph.co.uk/
The Guardian -Jobs	http://jobs.guardian.co.uk/
The Monster Board, UK	http://www.monster.co.uk/
The Times	http://www.timesonline.co.uk/
Top Jobs	http://www.topjobs.co.uk/

USA

Adguide's College Recruiter	http://www.adguide.com/
Financial Times	http://www.usa.ft.com/
Internship Programs	http://internships.wetfeet.com/
Job Hunt	http://www.job-hunt.org/
Jobweb	http://www.collegejournal.com/
Nation Job Network	http://www.nationjob.com/
Net Temps	http://www.net-temps.com/
The New York Times	http://www.nytimes.com/
The Wall Street Journal – College	http://www.collegejournal.com/
USA Today	http://www.usatoday.com/
US Government official site	http://www.usajobs.opm.gov/

Vietnam

Vietnam Works	http://www.vietnamworks.com/

United Arab Emirates

Jobs in Dubai	http://www.jobsindubai.com/
The Emirates Network	http://www.theemiratesnetwork.com/business/jobs.htm

International Organizations

OECD	http://www.oecd.org/
Inter-American Development Bank	http://www.iadb.org/
International Labour Organisation	http://www.ilo.org/
International Monetary Fund	http://www.imf.org/
Red Cross	http://www.redcross.org/
UNESCO	http://www.unesco.org/
United Nations	http://www.un.org/
The World Bank Group	http://www.worldbank.org/
World Health Organisation	http://www.who.org/
World Trade Organisation	http://www.wto.org/
Worldwide Corporate Information	http://www.corporateinformation.com/

Few More North American Job search Websites

ACCOUNTING/BANKING/FINANCE --
ACCOUNTING AND FINANCE JOBS – http://www.accountingjobs.com
ACCOUNTING.COM -- http://www.accounting.com
ACCOUNTING.NET -- http://www.accounting.net
AMERICAN BANKER ONLINE'S CAREERZONE -- http://www.americanbanker.com/careerzone
BLOOMBERG – http://www.bloomberg.com
CFO'S FEATURED JOBS -- http://www.cfonet.com/html/cfojobs.html
FINANCIAL, ACCOUNTING, AND INSURANCE JOBS PAGE --
http://www.nationjob.com/financial
FINCAREER -- http://www.fincareer.com
JOBS FOR BANKERS ONLINE -- http://www.bankiobs.com
NATIONAL BANKING NETWORK – http://www.banking-financejobs.com
ADVERTISING/MARKETING/PUBLIC RELATIONS –
ADWEEK ONLINE – http://www.adweek.com
DIRECT MARKETING WORLD – http://www.dmworld.com
MARKETING JOBS – http://www.marketingjobs.com

AEROSPACE
AVIATION AND AEROSPACE JOBS PAGE – http://www.nationjob.com/aviation
AVIATION EMPLOYMENT – http://www.aviationemployment.com
SPACE JOBS – http://www.spacejobs.com

ARTS AND ENTERTAINMENT
THE INTERNET MUSIC PAGES -- http://www.musicpages.com
ONLINE SPORTS -- http://www.onlinesports.com/pages/CareerCenter.html

BIOTECHNOLOGY/SCIENTIFIC
BIO ONLINE – http://www.bio.com
SCIENCE PROFESSIONAL NETWORK – www.recruitsciencemag.org

CHARITIES AND SOCIAL SERVICES
THE NONPROFIT TIMES ONLINE -- http://www.nptimes.com/classified.html
SOCIAL SERVICE – http://www.socialservice.com
SOCIAL WORK AND SOCIAL SERVICES JOBS ONLINE –
http://www.gwbweb.wustl.edu/jobs/index.html

COMMUNICATIONS
AIRWAVES MEDIA WEB – http://www.airwaves.com/job.html
THE JOBZONE – http://www.internettelephony.com/JobZone/jobzone.asp

COMPUTERS
COMPUTER – http://www.computer.org/computer/career/career.htm
THE COMPUTER JOBS STORE – http://www.computerjobs.com
COMPUTERWORK – http://www.computerwork.com
DICE – http://www.dice.com
DIGITAL CAT'S HUMAN RESOURCE CENTER – http://www.jobcats.com
IDEAS JOB NETWORK -- http://www.ideasjn.com
I-JOBS -- http://www.I-jobs.com

JOBS FOR PROGRAMMERS -- http://www.prgjobs.com
JOBS.INTERNET.COM -- http://jobs.intemet.com
JOB WAREHOUSE -- http://www.jobwarehouse.com
MACTALENT -- http://www.mactalent.com
SELECTJOBS -- http://www.seIectjobs.com
TECHIES -- http://www.techies.com

EDUCATION
ACADEMIC EMPLOYMENT NETWORK -- http://www.academploy.corn
ACADEMIC POSITION NETWORK -- http://www.apnjobs.com
AECT PLACEMENT CENTER -- http://www.aect.org/employment/empIoyment.htm
THE CHRONICLE OF HIGHER EDUCATION CAREER NETWORK – http://chronicle.com/jobs
DAVE'S ESL CAFÉ – http://www.eslcafe.com
HIGHEREDJOBS ONLINE – http://www.higheredjobs.com
JOBS IN HIGHER EDUCATION -- http://www.gsIis.utexas.edu/~acadres/jobs/index.html
LIBRARY & INFORMATION SCIENCE JOB SEARCH – http://www.carousel.lis.uiuc.edu/~jobs
THE PRIVATE SCHOOL EMPLOYMENT NETWORK – http://www.privateschooljobs.com
TEACHER JOBS – http://www.teacherjobs.com

ENGINEERING
ENGINEERJOBS -- http://www.engineerjobs.com

ENVIRONMENTAL
ECOLOGIC -- http://www.rpi.edu/dept/union/pugwash/ecojobs.htm
ENVIRONMENTAL JOBS SEARCH PAGE –
http://ourworld.compuserve.com/homepages/ubikk/env4.htm
WATER ENVIRONMENT WEB – http://www.wef.org
GOVERNMENT
CORPORATE GRAY ONLINE -- http://www.greentogray.com
FEDERAL JOBS CENTRAL -- http://www.fedjobs.com
FEDERAL JOBS DIGEST -- http://www.jobsfed.com
FEDWORLD FEDERAL JOB ANNOUNCEMENT SEARCH --
http://www.fedworld.gov/jobs/jobsearch.htmI
THE POLICE OFFICERS INTERNET DIRECTORY -- http://www.officer.com/jobs.htm

HEALTHCARE
HEALTH CAREER WEB -- http://www.heaIthcareerweb.com
HEALTH CARE JOBS ONLINE -- http://www.hcjobsonIine.com
HEALTH CARE RECRUITMENT ONLINE – http://www.healthcarerecruitment.com
MEDHUNTERS -- http://www.medhunters.com
MEDICAL-ADMART -- http://www.medicaI-admart.com
MEDICAL DEVICE LINK -- http://www.devicelink.com/career
MEDZILLA -- http://www.medziIIa.com
NURSING SPECTRUM CAREER FITNESS ONLINE – http://www.nursingspectrum.com
PHYSICIANS EMPLOYMENT – http://www.physemp.com
SALUDOS HISPANIS WEB CAREER CENTER – http://www.saludos.com/cguide/hcguide.html

HOTELS AND RESTAURANTS
ESCOFFIER ONLINE – http://www.escoffier.com/nonscape/employ.shtml

AMERICAN JOBS -- http://www.arnericanjobs.com
BEST JOBS USA – http://www.bestjobsusa.com

We would appreciate your help in keeping this resource up to date! mail your feedback at tariq_nadeem@selfhelppublishers.com

List of Suggested Job Search Web Sites in Canada

Canada Job search	www.canadajobsearch.com
Canada Wide	www.canada.com
Canada Work Info Net (B)	http://workinfonet.ca
Canada Work Infonet	www.workinfonet.com
Canadian Career Page	www.canadiancareers.com
Career Bookmarks	www.careerbookmarks.tpl.toronto.on.ca
Career Exchange	www.creerexchange.com
Career Mosaic	www.careermosaic.com
Career Networking	www.careerkey.com
Contractors Network Corporation	www.cnc.ca
Culture Net Announcement Board	www.culturenet.ca
Electronic Labour Exchange	www.ele-spe.org
E-Span	www.espan.com
Head Hunter	www.HeadHunter.net
HEART/Career Connections	www.career.com
Hot Jobs	www.hotjobs.com
HRDC Canada(B)	www.hrdc-drhc.gc.ca
Job Bus Canada	www.jobbus.com
Job Find	www.jobfind2000.com
Job Hunters Bible	www.jobhuntersbible.com
Job Search Canada	www.jobsearchcanada.about.com
Job Search Engine	www.job-search-engine.com
Job Shark	www.jobshark.com
Monster Board	www.monster.ca
Net Jobs	www.netjobs.com
Ontario Government (B)	www.gojobs.gov.on.ca
Public Service Commission of Canada(B)	http://jobs.gc.ca
SERN	www.sern.net
Toronto HRDC Jobs and Links	www.toronto-hrdc.sto.org
Toronto Job Ads	www.workwaves.com
University of Toronto Job Board	www.utoronto.ca/jobopps
Work Search (B)	www.worksearch.gc.ca
Workink(B)	www.workink.com
Work Insight	www.workinsight.com
Workopolis	www.workopolis.com

HI TECH

Hi Tech Career Exchanges	www.hitechcareer.com
IT Career Solutions	www.vectortech.com
Position Watch	www.positionwatch.com
Ward Associates	www.ward-associates.com

ENGINEERING

Canadian Society for Mechanical Engineers	www.csme.ca
Engineering Institute of Canada	www.eic.ici.ca

NON PROFIT ORGANIZATION

Canadian International Development Agency	www.acdi-cida.gc.ca
Charity Village	www.charityvillage.com
Human Rights-Job Bank	www.Hri.ca/jobboard/joblinks.shtml
Law Now's Resource for Charity/Non Profit	www.extension.ualberta.ca/lawnow/nfp
Online Resource for Non Profit	www.onestep.on.ca

HEALTH

Canadian Medical Placement Service	www.cmps.ca
Hospital News	www.hospitalnews.com
Med Hunters	www.medhunters.com

EDUCATION

Jobs in the Educational Field	www.oise.utoronto.ca/~mpress/jobs.html

WOMEN

Wired Women	www.wiredwoman.com

MULTI MEDIA

MultiMediator	www.multimediator.com

TOURISM AND HOSPITALITY

Cool Jobs Canada	www.cooljobscanada.com
Hospitality Careers	www.hcareers.com

AGRICULTURE

Caffeine	www.caffeine.ca
The Farm Directory	www.farmdirectory.com/employment.asp

ARTS AND ENTERTAINMENT

Acting	www.madscreenwriter.com
ACTRA (film)	www.actra.com
Canadian Actor Online	www.canadianactor.com
Canadian Actors Equity Association	www.caea.com
Canadian film @ TV Production Association	www.cftpa.ca
Canadian Film Centre	www.cdnfilmcentre.com
Mandy	www.mandy.com
National Film Board	www.nfb.ca
Ontario Theatre	www.theatreontario.org
Playback Magazine	www.playbackmag.com

SPECIALIZED

Canadian Federation of Chefs & Cooks	www.cfcc.ca
Canadian Human Resource Counsellors	www.chrp.ca
Contact Point – Counsellors	www.contactpoint.ca
Oil and Gas Industry	www.pcf.ab.ca
Social Workers of Toronto	www.swatjobs.com

PEOPLE WITH DISABILITIES

Canadian Council for Rehabilitation & Work	www.ccrw.org
Canadian Hearing Society	www.chs.ca
Canadian Mental health Association	www.cmha.ca
Canadian Paraplegic Association	www.canparaplegic.org
Job Accommodation Network	http://janweb.icdi.wvu.edu
TCG for People with Disabilities	www.tcg.on.ca
U of T Adaptive Tech ERC	www.utoronto.ca/atrc

WEB SITES FOR YOUTH AND RECENT GRADUATES

Bridges	www.bridges.com
Canadian Youth Business Foundation	www.cybf.ca
Canadian Youth Business Foundation (B)	www.cybf.ca
Career Owl	www.careerowl.ca
Career Planning	www.alis.gov.ab.ca

Cdn.International Development Agency(B)	www.acdi-cida.gc.ca
Fedeal Student Work Experience Program (B)	www.jobs.gc.ca
MazeMaster	www.mazemaster.on.ca
National Graduate Register	http://ngr.schoolnet.ca
Strategies Business Info – By Sector (B)	Strategis.ic.gc.ca/sc_indps/engdoc/homepage.html
Summer Jobs	www.summerjobs.com
Work Web (B)	www.cacee.com
Youth Canada (B)	www.youth.gc.ca
Youth Info-Job (B)	www.infojob.net
Youth Opportunities Ontario (B)	Youthjobs.gov.on.ca
Youth Opportunities Ontario (B)	www.edu.gov.on.ca

NEW COMERS

Citizenship and Immigration Canada	www.cic.gc.ca
Settlement.org	www.sttlement.org
Skills for change	www.skillsforchange.org
World Educational Services/Foreign Credentials Assessment	www.wes.org/ca

CAREER PLANNING AND JOB SEARCH STRATEGIES

Bridges	www.cxbridges.com
Career Cruising	www.careercruising.com
Counsellor Resource Centre (B)	http://crccanada.org
Essential Skills	www.essestialskills.gc.ca
Job Futures	http://jobfutures.ca
National Occupational Classification (NOC)(B)	www.hrdc.gc.ca/noc
Toronto Public Library	http://careerbookmarks.tpl.vrl.toronto.on.ca
What Colour is your parachute:	www.jobhuntersbible.com

LABOUR MARKET / INDUSTRY INFORMATION

Canada News Wire	www.newswire.ca
Canada Work InfoNet (B)	www.workinfonet.ca
HRDC Metro Toronto(B)	www.toronto-hrdc.sto.org
HRDC Sector Studies (B)	www.on.hrdc-drhc.gc.ca/english/lmi
Industry Canada	http://strategis.ic.gc.ca
Labour Market Information: Salary Ranges	www.Canadavisa.com/documents/salary.htm
Ontario Wage Information	www.on.hrdc-drhc.gc.ca

Workwaves Toronto	www.workwaves.com

NEWSPAPERS/MAGAZINE

Eye Magazine	www.eye.net/classifieds.
Globe and Mail	www.theglobeandmail.com
National Post	www.careerclick.com
Newswire	www.neweswire.ca
Toronto Star	www.thestar.com
Toronto Star / Globe and Mail	www.workpolis.com
Toronto Sun	www.canoe.ca

SMALL BUSINESS INFORMATION

Business Development Bank of Canada (B)	www.bdc.ca
Canada Business Service Centres (B)	www.cbsc.org
Canadian Company Capabilities (B)	Strategis.ic.gc.ca/engdoc/main.htm l
Canadian Women's business Network	www.cdnbizwomen.com
Educated Entrepreneur	www.educatedentrepreneur.com
Enterprise Toronto	www.enterprisetronto.com
Self Employment Assistance	http://www.sedi.org/html/prog/fs1_ prog.html
Toronto Business	www.city.toronto.on.ca/business/in dex.htm

WEB SITES WHERE YOU CAN POST YOUR RESUME

Electronic Labour Exchange	www.ele-spc.org
Job Canada	www.jobcanada.org
Job Shark (B)	www.jobshark.com
Monster Board (B)	www.monster.ca
National Graduate Register (B)	www.campusworklink.com
NetJobs	www.netjobs.com
Worklink	www.workink.com
Workopolis	www.workopolis.ca

TRAINING

Can Learn	www.canlearn.ca
Ellis Chart/Apprentice Training Programs	www.hrdc.gc.ca/hrib/hrpprh/redseal/ ndex.shtml
Interactive Training Inventory (B)	www.trainingiti.com
Ministry of Eduction & Training	www.edu.gov.on.ca/eng/welcome.ht ml
Onestep	www.onestep.on.ca

Ontario Universities' Application Centre	www.ouac.on.ca
Scholarships and Exchanges (B)	www.homer.aucc.ca
School finder(B)	www.schoolfinder.com

TUTORIAL SITES

Internet Stuff	www.webteacher.com
Learn the Net	www.learnthenet.com
Microsoft Office: word, excel, powerpoint	www.utexax.edu/cc/training/handouts
Mouse Tutorial	www.albright.org/Albright/computer-Lab/tutorials/mouse/

RELEVANT INFORMATION

City of Toronto	www.city.toronto.on.ca
Employment Resource Centres	www.tcet.com/ercs
Possibilities Project	www.possibilitiesproject.com

VOLUNTEER SITES

Charity Village	www.charityvillage.com
Rehabilitation	www.voc-reb.org
Volunteers	www.volunteer.ca

FREE EMAILS SITES

Excite	www.excite.com
Hotmail	www.hotmail.com
Mail City	www.mailcity.com
Yahoo	www.yahoo.com

SINGLE SEARCH ENGINES

www.google.com	www.altavista.com
www.excite.com	www.go.com
www.hotbot.com	www.yahoo.ca

META SEARCH ENGINES

www.search.com	www.profusion.com
www.megaweb.com	www.metacrawler.com
www.dogpile.com	

TIPS:

- Post your multiple versions of resume on-line where ever possible and register with as many recruiting agencies as you can. Services of these agencies are free for candidates because they are being paid by the employer if they find them an employee of their choice.

- Your resume should not be more then 2 pages of MS Word. The average time spent by an employer in Canada to shortlist resume is 10-15 seconds. So the first page of your resume should carry the most important information that you want to be noticed by HR managers.

- Access your resume by response, If you apply against 100 jobs and you receive 5-10 interviews that mean your resume is fine and you are doing a good job.

- After arriving in Canada attend job search workshops and trainings organized by your nearest HRDC (Human Resource Development Canada) office or by HRDC sponsored agencies free of charge. You will learn how job search techniques are different in Canada from rest of the world.

- When you are in Canada, do your networking, let as many people know as possible that you are looking for a job and learn making cold calls. These are the highly successful and result oriented methods of job search in Canada.

- Mail at least 5-10 resume and make 5 cold calls everyday for quick results.

- www.workopolis.com, www.monster.ca & www.hotjobs.com are the most commonly visited websites for job search.

Some Useful Toll-Free Numbers

For USA and Canada only

Information on the Government of Canada	1 800 622-6232
Canada Business Service Centres	1 800 576-4444
Canada Child Tax Benefit	1800 387-1193
Canada Education Saving Grant	1 888 276-3624
Canada Saving Bonds	1 800 575-5151
Citizenship and Immigration Canada	
In Montreal (local call)	1 54 496-1010
In Toronto (local call)	1 416 973-4444
In Vancouver (local call)	1 604 666-2171
Elsewhere in Canada	1 888 242-2100
Customs Information Service	1 800 461-9999
Employment Insurance and Social Insurance Number	1 800 206-7218
Old Age Security and Canada Pension plan	1 800 277-9914
Passport Office	1 800567-6868
Tax Enquiries-personal	1 800 959-8281
Youth Info Line	1 800 935-5555

Glossary of Terms

Find definitions of terms used frequently in *this book.*

Business Immigrant

Business immigrants include three classes of immigrants — investors, entrepreneurs and self-employed people. Business immigrants become permanent residents on the basis of their ability to become economically established in Canada. The spouse and children of the business immigrant are also included in this category.

Convention Refugee

A person who, by reason of a well-founded fear of persecution for reasons of race, religion, nationality, membership in a particular social group or political opinion, is (a) outside each of their countries of nationality and is unable, or by reason of that fear, unwilling to avail themselves of the protection of each of those countries; or (b) not having a country of nationality, is outside the country of their former habitual residence and is unable, or by reason of that fear, unwilling to return to that country.

Dependant

The spouse, common-law partner or conjugal partner and children of a landed immigrant. A dependent child is either a biological child or an adopted child. Children can be dependent if they meet one of the following conditions:

- they are under age 22 and unmarried or not in a common-law relationship;
- they have been full-time students since before age 22, attend a post-secondary educational institution and have been substantially dependent on the financial support of a parent since before age 22 and, if married or a common-law partner, since becoming a spouse or a common-law partner; or

- they are age 22 or over and have been substantially dependent on the financial support of a parent since before age 22 because of a physical or mental condition.

Before June 28, 2002, dependants were defined as the spouse of a landed immigrant and the children of that immigrant who were unmarried and under 19 years of age; or continuously enrolled as full-time students in an educational institution and financially supported by their parents since reaching age 19 (or if married before age 19, from the date of their marriage); or due to a medical condition, unable to support themselves and are dependent on their parents for financial support.

Economic Immigrant

People selected for their skills and ability to contribute to Canada's economy, including skilled workers, business people and provincial nominees.

Entrepreneur

An immigrant who has been admitted to Canada by demonstrating that they:

- have managed and controlled a percentage of equity in a qualifying business for at least two years in the period beginning five years before they apply; and
- have a legally obtained net worth of at least $300,000 Canadian.

Family Class

A class of immigrants to Canada made up of close relatives of a sponsor in Canada, including a spouse, common-law partner or conjugal partner; dependent children; parents and grandparents; children under age 18 whom the sponsor intends to adopt in Canada; children of whom the sponsor is the guardian; brothers, sisters, nephews, nieces and grandchildren who are orphans under age 18;

and any other relative, if the sponsor has no relative as described above, either abroad or in Canada.

Flows

Based on the initial entry method, the number of people identified as entering the CIC system (and presumably the country) for the first time. CIC commonly measures foreign student flows and foreign worker flows. Flows are calculated based on the earliest effective date of any valid permit issued to a foreign student or a foreign worker. *The Monitor's* quarterly figures measure foreign student flows and foreign worker flows as opposed to stocks (see stock definition for more details).

Foreign Student

A temporary resident who has been approved by an immigration officer to study in Canada. The study permit identifies the level of study and the length of time the individual may study in Canada. Students do not need a study permit for courses of six months or less if they will finish the course within the period of stay authorized upon entry, which is usually six months. Before June 28, 2002, students did not need a study permit for English and French as a second language courses of three months or less. Every foreign student must have a student authorization, but may also have been issued other types of permits or authorizations.

Foreign Worker

A foreign national who has been authorized to enter and remain in Canada, on a temporary basis, as a worker. This category excludes foreign students and people who have been issued employment authorizations for humanitarian reasons. Every foreign worker must have an employment authorization, but may also have other types of permits or authorizations.

Government-Assisted Refugees

People who are selected abroad for resettlement to Canada as Convention refugees under the *Immigration and Refugee Protection Act* or as members of the Humanitarian-protected Persons Abroad Classes, and who receive resettlement assistance from the federal government.

Investor

An immigrant who has been admitted to Canada because they:

- have business experience as defined in the Regulations;
- have a legally obtained net worth of at least $800,000 Canadian; and
- have invested $400,000 Canadian before receiving a visa.

The Canadian government allocates the investment to participating provinces and territories, which guarantee the investment and use it to develop their economies and create jobs. The investment is repaid, without interest, after five years.

Joint Assistance Sponsorship (JAS)

A joint undertaking by a sponsoring group and CIC to sponsor refugees requiring special assistance and whose admissibility depends upon the additional support of a sponsor. In order to resettle successfully, these refugees may require more than a 12-month sponsorship. Under the JAS Program, CIC provides financial assistance to cover the cost of food, shelter, clothing and essential household goods. The sponsor's role is to provide orientation, significant settlement assistance and emotional support. Refugees sponsored under the JAS program are identified as having special needs that will likely result in a longer or more difficult period of integration.

Landing

The permission given to a person to live in Canada as a permanent resident. An immigrant who has been "landed" is a permanent resident.

Level of Skill

Skill levels for foreign worker occupations are derived from the National Occupational Classification (NOC) system. They are:

0	–	Managerial
A	–	Professionals
B	–	Skilled and Technical
C	–	Intermediate and Clerical
D	–	Elemental and Labour
E	–	Not Stated (This category is the result of special programs and of foreign workers who were able to enter Canada initially with no requirement for a foreign worker permit)

Level of Study

There are five levels of study shown for the foreign student population in Canada. They are:

1. **University** — Foreign students pursuing undergraduate, postgraduate (master's and doctoral) and other studies at university institutions in Canada.
2. **Trade** — Foreign students pursuing education in a vocational trade at non-university educational institutions in Canada (such as technical and vocational institutions, CEGEP, and colleges).
3. **Other Post-Secondary** — Foreign students pursuing a post-secondary level of study, not specifically university or trade level. This category may include language institutions, private institutions and university qualifying programs.
4. **Secondary or Less** — Foreign students attending primary or secondary educational institutions in Canada.
5. **Other** — Foreign students who could not be classified at any of the above levels of study.

Live-in Caregiver

A temporary resident of Canada who has successfully completed the equivalent of Canadian secondary school; has six months of full-time training in a field or occupation related to that for which they are seeking a work permit; is able to speak, read and understand English or French at a level sufficient to communicate effectively in an unsupervised situation; and signs an employment contract with the future employer.

Participants in this program may apply for permanent resident status in Canada after completing two years of live-in caregiving employment within three years of arrival in Canada.

Other

This category includes people classified as Post-Determination Refugee Claimants or members of the Deferred Removal Order Class.

Permanent Residence for Protected Persons in Canada

People who have been determined to be Protected Persons by the Immigration and Refugee Board in Canada or through the Pre-Removal Risk Assessment, and who have been granted permanent residence as a result.

Provincial Nominee

An immigrant selected by the provinces and territories for specific skills that will contribute to the local economy. The Regulations establish a provincial nominee class, allowing provinces and territories that have agreements with CIC to nominate a certain number of workers. A nominee must meet federal admissibility requirements, such as those related to health and security.

Principal Applicant (Business Applicant)

The person who best meets the definition for one or more of the types of business immigrants and in whose name the application for immigration is made.

Principal Applicant (Economic Applicant)

The person who is likely to earn the most points in the self-assessment and in whose name the immigration application is made.

Privately Sponsored Refugees

Refugees selected abroad for resettlement to Canada who receive resettlement assistance from private sources.

Refugee Protection Claimant

A person who has arrived in Canada and who seeks the protection of Canada. If such a person receives a final determination that he or she has been determined to be a Protected Person, he or she may then apply for permanent residence.

Self-Employed People

An immigrant who has (a) shown that they can and intend to create their own employment in Canada and (b) that they can contribute significantly either to the Canadian economy as farmers or to the cultural or athletic life of Canada.

Skilled Worker

Immigrants selected for their skills, which will ensure their success in a fast-changing labour market and benefit the Canadian economy. The Regulations stress education, English or French language abilities, and work experience involving certain skills, rather than specific occupations.

Stocks

Stock statistics measure the number of people present in the CIC system on a specific date in each year of observation. CIC commonly measures foreign student stocks and foreign worker stocks. For a foreign student or a foreign worker to be counted as present in the stock, he or she must have a valid student or work authorization on that date. Any foreign student or foreign worker who has been granted landed status on or before the observation date is excluded from the stock count from that date forward.

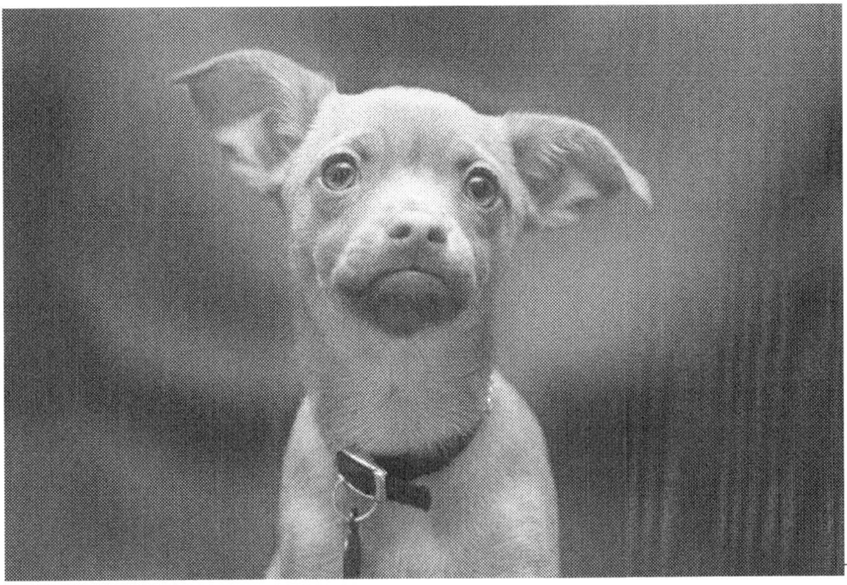

I wish to migrate to Canada too, under skilled worker class. I am trained to work at airports. I will prepare my application by myself. I heard that my rights are very well defined and respected in Canada.

Bibliography

Introduction to Canada, facts and figures – CIA -The world factbook

Manage your impression – Put Your Best Foot Forward.

World-wide quality of living survey
http://www.mercerhr.co.uk/pressrelease/details.jhtml?idContent=1173105

Canadian Economy in Brief
http://www.fin.gc.ca/ECONBR/ecbr06-03e.html

Budget in Brief
http://www.fin.gc.ca/budget06/brief/briefe.htm

Where Does Your Tax Dollar Go
http://www.fin.gc.ca/taxdollar/text/html/pamphlet_e.html

Top Ten Ways to Get Canadian Experience - Do You Have International Experience By Shawn Mintz of A.C.C.E.S
www.accestrain.com.

"Strategizing for Employment in the Canadian Workplace" Ms. Irena Valenta

About the Author

The author has an electro-mechanical engineering background in turnkey thermal power station/oil and gas contracting business. He has more than 14 years of experience with multi-national companies especially in site/project management and coordination by leading multi-discipline engineering teams. He was also a Cisco certified network and design professional (CCNP, CCDP, A+). He arrived in Canada as a skilled worker immigrant and faced numerous surprises and challenges as well as suffered a number of losses.

The author has a flare to help and teach. He wishes to save new immigrants from potential losses and miseries by sharing the wealth of information that he has gathered while immigrating and settling in Canada. After interviewing hundreds of new immigrants, especially internationally trained professionals from various countries, the author has come to the conclusion that the root cause of all the problems and loss of hard earned money and precious time is the lack of information and training before arriving to Canada.

In this book, the author provides everything to new or potential immigrants to not only prepare and submit their immigration application under every federal immigration class in a professional manner but to start working towards their eligibility for employment in Canada. He encourages them to explore employment opportunities or secure a job offer while their applications are in process.

For the people who are interested in starting their own small business in Canada, he also published a book titled "**How to Start a Small Business in Canada**". It is the 5th book under his belt. In this book he provides all the necessary tools, guidance and information to men and women who are on paid jobs and wishes to start their own small business. He encourages and motivates foreign trained professionals to be self-employed, who are facing numerous barriers during their job search efforts and struggling for an opportunity where they can utilize their talent and skills to their full competence.

He has also designed a part-time business strategy with $50-$500 of investment for those who want to retire early in Canada.

You can reach him at tariq_nadeem@sympatico.ca or info@selfhelppublishers.com or tariqnadeem.tariq@gmail.com for feedback/advise.